Discourses and Counter-discourses on Europe

The European Union plays an increasingly central role in global relations from migration to trade to institutional financial solvency. The formation and continuation of these relations – their narratives and discourses – are rooted in social, political, and economic historical relations emerging at the founding of European states and then substantially augmented in the Post-WWII era. Any rethinking of our European narratives requires a contextualized analysis of the formation of hegemonic discourses.

The book contributes to the ongoing process of 'rethinking' the European project, identity, and institutions, brought about by the end of the Cold War and the current economic and political crisis. Starting from the principle that the present European crisis goes hand in hand with the crisis of its hegemonic discourse, the aim of the volume is to rescue the complexity, the richness, the ambiguity of the discourses on Europe as opposed to the present simplification. The multidisciplinary approach and the long-term perspective permit illuminating scope over multiple discourses, historical periods, and different 'languages', including that of the European institutions.

This text will be of key interest to scholars and students of European Union politics, European integration, European history, and, more broadly, international relations.

Manuela Ceretta is Professor of History of Political Thought at the University of Turin, Italy. She is a member of the Scientific Board of *Studi Irlandesi, A Journal of Irish Studies* and of the Editorial Board of *Storia del Pensiero Politico*.

Barbara Curli is Professor of Contemporary History and Global History at the University of Turin, Italy. She was Jean Monnet Chair in History of European Integration at the University of Calabria, Italy, Fulbright Distinguished Chair in Italian and European History at Georgetown University, USA, and Editor-in-chief (2011–2015) of *Il Mestiere di Storico*.

Critical European Studies
Edited by Hartmut Behr
University of Newcastle, UK
and
Yannis A. Stivachtis
Virginia Tech, USA

Discourses and Counter-discourses on Europe

From the Enlightenment to the EU

Edited by
Manuela Ceretta and
Barbara Curli

LONDON AND NEW YORK

First published 2017
by Routledge
2 Park Square, Milton Park, Abingdon, Oxon OX14 4RN

and by Routledge
711 Third Avenue, New York, NY 10017

Routledge is an imprint of the Taylor & Francis Group, an informa business

British Library Cataloguing in Publication Data
A catalogue record for this book is available from the British Library

Library of Congress Cataloging in Publication Data
Names: Ceretta, Manuela, editor. | Curli, Barbara, editor.
Title: Discourses and counter-discourses on Europe from the Enlightenment to the EU / edited by Manuela Ceretta and Barbara Curli.
Description: Milton Park, Abingdon, Oxon ; New York, NY : Routledge, 2017. | Series: Critical European studies | Includes bibliographical references and index.
Identifiers: LCCN 2016035805| ISBN 9781138640726 (hardback) | ISBN 9781315636474 (ebook)
Subjects: LCSH: Political culture–Europe–History. | Political culture–European Union countries–History. | Europe–Politics and government. | European Union countries–Politics and government.
Classification: LCC JN94.A91 D57 2017 | DDC 341.242/2–dc23
LC record available at https://lccn.loc.gov/2016035805

ISBN: 978-1-138-64072-6 (hbk)
ISBN: 978-1-315-63647-4 (ebk)

Typeset in Times New Roman
by Wearset Ltd, Boldon, Tyne and Wear

Contents

Figures

Tables

Contributors

Marinella Belluati is Assistant Professor of Media Analysis at the University of Turin. She is a member of the Italian Political Communication Association and of the research team of the 'Osservatorio sulla Comunicazione Politica e pubblica' of Turin (www.politicalcommunicationmonitor.eu). Recent publications include: 'The Mediatization and Framing of European Parliamentary Election Campaigns' (with others) in M. Maier, J. Strömbäck, and L. Lee Kaid *Political Communication in European Parliamentary Elections* (Farnham: Ashgate 2011); with P. Caraffini (eds), *L'Unione Europea tra istituzioni e opinione pubblica* (Roma: Carocci); 'Signs of Europeanization? The 2014 EP Election in European Newspapers', *Italian Political Science Review/Rivista Italiana di Scienza Politica* (forthcoming).

Maria Cristina Caimotto, PhD, is Assistant Professor of English Language and Translation at the University of Turin. Her research interests include Translation Studies, Political Discourse, and Environmental Discourse. In her works, the compared analysis of texts in different languages (translated or comparable) is employed as a tool for critical discourse analysis. She is a member of the Environmental Humanities International Research Group and she is currently collaborating with Lancaster University (CASS) on the Changing Climates project.

Paolo Caraffini is Assistant Professor of History of European Integration and Democracy and Representation in the EU at the University of Turin. His main areas of research are Italian and French Europeanism, French politics in Africa and its relationship with European integration, the role of parties, and pro-European movements. Among his publications: *Costruire l'Europa dal basso. Il ruolo del Consiglio italiano del Movimento europeo (1948–1985)* (Bologna: il Mulino 2008); *Un grand commis e la dimensione internazionale: Giuseppe Petrilli e il processo di integrazione europea (1950–1989)* (Milan: Guerini, 2015); *L'Unione Europea tra istituzioni e opinione pubblica* (co-edited with M. Belluati) (Rome: Carocci 2015).

Cristopher Cepernich is Assistant Professor of Sociology at the University of Turin, where he teaches Sociology of Communication and Media Systems and ICT. He conducts investigations in the field of sociology of media and political communication. He is Director and Co-founder of the Oseervatorio della Comunicazione Politica e Pubblica of the University of Turin. Among his recent publications about the EU: 'L'Europa nella comunicazione dei partiti su Twitter alle Europee 2014', in M. Belluati and P. Caraffini (eds), *L'Unione Europea tra istituzioni e opinione pubblica* (Rome: Carocci (forthcoming)); 'La notiziabilità dell'Europa. Attori, eventi e temi nella copertura della stampa (1992–2002)', in C. Marletti and J. Mouchon (eds), *La costruzione mediatica dell'Europa* (Milan: Franco Angeli 2009).

Manuela Ceretta is Professor of History of Political Thought at the University of Turin. She has researched eighteenth-century Irish political thought and she contributed to *The Irish Act of Union: Bicentennial Essays* (Kildare: Irish Academic Press 2002) and to the *Dictionary of Irish Biography* (Cambridge: Cambridge University Press 2009). Recently, her research interests have focussed on French–Irish political relations and on French counter-revolutionary thought. Her recent publications include *Il Momento Irlandese. L'Irlanda nella cultura politica francese fra Restaurazione e Secondo Impero'* (Rome: Edizioni di Storia e Letteratura 2013) and '*Je meurs avec l'Europe'*: *Joseph de Maistre, ou de la force de l'espace public européen et de la fin de l'Europe* (Brussels: Peter Lang 2016).

Michelangelo Conoscenti is Professor of English Linguistics at the University of Turin. He has researched and served as external consultant for several military institutions (NATO NRDC-ITA HQ Commander, the Defence Language Institute, Monterey, CA, Fort Bragg, NC, the West Point Academy and Joint Staff Schools of the Italian Army). His research interests focus on the communicative strategies adopted by national and international civilian and military organizations towards mass media. Among his publications; *Media in the Mediterranean Area: Communication Codes and Construction of Dialogue. Problems and Outlook* (La Valletta, Malta: Midsea Books 2005) (translated into Arabic, French, Italian and Spanish).

Barbara Curli is Professor of Contemporary History and Global History at the University of Turin. She has been Jean Monnet Chair in History of European Integration at the University of Calabria and Fulbright Distinguished Chair in Italian and European History at Georgetown University. She is co-founder of NIREG (Nuclear Italy Research Group). Publications on nuclear history and European integration include: *Il progetto nucleare italiano, 1952–1964. Conversazioni con Felice Ippolito*, (Soveria Mannelli: Rubbettino 2000); 'Italy, Euratom and Early Research on Controlled Thermonuclear Fusion, 1957–1962', in E. Bini (ed.), *Nuclear Italy: An International History of Italian Nuclear Policies during the Cold War* (Trieste: EUT 2016).

Patrizia Delpiano is Professor of Early Modern History at the University of Turin. She has been *Chercheur invité* at the Centre Koyré, Paris (2008) and research fellow at the Herzog August Bibliothek, Wolfenbüttel (2014). She is the author of *Il governo della lettura. Chiesa e libri nell'Italia del Settecento* (Bologna: il Mulino 2007), *La schiavitù in età moderna* (Roma–Bari: Laterza 2009, Arabic translation Abu Dhabi: Kalima 2012), *Liberi di scrivere: La battaglia per la stampa nell'età dei Lumi* (Roma-Bari: Laterza 2015) and co-editor of 'Servants, Domestic Workers and Children', *Paedagogica Historica* (2007, with R. Sarti) and 'Les journaux savants dans l'Europe des XVIIe et XVIIIe siècles', *Archives internationales d'histoire des sciences* (2013, with J. Peiffer and M. Conforti).

Marco Di Giovanni is Assistant Professor of History of Military Institutions and History of War Crimes at the University of Turin and Vice President of the Strategic Sciences Study Program. He is now working on the integration processes and identity of military institutions in the Western World during the Cold War. His publications include *Le regole della battaglia* (Perugia: Morlacchi 2013) (ed.); 'Il soldato virtuale. I blog dei militari', in Nicola Labanca (ed.), *Gli Italiani in Guerra: Conflitti, identità, memorie dal Risorgimento ai nostri giorni. Vol. 5 Le armi della Repubblica: dalla Liberazione a oggi* (Turin: UTET 2009); 'Ufficiali o tecnocrati? La formazione dei quadri della Marina Militare italiana nel secondo dopoguerra', in Giuliana Gemell (ed.), *Politiche scientifiche e strategie d'impresa: le culture olivettiane ed i loro contesti* (Fondazione Adriano Olivetti 2005).

Rosita Di Peri is Assistant Professor in Political Science and International Relations in the Department of Culture, Politics and Society at the University of Turin. Her research interests are on democracy and authoritarianism in the Middle East with a focus on Lebanon and on the relations between power and tourism in the Mediterranean region. She has published several articles in national and international journals and a book on the politics of contemporary Lebanon. Her recent publications include: 'Islamist Actors from Anti-system Perspective: The Case of Hizbullah', *Journal of Politics, Religion and Ideology*, 2014; 'An Enduring "Touristic Miracle" in Tunisia? Coping with Old Challenges after the Revolution', *British Journal of Middle Eastern Studies*, 2015.

Giovanni Finizio is Adjoint Professor of EU Foreign Policy at the University of Turin and of History of International Relations at the Universidad Nacional de Tres de Febrero, Buenos Aires, Argentina. He is also Researcher at the Centre for Studies on Federalism, where he served as Scientific Coordinator of the *International Democracy Watch*. He is member of the Editorial Board of the *Bibliographical Bulletin on Federalism* and of the online peer-reviewed journal *Perspectives on Federalism*. Among his recent publications; *The Democratization of International Institutions. First International Democracy Report* (co-edited with L. Levi and N. Vallinoto) (London: Routledge 2014), and *Democracy at the United Nations. UN Reform in the Age of Globalisation* (co-edited with E. Gallo) (Brussels: Peter Lang 2013).

Filippo Maria Giordano graduated from the University of Pavia in Literature and Philosophy. In 2009 he received his PhD from the University of Pavia with a thesis on the relationship between Reformed Protestantism and Federal Ideology. His doctoral thesis won an award within Historical Studies on Piedmont in the Nineteenth Century. He is now a research fellow at the Scuola Sant'Anna of Pisa and a researcher at the Centre for Studies on Federalism of

Turin. His main research interests are in the fields of International Relations History, Regional Integrations and European Integration History.

Umberto Morelli is Professor of History of International Relations and of Global Governance and Regional Integration at the University of Turin and the President of the Centro di studi sull'Europa. He is also a member of the Editorial Board of *Storia del Pensiero Politico* and editor of the Book Series 'Federalism' published by Peter Lang (Brussels). Recent publications include 'European Federalists in the 1960s' in *Générations de fédéralistes européens depuis le XIXe siècle. Individus, groupes, espaces et réseaux*, edited by G. Duchenne and M. Dumoulin (Brussels: P.I.E. Peter Lang 2012); 'Crises as the Driving Force of European Integration' in *Hommes et réseaux: Belgique, Europe et Outre-Mers*. Liber amicorum edited by Michel Dumoulin, V. Dujardin, and P. Tilly (Brussels: P.I.E. Peter Lang 2013).

Rachele Raus is Assistant Professor of French Linguistics at the University of Turin. She obtained her PhD at the University of Trieste. Since 2002, she has taught French linguistics at the University of Turin. From 2009 to 2012, she was the Directress of the Research Centre for Women's and Gender Studies (CIRSDe) at the University of Turin. She has published widely on French discourse analysis and on translation, especially in a gender perspective. She has edited the book *Multilinguismo e terminologia nell'Unione Europea. Problematiche e prospettive* (Milan: Hoepli 2010) and is the author of *La terminologie multilingue. La traduction des termes de l'égalité H/F dans le discours international* (Brussels: De Boeck 2013).

Giuseppe Sciara received an MA in European Studies (summa cum laude) and a PhD in Political Studies at the University of Turin. He is currently a PhD candidate in Political Sciences, Political Thought, and Political Communication at the University of Genoa and at the University of Paris VIII. He is also Adjunct Professor of History of Political Thought at the University of Turin. His research focuses on post-revolutionary French liberalism and the presence of Machiavelli in French culture in the nineteenth century. He has published articles, essays, reviews, and, recently, a book on the political thought of Benjamin Constant.

Federica Zardo is Assistant Professor at the University of Vienna, Institute for European Integration Research. She received a PhD in Political Science and International Relations at the University of Turin. In 2012–2013 she was visiting PhD student at the KFG Transformative Power of Europe, Freie Universität Berlin. Her research interests revolve around European diplomacy, EU external action, Euro–Mediterranean and EU–Tunisia relations. In 2013 she worked for the European External Action Service at the EU Delegation in Tunis, where she was assistant to the political section. From 2008 to 2013 she was EU project manager and evaluator for a private consultancy and in 2008 she worked for the Italian Representation of Italy to the EU, Brussels.

Introduction

Rescuing Europe from its rhetoric

Manuela Ceretta and Barbara Curli

I This book is intended as a contribution to the ongoing process of rethinking the European project and to the debate on its 'constitutive' foundations brought about by a series of historical events and geopolitical changes which have occurred in these past thirty years. It assumes that the present European crisis goes hand in hand with the crisis of its hegemonic discourse, and that the more hegemonic such a discourse has become, the more it has turned flat and impoverished: the rhetoric on Europe is an integral part of its present crisis. The volume deals with the manifold discursive dimensions of Europe's history and identity by adopting a multidisciplinary approach and taking a long-term perspective from the mid-eighteenth century to the present. Its aim is to rescue the complexity, the richness, and the ambiguity of the discourses on Europe from their present simplification.

The end of the Cold War marked a systemic turning point in European history, and once again raised – albeit in a novel manner – the issue of Europe's 'borders'. After the fall of the Iron Curtain, a newly 'unbound' Europe[1] was compelled to question not only its geographical and geopolitical frontiers, but also its political, economic, and cultural boundaries. At the same time, such events prompted a redefinition of the institutional construction of the European Community, which had begun before the fall of the Berlin Wall. The Single European Act of 1986 and the launching of the single market project, in fact, had opened a new phase of structural transformation in the continent's economy and initiated a process (which will be carried on by subsequent treaties) of unprecedented enlargement of the policy-making competences of the Community with direct effects on the lives of European citizens. These changes redefined – at both the national and supranational level – the question of the state and its role in regulating the economy, that were now to be recast on a European scale.[2] The birth of the EU at Maastricht, the establishment of monetary union (also as a consequence of the events of 1989), and the process of Eastern enlargement which culminated in 2004–2007 were important phases in the redefinition of boundaries and institutional re-foundation.

This was a long, ambitious, and in many ways successful project. However, the onset of the current economic crisis, massive migratory waves, and new security and strategic issues (e.g. the rise of ISIS) represent a challenge for the institutions and the arrangements put in place after 1989. In fact, these issues appear increasingly to strain the resilience of those arrangements. The extent to which institutions like the European Central Bank or the Schengen rules are adequate responses to the challenges and threats to today's Europe is an open question. What is certain, however, is that the present dramatic circumstances have highlighted two important elements: first, the weaknesses in the mechanisms of integration; second, the change that has occurred within the European public sphere in just over a decade. Some great themes (e.g. 'European values', 'Europe's cultural and religious roots', 'a European constitution', the notion of 'citizenship') debated until a few years ago by eminently institutional actors have rapidly become part of the everyday conversations of millions of European citizens, acquiring a new urgency. The rigours of the economic crisis and the perceived inadequacy of institutional responses have for the first time raised the possibility of exit by a member country from the Monetary Union (the so-called 'Grexit'); while the perception of Europe as an area unable to address questions related to democracy, security and growth has actually engendered the decision by a member state to 'withdraw from the Union' (the so-called 'Brexit') – as provided for by art. 50 of the Lisbon Treaty.

All these events have opened a stimulating new chapter in European studies, raising once again 'the very old subject of European identity' – as Jacques Derrida noted in *L'Autre Cap*, written in 1991 in the wake of the fall of the Berlin Wall. Its incisive English translation, *The Other Heading* (1992), meant simultaneously the search for a direction for the continent and for some new 'heading':

> The very old subject of European identity indeed has the venerable air of an old, exhausted theme. But perhaps this 'subject' retains a virgin body. Would not its name mask something that does not yet have a face? We ask ourselves in hope, in fear and trembling, what this face is going to resemble.[3]

It was not by coincidence that it was a scholar of 'language' like Derrida who promptly perceived how Europe's new boundaries inevitably called also for a 'discursive' adjustment:

> Something unique is afoot in Europe, in what is still called Europe even if we no longer know very well *what* or *who* goes by this name. Indeed, to what concept, to what real individual, to what singular entity should this name be assigned today? Who will draw up its borders?[4]

But was there something truly 'unique' in the changes cited by Derrida? In fact, the European identity has always been an elusive subject. On determining its essential features, European culture has to deal with Europe's changing and unstable borders. The end of the Cold War was only the last of a long series of momentous turning points that have marked European history. From the

Congress of Vienna, through the Treaty of Versailles, to the Yalta Conference, Europe has undergone systemic collapses that have reshaped its physiognomy and balances while redefining its constituent components: nations, empires, political and institutional systems. Nor is it the first time that a major economic crisis (as in 1929) has recast the social and institutional structures of European growth and the political content of the great continental market.

What is truly unique at this stage of Europe's history is that the systemic collapse of the 1990s, the current economic and social crisis, and the new security scenario have come about in the presence of a new set of actors: the supranational European institutions. For the first time in European history there are properly 'European institutions' which, by virtue of certain prerogatives, have taken over and helped to steer the process of creating new political structures (e.g. enlargement to the East); have instruments (e.g. the official interest rate) to act on the area's macroeconomic variables; or find themselves dealing with international emergencies (e.g. migration).

One must therefore inquire as to the difference made by this presence, and the extent to which these new actors, this new supranational institutional framework, contribute to making the current turn in European history so difficult to read and interpret if one wants to avoid easy simplifications.

If this is the specificity and, at the same time, the difficulty of this turn, in order to grasp ongoing developments it is useful, as Derrida understood, to start from the effects of the fall of the Berlin Wall. The re-opening of the Pandora's Box of European 'identity' has raised not only the *old question* of Europe's identity but also the *new* one of the identity of the European Community/Union institutions and their fragile legitimacy. Although connected, the two issues are not identical: they partially overlap and both have to do with the crisis. Yet the European Union does not coincide with Europe, although in the public discourse and in the media this equivalence is increasingly asserted, and the term 'Europe' is increasingly used to mean the European Union.

It is evident that the European institutions are faced by a legitimation problem different from that of other political entities/actors in the international system (e.g. nation-states), both because they are historically young institutions and because they have 'weak' identities compared with those of nation-states. As a result, the legitimation of the European institutions has followed distinctive pathways in which they have had mainly to enhance the discursive dimension. This is not only because identity is a discursive practice which does not exist without definitions or without the search for them; it is also because, as 'weak' institutions, European institutions have had a particular need to narrate their existence, to give it visibility and consistency. What has been correctly termed an 'identity turn' in European studies[5] has therefore become a 'discursive turn' as well. The EU discourse on Europe has thus become essential for its legitimacy. Europe 'as a discourse'[6] and 'as a discursive battleground'[7] has indeed become central to the current debates in European studies, to such an extent that a branch of critical discourse analysis has been developed with a specific focus on the EU,[8] and discourse theory has become an integral part of European integration theories.[9]

However, discourses on Europe have progressively diminished in appeal. As the European Commission's president Barroso declared in 2013, a 'new narrative' for Europe is needed in order to restore to European citizens the meaning of a project that has lost its significance, and is perceived solely as a 'European fatigue'. 'We cannot have a more effective Europe without more European legitimacy', said Barroso; and this is why the EU needs 'a new narrative'[10] as a basis for its new 'constitutionalisation'.

A new narrative for Europe is therefore a political project to construct a European public space.[11] However, despite the undeniable appeal of a new narrative, the discourses on Europe – those discourses that should give substance to this new narrative – increasingly sound like stale discourses or hackneyed rhetoric. In fact, how can a new narrative be developed with old discourses? That is, with discourses that neither oblige nor encourage Europe to rethink itself in a creative, suggestive, and future-oriented manner? With the Maastricht Treaty, the Union committed itself to protecting and enhancing the common European cultural heritage. Various attempts have been made to build a shared 'European memory' intended to forge a European *demos*, and, as a consequence, to mould a new legitimation of European institutions. However, as shown by a series of studies on the EU Commission's 'memory policies'[12] and attempts to museumize a shared European history and memory,[13] such initiatives have rarely produced the hoped-for results. Rather, they have in fact turned out to be an essentially conservative political operation, only able to look to the past,[14] and not infrequently with results contrary to those desired (e.g. the re-nationalization of memory in the East, the revival of deep cleavages related to European history, etc.).[15] Although also meant to fill the vacuum of the turn of the century's end of political ideologies and utopias, these cultural policies 'from above' have instead fostered the emergence of official narratives and a 'ritualistic rhetoric' that have impoverished the rich complexity of Europe.[16] Teleological and progressive narratives have proved to be fundamentally inadequate to Europe's contested pasts, plural historical memories, and conflicting experiences.

Moreover, the only voice really discordant with this flat rhetoric is that of the Eurosceptic position. There has consequently arisen a dialogue 'with two voices' – Euroscepticism and the official narrative – which has rigidified both positions and paradoxically further impoverished the debate and exacerbated the 'old' discourses. Essentially, Euroscepticism has only been able to revive a rhetoric of the traditional nation-state, with the aggravating circumstance that it propounds impracticable remedies which look only to the past (e.g. the return of national currencies, the erection of 'walls') and are inadequate to face present global challenges.

II It seems thus necessary to break this dichotomy and recover the complexity of rethinking Europe. This book[17] is set within the framework of this intellectual effort shared by scholars from diverse disciplines. The intent is to regain the richness of discourses that have been lost or marginalized, and of counterdiscourses able to query old narratives and put them in perspective.

The first narrative called into question by the 1989 turn was the historical narrative: Europe's past needed to be 'rewritten'[18]: 'after 1989 nothing – not the future, not the present, and above all not the past – would ever be the same', as Tony Judt effectively put it in one of the first comprehensive 'histories of Europe' written after the fall of the Berlin Wall.[19] New historical approaches were needed in order to grasp the meanings of Europe's shifting boundaries, and the questions related to them. 'The past now has no agreed narrative shape of its own. It acquires meaning only by reference to our many and often contrasting present concerns'.[20]

The first part of this book (*Thinking and regretting Europe*) indeed adopts a historical approach, and seeks to relinquish some consolidated certainties, including, for example, the narrative that depicts the Enlightenment as the cradle of Europe. According to the director of the Scientific Committee of the Museum of Europe in Brussels, the historian Krzystof Pomian, 'the Europe of today, while having many Christian foundations, was built by the Enlightenment'. However, as Patrizia Delpiano notes in Chapter 1 ('Thinking Europe in the age of enlightenment: *Philosophes* and *Antiphilosophes* between universalism and fragmentation'), the Enlightenment does not lend itself to a rhetorical, linear and simplistic interpretation of the building process of the 'House of Europe'. In fact, the thinkers of the Enlightenment – if their theses are investigated carefully and also viewed through the distorting but revealing lenses of their detractors, the *antiphilosophes* – appear to have thought of Europe not as a compact world but rather as part of a world without borders.

On analysing the discourse of counter-revolutionary thinkers, in Chapter 2 ('Evoking Europe against the French Revolution: the rhetorical tools of counter-revolutionary thinkers') Manuela Ceretta highlights the link between the idea of Europe and the concept of 'crisis' in what has been called the first 'European moment' of European history. When the French Revolution shook the political foundations of the old continent as a crisis of European magnitude, Europe was conceived as a refuge concept, a defensive notion, by those belonging to the world which the revolution was sweeping away.

> In the age in which the problematic relationship between Europe and its constituent nations arose, Europe became a weapon in the rhetorical arsenal of the counter-revolution: if 'nation' was the *mot de la Révolution*, which knew no middle term between nation and humanity, 'Europe' was the rallying cry of the counter-revolution.

In Chapter 3 ('Discourses on Europe and their political value in Restoration France') Giuseppe Sciara observes one of the turning points in the construction of modern Europe: the Restoration and the Congress of Vienna. To do so, he adopts an original historiographical perspective: paraphrasing Milward, he argues that Vienna provided a kind of 'European rescue' of the post-revolutionary nation-state. If observed without 'teleological' lenses, the discourses on Europe between the first and the second Restoration prove in many cases to have been pretexts to rebuild the monarchy and the nation ravaged by the revolutionary crisis. To say 'Europe is asking us to do it' is a practice by no means new: during the time of the Congress of Vienna, 'political ideas and actions were frequently legitimized "in the name of Europe" '.

Part II (*The burden of rhetoric: inside the European institutions*) tackles the issue of the 'novelty' introduced into European history by the existence of European supranational institutions. The post-1989 historiographical turn also prompted a change of approach in the historiography of European integration, in particular as regards notions and languages borrowed from ideal models on which, more or less consciously, many methodological assumptions had been based.[21] It was in fact evident that the traditional narratives on the construction of the European Community institutions were in need of profound revision with regard to periodizations and interpretative and theoretical approaches, especially amid Europeanization and globalization trends that made traditional state- and West-centred paradigms of little significance. Now deemed necessary was the 'opening out' of the historiography of European integration to broader topics and methods,[22] to transnational perspectives,[23] to the insertion of European supranational governance within the wider framework of the history of economic globalization, and the long-term material change and modernization of European societies.[24]

Part II of this book aims to contribute to the historiographical debate and current discussion on the nature of the European institutions. What emerges is primarily the essential 'conservatism' of early European institutions, whose legitimizing discourse was certainly aware of the new systemic challenges posed by the Cold War but at the same time constantly looked backwards. The Cold War changed the discourses on Europe and strengthened their conservatism. In Chapter 4 (A European framework for military institutions? International integration and European perspectives in military rhetorics after the Second World War) Marco Di Giovanni shows how recovery of discursive practices of the Italian and French military traditions (the blood shed for the fatherland) merged into the rhetoric of an identity defending (with anti-communist blood) a Europe squeezed between the two superpowers. In the military rhetoric, Europe became 'a set of values', which included anti-communism, and its strategic borders could thus be extended, for instance, to the *Union Française* as a 'bulwark of the West'. At the same time, the defence of Europe continued to be affected by 'the weight of the past', and in particular by the blood of the two world wars: 'The blood of Europe lost its unifying quality in order to nourish ancient and unappeased divisions'.

The weight of the past and the new Cold War rhetoric also combined to define the discourse on projects of post-war integration in an entirely new sector – atomic energy – which epitomized economic modernity and the social utopia of a postwar 'golden age'. As shown by Barbara Curli in Chapter 5 ('Nuclear Europe: technoscientific modernity and European integration in Euratom's early discourse'), Euratom's discursive practices rescued images and rhetoric borrowed from Europe's past primacy and adopted the language of scientific internationalism, now expressed on a regional European scale. At the same time, while Euratom's research centres were intended to be truly transnational places where a new modern European identity would take shape, nuclear Europe was given especial responsibility in the new Cold War competition between a 'communist' and a 'Western' science. Nuclear power was thus an emerging economic sector also afflicted 'ideologically' by the new political burden of the Cold War, in a precarious balance between conservatism and modernity.

The hybridization between the awareness of the new challenges and a conservative theoretical-rhetorical instrumentation may partly explain the difficulties encountered by the European institutions in adopting a forward-looking and constructive attitude. Whilst, for example, after the systemic breakdown of the early 1990s they were able to manage such demanding processes as enlargement to the East or the launch of the single currency, in other circumstances they have been substantially ineffectual. This is the case of the Yugoslavian crisis of the early 1990s, when the European institutions proved unable to produce a common and effective response to the disintegration of the country and a viable solution to a conflict that marked 'the return of war' on European soil for the first time since the Second World War. In Chapter 7 ('The political groups of the European Parliament in the face of Yugoslavia's disintegration and the discursive framing of EU Foreign Policy (1991–1995)') Giovanni Finizio and Umberto Morelli deal with the discussion of these complex issues which took place in the European Parliament at the time. They show how recourse to images such as a new German Reich in the Balkans, or of 'another blatant Munich', or the ambiguous political usage of the concept of self-determination, revealed a discursive framing certainly affected by the burden of the past but also by the political difficulty of facing present challenges. What in 1991 – in the words of the president of the Council of the EU Jacques Poos – seemed to be 'the hour of Europe' – that is, the opportunity for Europe to assume a new role in post-cold war world affairs – would in fact turn out to be another 'American hour'.

The dialectical relationship between conservatism and change is also evident in the activities of the European Parliament, where decisions are the outcome of processes involving multiple actors and variables – as emerges from recent research adopting a transnational socio-ethnographic approach to the study of MEPs' behaviour.[25] As Paolo Caraffini and Filippo Maria Giordano show in Chapter 6 ('Parliamentary groups and political traditions in the debates on EU institutional reform, (1979–1999)'), the debates on institutional reform that took place in the post-1979 European Parliament – the first to be elected by direct universal suffrage and therefore also endowed with a new legitimacy – from the Spinelli Project to Maastricht, showed discursive adjustments by the main parliamentary groups, whereby established political positions or ideological approaches (e.g. those of the Popular parties or of the Socialists) changed over time according to circumstances, domestic issues, and shifting political priorities – as did the meanings of the terms 'social' and European 'institutional change'.

Part III (*Communicating Europe*) addresses how discourses on 'Europe' are used and elaborated in linguistic and media communication in different settings, and how these discourses have been perceived from the outside through EU documents and policies. The chapters deal with recurrent topics in the history of Europe (the threat of the Other, the nature of the boundaries between Europe and its neighbours, the notion of 'European' public opinion, the menaces to Europe's security). These long-term issues have acquired today a new geopolitical dimension as a result of the profound changes that have occurred in communication and in the new media, involving new actors and audiences. In this respect the mechanisms producing the official discourse through various actors – even 'unintended' ones, such as translators – provide an interesting case-study. Translation is a form of communication within the institution. At the same time it constructs the discourse, the resulting political positions, and public rhetoric: it interprets the rhetoric and simultaneously creates it, and in so doing constructs/deconstructs/reinforces discursive practices and stereotypes. The case analysed in Chapter 8 by Maria Cristina Caimotto and Rachele Raus ('The alter-globalist counter-discourse in European rhetoric and translation: women's rights at the European Parliament') is particularly revealing of this role: the linguistic approach to the issue of women's rights in the European Parliament shows, for instance, how the discourse on patriarchy is constructed when drafting and translating EP reports, showing different attitudes – and ethnic prejudice – towards the patriarchy of 'other' cultures as opposed to the 'gender stereotypes' that characterize European modernity:

> The EP discourse concerning patriarchy turns on 'other' contexts: patriarchy is an issue for minorities, notably Roma, and underdeveloped areas (Mexico, developing countries), that is, countries lacking modernity, which can also be due to Muslim religious traditions (Turkey). [...] Discriminations that women suffer within 'modern' Europe are rather presented as the consequence of stereotypes that justify unequal power relationships.

In Chapter 9 ('Europe in the media space: the construction of the EU public sphere in Italy'), Marinella Belluati and Cristopher Cepernich analyse the relationship between media strategies and the construction of a European public sphere, with specific reference to Italian media attitudes to public discourses about Europe. They focus on the recent EU parliamentary elections, assuming that the public space is a communicative relation that involves all social actors capable of generating public discourse. Empirical research on communicative approaches to the European public sphere – they argue – sometimes produces counter-intuitive results. Although 'the signs of Europeanization in the public sphere, at least in Italy, can now be seen and are clearly reflected in the mainstream media',

> where it would be reasonable to expect greater championing of the European dimension – that is, in the communications of politicians on Twitter during the European election campaign – this in fact continues to be woefully insufficient in terms of time and technique.

In Chapter 10 ('ISIS' Dabiq communicative strategies, NATO and Europe: who is learning from whom?') Michelangelo Conoscenti further elaborates on communication strategies and the use of new media by analysing a new subject of the discourse on Europe, ISIS, whose 'terminologies, discourses and narratives of the "enemy", i.e. the West and Europe, are re-appropriated and spun in order to satisfy the organization's own needs'. Within this 'memetic' activity, where it is difficult to discern who learns from whom in a kind of 'game of mirrors', there comes about an informative process 'that is neither a narrative nor a counter-narrative, but rather a narrative against a specific enemy: Europe'.

The manner in which Europe is perceived from outside, however, may be multifaceted, and media strategies alone are not able to capture the profound transformations which have occurred in regions that have historically played a crucial role for Europe, namely the Mediterranean region. In Chapter 11 ('Changing perceptions of the European Union in the MENA region before and after the Arab uprisings: the case of Tunisia'), Rosita Di Peri and Federica Zardo present the case of Tunisia's negotiations with the EU on the issues of migration and mobility, in the larger framework of the Euro-Mediterranean dialogue. They show that, contrary to the widespread representation of the EU as a fragmented and non-unitary actor, the perceptions by the Tunisian elites during the negotiations of the migration dossier was that of a powerful and steady counterpart, in particular after the Jasmine revolution and the fall of the authoritarian regime. Above all, the chapter underlines that the way in which Europe is represented and perceived when negotiating issues strategic for its security and stability may affect domestic politics of its neighbouring countries.

III What conclusions can be drawn from this collection of different perspectives, and how can they contribute to the debates raised by the present European crisis? One of the main purposes of this book is to question teleological narratives and 'ritualistic rhetoric' about European integration, on the assumption that these are themselves part of the present crisis. As a result, the book focuses on discourses and counter-discourses from long and very long-term perspectives. For it was in the late eighteenth century – the pivotal moment of European political modernity – that a discursive rhetoric based on a Europe that does not exist, nor has ever existed, first developed. As Part I of the book suggests, at the origins of early debates on Europe were not only the Kantian notions of perpetual peace or the enlightened visions of *philosophes*, but also the fears and anxieties of *ancien régime* societies, which at that time were facing crisis and collapse. Although mainstream narratives would still generally think of Europe as the product of Enlightenment and the champion of progressive values,[26] in fact the first great debate on Europe unfolded as a result of the French Revolution and actually focussed on the issue of 'the nation'. 'Europe' was instead a concept that attracted the defeated, whose idealized recollection of a Christian and medieval Europe was intended as an extreme attempt to defend a European order. As a matter of fact, the notion of Europe as a 'desperate remedy', as a conservative 'shelter' of last resort – as Lucien Febvre depicted the intellectual foundations of the post-Versailles debate[27] – may be a suitable methodological tool with which to rethink and rewrite the history of Europe well before the First World War, as well as in subsequent systemic turning points, like the post-1945 period.

In fact, as Part II of the book suggests, the roots of the construction of the post-1945 Community institutions lay not only in the renewed visions of an enlightened European organization leading to peace and prosperity, but also in the political and social fears of postwar chaos. Unlike counter-revolutionary thinking, however, the conservative approach to European integration was by no means nostalgic, nor could it have been after two world wars, as there was no ideal, idyllic past that anyone could wish to return to. Instead, the creative, democratic conservatism on which postwar Europe was rebuilt was compatible with modernization and actually constituted a new condition for modernization in an ideologically exhausted continent.[28] This tension is overlooked by most teleological narratives of European integration, as the recent historiographical debate that questions the 'progressive story' of European integration has shown.[29] The second part of this book is intended as a contribution to this debate,[30] and enhances it by focusing on discourses, on the assumption that this tension is in fact a constitutive element of the ambivalence of institutional rhetoric. On the one hand, we deal with institutions that are new and play a fundamentally 'modernizing' role; and on the other, their discursive practices reveal either notions of Europe as 'remedy' (for example, to fears of either military or industrial decline in the new Cold War setting, as in the cases of NATO and Euratom) or an institutional incapacity to act in creative and forward-looking ways, as certain debates that took place in the European Parliament at different historical junctures show.

The progressive teleological approach not only does not stand up to historical evidence, but also offers little explanatory value, even if we refer to current events and trends. A new narrative for Europe also requires a better understanding of the ways Europe is communicated, both internally and externally, and how it is perceived from the outside. The book's third part deals with today's discourses and takes advantage of the contribution made by other social sciences to European studies from a multidisciplinary perspective. On the whole, Part III is an invitation to distrust the common assumptions on which most public discourse and mainstream representations of Europe are currently based, and can be seen as a counter-intuitive exercise which helps us to rescue Europe from its rhetoric. On the one hand, it reveals the substantial inadequacy of the concept of a European public sphere as it is communicated by the media, even in political circumstances when Europe ought to display a strong 'identity', as during the European elections. There is a striking imbalance between the proliferation of scholarly reflections on a European public sphere, and political campaigns for the European Parliament, when Europe is hardly mentioned. Even terrorist propaganda that defines Europe as the enemy dilutes it into a generic, undefined West: unlike America's, Europe's identity is perceived as fragile and divided, but might at the same play the role of a reliable counterpart (as the case of negotiations with Tunisia show), the economic crisis and apparent political fragmentation notwithstanding.

European integration is thus in need of being rescued from its rhetoric, as rhetoric can be paralyzing or – even worse, as current events are showing – may perpetrate commonly-held and exhausted notions of 'Europe' that lead to misinterpretations of reality and to confused decision-making. Above all, Europe's backward-looking rhetoric is unable to mobilize, much less to create, informed public opinion. As Foucault wrote in relation to a key text of the French Revolution, *Qu'est-ce que le Tiers Etat?* by the Abbé Seyès, one of the strengths of the revolutionary discourse lay in its ability to think about the future and to dare to break with claims rooted in past entitlements:

> [A]nd so we have an inversion of the temporal axis of the demand. The demand will no longer be articulated in the name of a past right that was established by either a consensus, a victory, or an invasion. The demand can now be articulated in terms of a potentiality, a future, a future that is immediate, which is already present in the present.[31]

While learning from its past, Europe should perhaps also invert its discourses and dare to think of itself as potentiality being oriented towards the future.

Notes

1 Zielonka 2002.
2 Wright and Cassese 1996.
3 Derrida 1992, 5–6.
4 Derrida 1992, 5.
5 Belot 2010; Bossuat 2012.
6 Stråth 2000a.
7 Diez 2001.
8 Hart and Cap 2014; Krzyżanowski 2010. The debate can be traced in Richardson *et al.* 2014.
9 Carta and Morin 2014; Waever 2009. For a general introduction to this debate see Niţoiu and Tomić 2013 and Radaelli and Schmidt 2005. On the 'metaphorization' of European politics see Musolff *et al.* 2001 and Musolff 2004.
10 Barroso 2013.
11 On the discussion of a European public space in a historical perspective, see Kaelble and Passerini 2002; Kaelble 2002; Frank *et al.* 2010; Foret 2008.
12 Among the many titles see Eder 2009; Stråth 2000b and 2005; Jarausch *et al.* 2007; Sierp 2014.
13 Mazé 2012; Charléty 2004.
14 Traverso 2009; Remotti 2010.
15 Eder and Spohn 2005; Foret 2008; Gensburger and Lavabre 2012; Wodak and Boukala 2015.
16 Woolf 2003.
17 This book is the outcome of a research project carried out by a group of scholars working in the Department of *Culture, Politica e Società* of the University of Turin. The group has recently created a *Centro Studi sull'Europa (TO-EU)*, which brings together scholars in several disciplines (early-modern and modern European history, European integration, sociology, communication and media, linguistics, political science, history of political thought). The purpose of the Centre is to promote, with an interdisciplinary approach, research, publications, consultancy, and training in the

field of European studies, and to encourage their dissemination within the scientific community, in schools of all levels, among public authorities, and in civil society.
18 Woolf 2003; Neri Serneri 1999.
19 Judt 2005, 3.
20 Judt 2008, 16–17.
21 Hobsbawm 1997.
22 Ludlow 2009.
23 Kaiser *et al.* 2009.
24 Loth 2005; Bussière *et al.* 2009.
25 Among the several titles on this topic see for example Busby 2013; Abélès 2004.
26 For a critical discussion on this point, see Bottici and Challand 2013: 87–111.
27 Febvre 1999: 260.
28 Mazower 2000.
29 For a critical discussion see Gilbert 2008.
30 On this debate see the special issue 'Political Myth, Mythology and the European Union', *Journal of Common Market Studies*, 2011, 48:1: in particular Vincent Della Sala: 1–19 and Ian Manners: 67–87.
31 Foucault 2003, 222.

References

Abélès, Marc. 2004. 'Identity and Borders: An Anthropological Approach to EU Institutions'. *Twenty-First Century Papers: On-Line Working Papers, The Center for 21st century Studies, University of Wisconsin, Milwaukee* 4.

Barroso, José Manuel. 2013. Speech by José Manuel Barroso, President of the European Commission, 'A new narrative for Europe', Brussels, 23 April 2013, http://europa.eu/rapid/press-release_SPEECH-13-357_en.htm. Accessed 21 September 2016.

Belot, Céline. 2010. 'Le tournant identitaire des études consacrées aux attitudes à l'égard de l'Europe. Genèse, apports, limites'. *Politique européenne* 30, 1: 17–44.

Bossuat, Gerard. 2012. 'Des identités européennes'. In *Pour l'histoire des relations internationales*, edited by Robert Frank, 663–86. Paris: PUF.

Bottici, Chiara, and Benoît Challand. 2013. *Imagining Europe. Myth, Memory and Identity*. Cambridge: Cambridge University Press.

Busby, Amy. 2013. '"Bursting the Brussels Bubble": Using Ethnography to Explore the European Parliament as a Transnational Political Field'. *Perspectives on European Politics and Society* 14, 2: 203–22.

Bussière, Eric, Michel Dumoulin, and Sylvain Schirmann. 2009. 'The Development of Economic Integration'. In *Experiencing Europe: 50 Years of European Construction 1957–2007*, edited by Wilfried Loth, 44–101. Baden-Baden: Nomos.

Carta, Caterina, and Jean-Frédéric Morin eds. 2014. *EU Foreign Policy through the Lens of Discourse Analysis: Making Sense of Diversity*. Farnham: Ashgate.

Charléty, Véronique. 2004. 'L'invention du musée de l'Europe. Contribution à l'analyse des politiques symboliques européennes'. *Regards sociologiques* 27–28: 149–66.

Della Sala, Vincent. 2011. 'Political Myth, Mythology and the European Union'. *Journal of Common Market Studies* 48, 1: 1–19.

Derrida, Jacques. 1992. *The Other Heading. Reflections on Today's Europe*. Bloomington, IN: Indiana University Press (original version: *L'autre cap* suivi de *La démocratie ajournée*. Paris: Les Éditions de Minuit, 1991).

Diez, Thomas. 2001. 'Europe as a Discursive Battleground'. *Cooperation and Conflict* 36, 1: 5–38.

Eder, Klaus. 2009. 'A Theory of Collective Identity Making Sense of the Debate on a "European Identity"'. *European Journal of Social Theory* 12: 427–47.

Eder, Klaus, and Willfried Spohn eds. 2005. *Collective Memory and European Identity: the Effects of Integration and Enlargement*. Aldershot: Ashgate.

Febvre, Lucien. 1999. *Europa. Storia di una civiltà*. Roma: Donzelli.

Foret, François. 2008. *Légitimer l'Europe: pouvoir et symbolique à l'ère de la gouvernance*. Paris: Presses de la fondation nationale des sciences politiques.

Foucault, Michel. 2003. *Society Must be Defended. Lectures at the Collège de France, 1975–76*. New York: Picador (first edition 1997).

Frank, Robert, Hartmut Kaelble, Marie-Françoise Lévy, and Luisa Passerini eds. 2010. *Building a European Public Sphere: From the 1950s to the Present*. Bruxelles and New York: P.I.E., Peter Lang.

Gensburger, Sarah, and Marie-Claire Lavabre eds. 2012. 'D'une "mémoire européenne" à "l'européanisation de la mémoire"'. *Politique européenne* 37. Paris: L'Harmattan.

Gilbert, Mark. 2008. 'Narrating the Process. Questioning the Progressive Story of European Integration'. *Journal of Common Market Studies* 46, 3: 641–62.

Hart, Christopher, and Piotr Cap eds. 2014. *Contemporary Critical Discourse Studies*. London and New York: Bloomsbury Academic.

Hobsbawm, Eric J. 1997. 'European Union at the End of the Century'. In *European Integration in Social and Historical Perspective*, edited by Jytte Klausen and Louise A. Tilly, 267–75. Lanham, New York, and Oxford: Rowman & Littlefield.

Jarausch, Konrad H. and Thomas Lindenberger eds. 2007. In collaboration with Annelie Ramsbrock, *Conflicted Memories. Europeanizing Contemporary Histories*. New York: Berghahn Books.

Judt, Tony. 2005. *Postwar. A History of Europe*. New York: Penguin.

Judt, Tony. 2008. *Reappraisals. Reflections on the Forgotten Twentieth Century*. New York: Penguin.

Kaelble, Hartmut. 2002. 'The Historical Rise of a European Public Sphere?'. *Journal of European Integration History* 8, 2: 9–22.

Kaelble, Hartmut, and Luisa Passerini. 2002. 'European Public Sphere and European Identity in 20th Century History'. *Journal of European Integration History* 8, 2: 5–8.

Kaiser, Wolfram, Brigitte Leucht, and Morten Rasmussen eds. 2009. *The History of the European Union: Origins of a Trans- and Supranational Polity 1950–72*. New York and London: Routledge.

Krzyżanowski, Michał. 2010. *The Discursive Construction of European Identities: A Multi-level Approach to Discourse and Identity in the Transforming European Union*. Frankfurt am Main and New York: Peter Lang.

Loth, Wilfried ed. 2005. *La gouvernance supranationale dans la construction européenne*. Bruxelles: Bruylant.

Loth, Wilfried ed. 2009. *Experiencing Europe: 50 Years of European Construction 1957–2007*. Baden-Baden: Nomos.

Ludlow, Piers. 2009. 'Widening, Deepening and Opening Out: Towards a Fourth Decade of European Integration History'. In *Experiencing Europe: 50 Years of European Construction 1957–2007*, edited by Wilfried Loth, 33–44. Baden-Baden: Nomos.

Manners, Ian. 2011. 'Global Europe: Mythology of European Union in World Politics'. *Journal of Common Market Studies* 48, 1: 67–87.

Mazé, Camille. 2012. 'Des usages politiques du musée à l'echelle européenne. Contribution à l'analyse de l'européanisation de la mémoire comme catégorie d'action publique'. In *D'une 'mémoire européenne' à 'l'européanisation de la mémoire'*, edited by

Sarah Gensburger and Marie-Claire Lavabre, 73–100. *Politique européenne* 37. Paris: L'Harmattan.

Mazower, Mark. 2000. *Dark Continent. Europe's Twentieth Century*. London: Vintage.

Musolff, Andreas. 2004. *Metaphor and Political Discourse: Analogical Reasoning in Debates about Europe*. New York: Palgrave Macmillan.

Musolff, Andreas, C. Good, P. Points, and R. Wittlinger eds. 2001. *Attitudes towards Europe: Language in the Unification Process*. Aldershot and Burlington, VT: Ashgate.

Neri Serneri, Simone ed. 1999. Forum discussion, 'L'Europa: identità e storia di un continente'. *Contemporanea* 1: 79–102.

Niţoiu, Cristian, and Nikola Tomić. 2013. 'Introduction'. *Perspectives on European Politics and Society* 14, 2: 165–71.

Radaelli, Claudio, and Viviene A. Schmidt. 2005. *Policy Change and Discourse in Europe*. London: Routledge.

Remotti, Francesco. 2010. *L'ossessione identitaria*. Roma–Bari: Laterza.

Richardson, John E., Michał Krzyżanowski, David Machin, and Ruth Wodak. 2014. *Advances in Critical Discourse Studies*. London: Routledge.

Sierp, Aline. 2014. *History, Memory, and Trans-European Identity: Unifying Divisions*. London: Routledge.

Stråth, Bo. 2000a. 'Introduction: Europe as a Discourse'. In *Europe and the Other and Europe as the Other*, edited by Bo Stråth, 13–43. Bruxelles: Peter Lang.

Stråth, Bo. 2000b. *Myth and Memory in the Construction of Community: Historical Patterns in Europe and Beyond*. Bruxelles: Peter Lang.

Stråth, Bo. 2005. 'Methodological and Substantive Remarks on Myth, Memory and History in the Construction of a European Community'. *German Law Journal* 6, 2: 255–71.

Traverso, Enzo. 2009. 'L'Europe et ses mémoires. Trois perspectives croisées'. *Raisons politiques* 4, 36: 151–67.

Waever, Ole. 2009. 'Discursive Approaches'. In *European Integration Theory*, edited by Antje Wiener and Thomas Diez, 197–216. Oxford: Oxford University Press.

Wodak, Ruth, and Salomi Boukala. 2015. 'European Identities and the Revival of Nationalism in the European Union: A Discourse Historical Approach'. *Journal of Language and Politics* 14, 1: 87–109.

Woolf, Stuart. 2003. 'Europe and its Historians'. *Contemporary European History* 12, 3: 323–37.

Wright, Vincent, and Sabino Cassese eds. 1996. *La recomposition de l'État en Europe*. Paris: La Découverte.

Zielonka, Jan ed. 2002. *Europe Unbound: Enlarging and Reshaping the Boundaries of the European Union*. London and New York: Routledge.

Part I

Thinking and regretting Europe

Introduction to Part I

Thinking and regretting Europe

The first part of this book examines the founding moment of modern Europe, the period which, foreshadowed by the Enlightenment, ran from the French Revolution to its most visible European outcome: the Congress of Vienna.

All three essays tackle the problem of the use of history in the contemporary rhetoric and historiography on Europe. All too often this has involved an approach that tends to see history, in particular the history of the Enlightenment, as a sort of a highroad towards European integration, and which is based a posteriori on a simplistic canon and an undeviating story free of exceptions and stumbling blocks. It is also a strategy that ignores periods and viewpoints deemed unhelpful to the progress of the European project. The three essays are thus an attempt to contribute to a reconsideration of the European project by reinterpreting certain distinct moments in the history of the continent.

The word 'thinking' is used in the title above because this first part of the volume focuses on the crucial period of European history in which the first great discourse on Europe emerged, namely the years spanning from the second half of the eighteenth century to the early decades of the nineteenth.

While the current political debate tends to depict the Enlightenment as the cradle of Europe and, conversely, characterizes the counter-Enlightenment (a much less studied movement) as the origin of anti-Europeanism, the first essay reveals how such theories are in fact anti-historical. Through a careful re-examination of the sources, Patrizia Delpiano's contribution explains how, even though Voltaire or Montesquieu did consider the salient features of European society and the constituent elements of Europe, on the whole the Enlightenment did not actually launch a discourse about Europe. Such a debate was instead constructed a posteriori by a historiography ideologically influenced by the post-1945 European project and its lofty vocation, but it was a debate that never actually took place at the time: Europe was not a hot topic even for the Enlightenment thinkers who dedicated some thought to it, nor were there shared positions about the continent. What instead prevailed in the eighteenth century was a plurality of voices and visions, which do not fit with traditional Orientalist or postcolonial theories about the birth of a European sense of superiority. Instead they provide arguments supporting the idea that discourses on Europe (and on other parts of the world) represented an important chapter in the development of a new way of writing history.

Thus the debate on Europe was not baptised by the Enlightenment nor indeed by its detractors. The task was instead left to the French Revolution and the Congress of Vienna, tackled by Manuela Ceretta and Giuseppe Sciara in the second and third chapters. Ceretta investigates the ideological rationale and polemical motivations underlying the counter-revolutionaries' appeal to medieval and Catholic Europe of Charlemagne, while Sciara analyses how discourses on Europe were used instrumentally during the Restoration in order to deal with the internal poltiical struggle. The debates on Europe that developed after 1789 were moulded by a political and historical context in which intellectuals, writers and political actors began to be ever more aware of the strict correlation between domestic politics and foreign policy.

As this European moment progressed, a new way of thinking about the continent closely linked to the concept imposed itself, of which the notion of regret became one of the key cognitive elements, hence the second keyword of our title. When the counter-revolutionaries began to attack the *nation* in the name of Europe and to fight the Revolution in the name of God, Europe began to be regretted for something that no longer existed (e.g. peace, social order) and which in fact had never existed. This manufactured nostalgia became a myth, a memory that would play an important polemical-rhetorical role and serve concrete political objectives. It was no coincidence that discourses on Europe intensified in the moments of greatest crisis, between the First and Second Restorations, when the clash between the old and new France was most ferocious, or following the revolts of the 1820s, when struggles for liberty or for national independence broke out in the east and west of the continent.

Thus the notion of Europe was built on crisis or, more accurately, on a combination of crisis and fear. This is of course an old theme: both Marc Bloch in 1935 and Lucien Febvre in 1944–1945 argued convincingly that these concepts are of key importance to understanding Europe, its hesitations and fragilities. So why listen again to the voices that animated counter-revolutionary circles and refocus on Restoration France? Perhaps, because doing so helps to dismantle, in Febvre's words, 'this seductive image of a completed Europe that has become the true home of the Europeans' and to remind us, in the middle of our own difficult moment, that while crisis and trepidation have been an integral part of European identity, they have also nurtured transformations and visions of change.

1   Thinking Europe in the age of Enlightenment

Philosophes and *antiphilosophes* between universalism and fragmentation

Patrizia Delpiano

Introduction

When talking of the 'House of Europe', the president of the European Parliament, Martin Schulz, recently said that it is 'the greatest achievement of our European civilisation since the Enlightenment'.[1] While there are many European leaders who invoke the Enlightenment movement, seeing it more or less explicitly as one of the founding moments of Europe, there are, on the other side, not a few politicians ready to support a 'Christian Padania, a new Vandea' against 'a Europe without God [...], daughter of the Enlightenment and the French Revolution',[2] as a representative of Italy's Northern League (Lega Nord) party put it. It is a well known fact that historical discourse is an integral part of political debate, but our concern here is rather to highlight how pro- and anti-Europeans alike, albeit with different objectives, make reference to the century of Enlightenment and the French Revolution, thereby establishing close links between the eighteenth and twenty-first centuries.[3] In other words, this chapter takes into account the ideas of eighteenth century *philosophes* and anti-*philosophes* as a tool to unveil how much some of today's discourses on Europe have a tendency to oversimplify its history considering the past a sort of unstoppable and unavoidable path towards the European Union.

These are discourses and counter-discourses that are to be found not only in the political sphere, but also in the historiographical debate. The end of the Cold War and the fall of the Berlin Wall favoured a rapprochement between Eastern and Western Europe that encouraged research into the links between the past and the present, an investigation further stimulated by the birth of the European Union. During the 1990s and the first years of the new century – in the wake of undisguised pro-Europeanist enthusiasm – studies of the idea of Europe and its historical construction in the early modern age multiplied. Thus there emerged renewed enquiries into the links, more or less direct, between certain *philosophes* and the European Union and/or Europe (the two terms are not always kept separate).[4] Indicative of that period are the words used by the historian Krzystof Pomian, director of the Scientific Committee of the Museum of Europe in Brussels, who was prepared to recall Christian traditions in the European Constitution 'on one crucial condition: add immediately that the Europe of today, while having many Christian foundations, was built by the Enlightenment'.[5] These correlations abound and, in some cases, relate to the origins of anti-Europeanism, whose matrices are brought back into the fold of anti-Enlightenment and anti-Revolutionary culture,[6] although resistance to Europe in reality involves a diversity of political orientations.

So is the European Union the daughter – for better or for worse – of the Enlightenment, while anti-Europeanism drinks from the wells of *antiphilosophie*? This discourse and counter-discourse are examined here by giving voice to men of the eighteenth century: the French Enlightenment thinkers (or the *philosophes*, to use the eighteenth-century term), in particular Montesquieu and Voltaire (given that nowadays their names recur persistently), and the *antiphilosophes*, who organized a vigorous opposition to the Enlightenment movement throughout Europe. The chapter is divided into three sections: the image of Europe in the culture of the Enlightenment is analysed (section 1) in particular as related to the specific features that, according to the Enlightenment thinkers, characterized Europe as compared to other civilizations (section 2); the last section is devoted to the *antiphilosophique* culture and to the link between the Enlightenment and Europe through the eyes of opponents of the Enlightenment, a theme underinvestigated so far by historiography.

For both *philosophes* and *antiphilosophes* – who looked suspiciously at the interest philosophes had in other cultures, especially China and the Turkish empire – the idea of an non-compact Europe, of a world divided by deep internal fractures, prevailed. Accordingly in reading their writings one inevitably ends up demolishing every rhetorical, linear and simplistic interpretation of the construction process of the 'House of Europe'. Indeed, this seems to be a good time to do so: with the fading of Europeanist ardour, the current political crisis of the European Union has cooled the passions of even the most fervent historians, making the subject less intense and thus also less conditioned by visions of a teleological character.[7]

To be sure, some of the values that appear to guide the European Union today can be ascribed to Enlightenment culture, from secularism to freedom of thought and of the press. Establishing close anachronistic-type relations between the past and the present is, however, an entirely different matter. A historian of the early modern period will, for example, read with some embarrassment the declaration that 'the eighteenth-century ideal of unifying Europe politically and institutionally was reactivated [...] by Jacques Delors' 1992 European Single Market Project'.[8]

The Europe of the Enlightenment: a pluralistic world

We should begin by making clear – without claiming to have made here a comprehensive state-of-the-art survey – that many studies present the link between Europe and the Enlightenment as a natural tie, albeit one that can be interpreted in different ways. Whereas many (the majority) focus on a literary Europe, anchored to the role of the *république des lettres* and therefore elitist, some see the *philosophes* as having offered 'an ideal of Europe as a harmonious system of balancing states',[9] and still others present a picture of an Enlightenment Europe 'in search of its identity'.[10] Calling this nexus into question is so difficult that even those who work in that direction (including myself) risk reflecting implicitly on the concept of European identity,[11] in other words taking it for granted when, for example, analysing the role of trade or when bringing to the fore the creation of the history of Europe as a product of the Enlightenment.[12]

The heterogeneity of the interpretation of the relationship between Europe and the Enlightenment cannot however be passed off with the quip that 'European history is whatever the historian wants it to be'.[13] This diversity is not only in the eyes of the historian who interprets it,[14] but is also found in the ideas of Europe that emerge from eighteenth-century sources: ideas that appear much more varied than what has so far resulted from historiography. In fact, a closer look shows that no single image of Europe arises from *philosophique* culture and, furthermore, that Europe does not seem to be a compact world at all. It should also be noted that for the *philosophes* (as well as *antiphilosophes*) Europe was not a burning issue of debate about which they needed to direct public opinion. In other words, there was no 'problem of Europe' equivalent to the questions that engaged many *philosophes*, from education (private or public) to the death penalty. Studying the relationship between the Enlightenment and Europe therefore does not mean piecing together this (hypothetical) debate, but rather it means reflecting on images of Europe derived from the words of the *philosophes*, without ever claiming to be able to identify specific standpoints about a subject which, in fact, is an object of analysis constructed by present-day scholars.

Heterogeneity, then. In effect, the *siècle philosophique* was not marked only by the plans for a unified Europe theorised by men like the Abbé de Saint-Pierre, Jean-Jacques Rousseau or Immanuel Kant. In the work of some thinkers we find more complex ideas, which can only be understood by adopting, transversely, two perspectives: on the one hand, that which leads us to consider how the *philosophes* thought of Europe and, on the other, that which leads us to wonder what they thought about the other three parts of the known world (Africa, America, Asia). These two approaches have till now been kept virtually separate in the studies conducted so far, hence they have centred on just one aspect despite the fact that a broad-based view can be obtained only by weaving the two together.

It is well known that both Montesquieu and Voltaire ascribed specific traits to European civilization. In Montesquieu's work the continent is characterized over time by a power that was completely different, both in its republican form as in its monarchies, to the despotism that typified Asia: 'liberty', according to the *Lettres persanes* (1721), 'seems to be calculated to the genius of the nations of Europe, and slavery adapted to that of the Asiatics'.[15] A clear distinction is also drawn in the *Esprit des lois* (1748), where 'the liberty of Europe', is compared to 'the slavery of Asia'.[16] Voltaire, for his part, in *Le siècle de Louis XIV* (1751) offered an image that would enjoy considerable success:

> Christian Europe, all except Russia, might for a long time have been con-
> sidered as a sort of great Republic, divided into several states, some monarchi-
> cal and others mixt. Of the latter, some were aristocratic, and other popular;
> but all connected with one another; all professing the same system of religion,
> though divided into several sects; all acknowledging the same principles of
> public justice and policies, unknown to the other nations of the world.[17]

Thus we must observe, against any unifying vision of the relationship between
Europe and the Enlightenment, the difference that emerges between the two
authors who are often considered to be the founding fathers of the 'House of
Europe'. For Montesquieu, Europe was identified primarily with political
freedom; for Voltaire, the European states were instead unified by the Christian
religion and their political principles, a view that is also found in the 'Europe'
entry of the *Encyclopédie*, written by Louis de Jaucourt.[18]

Second, though the *philosophes* identified certain common traits in Europe,
they did not fail to point out its internal differences. In their eyes these distinctions were no less important than those that they recognized between Europe and
other parts of the world. What we see in the many *philosophique* texts, starting
with the *Lettres persanes*, are several distinct Europes. For Montesqueu, Asia
was a politically compact world 'where the rules of policy are every where the
same', while Europe was noted precisely for its contrasting governments, some
'mild', others 'severe';[19] some powerful (like the Holy Roman Empire and the
kingdoms of France, Spain and England), others subdivided into small states,
like those of Italy, described by a metaphor that recalled the world of the Turks
('caravanserials, where they are obliged to lodge their first comers').[20] While
Europe was marked on the political level by the presence of republics, a form of
government unknown in Asia,[21] and by monarchies devoid of the absolute power
held by the sultans,[22] in the European past there had been a 'military and violent
government' (a reference to the Roman empire under Caesar).[23]

Of particular significance were the differences between the various European
states in terms of freedom, as the *Lettres philosophiques* (1734) pointed out.
According to Voltaire, England was the home par excellence of religious freedom,
which was ensured by the presence of a variety of sects that managed to coexist
peacefully: 'This is the country of sects. An Englishman, as a free man, goes to
heaven by whatever road he pleases'.[24] Despite the presence of two dominant religions – the Anglicans and the Presbyterians (in Scotland) – all the others were
'welcome there and live[d] pretty comfortably together', to the extent that Jews,
Muslims and Christians traded with each other without conflict (here he used the
famous metaphor of the London stock exchange).[25] As for political freedom, this
was firmly rooted in the Magna Carta.[26] The country of the freedom of the press,
Britain was differentiated from the European countries that did not enjoy such a
right. At the other extreme there was the Italian peninsula, characterized by the presence of the Inquisition, where 'the miserable inhabitants are damned in the midst of
paradise'.[27] And France, too, was portrayed negatively, on account of its religious
censorship against the theatre, described as an authentic 'gothic barbarity'.[28]

The existence of internal frontiers is confirmed by the analysis of the *Esprit des lois*, where Montesquieu outlined a Northern Europe distinguished by its energy and freedom and a Europe of the *Midi*, marked by 'indolence' and 'slavery': a conception, then, which Montesquieu did not reserve exclusively for the Asiatic world.[29] And, again, the identification of commonalities in Europe did not deter Voltaire, in *Le siècle de Louis XIV*, from pointing out the abyss separating Spain, whose sovereigns had used their absolute power to sow terror,[30] from a country like the United Provinces, 'a singular example in the world, of what can be effected by the love of liberty, and indefatigable labour'.[31] What emerges from the works of Montesquieu and Voltaire, therefore, is a diverse Europe whose internal boarders were not even the same: while Montesquieu was consistently inclined to separate *les pays du nord* from *les pays du Midi*, two groups of striking contrast in terms of political and intellectual freedom, Voltaire does not appear to present an image of long-term stability. In the *Essai sur les moeurs* (1756) he described the *peuples du Nord*, united by their shared *esprit républicain*,[32] while in the *Dictionnaire philosophique* (1764) he instead thought in terms of states.

An example of this is the entry *Liberté de penser*, based on an imaginary dialogue between an impressively named English general officer, Lord Boldmind, and an equally significantly named Spaniard, Count Medroso ('fearful' in Spanish). The latter, a member of the Inquisition, had preferred – as he explained – to be the Inquisition's 'servant' rather than its 'victim'. Thus a strong contrast is drawn between the Europe of freedom (England and the United Provinces), linked to the classical literary tradition, and the Europe of the Inquisition (Spain and Portugal), associated with the triumph of hagiography. 'The Holy Office has clipped your wings', Lord Boldmind says to Medroso, who admits that in fact,

> it is not permitted us either to write, speak, or even to think [...]; and as we cannot be condemned in an *auto-da-fé* for our secret thoughts, we are menaced with being burned eternally by the order of God himself.

Medroso later receives from the English officer the well-known Horatian challenge to 'dare to think for yourself'.[33] The attack on censorship, moral and institutional, that also existed in France, was thus direct and expressed through a discourse on the condition of the *hommes de lettres* that included a long list of the persecuted, from Descartes to the *philosophes*.[34]

The Europe of the Enlightenment thinkers was therefore a sum of heterogeneous discourses, that is, a pluralized world where the languages of freedom were English and Dutch, while the old humanist countries, especially Italy, had become the hunting grounds of Inquisitors and places of intellectual conformism.

Crossed perspectives on changing civilizations

Turning now to trace the *philosophes*' perspective on the other three parts of the world, it must immediately be noted that this field of enquiry has long been influenced by the reading of Edward Said and his idea of 'orientalism', a term that, as is well known, refers in the works of this scholar and his followers to an attitude of disdain mixed with a sense of superiority on the part of the Europeans and/or Westerners towards the Orient, an attitude whose origins lie in the culture of the Enlightenment.[35] Having become a sort of academic orthodoxy *à la mode*, Said's analysis, propounded mainly in the context of postcolonial studies and gradually extended in space and time, has resulted – in its most negative outcomes – in an insistence on the malign face of the European identity, an identity (here again taken for granted) that was constructed on the exclusion of the Other, with a surprising continuity over the years, running from the Crusades to the genocide of the Jews.[36]

It is not difficult to find proof to support this notion by taking phrases from the works of the *philosophes* out of context and choosing not to offer a comprehensive interpretation of their ideas, which were in fact wide-ranging. It is, however, at least to those who read the sources in question in their entirety, that this approach is unfounded, as several historians have noted.[37] The attitude of the *philosophes* was not at all steeped in the Eurocentrism that purportedly constituted a sort of premise for nineteenth-century colonialism. It was in actual fact a universalistic outlook that prompted many *philosophes* to pursue a comparative analysis both of the different countries in Europe and between Europe and the other parts of the world, which in their opinion were also internally composite structures. This was a transversal comparison that surpassed internal and external frontiers to reflect on differences and similarities within and outside Europe. When Montesquieu considered questions such as justice, for example, he set Turkey side by side with Persia and, at the same time, with the republics of the United Provinces and Venice, not to mention the English monarchy.[38] Similarly, when Voltaire deliberated on the best form of government in the world, he did not fix his attention only on Europe but extended it to other parts of the world, in particular Asia, from India to Tartary. Indeed, his dialogue between the European, Indian and Brahmin ended with an affirmation that found all the protagonists in agreement: the best government was to be found 'where only the laws are obeyed', a government that did not exist, for which reason, we read, 'we must look for it'.[39]

It is true that thinkers like Montesquieu and Voltaire discussed the merits and defects of other parts of the world so as to talk about their own, in other words to improve the institutions of Europe. Yet this did not keep them from providing a generally balanced and unprejudiced survey, as is demonstrated by the journey presented by Montesquieu in the *Lettres persanes*, to which we return in order to demonstrate the impossibility of reducing his view of the world to simplifications. Africa – largely unknown beyond its coastal areas – appeared to him to be a world populated by 'savages' ill-disposed to work,[40] but the author was not silent on the issue of the trafficking of slaves to America. Quite the reverse, he denounced the willingness

> to fling away the lives of infinite numbers of men, to get out of the bowels of the earth gold and silver: those metals in themselves so useless, and which are Riches only because they have been chosen for the marks of them.[41]

As for Asia, this was broken down into its various regions. The Persian court from where Usbek had set out appeared corrupt.[42] And the Turkish empire – 'that huge distemper'd body' built on severe laws and a despotic government – was populated by 'barbarians' that had abandoned the arts: 'While the nations of Europe grow more and more knowing every day, they [these barbarians] remain in their ancient ignorance'.[43] Nevertheless, Montesquieu levelled equally strong criticism at European sovereigns, who were either religious or political leaders. Suffice it to recall the ironic depiction of the king of France as the 'great magician', able to exercise power over his subjects to the point of making them think 'just as he wou'd have them' (the reference was to the supposed healing power of the king, linked to the touching of those affected by scrofula). No less scathing was his depiction of the pope, 'another magician stronger than him'.[44] When the discussion turned to the treatment of heretics ('those who publish any new proposition') in certain parts of Europe, the roles were reversed, given the Spanish and Italian inclination to 'burn a man as they would burn straw'.[45]

What we see by analysing the ideas of the *philosophes* about other parts of the world, is, once more, the diversity of their positions. China is a case in point. While Montesquieu highlighted its negative aspects in matters of ethics and government practice, Voltaire offered a very different picture.[46] He admired the Chinese civilization's antiquity and its prowess in the field of inventions (one thinks of gunpowder, for example) – considered at length in his *Essai sur les moeurs* – even if that inventiveness did not appear to him to be always matched by an ability to perfect their discoveries. He saw as adverse factors the Chinese people's excessive respect for tradition and their extremely difficult language, but, in contrast, considered the Chinese unbeatable on the level of morals and laws.[47]

Voltaire was even more explicit in the *Dictionnaire philosophique*, where he defended the Peking government from the accusation of atheism: here the antiquity of China implied the awareness of a 'we' long linked to 'our savage territories'.[48] The Chinese certainly did not excel in the sciences: on the contrary, to Voltaire they seemed to be at the stage where the Europeans ('we') had been two centuries earlier. Yet this did not prevent him from acknowledging that Chinese civilization had the world's best 'constitution', thanks to the presence of a power exercised paternalistically and the role accorded to virtue. The wisdom and tolerance of the Chinese government in particular pointed to a possible escape route from the dogmatism of certain European states. As to fanaticism, in fact, if ever there was a religion that had shown general disregard for the concept of tolerance, it was certainly Christianity.[49] For Voltaire, the homeland of tolerance was Asia[50] and definitely not Europe, which during the religious wars had employed – in terms of methods used against heretics, from the stake to massacres – various forms of torture worthy of the worst barbarism.[51] This thought concerned the present as well as the past, since religious freedom in Voltaire's time was guaranteed only in a few countries, namely Germany, England and the United Provinces.[52]

What linked the *philosophes'* twofold perspective on Europe's internal and external frontiers seems clear: it was a new way of writing history. This was not so much because the Enlightenment thinkers had invented the history of Europe,[53] but rather because they experimented with a new history, one that was no longer tied to the idea of a providential plan but was instead secular and universal. In so doing, they also gave Europe a historical foundation within the framework of a far more expansive, spacious world that corresponded to all known human life. The attention to history, furthermore, could not fail to be accompanied by an awareness of change: the *philosophes'* position did not pin down any European country or any of the other three parts of the world into a definitive phase of development, and it did not recognize any immutable hierarchies of supremacy of one over the others.[54] In this sense, the aforementioned entry in the *Encyclopédie* by de Jaucourt is explicit, clearly showing the difficulty of extricating oneself from what he defined as a 'labyrinth' because Europe had never been known by a single name, nor the same divisions: it was, in fact, a reality experiencing change.[55]

The universalism of the Enlightenment mirrored by *antiphilosophie*

In turning our attention to the opponents of the Enlightenment active in the Catholic countries, men of state and of the church much less well known than the *philosophes*, the first point to underline is that their counter-discourse on Europe also did not see the continent as a problem to be placed at the centre of public debate. The scholars who identified a cornerstone of Anti-Europeanism in the *antiphilosophique* culture effectively use the word *antiphilosophie*, or the more prevalent *Counter-Enlightenment*, ahistorically: in other words they refer not to the period in which this movement was expressed (the second half of the eighteenth century) but to an orientation – subsequently still detectable – based on strong anti-cosmopolitan attitudes, on the role of the Catholic religion in public life, on the link between throne and altar, and on the defence of the duties of man (as opposed to the idea of rights).[56] Examining certain themes tackled by these thinkers thus helps, on the one hand, to bring to light their image of Europe and, conversely to think about the link between the Enlightenment and Europe. The fears stoked by the *antiphilosophes* in fact serve as a lens, albeit one deformed by the prejudices of the enemy, through which to verify what Enlightenment thinkers thought about Europe and the world.

Leaving aside various issues that are central to the historiographical debate but beyond the scope of this chapter,[57] it should first of all be noted that the pluralized image of Europe which can be traced in the works of the *philosophes* can also be found in *antiphilosophique* literature, albeit with a reversal of perspective. The countries which thinkers such as Montesquieu and Voltaire associated with political and intellectual freedom (England and the United Provinces) were here given destructive connotations, being defined as dangerous hotbeds of free thinking: damned places, to steer clear of. These are ideas that characterize a large part of *antiphilosophique* cultural output and which we will delve into here with some examples related to the Catholic world.

It will be helpful to begin with France, where the *antiphilosophique* movement – in close contact with the men and books of the Enlightenment – developed early on and organized, by means of an extraordinary use of the press (books, periodicals and dictionaries), a sort of trial of the *philosophes* who were accused of constituting a party variously described as a 'sect'[58] or an 'audacious cabal'.[59] Few doubted that there were already enemies within the borders of the kingdom. Enlightenment thinkers were, however, the descendants of Luther and Calvin, as well as Protestant thinkers such as Bayle and Collins, Newton and Locke, who shared an accursed origin because they all came from countries infected by the disease of heresy. This was a heresy which, moreover, contained another equally damaging virus: that of religious tolerance.[60] Having assimilated the principle of private interpretation, which was extended into every field of knowledge, those who lived in England and the United Provinces had more easily absorbed the *philosophique* poison. The French who had visited these countries or who had read the books produced in them had met the same fate. What was more, the picture painted of the *philosophe* was eloquent: he loved the republican countries, where tolerance – which in the eyes of the *antiphilosophes* represented unbridled recklessness – implied contempt for the throne and the altar.[61]

The memory of the religious schism of the sixteenth century was even more significant on the Italian peninsula, where the consolidation of the Church of Rome was closely interwoven with the victory over Protestant heresy. Even if the times were very different from those in which fires were lit not only to burn books, in the eighteenth century censors still continued to act against Protestantism, being required to condemn works that smacked of heresy on behalf of the two courts in charge of censorship (the Holy Office or Inquisition and the Congregation of the Index of Forbidden Books). Many *antiphilosophes* shared the opinion of the Dominican, Daniello Concina, according to whom books extolling deism or, worse, atheism, all published in England and the United Provinces (a claim that was in fact untrue), were 'a monstrous progeny [...] of the new reform of the Protestants'. Italian literature also defined the *philosophe* in accordance with his provenance: he arrived from the North, the land of the Protestants, a land generically situated over the Alps and depicted as a unified world that drew no distinction between the Calvinist United Provinces or Anglican England. The same was true of dangerous books which – produced 'over the mountains' – came 'among us to massacre'[62] and which were mostly written in an 'affected foreign language'.[63]

If the *philosophes* were dangerous, they were so – according to the *antiphilosophes'* judgment – not because they aimed to create unions of states within Europe. There was of course a risk that dangerous lines of communication would be opened between a Protestant North and the Catholic countries: the fear was, in fact, that the circulation of *philosophique* principles throughout Europe might help extend freedom of thought and of the press as well as religious tolerance (to say nothing of a *tout court* attack on the very idea of a creator God) from the North to the South. But the aspect most worth drawing attention to is the importance given by many *antiphilosophes* to the historical reconstruction offered by the Enlightenment. A prime example of this, because it is drenched in the *topoi* that can be traced in other authors (of then and later), is the work of the Jesuit Claude-François Nonnotte, *Les erreurs de Voltaire* (1762), which enjoyed an extraordinary circulation in eighteenth-century Europe and which we will analyse as a depository of opinions that were then widely shared.[64]

Many of the mistakes challenged in the book related in effect to the historical work of the *philosophe*, who was accused – with reference to the *Essai sur les moeurs* – of writing 'in the spirit of an ignorant Hottentot, or a blind Muslim'.[65] In the eyes of their opponents the *philosophes* were violating completely different limits to those of interest to the *antiphilosophes*, who feared the spread of the *libertas philosophandi* from the Protestant North to the Catholic South. These were confines that were outside of Europe and which were conceived in different ways (Muscovy and Turkey, for instance, were positioned differently by individual thinkers). If within Europe the Enlightenment demonstrated a clear preference for Protestant countries to the detriment of Catholic ones, worse was done externally. Barely respectful of religion in general, they never missed a chance to denigrate the faith in Christ for the benefit of other religions, which they deemed more tolerant than Christianity.[66] Being anything but promoters of a Eurocentric vision of the world or of a superior attitude towards the Other, the thinkers of the Enlightenment – again according to the *antiphilosophes* – did nothing but denigrate national habits and customs and commend foreign ones to the point that there was no lack of suspicion of 'a veritable contempt [...] for their nation'.[67] As if that were not enough, the *philosophes* praised other civilizations, especially China, but also the Turkish empire: Voltaire, who condemned the 'fanaticism of Europe'[68] dared to discern wisdom and reason among the infidels and idolaters.[69] And worst of all, he considered Mohammed to be 'a sublime genius' and portrayed the Turkish government as 'gentle, moderate, fair'.[70]

It was thus the absence of prejudice towards other civilizations, towards their habits and customs and religions, on the part of the Enlightenment that really disturbed the sleep of eighteenth-century conservatives. Ready to defend a supposed order built in large part against the principles of the Enlightenment, the *antiphilosophes* abhorred the *philosophique* sympathy towards other civilizations and cultures, a propensity that risked calling into question the central role of the Christian religion, considered the only one worthy of veneration.

Conclusions

Neither the *philosophes* nor the *antiphilosophes* considered Europe in terms of a problem. As regards the first, the baselessness of the idea that they would introduce and, indeed, invent a European sense of superiority over other civilizations should be underscored. Such a feeling would in fact presuppose a unified image of Europe, which did not exist at all in the minds of the Enlightenment thinkers, who were instead at pains to compare different internal parts of the known world and to apply to both the opposing concepts of wisdom and barbarity. They were able to do so because they devised a new way of looking at the history of mankind, thereby providing Europe and the other parts of the world with a historical foundation without, however, Europe becoming a topic of political debate. That in fact would occur in different ways only after 1789, in the thoughts of the revolutionaries and counter-revolutionaries. The latter would evoke the notion of a Europe which in effect never existed, a Europe of the *ancien régime* which, to their minds, had been swept away by the Revolution.[71]

Just as it is impossible to find a legacy of images of Europe that endured over the long term,[72] so it is impossible to trace a single representation with reference to the eighteenth century. However, the 'House of Europe' was never envisaged by the *philosophes* who – in support of the values of cosmopolitanism – thought of much broader boundaries: indeed, even of a world without borders. And the point of the principles that the European Union can inherit or has inherited from the Enlightenment, from secularism to the freedom of conscience, is altogether another thing, another story.

Notes

1 Schulz 2015.
2 I am quoting the declaration made in April 2003 by the then Member of the European Parliament for the Northern League, Mario Borghezio, as published in the party's newspaper. The article, 'Il governo boccia l'Europa senza radici cristiane', *La Padania*, 31 May 2003, is quoted by Pivato 2007. From a geographical point of view, Padania is the Po Valley, the plain in the North of Italy (Padus is the Latin name of the Po river). This word is used today by the Northern League, a federalist political party, with a political connotation as a possible name for an independent State or territorial unit in Northern Italy.
3 For a consideration of the use of the eighteenth century in the current political debate on the crisis of the European Union, see Rosenfeld 2014.
4 See, for example, Rolland 1994; Postigliola and Bottaro Palumbo 1995. On the European Union and historical studies see Verga 2003.
5 Pomian 2004.
6 This is the interpretation proposed by Holmes 2000, 83–85.
7 In this direction see Pocock 2002, but also Pocock 1994. See also Passerini 2012; Lilti and Spector 2014.
8 Ishay 1994, 210.
9 O'Brien 1997, 2.
10 This is the title of the first part of the volume by Py 2004.
11 On the relationships between European history and the expansion of trade in Montesquieu (who in fact had reservations about the latter) see Spector 2014.
12 Lilti 2014, 140. On the role of history see also, amongst others, O'Brien 1997. On histories of Europe in the Enlightenment era see Verga 2008 as well as Verga 2004.
13 This affirmation, by the historian Alan John Percivale Taylor, was made in an article published in the magazine *History Today* in 1986 and is quoted in Evans 2010, 593.
14 For a historiographical assessment that also pays attention to the uses of the word 'Europe' by the historians of the eighteenth century, see Albertone 2008.
15 Montesquieu 1721, II, Lettre CXXV, 226–233, 230; Montesquieu 1972, II, 202–208, 206.
16 Montesquieu 1973, I, XVII, 3, 296–298, 298; Montesquieu 1777, I, 351–354, 353.
17 Voltaire 1751, I, 11; Voltaire 1779, 7.
18 De Jaucourt 1756.

19 Montesquieu 1721, II, Lettre LXXVIII, 30–34, 30–31; Montesquieu 1972, II, 30–33, 30–31.
20 Montesquieu 1721, II, Lettre XCIX, 109–114, 110; Montesquieu 1972, II, 99–103, 99.
21 Montesquieu 1721, II, Lettre CXXV, 226–233, 226; Montesquieu 1972, II, 201–208, 202.
22 Montesquieu 1721, II, Lettre XCIX, 109–114; Montesquieu 1972, II, 99–103.
23 Montesquieu 1721, II, Lettre CXXV, 226–233; 231; Montesquieu 1972, II, 202–208, 206.
24 Voltaire 1734, Lettre V, 44–51, 44; Voltaire 1961, 22–24. The work was published in English for the first time under the title *Letters Concerning the English Nation* (Voltaire 1733).
25 Voltaire 1734, Lettre VI, 52–57, 55; Voltaire 1961, 25–26, 26.
26 Voltaire 1734, Lettres VIII-IX, 64–73, 74–86; Voltaire 1961, 30–33, 34–38.
27 Voltaire 1734, Lettre XX, 237–242, 241; Voltaire 1961, 95–98, 97.
28 Voltaire 1734, Lettre XXIII, 265–274, 274; Voltaire 1961, 110–113, 113.
29 Montesquieu 1973, in particular I, XIV, 2, 245–248, 248; Montesquieu 1777, 293–297, 296. See Rétat 1995.
30 Voltaire 1751, I, 19; Voltaire 1779, 11.
31 Voltaire 1751, I, 23; Voltaire 1779, 12.
32 Voltaire 1963; II, 370–371. Regarding the publishing history of the *Essai*, revised and republished by the author until his death (a posthumous edition was issued in 1785), see Voltaire 1963. See the recently published edition Voltaire 2009–2015.
33 The entry appears in the second, expanded edition of 1765. Voltaire, *Liberté de penser*, in Voltaire 1765b, 224–228; *Liberty of opinion*, in Voltaire 1901 (https:// ebooks.adelaide.edu.au/v/voltaire/dictionary/chapter307.html). On the publishing history of the work, see Mervaud 2008 (second edition), 13–42.
34 See, in particular, Voltaire, *Lettres, gens de lettres, ou lettrés*, an entry included for the first time in the following edition: Voltaire 1765a, II, 85–88; Voltaire, *Philosophe*, in Voltaire 1765b, 283–288; *Letters (men of)*, in Voltaire 1901 (https://ebooks. adelaide.edu.au/v/voltaire/dictionary/chapter304.html); *Philosopher*, in Voltaire 1901 (https://ebooks.adelaide.edu.au/v/voltaire/dictionary/chapter361.html).
35 Said 1978. See, for example, den Boer 1995, 58: 'European feelings of superiority were based on a conglomeration of ideas proceeding from the Enlightenment which, in turn, came to be associated with the notion of civilization'.
36 This is hypothesized by, amongst others, the political theorist Delanty 1995.
37 For a critical discussion of the notion of orientalism, see Clarke 2006 and Minuti (who correctly insists on the specificity of seventeenth- and eighteenth-century culture) 2006; Harvey 2012.
38 Montesquieu 1721, II, Lettre LXXVIII, 30–34, 32; Montesquieu 1972, II, 215–219.
39 Voltaire, *État, gouvernements. Quel est le meilleur?* in Voltaire 1764, 178–183; *States, governments*, in Voltaire 1901, https://ebooks.adelaide.edu.au/v/voltaire/ dictionary/chapter430.html.
40 Montesquieu 1721, II, Lettre CXVI, 187–189; Montesquieu 1972, II, 166–168.
41 Montesquieu 1721, II, Lettre CXIV, 181–183, 182–183; Montesquieu 1972, II, 161–163, 162–163.
42 Montesquieu 1721, I, Lettre VIII, 26–29; Montesquieu 1972, I, 24–27.
43 Montesquieu 1721, I, Lettre XVIII, 75–78; Montesquieu 1972, I, 66–69.
44 Montesquieu 1721, I, Lettre XXII, pp. 89–96; Montesquieu 1972, I, 78–85.
45 Montesquieu 1721, I, Lettre XXVII, 116–121, 118, 119; Montesquieu 1972, I, 100–105, 102, 103.
46 On the despotism of China, see Montesquieu 1973, I, VIII, 21, 138–140; Montesquieu 1777, 162–165. On the varied positions taken by the *philosophes* in relation to China, see Jones 2001. On Montesquieu see pages 30ff.
47 Voltaire 1963, I, 215–216.
48 Voltaire, *De la Chine*, in Voltaire 1764, 87–91, 90; *China*, in Voltaire 1901 (https:// ebooks.adelaide.edu.au/v/voltaire/dictionary/chapter114.html).

49 Voltaire, *Tolérance*, in Voltaire 1764, 338–341; *Toleration*, in Voltaire 1901 (https://ebooks.adelaide.edu.au/v/voltaire/dictionary/chapter452.html).
50 'Go into India, Persia, and Tartary, and you will meet with the same toleration and the same tranquility'. Voltaire 1764a (4 *Si la tolérance est dangereuse; et chez quel peuples elle est pratiquée*), 28–42, 36; Voltaire 1764b (4 *Whether Toleration is dangerous and among what Nations it is practised*), 37–52, 46.
51 Voltaire 1764a (3 *Idée de la Réforme du seizième siècle*), 22–28; Voltaire 1764b (3 *A Sketch of the Reformation in the Sixteenth Century*), 28–36.
52 Voltaire 1764a, *passim*; Voltaire 1764b, *passim*. On the role of China in the *philosophique* debate on tolerance see Clarke 2006, who insists, more generally, on the importance of the oriental tradition on the evolution of Western thought.
53 Lilti 2014.
54 On the search for a science of man capable of unifying all the people of the world, in the context of Enlightenment culture, see Harvey 2012. Still of great importance is Diaz 1958. On the shift in the eighteenth century, a period in which America also came to influence the writing of history in Europe, see Burke 1995; Armitage 1995.
55 De Jaucourt 1756.
56 Holmes 2000, who sees a link between today's anti-Europeanism and the Counter-Enlightenment, referring also to other politicians such as Yvan Blot, *maitre à penser* of Jean-Marie Le Pen.
57 I refer above all to the question of the consistency or heterogeneity of the *antiphilosophique* movement, on which see Masseau 2000 and Masseau 2014. See also McMahon 2001; Israel 2011, 140ff. In relation to the Italian space and its relations between the French and Italian worlds, see Delpiano (forthcoming) and Delpiano 2015.
58 Gauchat 1754–1763 [1758], *Avertissement*, III–IX.
59 Ferlet 1773.
60 Gauchat 1754–1763 [1759], II, XIII, *Lettre CXXXIV*, 261 and [Pinault], 1770.
61 Gauchat 1754–1763 [1757], II, VIII, *Lettre LXXXIV*, 194–215, 195, 200.
62 Concina 1754, I, 13.
63 Viganego 1772–1774, I, *Prefazione*, III–XXXIV, XXVIII.
64 Nonnotte 1762. Among the various editions, see the following: Nonnotte 1766; Nonnotte 1767; Nonnotte 1770. Italian editions, entitled *Gli errori di Voltaire* were published in, among other places: Nonnotte 1773 and Nonnotte 1774 and 1778.
65 The quotations are taken from the following edition: Nonnotte 1766, I, *Discours préliminaire*, X–XI. On the attack on Voltaire's *Essai*, see Gembicki 1997.
66 Nonnotte 1766, XV.
67 Nonnotte 1766, XXVIII.
68 Nonnotte 1766, 202.
69 Nonnotte 1766, XVII–XVIII and *passim*.
70 Nonnotte 1766, 80, 256–257.
71 See M. Ceretta, Chapter 2 in this volume.
72 For a reflection on the discontinuities between the mental representations of Europe, see Passerini and Nordera 2000.

References

Albertone, Manuela. 2008. 'The Idea of Europe in the Eighteenth Century in History and Historiography'. *History of European Ideas* 34, 4: 349–352.
Armitage, David. 1995. 'The New World and British Historical Thought. From Richard Hakluyt to William Robertson'. In *America in European Consciousness*, 1493–1750, edited by Karen Ordahl Kupperman, 52–75. Chapel Hill, NC: University of North Carolina Press, Published for the Institute of Early American History and Culture.

Boer den, Pim. 1995. 'Europe to 1914: The Making of an Idea. Introduction'. In *The History of Idea of Europe*, edited by Kevin Wilson and Jan van der Dussen, 13–82. London and New York: Routledge.

Burke, Peter. 1995. 'America and the Rewriting of World History'. In *America in European Consciousness, 1493–1750*, edited by Karen Ordahl Kupperman, 33–51. Chapel Hill, NC: University of North Carolina Press, Published for the Institute of Early American History and Culture.

Clarke, John J. 2006 (First edition 1997). *Oriental Enlightenment. The Encounter between Asian and Western Thought*. London: Routledge.

Delanty, Gerard. 1995. *Inventing Europe. Idea, Identity, Reality*. New York: St. Martin Press.

Delpiano, Patrizia. 2015. *Liberi di scrivere. La battaglia per la stampa nell'età dei Lumi*. Roma–Bari: Laterza.

Delpiano, Patrizia. *forthcoming*. 'Censure et guerre des livres: l'antiphilosophie, de la France à l'Italie'. In *La traduction comme dispositif de communication dans l'Europe moderne*, edited by Patrice Bret and Jeanne Peiffer. Paris: Hermann.

Diaz, Furio. 1958. *Voltaire storico*. Turin: Einaudi.

Evans, Richard J. 2010. 'What is European History? Reflections of a Cosmopolitan Islander'. *European History Quarterly* 40, 4: 593–605.

Gembicki, Dieter. 1997. 'La polémique autour de l'Essai sur les mœurs (de Bury, Verney, Nonnotte)'. In *Voltaire et ses combats*, edited by Ulla Kôlving and Christiane Mervaud, 2 vols; II, 1289–1344. Oxford: Voltaire Foundation.

Harvey, David Allen. 2012. *The French Enlightenment and Its Others: The Mandarin, the Savage, and the Invention of the Human Sciences*. New York: Palgrave Macmillan.

Holmes, Douglas R. 2000. *Integral Europe Fast-capitalism, Multiculturalism, Neofascism*. Princeton, NJ: Princeton University Press.

Ishay, Micheline. 1994. 'European Integration: The Enlightenment Legacy'. *History of European Ideas* 19, 1–3: 207–213.

Israel, Jonathan I., 2011. *Democratic Enlightenment. Philosophy, Revolution, and Human Rights 1750–1790*. Oxford: Oxford University Press.

Jones, David Martin. 2001. *The Image of China in Western Social and Political Thought*. New York: Palgrave.

Lilti, Antoine. 2014. 'La civilisation est-elle européenne? Écrire l'histoire de l'Europe au XVIIIe siècle'. In *Penser l'Europe au XVIIIe siècle. Commerce, civilisation, empire*, edited by Antoine Lilti and Céline Spector, 139–166. *Oxford University Studies in the Enlightenment*, 10.

Lilti, Antoine, and Céline Spector, eds. 2014. 'Introduction: l'Europe des Lumières, généalogie d'un concept'. In *Penser l'Europe au XVIIIe siècle. Commerce, civilisation, empire*, edited by Antoine Lilti and Céline Spector, 1–15. *Oxford University Studies in the Enlightenment*, 10.

Masseau, Didier. 2000. *Les ennemis des philosophes. L'antiphilosophie au temps des Lumières*. Paris: Albin Michel.

Masseau, Didier. 2014. 'Qu'est-ce que les anti-Lumières?' *Dix-huitième siècle* 46, 1: 107–123.

McMahon, Darrin M. 2001. *Enemies of the Enlightenment. The French Counter-Enlightenment and the Making of Modernity*. Oxford: Oxford University Press.

Mervaud, Christiane. 2008. *Le Dictionnaire philosophique de Voltaire* (second edition). Paris, Oxford: Presses de l'Université Paris Sorbonne-Voltaire Foundation.

Minuti, Rolando. 2006. *Orientalismo e idee di tolleranza nella cultura francese del primo '700*. Florence: Olschki.

O'Brien, Karen. 1997. *Narratives of Enlightenment. Cosmopolitan History from Voltaire to Gibbon.* Cambridge and New York: Cambridge University Press.

Passerini, Luisa. 2012. 'Europe and its Others: Is there a European Identity?' In *The Oxford Handbook of Postwar European History*, edited by Dan Stone, 120–138. Oxford: Oxford University Press.

Passerini, Luisa, and Marina Nordera, eds. 2000. *Images of Europe.* European University Institute, Florence, Working Paper HEC 2000, 5, 5.

Pivato, Stefano. 2007. *Vuoti di memoria. Usi e abusi della storia nella vita pubblica italiana.* Roma–Bari: Laterza.

Pocock, John Greville Agard. 1994. 'Deconstructing Europe?' *History of European Ideas* 18, 3: 329–345.

Pocock, John Greville Agard. 2002. 'Some Europes in Their History'. In *The Idea of Europe from Antiquity to the European Union*, edited by Anthony Pagden, 55–71. Cambridge: Woodrow Wilson Center and Cambridge University Press.

Pomian, Krzystof. 2004. 'L'Europe, fille de l'Église et des Lumières'. *L'Express,* 1 October. http://lexpansion.lexpress.fr/actualite-economique/l-europe-fille-de-l-eglise-et-des-lumieres_1340094.html.

Postigliola, Alberto and Maria Grazia Bottaro Palumbo, eds. 1995. *L'Europe de Montesquieu.* Naples: Liguori; Paris: Universitas; Oxford: Voltaire Foundation.

Py, Gilbert. 2004. *L'idée d'Europe au XVIIIe siècle.* Paris: Vuibert.

Rétat, Pierre. 1995. 'La représentation du monde dans L'esprit des lois. La place de l'Europe'. In *L'Europe de Montesquieu*, edited by Alberto Postigliola and Maria Grazia Bottaro Palumbo, 7–16. Naples: Liguori; Paris: Universitas; Oxford: Voltaire Foundation.

Rolland, Patrice. 1994. 'Montesquieu et l'Europe'. In *L'Europe entre deux tempéraments politiques. Idéal d'unité et particularismes régionaux. Études d'histoire des idées politiques*, edited by Michel Ganzin and Antoine Leca, 41–60. Aix-en-Provence: Presses Universitaires d'Aix-Marseille.

Rosenfeld, Sophia. 2014. 'Postface. L'Europe des cosmopolites: quand le XVIIIe siècle rencontre le XXIe'. In *Penser l'Europe au XVIIIe siècle. Commerce, civilisation, empire*, edited by Antoine Lilti and Céline Spector, 203–233. *Oxford University Studies in the Enlightenment*, 10.

Said, Edward W. 1978. *Orientalism.* London and Henley: Routledge and Kegan Paul.

Spector, Céline, 2014. 'Civilisation et empire: la dialectique négative de l'Europe au siècle des Lumières'. In *Penser l'Europe au XVIIIe siècle. Commerce, civilisation, empire*, edited by Antoine Lilti and Céline Spector, 93–115. *Oxford University Studies in the Enlightenment*, 10.

Verga, Marcello. 2003. 'La Comunità europea, la "politica della storia" e gli storici'. *Meridiana* 46: 31–61.

Verga, Marcello. 2004. *Storie d'Europa, secoli XVIII–XXI.* Rome: Carocci.

Verga, Marcello. 2008. 'European Civilization and the "Emulation of the Nations". Histories of Europe from the Enlightenment to Guizot'. *History of European Ideas* 34: 353–360.

Primary sources

Concina, Daniello. 1754. *Della religione rivelata contra gli ateisti, deisti, materialisti, indifferentisti, che negano la verità de' misteri.* Venice: Simone Occhi, 2 vols.

De Jaucourt, Louis. 1756. Europe (*Géog.*). In *Encyclopédie ou dictionnaire raisonné des sciences, des arts et des métiers, par une société de gens de lettres, mis en ordre et publié par M. Diderot et M. d'Alembert*, VI, 211–212. Paris: Briasson, David, Le Breton et Durand.

Ferlet, Edme. 1773. *De l'abus de la philosophie par rapport à la littérature*. Nancy-Paris: Imprimerie de Claude Leseure et J. Barbou.

Gauchat, Gabriel. 1754–1763. *Lettres critiques ou analyse et réfutation de divers écrits modernes contre la religion*. Paris: Claude Hérissant, anastatic reprint, Geneva: Slatkine reprints, 1973, 3 vols.

Montesquieu. 1721. *Lettres persanes*. Amsterdam: Pierre Brunel, 2 vols.

Montesquieu. 1777. *The Spirit of the Law*. In Montesquieu, *Complete Works*. London: Printed for T. Evans in the Strand, and W. Davis, 4 vols.

Montesquieu. 1972. *Persian Letters*. New York, London: Garland Publishing, 2 vols.

Montesquieu. 1973. *De l'esprit des lois*, edited by Robert Derathé. Paris: Garnier, 2 vols.

Nonnotte, Claude-François. 1762. *Les erreurs de Voltaire*. Paris: Antoine-Ignace Fez.

Nonnotte, Claude-François. 1766. *Les erreurs de Voltaire*. Amsterdam: La Compagnie des libraries.

Nonnotte, Claude-François. 1767. *Les erreurs de Voltaire*. Lyon: Imprimerie Jaquenod, père et Rusand.

Nonnotte, Claude-François. 1770. *Les erreurs de Voltaire*. Lyon: V. Reguilliot.

Nonnotte, Claude-François. 1773. *Gli errori di Voltaire*. Florence: Francesco Moucke.

Nonnotte, Claude-François. 1774. *Gli errori di Voltaire*. Venice: Guglielmo Zerletti, 1774 and 1778.

[Pinault, Pierre-Olivier]. 1770. *La nouvelle philosophie dévoilée et pleinement convaincue de lèse-majesté divine et humaine*. France: no publisher.

Schulz, Martin. 2015. *Speech by Martin Schulz, President of the European Parliament, to Mark his Receipt of the International Charlemagne Prize in Aachen*, 14 May 2015: www.europarl.europa.eu/the-president/en/press-room/speech-by-martin-schulz-president-of-the-european-parliament-to-mark-his-receipt-of-the-international-charlemagne-prize-in-aachen. Accessed 20 September 2016.

Viganego, Carlo Emanuele. 1772–1774. *Il filosofo moderno convinto, e ravveduto. Dissertazioni divise in dialoghi*. Turin: Eredi Avondo, 5 vols.

Voltaire. 1733. *Letters Concerning the English Nation*. London: C. Davis and A. Lyon.

Voltaire. 1734. *Lettres philosophiques*. Amsterdam: chez E. Lucas, au Livre d'or.

Voltaire. 1751. *Le siècle de Louis XIV*. Berlin: C. F. Henning, Imprimeur du Roi.

Voltaire. 1764. *Dictionnaire philosophique*. London: no publisher.

Voltaire. 1764a. *Traité sur la tolérance*. No place: no publisher.

Voltaire. 1764b. *A Treatise on Religious Toleration*. London: Printed for J. Newbery.

Voltaire. 1765a. *Dictionnaire philosophique portatif, nouvelle édition, avec des notes, beaucoup plus correcte et plus ample que les précédentes*. Amsterdam [actually Geneva]: Varberg, 2 vols.

Voltaire. 1765b. *Dictionnaire philosophique*. London: no publisher.

Voltaire. 1779. *The Age of Louis XIV*. London: Fielding and Walker.

Voltaire. 1901. *Philosophical Dictionary*. New York: E. R. DuMont.

Voltaire. 1961. *Philosophical Letters*, edited by Ernest Dilworth. Indianapolis: A Liberal Arts Press Book.

Voltaire. 1963. *Essai sur les moeurs et l'esprit des nations et sur les principaux faits de l'histoire depuis Charlemagne jusqu'à Louis XIII*, edited by René Pomeau. Paris: Garnier, 2 vols.

Voltaire. 2009–2015. *Essai sur les moeurs et l'esprit des nations et sur les principaux faits de l'histoire depuis Charlemagne jusqu'à Louis XIII*, edited by Bruno Bernard, John Renwick, Nicholas Cronk, and Janet Godden. Oxford: Voltaire Foundation.

2 Evoking Europe against the French Revolution

The rhetorical tools of counter-revolutionary thinkers

Manuela Ceretta

Introduction

In a volume dealing with discourses and counter-discourses on Europe, a chapter devoted to counter-revolutionary thought seems almost obligatory.[1] At once desperate and militant, aware of its own defeat yet incapable of surrender, counter-revolutionary thought was the 'counter' thought par excellence: the beginning of an intellectual tradition variously described, over time, as reactionary, conservative, anti-modern and intransigent.[2] Hostile to the Enlightenment, in revolt against rationalism, distrustful of the idea of progress, counter-revolutionary thought was born during the Revolutionary crisis and was fuelled by it.[3] Along with the French Revolution, it founded political modernity,[4] giving voice to the vanquished of history, and came to terms with the fragility of the secularized political structures and the pathologies of what, a few decades later, Tocqueville would call the 'democratic revolution'. As Antoine Compagnon wrote, counter-revolutionaries, untimely and outdated, pessimistic and sceptical, now appear, with their disenchantment, to be our real contemporaries.[5]

Being forced to stand on enemy ground and to confront the issues and language of the Revolution, counter-revolutionary thought organized its discourse in reaction to its adversary. Its vocabulary, arguments and polemics were chosen for opposition and were dictated by the agenda of the Revolution.[6] When revolutionaries spoke on behalf of a sovereign people, counter-revolutionaries spoke in the name of God, the one true sovereign. When the Revolution invoked the language of the rights of man, the counter-revolution invoked those of duties. When the Revolution fought in the name of the nation, the counter-revolution fought in the name of Europe.

In the age in which the problematic relationship between Europe and its constituent nations arose, Europe became a weapon in the rhetorical arsenal of the counter-revolution: if 'nation' was *le mot de la Révolution*, which knew no middle term between nation and humanity, 'Europe' was the rallying cry of the counter-revolution. In the polemics and debates of those crucial years Europe thus appeared as a counter-discourse, a discourse *against* the very idea of Revolution and against a certain idea of mankind, of history and of man's role in history. The Europe of the counter-revolutionaries had its roots in the ground abandoned by their foes: history, religion, tradition. The outcome was the histo-riographical invention of a Christian medieval Europe, as a model of a balanced order characterized by spiritual harmony, strong social cohesion and respect for the established hierarchies. In other words, the creation of the myth of a peaceful medieval Europe, designed and conceived for the use and nurture of counter-revolutionary concerns and struggles. The Europe of the counter-revolutionaries took on the characteristics of a 'concept-refuge',[7] of a notional world in which to seek shelter from the revolutionary menace, which threatened to destroy its values, to wipe out its traditions and erase its history.

At the end of the eighteenth century Europe was certainly not a new subject in the history of political thought, but neither had it ever been the centre of a real political debate.[8] From Hesiod onwards, the intellectual, cul-tural, religious and political history of the West had been punctuated by allu-sions to Europe: however, these references had never really entered the political debate or been the object of a lively dispute.[9] It was only with the French Revolution that – to use Martyn P. Thompson's expression – the *Euro-pean moment* began,[10] and the subsequent debate on Europe was animated by the thinkers of the crisis. Nevertheless, with few exceptions, the contribution of counter-revolutionary thought to the development of the idea of Europe has so far remained in the shadows, squeezed out by the utopianism of the great projects for perpetual peace of the eighteenth century and by the realism of the Congress of Vienna.

After all, it was hard for the counter-revolutionaries to compete on the 'Euro-pean' ground with Napoleon and the Congress of Vienna. Napoleon's campaigns had upset the political balance and a centuries-old consolidated European physi-ognomy, following his dream and ambition of founding a European system, a European Code and a Supreme Court for all Europe.[11] The aspiration to turn Europe into 'a truly united nation' under the aegis of a French empire which, by military force, would succeed in bringing harmony and unity to Europe, was shattered after the Hundred Days.[12] Napoleon had, however, had time to com-mission Benjamin Constant's *Acte additionnel aux Constitutions de l'Empire*, whose preamble – written jointly by the Emperor and Constant – expressed the desire to give birth to a 'great European federal system'.[13] With the end of the Imperial adventure, the Congress of Vienna had run for cover, giving life and articulation to the political and diplomatic system whose importance for the history of Europe is unquestionable. Indeed, however one interprets the Restora-tion, it is impossible to deny its significance as a turning point in the construction of modern Europe.[14]

These factors, taken together, have to a large extent obscured the importance of the counter-revolutionary contribution to the conceptualization of Europe. With the exception of the analyses written by some distinguished contemporar-ies – in particular Edmund Burke and Novalis, author of *Christianity or Europe*[15] – counter-revolutionary thought has not been given an autonomous space of investigation. This is partly because the counter-revolution has interested and fascinated scholars more for its activities – the workings of its conspiracy and information networks, the various kinds of national and European uprisings, the itineraries and components of emigration – than for its theoretical features.[16]

In recent years, however, there has been a kind of turnabout: what was for a long time largely considered only as the reversal of the French Revolution is now seen as the voice speaking out against the tradition that inaugurated political-democratic modernity and at the same time laid the foundations for its recurring crises. Thus there has been a growing interest in the theoretical distinctiveness of the counter-revolution, and in its polemics, its conception of the world and its anthropology.[17] This contribution follows this trend, investigating the reasons that led the counter-revolutionaries to place 'Europe' at the centre of their discourses and analysing where and in what way this operation was carried out.[18]

The French Revolution as a European wound

During the Restoration Europe became the 'bulwark against revolution',[19] while in the counter-revolutionary years it was instead seen as the victim of the French Revolution. From its earliest stages the Revolution became, in the opinion of counter-revolutionary thinkers, a *European* revolution, not simply because of its extensive reach but also on account of its political objectives. It had been the Revolution, universalist and humanist in its theoretical inspirations, which in 1793 declared through the Convention that it would not stop until all Europe's kingdoms had been supplanted by republics.[20] The following year Joseph de Maistre had noted in one of his Carnets: 'Before leaving for Turin I burnt the manuscript of my *Lettres savoisiennes* that I wrote at the time when I didn't have the least *illumination* on the French Revolution or, perhaps I should say, on the European Revolution'.[21] Two decades later, Louis de Bonald would reiterate: 'The French Revolution or, rather, the European revolution, was a call to all the passions and faults; to use the force of a geometric expression, it was evil at its maximum strength'.[22]

It is precisely the perception of being face to face with an event of pan-European reach, shared by all counter-revolutionary thought, that explains why – in what might perhaps be considered to be the manifesto of the counter-revolution, the *Considérations sur la France* (1797) – Joseph de Maistre tackled the subject of the destructive power of the Revolution, highlighting, from the outset, the European scale of the event. Although it was a text completely immersed in the political struggles of France and in its dramatic uncertainties, Maistre began his reflections by warning his readers that the French Revolution was a European phenomenon, whose destructive force had gone beyond the borders of France and would, if not stopped, compromise the future course of events in all of Europe: 'All over Europe monarchy is benumbed! [...] Public opinion persecutes fidelity all over Europe!'[23]

This idea was not original and had become part of counter-revolutionary tools (whose networks, thanks to emigration, extended throughout Europe) since Burke had declared that 'it looks to me as if I were in a great crisis, not of the affairs of France alone, but of all Europe, perhaps of more than Europe'.[24] In the *Reflections on the Revolution in France*, he had presented a systematic series of arguments painting a coherent and extraordinarily intense picture by using ideas partly borrowed from the works of the *anti-philosophes*.[25] He had, however, introduced a new element, related to the very destiny of Europe. The *Reflections on the Revolution in France* in fact pointed out that the French Revolution had destroyed the edifice of old Europe, which rested on the twin pillars of aristocracy and religion: 'the age of chivalry is gone. That of sophisters, oeconomists, and calculators, has succeeded; and the glory of Europe is extinguished for ever.'[26] Europe, which Burke claimed had been in a 'flourishing condition'[27] on the eve of the Revolution – the Europe upheld by knightly virtue and Christian faith, by the nobility and the clergy, and which for centuries had been at the head of the process of *civilisation* without fear of comparison with either Asia or the ancient world – risked being lost for ever.[28] The Revolution had sown a mine in the soil of Europe which would eventually dynamite all the political constructions, *les droits de l'homme*, which, in concert with the destructive fury of the 'false Enlightenment', were now delivering the deathblow to the Europe inherited by Burke and his contemporaries.

This thesis resonated with the beliefs of the counter-revolutionaries. Jacques Mallet du Pan, Swiss by birth but French by adoption, had in his *Considérations sur la nature de la Révolution de France* – published in 1793 in Brussels – stated that whatever happened in France 'Europe cannot long bear without being infected'.[29] In fact, right from the start the end goal of the French Revolution had been 'the subversion of the social order throughout Europe'.[30]

It was a Europe-wide Revolution, an epochal cataclysm, and its objective was the radical transformation of the entire continent: so appeared the French Revolution to the counter-revolutionaries. As Maistre wrote to Costa de Beauregard, a Savoyard noblewoman, during the height of the Terror:

> we must have the courage to confess it, Madame: for a long time we have not understood in any way the revolution that we are witnessing; for a long time we thought of it as an *event*. We were wrong: it is an *epoch*; wretched are those generations that witness the epochs of the world.[31]

Violently tearing apart past and present, and uncritically rejecting the recent past, the French Revolution had produced a terrible simplification in the course of history. France had purported to wipe the slate clean of centuries of past events, considered relics of an era which, with an expression as new as it was revealing, would henceforth be called the *ancien régime*.[32] The Revolutionary calendar, in a gesture as blatant as it was loaded with symbolic consequences, had divided the course of events in two, thereby decreeing the sovereignty of the nation over time and history. The Revolutionary spirit had brought about a radical artificialization of individual and collective experience, a result of the false notion that everything could be moulded, manipulated and modified.[33]

The sacrilegious act performed by the Revolution also meant, to a certain extent, the end of Europe.[34] The dissipation produced by the Revolution of the immense patrimony of civilization amassed over time undermined the whole of European society and plunged the old continent into an endless spiral of decline. What the Revolution was staging, in the eyes of the counter-revolutionaries, was the drama of the disintegration of a 'metapolitical' Europe – as Maistre put it – which mortgaged every construction of the future, making it ephemeral and weak. The idea of rethinking the European political profile on the basis of national self-determination seemed pure folly: such a notion embodied the very essence of modernity, centred on the desire to break away from the authority of God and of tradition. The constitutional voluntarism of the Revolution, whose absurdity was represented by the useless succession of constitutions established in Revolutionary France, and the entirely modern pretension to recreate a political and social order without giving it a metaphysical foundation, were the crimes of the Revolutionaries and of political modernity.[35] The witty and stinging incipit of the *Essai sur le principe générateur des constitutions politiques et des autres institutions humaines*, published by Maistre in 1814, could not have been clearer: 'one of the biggest mistakes of a century that has made them all, was to believe that a political constitution could be written and created a priori'.[36]

From the French Revolution onwards, Europe had followed a road that was leading to suicide: as Maistre wrote in 1819, 'je meurs avec l'Europe, je suis en bonne compagnie'.[37] In fact, far from ending in 1815, from being buried under the principles of balance and legitimacy, the Revolution had also triumphed at the Congress of Vienna. The Holy Alliance, in the *Preamble* drafted by Tsar Alexander I, denounced the clear desire to found the Concert of Europe on the basis of religious indifference: the union of Christian sovereigns in Europe virtually affirmed equality between its different churches. Despite its name, the Holy Alliance appeared to the counter-revolutionaries to be the heir of Bayle, Voltaire and religious indifferentism. Hence the declaration made, somewhat paradoxically, by Maistre in 1817: 'The Revolution is much worse now than in the times of Robespierre'.[38]

The solvents of Europe: Protestantism, Enlightenment and the public sphere

According to the counter-revolutionaries, Europe's mortal wounds had not been inflicted only by the Revolution, with its many struggles and wars, but also by the Enlightenment and the false doctrines that had silently eroded the laws, customs and institutions that made up its time-honoured foundation. Europe, Bonald wrote:

[C]annot perish except by wasting away. The day when the atheistic dogma of the sovereignty of the people replaces in politics the sacred dogma of the sovereignty of God; the day when Europe ceases to be Christian and monarchical, she will perish, and the scepter of the world will pass to other hands.[39]

The legacy of the pernicious doctrines that had undermined Europe and its monarchies could be traced back to the *philosophes'* and Revolutionaries' limitless trust in the capacity of human reason, a confidence inculcated initially by Protestantism. There was a direct connection between Protestantism, the Enlightenment, the Revolution and the fragility of the exclusively human institutions that the Revolutionaries, with their irreligious and Promethean drive, believed they could establish.

In the ranks of the blameworthy a special place was reserved for Protestantism because it had infected Europe with the virus of discussion, the challenge made by individual reason to God and tradition. In *Du Pape* Maistre had written that in order to stem the impending misfortunes it was necessary to 'remove from the European dictionary this menacing word, PROTESTANTISM'.[40] And in the essay *Sur le protestantisme*, written at the height of the counter-revolution, he had insisted on the fact that Protestantism was the 'great enemy of Europe', and represented the 'mutiny of individual reason against general reason'.[41] By dint of attacking and corroding everything, Protestantism had undermined the principle of sovereignty and faith in God, placing Europe on a slippery and insecure slope, as slippery and insecure was anything that did not come from the hands of God.[42]

Enlightenment principles had amplified and broadened the senseless revaluation of individual reason advocated by Protestantism. As Chateaubriand wrote in his *Essai historique, politique et moral sur les revolutions anciennes et modernes, considérées dans leur rapports avec la Révolution Française* (1797), the principles of the *philosophes* 'have become the machines that demolished the edifice of the current governments of Europe'.[43] The Enlightenment, blamed for having promoted a form of reason capable only of destruction, was accused by all the major counter-revolutionary theorists of having ignored the nihilistic power of its own reason: 'What, therefore, was the spirit of this sect [the Encyclopaedists]? Destruction. To destroy was their aim; destroying their argument. What did they want to put in the place of what was already there? Nothing.'[44]

The explicit condemnation of Protestantism and of the Enlightenment was an implicit admission of the strength and weakness of the 'European public sphere', based on reason and on the corrosive criticism of individual opinions which might be considered to be a legacy of the Enlightenment.[45] Public opinion had revealed its strength before and during the Revolution, and had become not only 'the queen of the world' but also a political subject that had contributed a great deal to the crisis of the *ancien régime*.[46] However, since its only strength was its disruptive power, this was also its weakness, a fact which exposed its fundamentally nihilist premises. Human institutions displayed all their inadequacy when they claimed to replace – as a prerequisite for the legitimacy of power – tradition and authority with rational inquiry. As Maistre wrote with reference to the 'miracle' of the Church:

> No human institution has lasted eighteen centuries. This achievement, which would be surprising anywhere, is even more surprising in the bosom of

noble Europe. Idleness is anathema to the European and his character contrasts sharply with the immobility of the Oriental. For the European it is necessary to act, to strive, to innovate and change everything possible.[47]

The role that counter-revolutionaries gave to public opinion – an ominous role – was a grudging admission of the power acquired by the European public sphere, a power that was as extraordinary as it was destructive. And yet it was, moreover, a power that they themselves sought to harness when exploring every possibility of opposing the Revolution on its own rhetorical ground. The end of Europe was decreed by the characteristics that the public sphere had given itself, qualities that would eventually devour its own premises.[48] The offensive of the Enlightenment had targeted both religion and Europe, it had hatched 'a huge plot covering all of Europe',[49] had attacked everything that stood in its way – namely God, religion and the Church – and, so as to see the offensive through to the end, had had to strike against Europe: 'all the governments, all the institutions of Europe it [philosophy] abhorred because they were Christian'.[50]

The crisis unleashed by the Revolution had been primed by the European public sphere which, as a means of bringing about the discursive dissolution of power, turned out to be the lethal weapon which the *anti-philosophes* had accused it of being for almost half a century.[51]

The crisis of Europe was thus the product of the *bienfaits de la Révolution* (the emblematic title given by Maistre to one of his works) and of the unbridled power of the Enlightenment. In its diagnosis of the long-term causes of the European crisis, counter-revolutionary discourse deemed Europe to be the victim of the processes of pluralization and secularization. As Bonald's words also made clear, there was an understanding that an epochal crisis was coming that jeopardized Europe: 'but today [...] it is the Christian religion that must be defended, it is the civilization of Europe and of the world that must be preserved; it is order, justice, peace, virtue, truth'.[52]

In contrast to this Europe, wounded and pursuing the path of decadence, counter-revolutionary discourse proposed another, that of Christian-medieval Europe. In opposition to the Europe of the people and nations, and against the society of the future envisioned by the Revolutionaries and built on abstract notions of human rights, freedom, equality and fraternity, counter-revolutionary discourse proposed the tangible society of the past, built on the solid ground of history, authority, tradition and religion. Within this clash, which turned history into a polemical discipline and the pivot of the counter-revolutionary argument, was born the myth of medieval Europe.

Charlemagne's Europe, or the counter-revolutionary Middle Ages

As we know, during the nineteenth century historiography and literature built a hugely successful political and cultural paradigm around the concept of the Middle

Ages. This undertaking, driven by highly ideological cultural and political motives, led to commendable advances and the establishment of research institutions and repositories of sources of lasting value. In this process of reassessment of the Middle Ages, the role of *trait d'union* played by counter-revolutionary thought was of enormous importance. The nineteenth century, fascinated by mores, by the great waves of migration and the encounter-clash between peoples and cultures, discovered the cradle of Europe in the Middle Ages.[53]

Professional medievalists have vouched for the strength of that nineteenth-century intuition, a theoretical construction which, apart from some fanciful elements, was based on an essentially correct idea: that of a Europe in which the Carolingian age functioned as a memory of an era characterized by a learned unity, harmony and peace. But this nineteenth-century perception, confirmed by the most recent historical research, is indebted to the myth of medieval Christianity, a model of a balanced order that owed much to the writings of the counter-revolutionaries and the origin of which is attributable to the controversy concerning the French Revolution.

In the age of the Revolution, medievalism acquired a specific political significance, allowing supporters of the monarchy to disguise their enthusiasm for the restoration of the throne (which in fact dated from the Middle Ages) as erudite investigations, without exposing themselves to the risk of censure or violent attack.[54] Furthermore, medievalism – like much of the rhetorical arsenal of the counter-revolution – found, for opposition, its *raison d'être* in the Enlightenment attitude towards the Middle Ages.

It is now well-known that the verdict of the Enlightenment on the Middle Ages was far from unique. The *querelle* between ancients and moderns and the clash over the Frankish or Germanic history of France, which pervaded and divided French political thought during the seventeenth and eighteenth centuries, had seen the defenders of the freedom of medieval communes and the supporters of absolutism take opposite sides, with the latter accused by the former of having expunged medieval freedoms. Some recent studies have also pointed out convincingly that the medieval age was a key reference point during the eighteenth century which, at least until 1775, produced articulate and diverse readings of the Middle Ages which were anything but entirely negative.[55]

Two things, however, cannot be ignored. First, the self-representation of the *philosophes* and the cliché that they built around the eighteenth century: that of the *siècle des Lumières*, illuminated by the light of reason and in rhetorical and polemical opposition to the dark centuries of the Middle Ages, living in the shadow of prejudice. Second, the trenchant judgment on the medieval period expressed by the century's *maître à penser*, Voltaire, whose mortal remains were transferred to the Panthéon in 1791 with the most imposing of ceremonies. For him, the Middle Ages symbolized dogmatism, fanaticism, intolerance: an age marked by 'ignorant superstition' during which 'all was confusion, tyranny, barbarism and poverty'.[56] And this would be the case also for men and women of the Revolution, who, when choosing political models from the past to inform their present, leapt over the Middle Ages to draw inspiration from the antiquity of republican Rome.

It is reasonable to argue that the anti-medievalism of Voltaire and the Revolutionaries prompted the counter-revolutionaries to explore the argumentative potential of recalling a medieval Europe, described with lamenting and
nostalgia for something lost. Such an argument was in fact a double-edged
sword. On the one hand, it brought with it the obvious reference to a historic
period before the rupture of the Reformation, a period imbued with Christian
religious sentiments in which the power of the pope and the Church was at its
zenith. An age consequently presented in counter-revolutionary discourses as
the highest point of European civilization. On the other hand, the evocation of
the Middle Ages as a golden age of European society went hand in hand with
a severe verdict on modernity, which far from being a path of progress,
equated to gradual degeneration. In this respect, the rediscovery of the medieval period by counter-revolutionary thought should not be seen as a prolon-
gation of the *querelle* between ancients and moderns, in other words it should
not be considered to be fully consistent with the positive reappraisal of the
Middle Ages made by Henry de Boulainvilliers and Montesquieu. On the contrary, it represented a break with those eighteenth-century conceptualizations:
the counter-revolutionary Middle Ages were intended to be anti-modern, since
the Protestant reformation, the Enlightenment and the French Revolution were
conceived as embodiments of modernity.[57]

Thus, for example, Bonald in his *Discours politique sur l'état actuel de
l'Europe*, written in 1800, identified Charlemagne, Christianity, the papacy, the
Crusades and the nobility as the drivers of a process of civilization that was led
by France: 'France has been, since Charlemagne, the center of the civilized
world, and the point around which the social system of Europe turns'.[58] Maistre,
meanwhile, in the *Essai sur le principe générateur des constitutions politiques et
des autres institutions humains*, argued:

> there will come a time in which the popes that we have recriminated against,
> like Gregory VII, will be considered in all countries as the friends, the
> tutors, the saviours of the human race, as the true founding geniuses of
> Europe.[59]

Behind the discourse on medieval Europe lay three themes that were typically
counter-revolutionary. The first was the desire to restore the centrality of God
and his vicar on Earth in defiance of the sacrilegious *hubris* of the revolutionaries, which impelled the 'prophets of the past' to insist on religion as the indispensable source of legitimacy of socio-political institutions and as the guarantee
of their lasting duration:

> We see, on the one hand, how the men we call *barbarians* created, in the
> darkness of the Middle Ages, institutions that lasted fourteen centuries and
> in the end yielded only to the repeated efforts of an innumerable crowd of
> madmen who had all the vices of the universe and of Hell as their allies.[60]

And, Maistre continued: 'how, on the other hand, all the science, all the resources of the century of philosophy [...] have produced an edifice that lasted fourteen minutes, only to collapse ignominiously in the fifteenth, like a squashed pumpkin'.[61]

The second theme was the post-Revolutionary concern for the dissolution of social ties, for the decline of social hierarchies and the birth of the entirely modern 'passion' that was individualism, jointly produced by Protestantism, the Industrial Revolution and the French Revolution.[62] In the case of Bonald it can be said that his 'medievalism – a highly selective, even fantastic, interpretation of the civilization of the Middle Ages – functions as the obverse of the modern individualism he reviled'.[63] This theme obviously overlaps the first, to the degree that the decline of religious feelings, in the original meaning of *religo*, also involved the weakening of the social glue *par excellance*, although counter-revolutionary thought developed the argument in a new direction, that of an examination of the fabric of modern society, which, as Bonald wrote, was made from grains of sand.[64]

The third theme was a new kind of historical attitude generated by the excesses of the Revolution which railed against the historical ruins that symbolized Catholic France and the *ancien régime*. This led the counter-revolutionaries, generally favourable to the early stages of the Revolution, to look backwards, to resort to the worship of ruins and of the past, thus leaning towards the veneration of the monarchy and the martyred king.[65] In this respect, the *Génie du Christianisme* probably offered the most influential representation of a medieval Europe identified with *Christianitas*, marked by order and harmony that nurtured unity of thought and belief. The book, written by Chateaubriand in 1802, while the ruins of France's 1,000-year religious history were strewn throughout the land, as testimony to the work of destruction perpetrated in the name of the principles of the French Revolution, was designed as a refutation of Enlightenment doctrines and it was a resounding success. Its aim was to show that, in opposition to the monstrous campaign waged by the Enlightenment, Christianity had played an extraordinary role as a civilizing force, from its first appearance and throughout the succeeding centuries. The pages of the *Génie du Christianisme* painted a picture of a mythologized Middle Ages, described as the laboratory of freedom, an image barely credible from a historical point of view, but one that worked polemically in reference to a lost past devoured by the Revolution.[66]

Last but not least, medieval and counter-revolutionary Europe was a continent that had over time rid itself of the propensity for violence and conquest: it was a peaceful Europe perceived in open contrast to the bloodiest days of the Revolution and the years of the Napoleonic wars. Bonald wrote in his *Réflexions sur l'intérêt général de l'Europe*:

> Europe until the sixteenth century lived by these two principles of monarchy and Christianity. Peace was interrupted by wars between neighbors. But such wars without hate, these passing struggles between two peoples united by the same political and religious doctrines had only served as an outlet for the forces of states, without any danger to their power and independence.[67]

It is difficult to say whether the medievalism of the counter-revolutionary discourse could be seen as an indicator of a *passéiste* attitude, reactionary, nostalgic and melancholy or, on the contrary, as an expression of the belief in the possibility of returning to a path interrupted by modernity, there to search for a distinct variety of modernity, or an alternative modernity. In other words, it is hard to decide whether to side with those who include the counter-revolutionaries among the antimodernists and those who instead consider them to be the heralds of another idea of modernity, different to the one that imposed itself. What is certain is that their counter-discourse on Europe appears to us distant and unattainable.

Conclusions

In an intellectually stimulating study of counter-revolutionary thought, Gérard Gengembre wrote that 'the definitive laicisation of our modernity convicts the Counter-revolution of unreality'.[68] To the Europeans of the third millennium, who are incredulous and frightened observers of the 'revenge of God',[69] the first part of this affirmation sounds dubious: the process of the 'definitive laicisation of our modernity' appears to be regressing a little every day, pushed back by the blows of new and old fundamentalisms that have brought about a new and dramatic crisis of Europe. It is for this reason that counter-revolutionary thought may still have something to teach us: not the model of Charlemagne's Europe, but the legacy of thought born in a moment of crisis and capable of looking the crisis in the eyes. The legacy of thought that in the middle of the worst crisis ever faced by modern Europe did not remain silent or shift its gaze elsewhere; thought that attempted to understand and explain the crisis, accepting fear and menace as its horizon; thought that was not steamrollered by its present, but held to the long-term view imparted by its history and values.

And for historians there remains the awareness that all discourses and counter-discourses on Europe have been the result of one or more crises. The outcome of reflections on the history of Europe and against the history of Europe.

Notes

1 I have adopted the distinction between counter-revolution (defined both as an intellectual resistance movement and as a form of political opposition to the French Revolution, specific to the elites but varied in its expressions) and anti-revolution (a spontaneous and popular form of resistance, diversified and essentially practical, against the changes, the laws, the decrees and the symbols and practices introduced by the Revolution): on this subject, see Mazauric 1987, 237–244.

2 See Hirschman 1991; Shorten 2015, 179–200.

3 Valade 2013, 307.

4 Zeev Sternhell insists on this point, seeing counter-revolutionary thought as the harbinger of a different idea of modernity that coexisted and conflicted with rational modernity, rather than as the expression of anti-modern thought. See Sternhell 2010, Chapter 2.

5 Compagnon 2005, 19.

6 The language, words and discourses of the Revolution have been investigated in depth. Among the many available studies, I refer in particular to Jacques

Guilhaumou's historiographical overview of the research into the political culture of the French Revolution: Guilhaumou 2005, 63–92. See also: Brasart 1988; Équipe 18ème et Révolution 1995.

7 On Europe as 'a notion of crisis' and as 'refuge', see Verga 2004, 88–120.

8 See Chapter 1 of this volume, P. Delpiano, 'Thinking Europe in the Age of Enlightenment: *Philosophes* and *Antiphilosophes* between Universalism and Fragmentation'.

9 Despite the impression that one might obtain by reading some of the most fascinating histories of the concept of Europe: see the classic studies by: Hay 1957; Curcio 1958; Chabod 1962; Rougemont 1961; Duroselle 1990; Geremek 1991. On the teleological 'vice' of most histories of Europe, see Woolf 2013, 327.

10 Thompson 1994, 38.

11 See Las Cases 1961, 220.

12 See Fontana 2002, 116–138.

13 See Constant 2001; on this subject, see Woolf 1992.

14 In the months preceding the Congress of Vienna 'the whole of Europe thus began to talk about Europe in opposition to Napoleon, who had attempted to create it': Rougemont 1961, 199; there is a very extensive literature on the Congress of Vienna and the definition of the new European order. See, most recently, Lentz 2013.

15 Novalis 1993, 581–611.

16 On these characteristics of the studies of the counter-revolution, see Tulard 1990, 10. This historiographical tradition, which has favoured the analysis of the various forms of resistance to Revolutionary reforms, included, most recently, Sutherland 1986. There exist, obviously, significant exceptions, for example the attention showed by Carl Schmitt towards counter-revolutionary thought and the seminal work by Jacques Godechot, who reconciled an investigation into its networks of conspiracy with an interest in the different theoretical components of counter-revolutionary thought: Schmitt 1985; Godechot 1961.

17 See Rials 1987, 13.

18 This chapter covers the period running from 1789 to 1814 when the Congress of Vienna opened a new phase in the relationship between Revolution and counter-Revolution and in reflection on Europe. On the counter-revolutionaries' discourses during the first stages of the Revolution, see Middell 1991, 67–77.

19 Proietti 2014, 41.

20 Martin 2011, 54.

21 Quoted in Rials 1987, 31.

22 Bonald 1817, t. VI, 78.

23 Maistre 1994, 4 and again:

> France exercises over Europe a veritable magistracy that it would be useless to contest and that she has most culpably abused. [...] And so, since she has used her influence to contradict her vocation and demoralize Europe, we should not be surprised if she is brought back to her mission by terrible means.
>
> (Maistre 1994, 9)

24 Burke 1986, 92.

25 See McMahon 2001, 68; Chiron 1990, 85–97.

26 Burke 1986, 170.

27 Burke 1986, 173.

28 Burke 1986, 170.

29 Mallet du Pan 1793, 3 (English edition).

30 Mallet du Pan 1793, 12 (English edition).

31 Maistre 1794, 273.

32 Furet 1994, 707.

33 On the characteristic traits of the revolutionary mentality, Michel Vovelle's considerations continue to be illuminating: Vovelle 1985.

34 Furet 1986, 56–66.
35 On the counter-revolutionary polemic against constitutional voluntarism, see Rials 1987, 13–17. The critique of constitutional voluntarism lived within a wider polemic towards the primacy of the law, of the modern state and more generally the role taken by writing in modernity. See Maistre's thesis which, quoting Plato's *Phaedrus*, stated:

> ancient philosophers have heard clearly the weakness, I would say almost the absence, of writing in the great institutions; but nobody saw and expressed this truth better than Plato [...]. According to him, first of all, 'the man who owes all his education to writing will never have anything more than the appearance of knowledge.' 'The written word' – he added – 'is to man as a man is to his portrait'.
>
> (Maistre 1814, 254–255)

On this subject, see Battini 1995, 51–65.
36 Maistre 1814, 235.
37 Maistre to Count de Marcellus, 9 August 1819, in *Œuvres Complètes*, t. XIV, 183.
38 Maistre to M. le Chavalier d'Olry, 5 September 1818, in *Œuvres Complètes*, t. XIV, 148.
39 Bonald 1815, 22.
40 Maistre 1819, 524.
41 Maistre 1798, 64.
42 See Maistre 1814, 223–308.
43 Chateaubriand 1797, 369.
44 Chateaubriand 1797, 359.
45 The literature on the European public sphere is extensive. For summary of the recent debate, see Bärenreuter *et al.* 2009; Doria and Raulet 2016.
46 Ozouf, 1987.
47 Maistre 1819, 431.
48 Heller 1999, 61–79.
49 Maistre 1814, 305.
50 Maistre 1814, 306.
51 McMahon 2001.
52 Bonald 1806, 240.
53 Artifoni 1997; Bernard-Griffiths *et al.* 2006; Wood 2013.
54 See Armenteros 2014, 20–21.
55 See the work by Alicia C. Montoya and the related bibliography: Montoya 2013.
56 Voltaire 1963.
57 For a contrasting interpretation, see Bordone 2002, 11–18. On this subject see also Montoya 2013, 43–68.
58 Bonald 1800, 113.
59 Maistre 1814, 261.
60 Maistre to M. le Comte de d'Avaray, 12 (24) July 1807, in *Œuvres Complètes*, X, 435.
61 Maistre to M. le Comte de d'Avaray, 12 (24) July 1807, in *Œuvres Complètes*, X, 435–436.
62 Reedy 1995; Pranchère 2001.
63 Reedy 1995, 53.
64 Bonald 1796.
65 See on this theme, Gengembre 1989, 234–238. In the introduction to the 1828 edition, Chateaubriand placed his work within this cultural climate: 'It was therefore, so to speak, in the midst of the ruins of our temples that I published the *Genius of Christianity*, to call back to these temples the grandness of the rituals and the servants of the altars': Chateubriand 1803, 459.

66 On the allure of ruins, see, in particular, Chateaubriand 1803, *Génie du Christianisme*, part III, book V, ch. 3–4, 881–887; on this subject, see Berchet 2006, 306.
67 Bonald 1815.
68 Gengembre 1989, 14.
69 Kepel 1994.

Bibliography

Armenteros, Carolina. 2014. 'Royalist Medievalisms in the Age of Revolution: From Robert de Lézardière to Chateaubriand, 1792–1831'. *Relief* 8, 1: 20–47.

Artifoni, Enrico. 1997. 'Il medioevo nel Romanticismo. Forme della storiografia tra Sette e Ottocento'. In *Lo spazio letterario del medioevo. Il medioevo latino* edited by Silvio Avalle D'Arco, Walter Berschin, Enrico Campanile, Franco Cardini, Donatella Frioli, Alessandro Ghisalberti, Sante Graciotti, *et al.*, 6 vols., IV, 75–221. Rome: Salerno editrice.

Bärenreuter, Christoph, Brüll, Cornelia, Mokre, Monica and Wahl-Jorgensen, Karin. 2009. 'An Overview of Research on the European Public Sphere'. *Eurosphere. On line working paper series*, n. 3. http://eurospheres.org/files/2010/08/Eurosphere_Working_Paper_3_Barenreuter_etal.pdf. Accessed 9 March 2016.

Battini, Michele. 1995. *L'ordine della gerarchia. I contributi reazionari e progressisti alle crisi della democrazia in Francia, 1789–1914*. Turin: Bollati Boringhieri.

Berchet, Jean-Claude. 2006. 'François de Chateaubriand'. In *La fabrique du moyen âge au XIXe siècle: representations du Moyen âge dans la culture et la litterature françaises du XIXᵉ siecle*, edited by Siomone Bernard-Griffiths, Pierre Glaudes and Bertrand Vibert, 297–311. Paris: Champion.

Bernard-Griffiths, Simone, Glaudes, Pierre and Vibert, Bertrand, eds. 2006. *La fabrique du moyen âge au XIXe siècle: representations du Moyen âge dans la culture et la litterature françaises du XIXᵉ siecle*. Paris: Champion.

Bordone, Renato. 2002. 'Le radici della rivisitazione ottocentesca del medioevo'. In *Medioevo reale, medioevo immaginario. Confronti e percorsi culturali tra regioni d'Europa*, edited by Musei Civici Torino, 11–18. Turin: Musei Civici Torino.

Brasart, Patrick. 1988. *Paroles de la Révolution (les assemblees parlementaire 1789–1794)*. Paris: Minerve.

Chabod, Federico. 1962. *Storia dell'idea di Europa*. Bari: Laterza.

Chiron, Yves. 1990. 'Edmund Burke'. In *La Contre-Révolution: origines, histoire, post-herité*, edited by Jean Tulard, 85–97. Paris: Perrin.

Compagnon, Antoine. 2005. *Les antimodernes de Joseph de Maistre à Roland Barthes*. Paris: Gallimard.

Curcio, Carlo. 1958. *Europa. Storia di un'idea*, 2 vols. Florence: Vallecchi.

Doria, Corinne and Raulet, Gerard, eds. 2016. *Histoire et méthodologie*. Brussels: Peter Lang.

Duroselle, Jean-Baptiste. 1990. *Europe: A History of its People*. Harmondsworth: Viking Penguin Books.

Équipe 18ème et Révolution, eds. 1995. *Langages de la révolution (1770–1815). Actes du 4éme colloque international de lexicologie politique*. Paris: Klincksieck.

Fontana, Bianca Maria. 2002. 'The Napoleonic Empire and the Europe of Nations'. In *The Idea of Europe: from Antiquity to the European Union*, edited by Antony Pagden, 116–138. Cambridge: Cambridge University Press.

Furet, François. 1986. 'Burke ou la fin d'une seule histoire de l'Europe'. *Le débat* 39: 56–66.

Furet, François. 1994. 'Ancien Régime'. In *Dizionario critico della Rivoluzione francese*, edited by François Furet and Mona Ozouf, 2 vols, II, 705–716. Milan: Bompiani.

Gengembre, Gérard. 1989. *La contre-révolution, ou l'histoire desesperante: histoire des idees politiques*. Paris: Imago.

Geremek, Bronislaw. 1991. *Le radici comuni dell'Europa*. Milan: Il saggiatore.

Godechot, Jacques. 1961. *La contre-revolution. Doctrine et action, 1789–1804*. Paris: Puf.

Guilhaumou, Jacques. 2005. 'La langue politique et la Révolution française'. *Langage et société* 113: 63–92.

Hay, Denys. 1957. *Europe: The Emergence of an Idea*. Edinburgh: Edinburgh University Press.

Heller, Agnes. 1999. 'La modernità onnivora'. Agnes Heller, *Dove siamo a casa: Pisan Lectures 1993–1998*, edited by Debora Spini, 61–79. Milan: FrancoAngeli.

Hirschman, Albert O. 1991. *The Rhetoric of Reaction: Perversity, Futility, Jeopardy*. Cambridge, MA: The Belknap Press.

Kepel, Gilles. 1994. *The Revenge of God. The Resurgence of Islam, Cristianity and Judaism in the Modern World*. Cambridge: Polity Press.

Lentz, Thierry. 2013. *Le congrès de Vienne. Une refondation de l'Europe 1814–1815*. Paris: Perrin.

Martin, Jean-Clément, ed. 2011. *Dictionnaire de la Contre-Révolution*, Paris: Perrin.

Mazauric, Claude. 1987. 'Autopsie d'un échec, la resistance à l'anti-Révolution et la defaite de la Contre-Révolution'. In *Les Resistences à la Révolution. Actes du Colloque de Rennes*, edited by F. Lebrun and R. Dupuy, 237–244. Paris: Imago.

McMahon, Darrin D. 2001. *Enemies of the Enlightement. The French Counter-Enlightenment and the Making of Modernity*. Oxford: Oxford University Press.

Middel, Matthias. 1991. 'La Révolution française vue par les contre-révolutionnaires à l'assemblée nationale de 1789 à 1791'. *Annales historiques de la Révolution française* 283: 67–77.

Montoya, Alicia C. 2013. *Medievalist Enlightenment: from Charles Perrault to Jean-Jacques Rousseau*. Cambridge: Boydell and Brewer.

Ozouf, Mona. 1987. 'L'opinion public'. In *The French Revolution and the Creation of Modern Political Culture*, 3 vols, *The Political Culture of the Old Regime*, I, edited by Keith Michael Baker, 419–434. Oxford: Pergamon Press.

Pranchère, Jean-Yves. 2001. 'The Social Bond According to the Catholic Counter-Revolution: Maistre and Bonald'. In *Joseph de Maistre's Life, Thought and Influence: Selected Studies*, edited by Richard A. Lebrun, 190–219. Montreal, Kingston: McGill-Queen's University Press.

Proietti, Fausto. 2014. 'La réorganisation de l'Europe nel dibattito politico francese tra Prima e seconda Restaurazione (1814–1815)'. In *Il Congresso di Vienna 1814–1815. Storia, politica e diplomazia*, edited by Francesco Randazzo, 41–59. Tricase: Libellula.

Reedy, W. Jay. 1995. 'The Traditionalist Critique of Individualism in Post-Revolutionary France: The Case of Louis de Bonald'. *History of Political Thought* 26:1: 49–75.

Rials, Stéphane. 1987. *Révolution et contre-révolutions au XIXe siècle*. Paris: D.U.C./ Albatros.

Rougemont, Denis de. 1961. *Vingt-huit siècles d'Europe: la conscience européenne à travers les textes: d'Hésiode à nos jours*. Paris: Payot.

Schmitt, Carl. 1985. *Political Theology. Four Chapters on the Concept of Sovereignity*, Cambridge and London: MIT Press.

Shorten, Richard. 2015. 'Reactionary Rhetoric Reconsidered'. *Journal of Political Ideologies* 20, 2: 179–200.

Sternhell, Zeev. 2010. *The Anti-Enlightenment Tradition*. New Haven, CT: Yale University Press.

Sutherland, Donald M. G. 1986. *France 1789–1815: Revolution and Counter-revolution*. Oxford: Oxford University Press.

Thompson, Martyn P. 1994. 'Ideas of Europe during the French Revolution and Napoleonic Wars'. *Journal of the History of Ideas* 55, 1: 37–58.

Tulard, Jean. 1990. Preface to *La Contre-révolution: origine, histoire, postherité*, edited by Jean Tulard, 9–11. Paris: Perrin.

Valade, Bernard. 2013. 'Les théocrates'. In *La Contre-Révolution. Origines, histoire, postèrité*, edited by Jean Tulard, 286–309. Paris: Perrin.

Verga, Marcello. 2004. *Storie d'Europa. Secoli XVIII-XXI*. Rome: Carocci.

Vovelle, Michel. 1985. *La mentalité révolutionnaire*. Paris: Editions sociales.

Woolf, Stuart. 1992. 'The Construction of a European World-View in the Revolutionary-Napoleonic Years'. *Past and Present* 137: 72–101.

Woolf, Stuart. 2013. 'Europe and its Historians'. *Contemporary European History* 12, 3: 323–337.

Wood, Ian. 2013. *The Modern Origins of the Early Middle Ages*. Oxford: Oxford University Press.

Primary sources

Bonald, Louis de. 1796. *Théorie du pouvoir politique et regieux dans la société civile démontée par le raisonnement et par l'Histoire*. In *Œuvres complètes*. 1982, 9 vols, t. XIII–XV. Geneva: Slatkine.

Bonald, Louis de. 1800. *Discours politique sur l'état actuel de l'Europe*. In *Œuvres complètes*. 1982, 9 vols, t. IV, 113–339. Geneva: Slatkine.

Bonald, Louis de. 1806. *De l'unité religieuse en Europe*. In *Œuvres complètes*. 1982, 9 vols, t. X, 229–283. Geneva: Slatkine.

Bonald, Louis de. 1815. *Réflexions sur l'intérêt général de l'Europe, suivies de quelques considérations sur la noblesse*. Paris: Le Normant.

Bonald, Louis de. 1817. *Pensées sur divers sujets et discours politique*. In *Œuvres complètes*. 1982, 9 vols, t. VI–VII. Geneva: Slatkine.

Burke, Edmund. 1986. *Reflections on the Revolution in France* [1790]. London: Penguin.

Chateaubriand, François René de. 1797. *Essai historique, politique et moral sur les révolutions anciennes et modernes, considérées dans leur rapports avec la Révolution Française*, edited by Maurice Regard, 3–455. Paris: Gallimard, 1978.

Chateaubriand, François René de. 1803. *Génie du Christianisme*, edited by Maurice Regard, 459–1367. Paris: Gallimard, 1978.

Constant, Benjamin. 2001. *Acte Additionnel aux constitutions de l'Empire* [Texte adopté par le Conseil d'État] (1815). In *Œuvres complètes de Benjamin Constant, Série Œuvres*, vol. IX-2, edited by Olivier Devaux and Kurt Kloocke, 611–622. Tübingen: Niemeyer.

Las Cases, Emmanuel de. 1961. *Mémorial de Sainte-Hélène*, texte établi avec introduction, bibliographie et notes par André Fugier, 2 vols. Paris: Garnier.

Maistre, Joseph de. 1794. *Discours à Mme la marquise de Costa sur la vie et la mort de son fils*. In *Œuvres Complètes*. 1979–1980, 7 vols, t. VII, 234–278. Geneva: Slatkine.

Maistre, Joseph de. 1797. *Considérations sur la France*. In *Œuvres complètes*. 1979–1980, 7 vols, t. I, xlvii–184. Geneva: Slatkine.

Maistre, Joseph de. 1798, posthumous. *Réflexions sur le protestantisme*. In *Œuvres complètes*. 1979–1980, 7 vols, t. VIII, 61–97. Geneva: Slatkine.

Maistre, Joseph de. 1814. *Essai sur le principe générateur des constitutions politiques et des autres institutions humaines*. In *Œuvres complètes*. 1979–1980, 7 vols, t. I, 221–308. Geneva: Slatkine.

Maistre, Joseph de. 1819. *Du Pape*. In *Œuvres complètes*. 1979–1980, 7 vols, t. II, v–544. Geneva: Slatkine.

Maistre, Joseph de. 1994. *Considerations on France*. Cambridge: Cambridge University Press.

Mallet du Pan, Jacques. 1793. *Considérations sur la nature de la Révolution de France et sur les causes qui en prolongent la durée*. London: Flon.

Mallet du Pan, Jacques. 1793. *Considerations on the nature of the French revolution and on the causes which prolong its duration*. London: J. Owen.

Novalis. 1993. *La cristianità ovvero l'Europa*, in Novalis, *Opera filosofica*, 2 vols, II. Turin: Einaudi.

Voltaire. 1963. *Essai sur les moeurs et l'esprit des nations et sur les principaux faits de l'histoire depuis Charlemagne jusqu'à Louis XIII*, 2 vols, edited by René Pomeau. Paris: Garnier.

3 Discourses on Europe and their political value in Restoration France

Giuseppe Sciara

Introduction

'Europe is asking us to do it': in contemporary political debates it is now commonplace for politicians, commentators and journalists to make reference to Europe to justify unpopular measures or to legitimize their own political positioning on domestic issues or specific interests.[1] The practice is by no means new: more than a century before the start of the process of European integration, at the time of the Congress of Vienna – the foundational moment of contemporary Europe – political ideas and actions were frequently legitimized 'in the name of Europe'.[2]

This chapter will investigate the discourses and representations of Europe in the French political debates of the Restoration, not so much with the aim of contributing to the reconstruction of a history of the idea of Europe, a theme that has been the object of important studies for quite some time,[3] but rather to shed light on a matter that has been overlooked by historiography: the way in which various intellectuals, polemicists and political players used different 'images' of the continent to pursue national political objectives, those closely linked to the historical and political context of the France of Louis XVIII and Charles X. The Restoration, having long been undervalued by historiography and reduced, at best, to a transition period, is now more convincingly regarded as a laboratory of ideas and of political experiences worth investigating in order to shed light on the origins of our political and cultural identity.[4]

This chapter will concentrate in particular on two crucial moments of crisis during which discourses on Europe played a primary role in French political debates: the biennium of 1814–1815 and the years 1822–1825. The first period was characterized by a rescaling – after the devastating effects of the Napoleonic campaigns – of France's role on the European chessboard and by constant institutional upheavals: in the space of sixteen months the Bourbons returned to power twice, while the country sought, with difficulty, to put an end to the Revolution, without managing to resolve the conflict between the old and new France. While, during the First Restoration, Louis XVIII granted the *Charte* of 4 June 1814 along with freedom of the press to try to rally support for his political project, after the brief parenthesis of the Hundred Days and the election of a parliament made up mostly of counter-revolutionaries, the political contest became increasingly bitter, provoking the various political forces in the field to clash on the fronts of the constitution, the economy and religion.[5] In the political pamphlets and tracts of this time there was a discussion about the new continental order that must emerge from the Congress of Vienna, and a variety of images were drawn of Europe deriving from the multifarious world views and political, philosophical and religious stances that reflected the polarity between the advocates and opponents of Revolutionary principles. Analysing the different ways of portraying the continent in the aftermath of the Imperial period and the different ways of formulating plans for its political and cultural re-establishment brings into focus the ideologies of the different political forces, and allows a better understanding of some interesting dynamics of Restoration France.

The chapter is organized into five sections. The first considers the discourses of the so-called royalists *exagérés* who depicted a Europe gripped by chaos and desolation that could only reestablish peace and morality by returning to the political order of the *ancien régime* and to a medieval continental system. The second analyses the arguments put forward by the moderate royalists and their proposal for a Europe reorganized around principles of legitimism and religion that would nevertheless retain certain important achievements of the Revolution. The third section focuses on the liberals, who imagined a Europe of the nations organized on the basis of the principles of representative government. The fourth section is dedicated to the defenders of Bonaparte, who during the Hundred Days led an attack against illiberal Europe in order to create consensus around Napoleon's new political project. Finally, the fifth section considers how this sharp contrast between different images of Europe appears to have dissipated following the 1821 uprisings, when the political debate centred on whether France should intervene in the Greek war of independence from Ottoman rule. This discussion shows that the representations of Europe, compared to the otherness of Turkey, somehow lost their polemical purpose but not their instrumental value: precisely because the common objective was that of pushing the government to intervene in the conflict and to reclaim the nation's role as a continental power, a shared discourse on Europe emerged among the different political forces.

The aim of this analysis is to reveal the complexity and ambivalence of the discourses and counter-discourses on Europe in a crucial period in the history of the continent. From this point of view, as has been underlined in the introduction to this volume, the current historical discourse on the European institutions appears dull and impoverished, not only because it does not take into due consideration the variety and vivacity of the debates taking place within the different nation states, which have run alongside the development of Europe, but also because it all too often forgets to interpret the history of those debates in relation to these internal political dynamics.

The Europe of the royalists *exagérés*: from the chaos of Bonaparte to the return to the *ancien régime*

In the majority of writings published both after the first return of the Bourbons to France and then in moments of great uncertainty and political tension, such as the Hundred Days and the months following Napoleon's defeat at Waterloo, Europe was depicted for the most part as a collection of sovereign states held together by a monarchical political order and a common religious identity. The proponents of this view were those who, in the French political landscape of the Restoration, can be generically termed royalists. Even so, a detailed analysis of these discourses on Europe enables us to distinguish two separate currents of *royalisme*.

Some pamphlets and circumstantial writings, for example, spread within public opinion the image of a Europe that had plunged into disorder and chaos not simply because of the hegemonic objectives of Napoleon, but also because of the false doctrines of the Revolution: bringing back into discussion the entire political, cultural and moral phenomenon that went under the name of Revolution, the authors of these works set forth the need not only for a political renovation of the continent, but also a moral one. The pamphlet by Mannoury d'Ectot, written under the captivating title, *La chute de l'impie, le Juste couronné, Rome rendue au Souverain Pontife, ou l'Europe pacifiée*, and published in the first half of 1814, saw the fall of Napoleon as an event desired by Providence. Its hope for all the European states was a rigidly monarchical order and, in this respect, it saw the Catholic Church as a driving and generating force for the entire continent. Moreover, the author believed that the salvation of the continent would be realized only by admitting that philosophy was not based on any law 'qui ne soit contenue dans la religion catholique'.[6] For such authors, who we may call 'pure' royalists and who after the Hundred Days were branded *exagérés* or *ultraroyalistes*, Europe was in special need of a moral reconstitution that stemmed from pre-Enlightenment philosophy. They identified in Catholicism – and not generally in Christianity – the bonding agent of the various states and a key principle for ensuring the continental balance. Taking inspiration from counter-revolutionary doctrines, they saw the Bourbon restoration and the return to the pre-1789 balance between states as an opportunity to re-establish the *ancien régime* in France and throughout the continent.

This position found a model theoretical formulation, not accidentally, in the works of one of the writers who, together with Joseph de Maistre, theorized the basic principles of counter-revolutionary thought, and on whom Manuela Ceretta focused her attention in the preceding chapter: Louis de Bonald. In his *Réflexions sur l'intérêt général de l'Europe, suivies de quelques considérations sur la noblesse*, published in October 1814 when the Bourbon regime was already acutely unstable (and at the same time as the opening of the Congress of Vienna), he pondered at length the post-Napoleonic situation in Europe, depicted as a desolate place of irreconcilable conflict and political and moral disorder. The negotiations of the Congress thus appeared to him the ideal instrument by which to destroy false philosophical doctrines and to reinstate the European balance of the *ancien régime*. In his opinion, it was not enough to identify religion and monarchy as the only forces that could bring back peace and tranquility and preserve Europe's leading role in world politics, since the main danger facing the continent was 'le dogme athée de la souveraineté du peuple'.[7] It was therefore necessary to return to an absolute power of sovereigns and to restore the leading role of the Holy See, from whose influence, superior to that of other European states, derived 'l'ordre et la paix des esprits et des cœurs'.[8]

France had to have a leading part in this process because it had 'toujours exercé une sorte de magistrature dans la chrétienté'.[9] Furthermore, Bonald explained, the dramatic events that marked the country's history in recent decades – the development of pernicious doctrines and the tyranny into which it had fallen – were not exclusive to it, but could be traced back to a more general movement of rebellion that originated in the Protestant Reformation and which pervaded the whole of Europe, but which now 'ne peut plus se reproduire'.[10] The counter-revolutionary intellectual therefore hoped that the countries of Europe 'parvenus à un haut degré de civilisation et de connoissance' would not harp on each other's mistakes, but would instead unite to fight 'contre le danger des fausses doctrines qui minent à petit bruit les lois, les mœurs, les institutions'.[11] Thus, according to Bonald, the restoration of monarchy in Europe had to move in tandem with a return to Catholicism and a consequent progressive reduction of Protestantism.

In addition, to restore the natural order, Bonald foresaw a wide-ranging overhaul of Europe's social organization and a return to the class system that preceded 1789. The guiding role was to be shared by the clergy and the hereditary nobility which 'est une institution *naturelle* et *nécessaire* de la société publique, aussi nécessaire, aussi ancienne que le pouvoir lui-même'.[12] Bonald, in fact, believed it was vital to rebuild what the Revolution had destroyed: 'instituer la noblesse dans son état politique, et même dans son état domestique; en faire réellement un ordre, c'est-à-dire un corps de familles dévouées au service public'.[13] The role of the nobles was of paramount importance because they 'participent partout de la nature du pouvoir', in other words, they were to cover the role of ministers and carry out certain 'fonctions publiques' that had become hereditary when the heritability of the crown came into being. This was a process inherent in the very nature of monarchy, a form of government that conferred dynastic rights on a single house, the royal one, and which constituted a society in which the individual did not dominate, as in a republic, but rather the family.

The *Réflexions sur l'intérêt général de l'Europe* must of course be placed in the specific context of the First Restoration and the political dynamics of France prior to the Hundred Days. Convinced that 'la politique se fortifie de tout ce qu'elle accorde à la religion',[14] Bonald and all the royalists *exagérés* rediscovered the Catholic identity of Europe in order to take sides in favour of a return to Catholicism as the state religion of France. The future *ultras* thus opposed the *Charte* granted by Louis XVIII, which listed religious freedom among its core principles, affirmed the formal equality of citizens and confirmed the irrevocability of the sale of national assets. In presenting a Europe predominated by the noble houses and the clergy, and in which the mechanisms of power were rooted in centuries-old tradition and dynamics, the discourses of the *ultras* had the specific objective of opposing any written constitution, since in their eyes France already had an unwritten one that dated back to the Middle Ages. Thus it is apparent that their political blueprint had a subversive significance in that it cast doubt on the validity of constitutional monarchy as a political model for France by asserting the preexistence of another monarchy, one of medieval and Carolingian vintage.[15] This idea went hand in hand with a certain image of Europe and 'the historiographical invention of a Christian medieval Europe', that Manuela Ceretta has considered above; medieval Europe was essentially conceived by the counter-revolutionaries as a rhetorical instruments with which to legitimize their rejection of the *Charte* in French domestic politics.

And yet for all that, during the Second Restoration, soon after the second return of the Bourbons to France, the *ultras*, having gained a large majority in the elections of August 1815 that brought about the famous *Chambre Introuvable*,[16] not only accepted the principles of representative government, convinced of eventually being able to exploit its mechanisms to bring back the *ancien régime*, but even fought for an expansion of the power of parliament over the prerogatives of the Crown.

The substance of the *ultras'* discourses on Europe never changed but the tone of their arguments did, however, become more radical. Two examples suffice as evidence: that of an anonymous counter-revolutionary whose pamphlet, with the plain-spoken title *Les principes de la révolution française sont incompatibles avec l'ordre social*, described, almost apocalyptically, a Europe in which, from 1789, chaos and desolation prevailed,[17] while the *ultra* Debauve, in a pamphlet entitled *Le Gouvernement légitime de Louis XVIII peut seul sauver la France et l'Europe*, expressed the hope that all Frenchmen would, in loyalty and devotion, gather around Louis XVIII who, in July 1815, had for the second time returned to the French throne. Debauve warned against the influence of the eighteenth-century *philosophes* with their republican and anti-Catholic ideas, which had allowed the continent to fall back into the wantonness of the Revolution.[18] The discourses on Europe, then, reflected the authentic vision of the world of the *ultras* while also, unwittingly, exposing the shrewdness of their political design: their representation of a legitimist, Catholic and pre-Revolutionary Europe was not entirely consistent with their choosing to embrace the principles of representative government and to fight for the prerogatives of parliament.

The Europe of the moderate royalists between legitimism and limited monarchy

As mentioned, the importance of religion was a key component of the representations of Europe made by all the royalists between April 1814 and the final months of 1815, but it is the value assigned to the process of a political reconstitution of the continent that forms the best litmus test for grasping the distance separating the *exagérés* or *ultraroyalistes* from those who may be called 'moderate'. The latter were firmly persuaded of the validity of the principle of legitimacy, that is, of the need to put the legitimate sovereigns of Europe back on their thrones, and they also accepted that religion – broadly understood – was fundamental to bringing peace to the continent. They were, however, willing to tolerate the effects of the Revolution.

Immediately after the fall of Bonaparte in March 1814, François-René de Chateaubriand, who in the Imperial era had penned *Génie du Christianisme*, unhesitatingly declared himself in favour of the return of the Bourbons, publishing one of his most famous works: *De Buonaparte et des Bourbons, et de la nécessité de se rallier à nos princes légitimes pour le bonheur de la France et celui de l'Europe.* In this, the continent is configured in a unified way as a grouping of monarchies 'à peu près filles des mêmes mœurs et des mêmes temps', led by sovereigns to be considered as 'frères unis par la religion chrétienne et par l'antiquité des souvenirs'.[19] The image of Europe drawn by Chateaubriand was therefore based essentially on the classic claims related to monarchical legitimism, while religion, which he also considered to be a constituent element of European civilization, was subordinate to the political and institutional affinity between the different European states and the family connections of the ruling dynasties, because 'il n'y a pas un roi en Europe qu'il n'ait pas du sang des Bourbons'.[20]

Because Chateaubriand's objective was to forge a broad consensus around the recently restored Bourbon regime, he deliberately drew an image of Europe that suited his purpose. For the whole of the First Restoration he acted as the spokesperson of the 'moderate' royalists who shared a disenchanted view of the historical period through which France and Europe were passing:[21] whereas on the one hand they maintained that the Bourbons' right to the throne was indisputable given that it was based on tradition (but certainly not on a divine legitimacy),[22] on the other they believed that Louis XVIII was the sovereign best fitted 'à l'esprit du siècle' and to the new European political order. Owing to their providential and deterministic conception of history, the entire Revolutionary phenomenon, assuredly European and not merely French in dimension, was seen by them to have been inevitable.[23] It was therefore impossible to wipe out twenty-five years of history and Revolutionary achievements and it was equally unrealistic to aspire to return the entire continent to the *ancien régime*. Rather, what needed to be done was to reconcile oneself to the changes that had occurred and, in order to once and for all ensure that Europe enjoyed order and tranquility, to establish in France and throughout Europe a state structure based on 'l'égalité des droits, de la morale, de la liberté civile, de la tolérance politique et religieuse'.[24]

Unsurprisingly, by 'monarchy' Chateaubriand intended a political regime in which a limited political power operated either by the concession of a constitutional charter or by intermediary bodies that ensured certain freedoms. A few months after the publication of *De Buonaparte*, he crystallized his ideas in the *Réflexions politiques sur quelques écrits du jour*, in which he presented a Europe that from the Middle Ages 'excepté peut-être l'Italie et une partie de l'Allemagne, eût à peu près la même constitution', that is, the 'système représentatif'.[25] For centuries the continent had marched in step towards a common civilization identified with the founding and refining of representative government; indeed, were it not for local events that had interrupted the flow of this movement, all European countries would have already reached the same level of political maturity as England. It is clear that when Chateaubriand spoke of representative government, knowingly conflating the English model and the French monarchy of the *ancien régime*, he was certainly not thinking of a Parliamentary monarchy, but rather of a system in which representation was granted on the basis of class and not the individual.[26] His depiction of a Europe in which the institution of representation had been in place since the Middle Ages was certainly forced, being made in pursuit of a political project belonging exclusively to the France of the First Restoration: to consolidate support for the regime of Louis XVIII, urging all royalists to accept the *Charte* of 4 June 1814 because it was *octroyée* by the sovereign, and discouraging them from exploiting the return of the Bourbons to go back to the *ancien régime*.

As for the Christian identity of Europe, Chateaubriand was a long way from seeing religion as an instrument of power or, to quote Maistre, as 'l'ami, le conservateur, le défenseur le plus ardent de tous les gouvernements'.[27] From the consular-imperial period, during which it heralded the concordat politics of Bonaparte, religion was conceived by Chateaubriand as something that could guarantee man full enjoyment of his freedom as well as protection from interference by political power.[28] This was why, despite making frequent reference, both in *De Buonaparte* and the *Réflexions*, to a Christian Europe, he was not thinking of religion as an *instrumentum regni*, but rather as a cultural factor of the continent or, at least, as a spontaneous force that could bring moral reform to post-Napoleonic Europe.

In short, while the royalists *exagérés'* discourse on Europe depended on an interpretation, so to speak, of principle, which did not permit any compromise with the Revolution and unavoidably collided with the politics of Louis XVIII, that of the moderate royalists was instead a discourse adapted to the defence of the Bourbon regime.

The liberals: the Europe of the people and of representative governments

As we know, the decisions of the Congress of Vienna were taken against a background of a vision of a legitimist and Christian Europe. Nonetheless, from 1814 onwards in pro-Revolutionary circles – that is, among that diverse political grouping composed of liberals, republicans and ex-Bonapartists, in other words by those who during the Second Restoration would form the party of the Independents – many works were produced that energized the debate on how to create a new European order based on the principles of 1789. The cult of the Revolution, with its aspiration to universalism, prompted these authors to regard the fundamentals of freedom and equality not only as a French achievement, but as one of the whole continent, and to formulate proposals for a federal or confederal reorganization of Europe for the peaceful coexistence of its different nations.

The idea of a European federation formed the basis of *Le Conservateur de l'Europe*, a script written towards the end of 1813 but published, anonymously, only in 1815. The author was Marc-Antoine Jullien, a former Bonapartist who from 1810 onwards gradually became an opponent of the Emperor in consequence of his contacts with liberal circles and Madame de Staël.[29] Having analysed the effects of the Napoleonic regime, considered an 'excès', a dangerous deviation compared to the 'direction primitive' of the French Revolution,[30] Jullien proposed restoring peace on the continent through the creation of a 'grande fédération européenne, à la tête de laquelle seront les principales puissances du continent',[31] the most prominent of which was England, considered 'le bouevard et la conservatrice de la civilisation européenne'.[32] Jullien had in mind a sort of confederation of federations including: the '*confédération* particulière *du nord*' made up of Russia, Poland and Prussia but also open to Denmark and Sweden; Italy 'organisée comme un *état fédératif indépendant*, sous la protection spéciale de l'Autriche';[33] the '*Confédération Germanique*'[34] of the German states and Austria; and, finally, France, organized as a '*union fédérative*' of all its provinces which, possessing a certain degree of independence, would be able to 'résister à l'influence dominatrice et malfaisante d'un seul chef'.[35] Jullien's intention was not to propose a plan of European unity, but simply to outline a system of balance based on sound military alliances between independent states.[36] Leaving aside the practicality or otherwise of his project, its most interesting aspect is the way in which the former Bonapartist general viewed Europe as an ensemble of peoples whose diverse characters and needs had to be recognized. In short, one can make out between the lines of his argument a recognition of the principle of nationality that Napoleon himself had helped to propagate in Europe, and which in the end led to the collapse of his empire.[37]

The most famous writing with regard to representations of Europe and proposals for establishing a stable and peaceful new order was *De la réorganisation de la société européenne* by Saint-Simon and Thierry, a work which is usually held by historians to be one of the first attempts to conceptualize a Society of Nations.[38] Implicitly aligning itself with Kantian pacifism, but also taking in some elements of the nascent Romanticism that was spreading in liberal circles largely thanks to the writings of Madame de Staël, the work started from the assumption that medieval Europe had much more solid foundations than the Europe of 1814. In the thirteenth century the 'confederate' structure of the continent was in fact grounded on Christian principles and the enormous influence of the papacy. It is worth noting, however, that, contrary to the view taken by counter-revolutionary intellectuals, for these two liberal authors medieval Europe simply provided a point of comparison and not a model to adopt as a goal, and the Christian religion was for them a political factor long since relegated to the continent's past. They supported without hesitation the principles of the Revolution and defended all its political, moral and social accomplishments, but they went on to argue that just as religion was at the heart of Europe in the fourteenth century, the new Europe must have at its core a common commitment to the political and institutional principles that could be traced back to the form of representative government first put into practice in seventeenth-century England.[39] It is no coincidence that after the introduction and preface the first part of the work was devoted entirely to the exposition 'de la meilleure forme de gouvernement', that is, parliamentary government.[40] It should, however, be noted that Saint-Simon and Thierry used the term *gouvernement parlamentaire* and not simply *gouvernement rappresentatif* precisely because their understanding was that the representative aspect of sovereignty, which naturally belonged to the people, was expressed in parliament. In this sense, despite their acceptance of the monarchical form, their political conception was much closer to that of the republicans than that of the moderate royalists *à la* Chateaubriand, who, like the liberals, supported the Bourbon government and the general idea of representation, but rejected the notion of popular sovereignty.

Saint-Simon and Thierry's proposal for the reorganization of Europe hinged on the progressive expansion of parliamentary government from England to the rest of the continent. France was ahead of other European states in this process – thanks to the Revolution it 'est libre ainsi que l'Angleterre'[41] – and so it was vital to create close ties between the two countries, forming an alliance to act as the driving force for peace building in Europe. The best political organization for Europe would thus be obtained if all the states accepted this form of government and 'reconnaissaient la suprematie d'un parlement général placé au-dessus de tous les gouvernemens nationaux'. The model of parliamentary monarchy, with its division of power between the sovereign, council of ministers, chamber of deputies and chamber of peers, had to be applied not only to individual states, but to the transnational continental system as well: all countries had to participate in the election of a European parliament that decided on the common interests of the continent.

In addition to Jullien, Saint-Simon and Thierry, many other defenders of Revolutionary principles who were active in the early years of the Restoration used terms like *confédération, fédération* or *pacte fédératif* to promote their Utopianist proposals for a united Europe or to present plans for peace-keeping by a European army.[42] What distinguished the discourses on Europe elaborated by these authors from those of the royalists – *exagérés* or moderates – was their vision of the continent not as a set of states led by kings and royal families, but as a group of free nations and peoples. For the liberals (and the republicans) the *conditio sine qua non* of any peace plan for post-Napoleonic Europe was the recognition of the sovereignty of the people by every European state. Jean-Pierre Pagès, a liberal who worked with Benjamin Constant on the periodical *Minérve Française*[43] insisted in his *Principes généraux du droit politique dans leur rapport avec l'esprit de l'Europe et avec la monarchie constitutionnelle* that any proposal for a European confederation 'ne peut être exécuté que par des êtats où la souveraineté est entre les mains de plusieurs'.[44]

Besides the patent criticism of the principles on which the great European Powers based the agreements of the Congress of Vienna, it is important here to underline that the projects for the 'réorganisation de la société européenne' appear to have been strongly influenced by the political positioning of authors in the French political arena. Jullien, Saint-Simon, Thierry and Pagès were among a large group of liberals who supported the Bourbon regime. During the First Restoration, Saint-Simon, in contrast to what would happen later when he propounded his industrialist and socialist views,[45] collaborated with the *Censeur* run by Charles Comte and Charles Dunoyer, a newspaper that supported Louis XVIII.[46] These authors identified representative monarchy rather than the republic as the system of government best suited to the European states for the taking of sides over domestic policy. However, the image of a Europe composed of states in which parliament figured as the most important institutional body was in reality also a critique of the recently restored Bourbon regime, which, despite the granting of the *Charte*, was little inclined to include parliamentary development among its policies. Finally, the liberals condemned the recently collapsed Napoleonic regime, which had exploited popular sovereignty through plebiscites and devalued the importance of representative institutions. In short, liberal discourses, which depicted a Europe of nations in which the people were sovereign, and a Europe ordered on the model of representative government, strove to bring the French Revolution to its conclusion, defending its primary inspiration from a drift towards Jacobinism and from attacks by the *ultras*.[47] Their liberalism, while deployed in support of Louis XVIII, held greatly advanced positions in comparison to those of other supporters of the Bourbon regime who firmly rejected the sovereignty of the people.[48]

The supporters of Napoleon during the Hundred Days: against the illiberal Europe of the Congress of Vienna

If on the *royaliste* front what distinguished the *exagérés* from the moderates was their different way of understanding the monarchical regime and religion, the advocates of Revolutionary principles were divided over their assessment of the Napoleonic experience, with obvious implications for how to represent Europe and the system of balance between the states. In the same months in which the European powers met in Vienna and Napoleon regained power in France for the Hundred Days, the discourses on Europe developed by those who intended to support the Emperor's new regime turned in effect into counter-discourses: the continent was no longer portrayed positively, on the basis of clear-cut political, cultural and religious principles, but was generally attacked in order to strike political opponents – that is, those who, inside and outside of France, were opposed to the Bonapartist regime.

If, as mentioned, the confederation projects described by the liberals were based on a strategic alliance between France and England, the Bonapartists instead saw England as Napoleon's chief enemy. Indeed, there circulated among the pro-Revolutionaries a brief *Projet de pacte fédératif des Français et de tous les peuples de l'Europe, contre les Anglais et les soi-disant souverains, assemblés en congrès à Vienne*. This overtly Bonapartist text was a denunciation of the political design of the European powers, especially England, that were hostile to the Emperor and were determined to return Louis XVIII to the throne.

The continent was thus seen as a collection of people subjugated to 'despotes [qui] ont violé les droits les plus sacrés de la nature et des gens',[49] while France remained the one true bastion of liberty.[50]

Even Benjamin Constant, proven adherent of liberalism, bona fide admirer of the English model, and bitter enemy of Napoleon throughout the Imperial period, found himself defending the Napoleonic regime with very similar arguments.[51] During the Hundred Days, in fact, he agreed to collaborate with Bonaparte by writing the *Acte Additionnel*[52] and, in an article entitled 'Politique européenne' and published anonymously in the *Indépendant* on 1 June, he admonished the European powers – 'cette coalition impie, perturbatrice du repos du monde'[53] – whose sole objective was 'de faire rétrograder l'esprit humain, d'anéantir les principes de liberté'.[54] He also vigorously attacked the English ministers 'qui ont coopéré à toutes les injustices du congrès de Vienne'.[55] Constant addressed the French nation because he was convinced that foreign forces were not at war with Napoleon but instead 'c'est la révolution elle-même qu'ils attaquent et dont il veulent anéantir les bienfaits'.[56] The French thus took up arms not in support of the ambition of their leader, nor for who-knows-what Imperialist aims, but simply to ward off despotism and to protect freedom. According to his line of reasoning, the French cause coincided with the Revolutionary one, with the progress and freedom of Europe as a whole, and that of all the human race.

Of course, it comes as a surprise to discover that only a year before, in his famous *De l'esprit de conquête et de l'usurpation dans leurs rapports avec la civilisation européenne*, Constant had provided a totally different portrait of Europe. In that long analysis of the peculiarities of the Bonapartist politico-military system, the continent was described as a place of progress, civilization and real-life freedom thanks to the Revolution, while Napoleon, unable to 'faire arriver au sein de l'Europe l'ignorance et la barbarie', was accused of having led 'des Européens en Afrique, pour voir s'il réussirait à les façonner à la barbarie et à l'ignorance'.[57] However, Constant had added significantly: 'and then, to preserve his own authority, [Napoleon] worked to ensure that Europe regressed to the same level'.[58] Here, then, is confirmation of the fact that the way in which discourses on Europe were used for political ends often changed, sometimes diametrically, for the sake of political expediency. The attempt to galvanize the French into actively supporting the government of Napoleon and to defend its actions led Constant to set aside, during the Hundred Days, the idea of a Europe of civilization and progress, in favour of an illiberal Europe that only Bonapartist France could save.

The confrontation with Turkish otherness: a united Europe of the nations, civilization and Christianity

During the 1820s discourses on Europe continued to have a significant political value for French domestic politics, and yet they were formulated in a situation that saw France re-appropriate, step by step, its leading role on the continental stage. In light of the revolts affecting several European countries between 1820 and 1821, the French began to discuss whether to intervene in the war of independence undertaken a year earlier by the Greek people against Ottoman rule. Leaving aside the geopolitical questions and the strategic interest that France retained in the Balkans, my aim is to examine here the discourses on Europe that appeared in certain writings published in the years immediately preceding 1826, when, thanks to Russia's armed intervention against the Sublime Porte and to public pressure, the *ultraroyaliste* government led by Villèle opted first to seek an independent diplomatic solution before then, at long last, taking direct action in the conflict.[59]

Liberal writers brought the Greek question to public attention in France during 1822, the year in which Dominique Dufour de Pradt published a brochure entitled *De la Grèce dans ses rapports avec l'Europe*. Having been a Bonapartist functionary and diplomat in the years of the Empire, during the Restoration Pradt became a member of the Independents, the left-wing party that after the turning point of 1820 – the year in which the murder of the Duc de Berry led France once again down the path of counter-revolution – formed the opposition to the right-wing *ultraroyaliste* governments. With this work, the liberal writer, whose interest in foreign policy and diplomatic relations between European states was first roused in the Imperial period, intended to oppose the growing influence of Russia on the continental scene, but, even more than that, wanted to ally himself with the Greek people in their fight for the fundamental right to independence.

In considering how to convince the government to intervene, Pradt wondered which of the two nations – the Greek or the Turkish – was most compatible with the European spirit, here defining Europe as an ensemble of states distinguished 'par la similitude de religion et des mœurs'.[60] There existed, therefore, in the eyes of this liberal author, a Europe with clearly prescribed political and cultural characteristics, markedly different from the Ottoman orient for one specific reason, which was referred to frequently in liberal journalism and which became vitally important to all later French historiography: 'civilization'. By this term Pradt meant everything that contributed to the scientific, moral and political progress of the European continent, albeit in his reasoning the process acquired distinct economic overtones, being identified with the capitalism that during the 1820s was making a notable impact on France. It was therefore not by chance that he underlined the perpetual need of civilization for new spaces in which to evolve, and thereby to constantly expand into new territories: 'armé d'une science toujours croissante, qu'en fera l'homme, s'il ne sait où il peut en placer les produits?' It was useless to continue to make scientific progress, 'si en même temps il ne multiplie pas les consommateurs, et s'il n'aiguise pas sans cesse leur goût pour de nouvelles consummations'.[61]

Pradt's argument was clearly posited on a political rationale: that of attacking the *ultraroyaliste* politics of the government led by Villèle – practically isolationist, or so it seemed – and that of pleading the cause of the bourgeois class composed of industrialists, merchants and bankers who required new spaces in which to do business. Pradt in fact painted a picture of a Europe of scientific and economic progress, a capitalist Europe but also a colonialist one which needed to find in a 'Turquie d'Europe', a 'Turquie d'Asie', and a 'Turquie d'Afrique' new markets for its products.[62] In short, the liberal author took the side of intervention not only to uphold the Greek people's right to independence, but also for straightforward reasons of economic interest. The Ottoman Empire, moreover, could never be a prosperous market for European goods, the reason being a simple matter of culture: 'le Turc est voué à une vie sobre; il consomme peu, sa nourriture est simple et ses vêtemens durables par sa vie sédentaire et par la gravité conservatrice de sa demarche'.[63] To Pradt, Turkey appeared as 'un cadavre', as 'le sépulcre de la population, des arts, des sciences': a static land in which the civilization process simply did not happen. On the contrary, it was 'un principe de mort d'autant plus actif qu'ils sont contenus dans les élémens mêmes de l'association musulmane'.[64] Here at last one of the factors that, according to Pradt, rendered the Ottoman Empire backward and incompatible with the European spirit was brought into the open: its religion, Islam.

In the French political landscape where the *ultraroyalistes* and the liberal Independents were in a state of conflict, not everyone was in favour of intervention. For example, in the text *Un mot sur la Grèce*, an anonymous author clearly took issue with Pradt's arguments. Recalling the traditional alliance between France and the Ottomans, he pointed out not only that 'la Turquie est pour nous une puissance amie'[65] but also that the Ottoman Empire had been recognized by the Congress of Vienna as an integral part of Europe. In addition, he rejected Pradt's liberal view of Europe: 'l'amour de la liberté n'ont rien de commun avec la civilisation', and a far more important factor for the social progress of a nation was 'discipline'.[66] Needless to say, the author, who wrote in defense of Villèle's government, had a counter-revolutionary conception of politics, but this led him, paradoxically, to defend the diversity of the Ottomans from liberal attacks, arguing that 'les Turcs ont leurs mœurs comme nous avons les nôtres'[67] and that having a different religion did not imply a despotic political disposition. At the root of this *ultraroyaliste* position there lay not only a need to defend the government's actions, but also concern over the liberal and national movements that from 1821 onwards had made inroads into half of Europe, affecting not only Greece, but also Italy, Spain and Portugal.[68] What is most striking here, however, is that in the early years of the debate on the Greek question there had been almost a reversal of the arguments on Europe that characterized the 1814–1815 period: the *ultras*, to defend the government's non-interventionism, seemed to minimize the importance of religion as a factor in European culture, while the liberals, although stressing the importance of the principle of nationality, appealed principally to Europe's Christian identity.

Confirmation of this can be found in *Appel aux nations chrétiennes en faveur des Grecs*, a brief text written in 1825 by Benjamin Constant. Faced with the massacre of the Greek people by the Turks and years of inaction by Villèle's government, which opportunistically complied with the non-interventionist stance of Russia and Austria, Constant became spokesman of a pro-Greek committee, set up by the 'Société de la Morale chrétienne', whose express aim was to 'secourir le peuple courageux et infortuné que l'indifférence persévérante des états chrétiens livre depuis quatre ans au glaive des Musulmans'.[69] The Holy Alliance, composed of the major European states, was accused of sanctioning the extermination of a glorious and profoundly European population and was urged to act in defence of its 'Greek brothers'. Plainly, the 'nations chrétiennes' evoked in the title of Constant's writing defined a fellowship, a fraternity of a religious nature between the European peoples and not between the sovereigns. The French liberals, in other words, laid claim to the Greeks' right to self-determination, representing Europe in terms of a distinction between a Christian 'us' and a Muslim 'them', and tracing back a vision of 'the Turk' that had its roots in the modern age.[70]

But by this time the liberals were not alone in fighting the Greek cause, partly because in the meantime France had dropped its foreign-policy indecisiveness, having used its armed forces in 1824 in Spain to put an end to the liberal triennium and restore Ferdinand VII to the throne. In 1825 Chateaubriand, a critical but extremely authoritative voice in the *ultra* party, not only became president of a 'Societé philanthropique pour l'assistance aux Grecs', but also spelled out his own position by publishing a *Note sur la Grèce*. While maintaining that the sovereignty of Turkey over territories it had possessed for centuries could not be challenged, Chateaubriand nevertheless invited his readers to ask themselves, with regard to the Sublime Porte, 'comme elle se place elle-même avec les autres peuples'[71]: the Ottomans did not recognize European international law, nor the law of nations in force on the continent. It was just to acknowledge the legitimate claims of Turkey – which had nothing of the European spirit – over the territories inhabited by Muslims, while 'dans ses provinces chrétiennes, là où elle n'a plus force, là elle a cessé de régner'.[72] Even Chateaubriand, then, saw the Christian religion as a decisive factor which established that Greece belonged to the European continent and thus legitimized its struggle for independence. Contrary to what one might expect, however, he also acknowledged the principle of nationality and the right of the Greek people to self-determination. In his opinion, 'les Grecs ont incontestablement le droit de choisir la forme de leur existence politique',[73] to the point that there was no need to fear a possible republican government because 'la plus grande découverte politique du dernier siècle [...] c'est la création d'une *république représentative*'.[74] In short, in this work Chateaubriand drew close to the idea of a Europe in which civilization coincided with an inevitable process of democratization.

Conclusions

I have tried to show how in France discourses on Europe, on its identity and on plans for its peaceful reorganization depended largely on the political objectives pursued by the various players with an eye on the domestic situation. This applied in particular to moments of great political and institutional crisis and those in which foreign policy affected domestic policy. The strong political and ideological distinctions in representations of Europe were at their sharpest in the two years between the First and Second Restorations, in other words when the split between the advocates and opponents of Revolutionary principles appeared irreconcilable. A few years later, however, when confronted by 'otherness', these distinctions gradually faded and there emerged an image of Europe shared by the different political forces in the field: that of a Europe of nations, civilized and Christian. And so it is perhaps not wrong to pick out a slender thread that links the discourses on Europe of the past to those of the present. This self-perception and self-representation for reaction to Muslim otherness is, in fact, a constant in the history of the idea of Europe and reaches up to the present day: we need only recall the recent debate on whether or not to accept Turkey's application to join the European Union. Even in that case, it would be interesting to investigate, perhaps in a comparative perspective, how commentators and politicians in different European countries used the image of a 'civilized' and Christian Europe that must be defended from the threat of the 'backward' and Muslim oriental world to implement strategies that benefit national political objectives.

Notes

1 Among its many meanings, the term 'Europeanization', now widely used by scholars, also indicates the influence of the European Union not only on the public policies of individual member states, but also on their internal political conflicts and the communication strategy of politicians and party activists. See Featherstone 2003; Schmidt and Radaelli 2004.
2 See Featherstone 2003.
3 For an overview of the history of the idea of Europe, see Saitta 1948; Duroselle 1965; Curcio 1978; Wilson and Van der Dussen 1995; Desbazeille 1996; Verga 2004.
4 The origins of the re-evaluation of the Restoration can be traced through the by now classic work of Bertier de Sauvigny 1999 (first edition 1955). The most important recent contributions have been the essays collected by Waresquiel 2015.
5 For an account of the fall of Napoleon, the birth of the Bourbon regime, the Hundred Days, and finally the return of Louis XVIII, see Bertier de Sauvigny 1999, 9–140; Waresquiel and Yvert 2002, 11–163.
6 Mannoury d'Ectot 1814, 4.
7 Bonald 1815, 22.
8 Bonald 1815, 49.
9 Bonald 1815, 18.
10 Bonald 1815, 21.
11 Bonald 1815, 22.
12 Bonald 1815, 53.
13 Bonald 1815, 76. On the political ideas of Bonald, see Klinck 1996; Chignola 1993.
14 Bonald 1815, 50.
15 On the political conception of the royalists *exagérés*, see Oechslin 1960; Sciara 2013, 41–44.
16 On the 'Chambre Introuvable' see Bertier de Sauvigny 1999, 126–140; Waresquiel and Yvert 2002, 165–196; Cassina 1989.
17 [Anonymous] 1816.
18 Debauve 1816.
19 Chateaubriand 1814 [a], 78.
20 Chateaubriand 1814 [a], 79.
21 On the positions taken by the moderate royalists during the first Restoration, see Sciara 2013, 28–35.

22 On Chateaubriand's conception of legitimism, see Holmes 1982, 172–176.
23 On Chateaubriand's conception of history, see Aureau 2001, 177–198.
24 Chateaubriand 1814 [a], 54.
25 Chateaubriand 1814 [b], 91.
26 On Chateaubriand's understanding of monarchy, see Sciara 2013, 187–193.
27 Maistre 1884, 90.
28 On Chateaubriand's conception of freedom and his way of understanding religion, see Clément 1987, 30–33.
29 Jullien 1815. The work does not include a date or name of publisher, but the *Avis de l'éditeur* is signed by Chevalier de Clendi. As a note in the frontispiece testifies, the text, despite being published in the summer of 1815, was written in October 1813 and sent by the author to Tsar Alexander.
30 Jullien 1815, 12.
31 Jullien 1815, 63.
32 Jullien 1815, 81.
33 Jullien 1815, 62
34 Jullien 1815, 71.
35 Jullien 1815, 79.
36 For a lucid analysis of Jullien's text, see Pancera 1991.
37 On this subject see Fontana 2013.
38 This is true above all for the period between the two World Wars in France, see Piguet 1993, 7. For a detailed analysis of this text, see Saitta 1948, 149–157; Carbonell 2001; Scuccimarra 2011; Proietti 2014, 51–57.
39 Saint-Simon and Thierry 1814, XV.
40 Saint-Simon and Thierry 1814, 19.
41 Saint-Simon and Thierry 1814, XVII.
42 For an interesting review of these texts, see Proietti 2014.
43 On this periodical and on the group of liberals that worked on it, see Harpaz 1968.
44 Pagès 1817, 225.
45 On Saint-Simon and his school see Larizza Lolli 1980.
46 On the *Censeur* see Harpaz 2000.
47 For a detailed analysis of the political thought of the liberals and the establishment of the Independent party, see Alexander 2003, 30–80. On the political position of the liberals close to the *Censeur* see Harpaz 2000; Sciara 2013, 193–202.
48 One thinks, for example, of the doctrinaires like Guizot and Royer-Collard. See Rosanvallon 1985.
49 [Anonymous] 1815, 2.
50 On Bonapartism, see Bluche 1980.
51 On Constant's political thought, see Holmes 1984; Kelly 1992; De Luca 2003; Rosenblatt 2009.
52 On Constant's political positioning between the First and Second Restoration and his choices during the Hundred Days, see Kloocke 1984, 181–215; Wood 1993, 215–229; Sciara 2013. For an enlightening account on Constant as a political figure, see Todorov 1997.
53 Constant 2001, 864.
54 Constant 2001, 865.
55 Constant 2001, 866.
56 Constant 2001, 865.
57 Constant 2005, 749.
58 Constant 2005, 749.
59 On the Greek question in relation to French politics, see Bertier de Sauvigny 1999, 400–408.
60 Pradt 1822, 67.
61 Pradt 1822, 56.

62 Pradt 1822, 58.
63 Pradt 1822, 65.
64 Pradt 1822, 61.
65 [Anonymous] 1822, 10.
66 [Anonymous] 1822, 21.
67 [Anonymous] 1822, 22.
68 The European revolts are analysed in a contemporary account from a moderate royalist perspective. See Salvo 1824.
69 Constant 1825, 5.
70 On the French view of the Turk in the modern era, see Rouillard 1940. See also Formica 2012.
71 Chateaubriand 1825, 20.
72 Chateaubriand 1825, 22.
73 Chateaubriand 1825, 27.
74 Chateaubriand 1825, 29.

References

Alexander, Robert. 2003. *Re-Writing the French Revolutionary Tradition: Liberal Opposition and the Fall of the Bourbon Monarchy*. Cambridge: Cambridge University Press.

Aureau, Bertrand. 2001. *Chateaubriand penseur de la Révolution*. Paris: Champion.

Bertier de Sauvigny, Guillaume. 1999. *La Restauration*. Paris: Flammarion.

Bluche, Frédéric. 1980. *Le bonapartisme: aux origines de la droite autoritaire (1800–1850)*. Paris: Presses Universitaires de France.

Carbonell, Charles Oilvier. 2001. *L'Europe de Saint-Simon*. Toulouse: Eìditions Privat.

Cassina, Cristina. 1989. 'I lavori parlamentari della "Chambre Introuvable"'. *Critica storica* 4: 573–610.

Chignola, Sandro. 1993. *Società e costituzione. Teologia e politica nel sistema di Bonald*. Milan: FrancoAngeli.

Clément, Jean-Pierre. 1987. 'Introduction. Chateaubriand ou la religion de la liberté'. In *De l'Ancien Régime au Nouveau Monde. Écrits politiques, textes choisis*, by François-René de Chateaubriand, 9–70. Paris: Hachette.

Curcio, Carlo. 1978. *Europa. Storia di un'idea*. Turin: Eri.

De Luca, Stefano. 2003. *Alle origini del liberalismo contemporaneo. Il pensiero di Benjamin Constant tra il Termidoro e l'Impero*. Lungro di Cosenza: Marco Editore.

Desbazeille, Michèle Madonna. ed. 1996. *L'Europe, naissance d'une utopie? Genèse de l'idée d'Europe du XVIe au XIXe siècles*. Paris: L'Harmattan.

Duroselle, Jean-Baptiste. 1965. *L'idée d'Europe dans l'histoire*, Paris: Denoel; Milan: Ferro.

Featherstone, Kevin. 2003. 'Introduction: In the Name of "Europe"'. In *The Politics of Europeanization*, edited by Kevin Featherstone and Claudio M. Radaelli, 3–26. Oxford: Oxford University Press.

Fontana, Bianca Maria. 2013. 'The Napoleonic Empire and the Europe of Nations'. In *Imagining Europe. Myth, Memory, and Identity*, edited by Chiara Bottici and Benoit Challand, 116–138. Cambridge: Cambridge University Press.

Formica, Marina. 2012. *Lo specchio turco. Immagini dell'Altro e riflessi del Sé nella cultura italiana d'età moderna*. Rome: Donzelli.

Harpaz, Efraïm. 1968. *L'Ecole libérale sous la Restauration, le Mercure et la Minerve, 1817–1820*. Geneva: Droz.

Harpaz, Efraïm. 2000. *Le Censeur, le Censeur Européen: histoire d'un journal liberal et industrialiste*. Geneva: Slatkine Reprints.

Holmes, Stephen. 1982. 'Two Concepts of Legitimacy: France after the Revolution'. *Political Theory* 10: 165–183.

Holmes, Stephen. 1984. *Benjamin Constant and the Making of Modern Liberalism*. New Haven, CT and London: Yale University Press.

Kelly, George Armstrong. 1992. *The Humane Comedy: Constant, Tocqueville and French Liberalism*. Cambridge: Cambridge University Press.

Klinck, David. 1996. *The French Counter-Revolutionary Theorist Louis de Bonald, (1754–1840)*. New York: Peter Lang.

Kloocke, Kurt. 1984. *Benjamin Constant. Une biographie intellectuelle*. Geneva: Droz.

Larizza Lolli, Mirella. ed. 1980. *Scienza, industria e società. Saint-Simon e i suoi primi seguaci*. Milan: Il Saggiatore.

Oechslin, Jean-Jacques. 1960. *Le mouvement ultra-royaliste sous la Restauration. Son idéologie et son action politique (1814–1830)*. Paris: Librairie Générale de Droit et de Jurisprudence.

Pancera, Carlo. 1991. 'Marc-Antoine Jullien de Paris et son projet de confédération entre les gouvernements européens (1813–1818)'. In *Le cheminement de l'idée européenne dans les idéologies de la paix et de la guerre*, edited by Marita Gilli, 179–194. Paris: Les Belles Lettres.

Piguet, Marie-France. 1993. 'L'Europe des Européens chez le comte de Saint-Simon'. *Mots* 34: 7–24.

Proietti, Fausto. 2014. 'La réorganisation de l'Europe nel dibattito politico francese tra Prima e seconda Restaurazione (1814–1815)'. In *Il Congresso di Vienna 1814–1815. Storia, politica e diplomazia*, edited by Francesco Randazzo, 41–59. Tricase: Libellula.

Rosanvallon, Pierre. 1985. *Le moment Guizot*. Paris: Gallimard.

Rosenblatt, Helena. ed. 2009. *The Cambridge Companion to Constant*. New York: Cambridge University Press.

Rouillard, Clarence Dana. 1940. *The Turks in the French History, Thought and Literature*. Paris: Boivin.

Saitta, Armando. 1948. *Dalla res publica christiana agli stati uniti di Europa: sviluppo dell'idea pacifista in Francia nei secoli XVII-XIX*. Rome: Edizioni di Storia e Letteratura.

Schmidt, Vivien A., and Claudio M. Radaelli. 2004. 'Policy Change and Discourse in Europe: Conceptual and Methodological Issues'. *West European Politics* 27: 183–210.

Sciara, Giuseppe. 2013. *La solitudine della libertà. Benjamin Constant e i dibattiti politico-costituzionali della prima Restaurazione e dei Cento Giorni*. Soveria Mannelli: Rubbettino.

Scuccimarra, Luca. 2011. 'Una costituzione per l'Europa. Saint-Simon e la *Réorganisation de la société européenne*'. *Historia Constitucional* 12: 1–20.

Todorov, Tzvetan. 1997. *Benjamin Constant. La passion démocratique*. Paris: Hachette.

Verga, Marcello. 2004. *Storie d'Europa. Secoli XVIII–XXI*. Rome: Carocci.

Waresquiel, Emmanuel de. 2015. *C'est la Révolution qui continue! La Restauration 1814–1830*. Paris: Tallandier.

Waresquiel, Emmanuel de, and Benoît Yvert. 2002. *Histoire de la Restauration 1814–1830. Naissance de la France moderne*. Paris: Perrin.

Wilson, Kevin, and Jan van der Dussen. eds. 1995. *The History of the Idea of Europe*, London and New York: Routledge, 1995.

Wood, Dennis. 1993. *Benjamin Constant. A Biography*. London and New York: Routledge.

Primary sources

[Anonymous]. 1815. *Projet de pacte fédératif des Français et de tous les peuples de l'Europe, Contre les Anglais, et les soi-disans Souverains, assemblés en congrès à Vienne.* Paris: Charles.

[Anonymous]. 1816. *Les principes de la révolution française sont incompatibles avec l'ordre social. Aussi longtemps que les Français ne seront pas soumis à leur souverain légitime, il ne peut y avoir ni bonheur pour la France, ni sûreté pour l'Europe. 3e partie d'un ouvrage destiné à l'impression en 1795.* Paris: Pachoud.

[Anonymous]. 1822. *Un mot sur la Grèce, ou Réflexions sur la dernière brochure de M. de Pradt, intitulée: 'De la Grèce dans ses rapports avec l'Europe'.* Paris: Imprimerie de Fain.

Bonald, Louis de. 1815. *Réflexions sur l'intérêt général de l'Europe, suivies de quelques considérations sur la noblesse.* Paris: Le Normant.

Chateaubriand, François-René de. 1814 [a]. *De Buonaparte, des Bourbons, et de la nécessité de se rallier à nos princes légitimes, pour le bonheur de la France et de celui de l'Europe.* Paris: Mame frères; Le Normant; H. Nicole.

Chateaubriand, François-René de. 1814 [b]. *Réflexions politiques sur quelques écrits du jour et sur les intérêts de tous les Français, par M. de Chateaubriand.* Paris: Le Normant.

Chateaubriand, François-René de. 1825. *Note sur la Grèce, par M. le vicomte de Chateaubriand, membre d'une société en faveur des Grecs.* Paris: Le Normant.

Constant, Benjamin. 1825. *Société de la morale chrétienne. Comité des Grecs. Appel aux nations chrétiennes en faveur des Grecs.* Paris: Treuttel et Würtz.

Constant, Benjamin. 2001. 'Politique européenne'. In *Œuvres complètes de Benjamin Constant, Seirie Œuvres*, vol. IX-2, edited by Olivier Devaux and Kurt Kloocke, 863–866. Tübingen: Niemeyer.

Constant, Benjamin. 2005. 'De l'Esprit de conquête et de l'usurpation, dans leurs rapports avec la civilisation européenne'. In *Œuvres complètes de Benjamin Constant, Seirie Œuvres*, vol. VIII-2, edited by Kurt Kloocke and Béatrice Fink, 687–801. Tübingen: Niemeyer.

Debauve, Bernard-Simon-Laurent. 1816. *Le Gouvernement légitime de Louis XVIII peut seul sauver la France et l'Europe.* Paris: Gueffier jeune, Belin et Delaunay.

Dufau, Pierre-Armand. 1822. *Du partage de la Turquie d'Europe entre la Russie, l'Autriche, l'Angleterre et les Grecs, sous la médiation de la France.* Paris: Chanson.

Jullien, Marc-Antoine. 1815. *Le Conservateur de l'Europe, ou Considérations sur la situation actuelle de l'Europe, et sur les moyens d'y rétablir l'équilibre politique des différens états, et une paix générale solidement affermie; Quelques Fragmens extraits du portefeuille politique de Buonaparte, ou Mémoires sur les intérêts politiques de l'Italie et sur ceux de la France; précédés d'un avertissement de l'éditeur.* Paris: Ch. de Clendi.

Maistre, Joseph de. 1884. 'Réflexions sur le Protestantisme, dans ses rapports avec la Souveraineté'. In *Œuvres complètes de Joseph de Maistre*, vol. 8. Lyon: Vitte et Perrussel.

Mannoury d'Ectot, Jean-Charles-Alexandre-François. 1814. *La chute de l'impie, le Juste couronné, Rome rendue au Souverain Pontife, ou l'Europe pacifiée.* Paris: Impr. de Porthmann.

Pagès, Jean-Pierre. 1817. *Principes généraux du droit politique dans leur rapport avec l'esprit de l'Europe et avec la monarchie constitutionnelle.* Paris: Béchet.

Pradt, Dominique Dufour. 1822. *De la Grèce dans ses rapports avec l'Europe.* Paris: Béchet aîné.

Pradt, Dominique Dufour. 1824. *Parallèle de la puissance anglaise et russe relativement à l'Europe; suivi d'un Aperçu sur la Grèce.* Paris: Béchet aîné.

Saint-Simon, Claude-Henri de, and Augustin Thierry. 1814. *De la réorganisation de la société européenne, ou De la nécessité et des moyens de rassembler les peuples de l'Europe en un seul corps politique, en conservant à chacun son indépendance nationale.* Paris: A. Égron; Delaunay.

Salvo, Charles de. 1824. *Considérations sur les dernières révolutions de l'Europe.* Paris: Béchet aîné.

Part II

The burden of rhetoric

Inside the European institutions

Introduction to Part II

The burden of rhetoric: inside the European institutions

After the Second World War, when the early institutional steps towards European regionalism were conceived, there was no European past to be 'regretted'. Nazi and fascist Europe, the great depression and the upheaval of total war could hardly be viewed as idyllic bygone times to which one might wish to return. On the contrary, that period of European history had optimistically and definitively been left behind, and substituted by a better and more humane society regulated by new 'enlightened' supranational institutions designed to contribute to peaceful coexistence, political stability and economic growth. The rhetoric of European 'unity' was an integral part of the recasting of postwar European discourse. However, despite expressing a fundamental discontinuity with the past and being embedded in a modernizing vision of European organization, the new regional institutions were also the outcome of a more general conservative attempt to 'contain' the postwar drive for social change in a divided Cold War Europe. This apparent contradiction, and the tension arising from it, partly explain the discursive ambivalence in which new-born European institutions were rooted, and somehow cast subsequent institutional rhetoric as a legitimizing device meant to compensate for the lack of a direct popular mandate. The second part of this volume is an attempt to develop an explanation for this ambivalence, and its four chapters deal with the role played by supranational European institutions in the discursive construction of an 'organized' Europe. They are based on the assumption that the burden of rhetoric is one of the conservative legacies of early European integration and among the enduring difficulties that prevent European institutions from adopting and communicating more forward-looking attitudes. As a result, and somehow paradoxically, institutional rhetoric has often turned out to be an obstacle to legitimization.

This second part is informally divided into two subsections. The first two chapters, focused on military institutions and nuclear energy, deal with the discursive rhetoric of early European integration in the immediate postwar years and in the 1950s.

In the aftermath of the Second World War, European countries engaged in a profound and unprecedented revision of the hierarchy of power and eroded the traditional references to homelands and nations, since the new security framework of the West was built on a Euro-Atlantic axis. However, military traditions, both national and continental, did not disappear, and a new European perspective was proposed as part of a rhetorical discourse that intended to offer an identity to integrated organizations that were called to stand alongside the American giant. Taking into consideration, with particular reference to the Italian and French contexts, the assumptions underpinning the plans made by military institutions prior to the failure of the EDC project in 1954, Chapter 4 shows that 'Europe' and the 'West' were notions that challenged the internal culture of national military institutions, and measures the resilience of the traditional reference to the 'fatherland' against the drive to give ideological content to the notion of 'the West'. While, in Italy, the internationalization of armed forces guaranteed a route towards a gradual reacquisition of sovereignty, the military in France was forced to confront imperial decline and the difficulty of integrating national priorities, European geopolitical imperatives and surviving ambitions of 'grandeur'. Until the end of the Algerian crisis, anti-communism mixed geopolitical issues and the surviving values of the old European and white ruling powers under the someway ambiguous brand of 'the West'.

The challenge of the Cold War also affected the discourse surrounding the launch of European techno-scientific integration through Euratom, the Community created in 1957 to develop a new European atomic energy capacity. Little investigated by historiography, the Euratom experience raises a series of questions on the ways atomic technology – the epitome of postwar modernization – contributed to a language of Europe and of European integration in an advanced industrial sector. The rhetorical construct at the origins of 'nuclear regionalism' in the early phase of Euratom sheds light on how the development of civilian nuclear power promoted discourses on Europe, both as a new regional institutional framework and as a project of modernity, albeit one embedded in a language that took up ideas dating from nineteenth-century scientific internationalism yet revisited in the light of Cold War confrontation.

The following two chapters concentrate on discursive practices in the European Parliament through analyses of the language of parliamentary debates in two different, more recent and heated discussions. Chapter 6 deals with the institutional reform of the European Community/European Union in the late 1980s and early 1990s, taking into consideration the shifting views and positions adopted by the two main political groups, the European People's Party and the European Socialists, from the first direct elections of the EP to the adoption of the Treaty of Amsterdam. Chapter 7 focuses on the disintegration of Yugoslavia between the outbreak of the crisis in 1991 and the Dayton Agreement of 1995, which marked the end of the war in Bosnia-Herzegovina. References to Europe's historical role in the Balkans, to the profound legacy of the Second World War, and to the role of the United States in that early post-Cold War phase show both the inadequacy of the Union's foreign policy tools when faced with the challenge of the return of war on Europe's borders, and how the resort to rhetorical practices was part of that inadequacy.

4 A European framework for military institutions?

International integration and European perspectives in military rhetorics after the Second World War

Marco Di Giovanni

After the 'turn of 1989' and in the late Nineties, the European Union was once again talking about a 'European Security and Defence Identity'. From the Cologne European Council to the Lisbon Treaty, the Union reaffirmed the willingness to develop capabilities for autonomous military action and to create a common ground for security among its member states, drawing on civilian and military assets. The end of the Cold War gave new strength to the idea of recasting defence policy on a European scale, alongside the mature path of economic integration. A common defence might be the essential support and main instrument of a common foreign policy, which was also yet to be determined. The strategic turn of the new century and the spreading of global and insidious threats, made the need for integration more urgent. 'Defence' joined 'security', multiplying the levels of interaction and integration of national systems, once again insufficient in the face of new challenges.

As happened at the dawn of the Cold War, European countries are called to face a common future, this time backed by strong Community institutions but still bound to national structures and national sovereignty traditions. Europe appears still incomplete, fuelling a new scepticism built on the recall of the past, and precautionary closures impatient for supranational logic.

A common 'Security and Defence Identity' has still to take root but it has been a part of the European project from its very beginning, as a response to the systemic turn at the end of the Second World War, which reshaped Europe's physiognomy and balances, recasting its components, nations and empires in a dominant Western perspective.

The discursive dimension of Europe in post-1945 military rhetoric that is dealt with in this chapter inevitably compares with the present, and raises the issue of the incapacity of individual European nation-states to face the new threats of global instability. The failure of EDC may represent a mirror for the future. However, beyond the path from that original failure of a European military community, stand the 'integrative effects' of NATO military structures in the making of Europe in a long-term perspective, until today. Under the rhetoric of the West and NATO integrated policy, shared practices have developed, essential to the common European structures of the future.

The military and Europe

Paul Marie de La Gorge, the historian and passionate witness of the French Army's decline, depicted the French military scenario at the end of the war, in 1945, in terms partly applicable to the Italian situation as well, at least as regards the uncertainty that surrounded the future role of the armed forces. Their national function seemed suddenly uncertain and hybrid. The huge crowds that watched the Liberation parades 'hardly recognized uniforms entirely similar to the British or American models; [...] they admired the material of completely foreign origin, but they were unable to decipher the military insignia of the new units, new divisions, and new weapons'.[1] Furthermore, the Italian troops of the liberation army – not to mention the partisan units – paraded through liberated cities dressed in uniforms which had nothing to do with the traditional colours of grey and green. The Italian army's survival would be effectively nourished by materials granted by foreign armies.[2]

The countries of Europe were confronted by a profound and unprecedented revision of power hierarchies which eroded the traditional references to the fatherland/nation and imposed a necessarily 'collective' security framework which, in the Western context, was to be constructed on a Euro–Atlantic axis.[3]

The national military traditions, however, did not disappear from the European perspective that was part of the integration processes envisaged at that time. A composite vision of Europe supported rhetorics intended to give a physiognomy to what flanked the American giant to the west of the Rhine (or Elbe).

The military sphere was entirely invested in those sovereignty redefinition processes because of the martial dimension that had been the central prerogative of sovereign statehood since the birth of a *Jus Publicum Europaeum*.[4]

The tradition of the fatherland-state, which had dominated, as a monumental ruler, the Great War, was demolished by the maelstrom of the 'second Thirty Years War', which swept away the structural elements that had determined and supported it.[5]

Nationalism and its crisis coexisted in the 'savage continent'[6] while the ruling classes of the reconstruction had to contend with the new scale of power, with the bipolar hardening of alignments, and with the uncertain fate of the old empires.

The delegation of security to the principal ally assumed a European dimension. The soldiers of the countries belonging to what was then being defined as the 'West' were required to confront the idea of Europe in the field of military internationalization. They reacted with opposition or solicitation according to the national context, sometimes technocratically welcoming the new professional opportunities that internationalization seemed to create.

This chapter describes this European approach to the construction of security by considering the plans and discourses produced by military institutions in the Italian and French contexts, which shared some cultural features but were in radically different situations: France as a 'victorious' country but in search of confirmation of its role; Italy as a defeated country in search of international

legitimacy and pursuing a 'complicated route of gradual reacquisition of sovereignty with the instruments and principles of interdependence' that 'connoted
the post-war transformation of Western Europe in its entirety'.[7]

We consequently witness the contradictory process of the internationalization
of military apparatuses during its first decade from the end of the war until the
failure of the project for a European Defence Community (EDC).

Studies at international level concentrate mainly on strategic-political aspects,
providing a broad background for national-level analyses.[8]

The French literature comprises a very rich array of works which frame
military affairs within the history of the Fourth Republic,[9] whilst in Italy studies
on the Republic's armed forces are still essentially in their infancy.[10] Less
developed however, even in France, is cultural and institutional analysis which
takes a comparative approach to the remodulation of the reference cultures and
traditions of the military corps undergoing the internalization of processes imposed
by the strategic context. Warranting particular investigation – especially in light
of the recent debate on an effective 'European Defence Policy' – is the 'European' declension of those processes.[11] 'Europe' and 'European' are lemmas that
imply challenging and interesting cultural references within the internal culture
of national military institutions, measuring the resilience of the traditional reference to the 'fatherland' or giving ideological content to the notion of 'the West'.

The strategic-political culture and public rhetorics conceived 'Europe' as an
operational space, an identity, a network of relations and traditions which had to
face the bipolar direction of history either by acquiescing to its effects or pro-
pounding potential alternatives. There loomed the disastrous prospect of Europe
once again becoming a battlefield in the titanic clash of the superpowers, leaving
disenfranchised peoples and nations perpetually divided and once again
overwhelmed.

'Europe' was, however, a common heritage so profoundly soaked with the
blood of two world wars that it now had to cope with the sense of its internal
divisions. It sought a common profile by welding the fatherland's traditions,
from regimental flags to the imperial dominions, with a substantial reshaping of
sovereignty. 'Europe' was a set of values that contributed to develop, and could
absorb, the very notion of the West, with its boundaries and interests. In the
military sphere, required directly to confront the Soviet threat, anti-communism
was a well-established value to be shared and transformed into a factor of
cohesion.

However, the national and identitarian components of the strategy could not
always be overcome. Among the other technocracies, often inclined to favour
the European and Community option, the army assumed a particular stance. It
was partly attracted by those prospects, and partly reluctant to abandon national
roots. Indeed, a recent essay[12] has shown that, among the junior officers of
today's European armies, those from military families are the most reluctant to
sacrifice their lives for the European Union.[13] The number of officers in the
family and support for European military forces are inversely correlated. It might
be suggested that this is a legacy of the reluctance which sixty years ago

contributed to the substantial abortion of a potential 'European' military policy. It is the heritage of Europe's original fragmentation into pieces which the common institutions – notoriously slow and laborious in their functioning – have still not been able to weave back together.

Military reconstructions: Atlantic Italy and (Franco-) European impotence – Europe as a battlefield

The first attempts at European political-military aggregation associated Great Britain with the continental democracies of France and the Benelux countries in the face of a possible revival of German aggression and more concrete Soviet totalitarianism. The Treaty of Dunkirk in 1947 and that of Brussels in 1948,[14] amid Britain's evident continental disengagement, manifested the substantial weakness of the countries of Europe in the event of possible attack. Given the strategic uncertainty of what was by now the 'Western' alignment, was this, one asks, a peripheral strategy which merely slowed the advance of the adversary, the purpose being to maintain bridgeheads on a continent to be rescued in the long term by American intervention. Or was it a strategy to make Europe a continental bulwark to maintain and protect under the umbrella of nuclear deterrence? France would have to consider its geostrategic centrality and the inalienable constraints of British, and especially American, alliances and guarantees, though never losing sight of its role as a major continental and (still in its aspirations) global partner. In dialogue with the allies and Europe, the *Union Française* was simultaneously an alleged resource, an unsustainable military burden and an anchorage (largely fanciful) for possible independent actions as a great power.

After defeat, Italy's position matured from being initially peripheral to inclusion in European initiatives and the construction of a preferential relationship with the United States. From 1943–1945 onwards, reorganization of the military instrument came about through this relationship, which fostered the reconstruction of a 'transition' army entirely oriented to homeland defence, and which then, albeit under the constraints of the peace treaty, opened prospects for development strongly characterized by interdependence. As Federico Romero wrote, 'Independence for Italy came about through acceptance of the constraint of belonging to the West'.[15]

Through inclusion in the mechanisms of alliance and supranational integration, Italy sought a new legitimacy.[16] De Gasperi, together with the country's technocratic elites, grasped the opportunities of the new situation. The military seemed to stand midway. It was culturally oriented to the past (nationalist and, in part, Eurocentric) but pragmatically willing to profit from the opportunities offered by external relationships, in particular those within the Atlantic alliance.

At the beginning of the post-war period, Italian military journalism acknowledged Italy's defeat and the new scales of power in international relations. While commentators initially concentrated on issues of domestic reorganization, they then turned their attention to the international dimension as a framework for the development of national armies.[17] The Atlantic relationship and the prospects of growth that it promised very soon acquired salience. Nevertheless, there were numerous analyses which referred, with varying emphases, to the specific role of the European space.

In regard to the internationalization of military planning, some commentators argued that a coalition was indispensable: no country, except for the great powers, could afford the costs and support the technological-industrial complexity of new military systems.[18] This applied in particular to sectors strongly dependent on technological advances, such as aeronautics, but also the Army. In 1947 General Zanussi published in *Rivista Militare Italiana* an article in which he analysed the strategic dimension of the European space and extolled the 'Euro-Mediterranean' arena as giving especial importance to Italy. Zanussi then referred, in vague terms, to a European horizon of military reconstruction: a 'Pan-Europe' – not better defined but resulting from the common destruction suffered – in which Italy should find its place.[19] The frequent vacillations to be found in these texts reflect the strategic uncertainty that affected the Old Continent, even though it was at the centre of the dynamics of the Cold War.

In fact, given Italy's absolute dependence in this first phase, the military regarded Europe as an actor still shapeless with respect to the more concrete prospects of bilateral cooperation with the United States. After the peace treaty, with the Atlantic shift accomplished, Italy also aligned with the processes of European integration. The face of the continent emerged from the fog. Between the end of 1947 and 1949, it was essentially an area of profound attrition in which the boundaries of the 'West' arose between the Greek civil war and the satellization of countries under Soviet control. Europe had become a potential battlefield dominated by the great powers.

Articles on the global strategic dimension of the new conflicts, such as those by Admiral Fioravanzo in the *Rivista Marittima*, described Europe's political weakness in the context of the peripheral strategy of its allies in regard to a possible Soviet attack:

> In any case, [it] would become a battlefield [...] and should provide for itself during the not brief period before America could intervene to free it.... The end result would be destruction of the last vestiges of European civilization [...]. In the war of great strategic spaces, Europe as it is now is bound to succumb.[20]

Also when, in 1950, the attack on South Korea prompted the initiatives leading to the project for a European Defence Community, intended to confer a more active role on Europe, commentators started from this dramatic strategic situation: the continent was going to become a battlefield once again. Amedeo Mecozzi (an author of considerable prestige)[21] invoked assumption of collective responsibility by the continent, also suggesting its role as a 'third force', given the intolerable subjection which that situation entailed: 'Europeans should unite with the sole purpose of ensuring that the two colossuses, whose rivalry looms

over the world, exclude the territories of Europe from the theatre of their competition'.[22] The army corps general Taddeo Orlando had in fact anticipated this
position in 1949. On discussing Paul Reynaud's book *La France a Sauvé
l'Europe*, he imagined 'a loyal and harmonious merger of European peoples
which generates an array of means and forces able to impose respect for a reso-
lute desire for peace'.[23]

Therefore, Europe as a renewed entity and acting as a balance between the
blocs was a prospect also envisaged by some Italian soldiers. In the meantime,
however, it was membership of the West which prevailed, and the decisive
borders were those defined by adherence to the Marshall Plan.

The predominance of an essentially bilateral conception of the Atlantic sphere
established the instruments and the objective (USA support for military reconstruction and a clear and well-defined role in anti-Soviet/anti-communist action)
able to confer a political role on the Italian armed forces. The transitional phase
now completed, they could once again act as an instrument of a foreign policy
whose dominant features were the national dimension and bilateral relations with
the USA.[24]

It was entry into NATO that fully reintegrated Italy into the international
community and thus initiated a process that would rebuild its role. 'The Italy
humiliated by the Diktat was succeeded by the free Italy which fraternally shook
hands with the other nations of the West, assuming a task of civilization and
peace before the world'.[25] The Atlantic Treaty was the real military arm of the
West and would provide for the military rebirth of the contractors. NATO had to
be the solid anchorage of Italy and the Western – in the strategic, cultural and
political sense – part of Europe.

The predominant view was that of a substantially secondary Europe, more a
strategic space and cradle of civilization than an actor defined in terms of power
politics. Discussed at the time was the 'Defence of Europe and defence of Catholicism' as conducive to the emergence of a stronger and shared identity.[26] Thus in
Italy 'Christian Europe' sounded like a synonym for a 'dam' against both the external enemy and the internal one, and it synthesized the universal values of a national
mission, while also the issue of the colonies would fall within the ambit of the
Atlantic strategy (which, moreover, included French Algeria). When military
journalism asserted Italy's 'good right' to manage the transition of its former
African dominions, it was accompanied by confirmation of the view of Europe as
the cradle of civilization.[27] But it did not adopt, as would instead occur in France, a
significantly polemical stance or oppose alternative strategies to the Atlantic one.

NATO, the authentic and innovative basis for military integration,[28] was
essentially flanked by an economic Europe which wanted, if anything, to equip
itself with instruments of defence, a project in which also the German economy
was enlisted.[29] Even when, in the autumn of 1950, the prospect of a European
military structure arose, the Euro-Atlantic dimension continued to prevail, and
with it the concreteness of the USA's indispensable support. A 'Euramerica'
opposed to a 'Eurasia' was the polarity that Colonel Fausto Monaco proposed
when discussing the modernization of national defence.[30]

In short, there was no apparent emphasis on Europe's potential 'third' role between the two blocs; nor on its 'competition' in the Western camp with the United States and the British Commonwealth, as would happen instead in France.

The situation in France, in fact, was troublesome in many respects. In 1947, the military authorities were forced to acknowledge that the impossibility of ensuring the country's adequate defence imposed a coalition on France. The Treaty of Brussels was the lame embodiment of this guarantee policy against both Germany (in essentially political terms) and the USSR. Britain appeared disengaged on the continent: the idea of the 'British redoubt' prevailed, and everything weighed on the shoulders of France, which, with the Benelux countries, acted as essentially a rampart before the Commonwealth.[31] France's continental centrality fostered a notion of European defence in which the country could find, or confirm, a leading international role, but it had to cope with the material and strategic limits of the present.

The Atlantic Treaty was therefore an indispensable complement to the Treaty of Brussels, and between the end of 1947 and the spring of 1948 – also in response to the Prague coup – France's request for American commitment became pressing. The compelling urgency of the present was felt. But envisaged for the long period was the full European/French assumption of responsibility as the third pole of the West. In these conditions of fragility, the Atlantic Pact was not, according to the official reassurances of Robert Schumann, the abandonment of a recognizable European identity, but rather the necessary condition for the existence, and the construction, of a strong Europe, 'insurance for the future of the values of European civilization'.[32]

According to defence minister Ramadier, it was necessary to create a 'solidarity [...] that will give us the strength to enforce respect of our independence'. The strong cultural resistance to forms of military integration that would compromise portions of national sovereignty had to be abated. According to the defence minister Teitgen, 'Independence in solitude will be for France independence in fragility'.[33]

The stance of the French military authorities comprised a pragmatic component, but it merged with an underlying Eurocentric perspective. It was embedded in an idealized vision of a Europe led by France. At the same time, it maintained a strong assertion of national sovereign prerogatives. Realism soon imposed the urgency of Germany's contribution to defence of the European space. In 1947, contacts and discussions concerning the Soviet threat between the senior French generals (Billotte and Revers) and their British (Morgan) and American (Ridgway) counterparts immediately placed Germany at the centre of European defence.

In concrete terms, the intention of the French chiefs of staff was to obtain reassurances from the United States concerning its commitment to Europe. It was essential to move 'our common defence system' eastwards to German territory 'largely beyond the Rhine',[34] thus ensuring that France would not be invaded once again from the east. Because of its weakness, Western Europe was designated an operational area that included Germany and required it to contribute 'blood'. The French officers in the NATO commands referred to Germans as 'a warrior people, fiercely anti-communist' and not just as the 'best infantry in Europe'.[35] The battle between the Rhine and the Elbe had to mingle German blood with the blood of Europe. The physical and ideal anti-communist space of the West was the terrain on which the grievous legacy of war and occupation, and the rigidity of French policy towards German rearmament, could also be overcome.

The ominous prospect of Europe once again becoming a battlefield persisted even with regard to subsequent processes of politico-military integration. The 'new look' of the American forward strategy announced by General Radford in December 1953 envisaged the use on the European battlefield of tactical nuclear weapons, and it required the creation of a coverage zone as a bastion beyond which nuclear war would be waged. Therefore, even after the failure to ratify the EDC Treaty in September 1954, the French military leaders argued that

> the German contribution is confirmed necessary from both the geographical and military point of view. It could ensure the most eastward possible displacement of the nuclear battlefield, and thus contribute to distancing French territory from the zone at risk of mass destruction.[36]

The strategic depth of the future battlefield enabled the French politicians and generals to promote the role of the *Union Française* in the defence of Europe and as a bulwark of the West, while positing France in its 'entirety' as leader of the processes of continental integration that were taking shape. In the array of ideological issues that formed around the failed project to create the EDC, France included its imperial vision and the strategic scope of its overseas territories in the European space. Thus designated was a zone of physical and ideal conflict which extended from the North Sea to the Mediterranean harbour of Mers el Kebir and then to the Atlantic beaches of Dakar. The borders of Europe became wider as the ideological meaning of European space became deeper.

The EDC project, the blood of Europe and the European perspective

The project of a European Defence Community prompted military circles to conceive an institutional, operational, but also political picture of Europe which revealed its potential but also dangers and weaknesses. The EDC question was particularly complex in France, where it generated a debate which condensed deep ideological issues, as the Dreyfus Affair had done.[37] The EDC project was born on France's initiative in order to respond to technical and political pressures, American or otherwise, to postpone Germany's rearmament no longer. The matter had been discussed since at least 1948, but it was made urgent by the Korean crisis. It was addressed by France with the Pleven Plan, which envisaged a Community that would create an integrated army among the democracies of the continent, thus furnishing the instrument for the United States to pledge its continental commitment in Europe. But it would also create the political and institutional means to control Germany's rearmament.[38] In France, this would be one of the key topics of the debate, together with such issues as identity/ divergence between France and Europe, the maintenance of national control over military structures, the role of the empire and French political autonomy. Elsewhere, as in Italy, although the EDC's problematic aspects in relation to the military tradition naturally mattered, the debate was less heated. It was more oriented to taking the opportunities offered by international integration.

In the autumn of 1950, the French military leaders, having acknowledged that German rearmament was necessary, had to deal with a government project that was fraught with unknowns. The danger of a Germany once again bearing arms was flanked by the perils of a transfer of sovereignty that seemed unprecedented and dangerous.

A rearmed Germany was acceptable to the military, which reflected fewer technical resistances of politicians and public opinion,[39] only by virtue of European embeddedness. This meant controlled German rearmament, operational integration of the German divisions into army corps with mixed command units, (but not the creation of a German high command or defence ministry), unquestioned French centrality in Western Europe and France's equal dignity with the United States and Britain. The nascent European Coal and Steel Community should dilute and curb the revival of German heavy industry.[40] The economic Europe was expected to absorb and control Germany's power, also maintaining imperial France's role as Europe's political leader in dialogue with the main allies. Envisaged for the cadres of the new German forces was a 'European' education whereby Europe would rehabilitate and redeem the German tradition of militarism.

The issue of the Wehrmacht's rebirth harmed the relationship, military and otherwise, between the French and the need to integrate European defence, burdening it with the weight of the past. The 'voice of the earth and the dead' was cited in 1953 by Foreign Minister Bidault when asserting the 'holy and sacred' function of nations in regard to the difficult challenge of the EDC.[41] The blood of two wars still determined the borders of Europe.[42] Jean Pierre Rioux points out that, in 1953, while the theme of the EDC assumed increasing importance in the public debate, the Bordeaux trial of some of the perpetrators (German and Alsatian) of the massacre of Oradour had reopened a deep and bloody wound. According to Chancellor Adenauer, in an interview with *Le Monde* on 14 January 1953, 'This trial [will] revive in the eyes of foreigners the image of a ferocious and bloodthirsty Germany'.[43] The blood of Europe lost its unifying quality in order to nourish ancient and unappeased divisions.

At the Radical Party congress of 1953, the aged Edouard Herriot delivered a speech that, in regard to that project, expressed all the weight of the twentieth-century tragedy: '...the European Union, let me say what I think on the threshold of death, is the end of France'. Others at the congress retorted to speeches by the Alsatian delegates in favour of the EDC by declaring: 'We are not here to defend the Krauts, we are here to defend France'. The German danger, its extraneousness to a certain idea of Europe, was real and motivating even for the supporters of the EDC. Pierre Henri Teitgen formulated the issue in exactly the terms in which it was perceived by important sections of the armed forces: 'If we do not create a European army, we shall inevitably have the Wehrmacht, and if we have the Wehrmacht, all is finished and there is no hope for Europe'.[44] The *Sonderweg* was still one of the nightmares haunting a contested and ambiguous Europe.

Mixing one's blood with the Germans might be less acceptable than digesting, with political realism, an inevitable alliance – which in fact came about, to the satisfaction of the French general staff, with Germany's entry into NATO a few months after the failure to ratify the EDC treaty.

The military authorities also saw as threatening the integration and denationalization entailed by the treaty, and which directly concerned the French units. The allocation of fourteen divisions to the Community, alongside which units of national/imperial interest would be maintained, undermined the compactness of the '*Armée*'. These aspects were strongly opposed, and they would be at the centre of a long comedy of military admonishments and political restructuring of the project. It was here that the continuity of the national dimension was developed. Its spokesman, was of course General de Gaulle. In October 1950 he declared: 'the possible participation of German contingents in the inter-allied Battle of the Elbe will not appear alarming for a stable and strong France in an organized Europe of which she represents the centre'.[45]

According to General Bethouart, notwithstanding realistic acceptance of the inevitability of the European military federation, the army:

> cannot be constructed from an amalgam of disparate and soulless elements, but through the federation of units deeply rooted in the national soil [...]. It will be necessary that our regiments, like those of our allies, enter with their numbers, their histories, their traditions, their uniforms, and their *esprit de corps.*[46]

An aged and celebrated general, Maxime Weygand, who feared German dynamism while difficulties in the French colonies increased, vehemently denounced the danger of denationalization. According to Weygand, what should be pursued was 'A confederation of strong nations, not a community of denationalized countries that will be dominated by the strongest'.[47] Also, General Juin argued that if France were confined within the European Defence Community, it would have to deal on an equal standing with a Germany not burdened by the weight of other commitments.[48]

The 'Europe of nations' would thus become the watchword of General de Gaulle in 1954, when he heightened his opposition to the EDC to reiterate the centrality of France in Europe: 'not the little Europe of six or a NATO totally subject to American strategy, or dependent on the Anglo-American axis'.

Amid a general easing of tensions with Stalin's death, and while France was being taught a harsh lesson in Indochina, de Gaulle pursued France's autonomy in the West. This was the objective that the French government secretly set itself in those months by starting a nuclear project which the provisions of the EDC agreement would not have permitted.[49] In August 1954, General Valluy, French delegate to the NATO Standing Group, had sent a report on the subject of nuclear weapons and Europe's role to the Minister, General Koenig, and the chief of general staff, General Guillaume:

> The West's defence, centred on nuclear weapons, is entirely dependent on American will. The only corrective to this subordination is the creation by the European nations of a nuclear arsenal which enables them to intervene with their own means in this new war and thereby assume a leading role in the coalition.[50]

In the labyrinth of the 'European homeland', the French nuclear programme would begin within the safe confines of the nation, from which it would draw its reason for existence and development, thus marking one of the political pathways of transition from the Fourth to the Fifth Republic.

The theme of Europe's autonomy also raised the difficult issues of its 'Atlantic' nature and definition of the concept of the 'West'. In 1953, the EDC affair had prompted the editor of *Esprit*, Jean-Marie Domenach, to denounce 'the false Europe of the six'. He urged the construction of a true 'Europe against the dual hegemony of the blocs, and above all a western Europe against American hegemony and its German intermediary'.[51] The afflictions of the empire would condense, as we shall see, in the ambiguities of the encounter among a 'civilizing' tradition, Europe, and the political meaning of the West.

From the Italian point of view, Germany's rearmament completed the international reintegration of the 'defeats' from which Italy had already benefited. The 'Western' and 'Atlantic' perspective which dominated the Italian view of these processes was confirmed by the political commentaries which associated this passage with Japan's realignment with the 'free nations'. German rearmament did not have the dramatic significance in Italy that it assumed in France: it marked the overcoming of the past, and it was essentially framed (with sporadic federalist outbursts) in a reformulation of the forward strategy of the NATO Commands.

The cycle begun by the Pleven Plan attracted the attention of military journalism, especially after the signing of the Treaty of Paris in May 1952. It guaranteed and completed the growth process through international integration that military Italy had pursued since the early post-war years. The EDC gained in strength and was conceived primarily as part of NATO strategy. It would continue, in a European setting, the modernization process that experience within NATO was consolidating, albeit in minor areas of the apparatus.[52]

The absence, in the military journals, of leading articles on the EDC until 1953 is indicative of markedly lukewarm interest in the political aspects of the project. Interest consolidated only after the signing of the Treaty of Paris. At that point, consideration could be made of the organizational and institutional consequences of the birth of the EDC, with some discussion concerning the role of the European tradition. The result was a project to be assessed, with scepticism but without radical preclusions, while maintaining the priority of NATO and Atlantic integration.[53]

The *Rivista Militare Italiana* published an article discussing the EDC in early 1953. In light of the government's decision, the article addressed the issues most problematic for the military culture and which Italy shared with France. It was essential that 'arousing a supranational sentiment' should not mean denationalising but rather, and especially, strengthening the instinctive patriotism of individuals and communities, which should gradually emerge among horizons wider than those of the past.[54] In short, patriotism should be channelled into a broader course which responded better to the urgent needs of the time. The article used the same arguments that De Gasperi had put forward a few months previously.[55]

Numerous commentators in the *Rivista Militare Italiana* emphasized the provisional nature of the organizational, regulatory and institutional framework of the envisaged Community. But some of them also stressed the specifically European significance of the EDC: 'The EDC is not just the equivalent of a European army within the NATO framework [...rather, it is] a manifestation of Europe, its first material form of unity'.

Europe and the homelands could cohabit and sustain the historical and political survival of their civilization: 'The possibility of surviving politically as Europeans is conditional upon our capacity to unite ourselves; that is, to achieve a political integration which does not erase our European homelands but instead prevents their disappearance'.[56]

However, despite the author's sincere federalism, he did not consider the intense and dramatic array of themes and values which was typical of the French debate, even though he grasped the negative impact that the EDC project's failure would have on the process of political unification.

Contributors to the *Rivista Marittima* more precociously engaged with the European dimension of military organization, and their attitude was open to the federalist prospect. The issue of a divided Europe – as both the cause and effect of a catastrophe to be overcome – was addressed by some articles as early as 1948.[57] It was accompanied, as said, by the perception of a shared condition of inferiority that might once again transform Europe into a battlefield.[58]

From early 1949 onwards, the *Rivista Marittima* published articles which (in certainly unusual manner) took a distinctly pro-European stance. Writing under the pseudonym of Altair, a high-ranking officer was not only a chronicler-participant of the federalist congress held in Rome in October 1948, and the prospects envisaged by De Gasperi and Spaak; he also emphasised the design of a European army produced by a group of Italian military officers belonging to the federalist movement. The idea that the external danger might accelerate the European integration project also suggested the unusual notion that the military authorities themselves, who apparently cleaved to traditions less open to supranational integration, could be front-line proponents of Europe's need to 'federate or perish'.[59]

The themes of the war of coalition and the standardization of materials, procedures, codes, and training consolidated,[60] and the EDC became part of an already-begun process of modernizing internationalization. The latter comprised both awareness that 'sovereignty seems today an illusion'[61] and the idea that, given the strength of the new superpowers,

> it is in the Union [...] that the free nations of our continent can find a guarantee of their independence. [It is] a categorical imperative for the countries of Western Europe to unite, sacrificing hatreds, grudges, and unlimited sovereignty on the altar of common salvation.[62]

The Navy's relatively greater openness can perhaps be explained by the fact that the EDC project did not directly involve naval forces in insidious processes of supranational merger. It should, however, be stressed that the Navy officers were probably more accustomed to participating in joint NATO operations, and that they were more willing to accept internationalization than the Army.[63]

For the Italian military authorities, therefore, the undoubted benefits of the Atlantic relationship and their traditional reluctance to engage in political debate, made European integration a military option to be evaluated in its technical aspects, and its effects in terms of careers and salaries, but less with regard to the crucial ideological issues: adherence to tradition did not overflow as in France but remained in the background, where it intertwined with scepticism concerning the undefined and controversial aspects of the project.[64] Europe was mainly regarded as the most sensitive sector of Western strategy and as terrain for recognition of Italy's military–political role, not as the basis on which to construct or recover a set of values.

At that stage, in military circles it was essentially figures and attitudes polemical against the framework defined by NATO that made Europe, as a set of values, a strong reference. They claimed spheres of interest and identitarian features that the Atlantic relationship and the policies of its largest stakeholder visibly neglected.

In Italy, this position was forcefully expressed by General Giacomo Carboni, who had by now left the Army but still had a certain influence. As a technician and soldier polemicist (who in the post-war turmoil aligned with the leftist parties), Carboni published a detailed pamphlet which envisaged the Europe of nations as the bastion, evidently ideologically usable by the Left as well, against external encroachments:

> The resistance of the old, civilized Mediterranean Europe against attempts brutally to turn it into a colony consolidated in 1953, although the struggle against the arrogance of the two Anglo-Saxon empires appears of formidable difficulty amid the constant pitfalls and dangers set to discourage those who want to wage it.[65]

In Carboni's view, like that of Domenach, mentioned above, if Europe represented a set of values (essentially nation-based), the EDC was an American imposition and a potential 'military Babel', 'where every principle and distinction of nationality would be submerged'. The armed Europe as proposed would have divided the nations and their armies, sweeping away the only flags worthy of self-sacrifice.[66]

Carboni's pamphlet mixed technical with nationalist opposition to the EDC. However, it gave measure, in its overlapping of issues between countries, of the extent to which the resilience of the national military institutions acted as a powerful structural antidote to unification of the armed forces.

Other points of view fuelled dissociation from the process of European integration that the EDC anticipated. In October 1953, *Rivista Marittima* published an article whose significant title combined the Euro-Mediterranean profile with alignment of old colonial prospects to modern times: *Eurafrica, Terza Forza Mondiale* by Paolo D'Agostino Orsini.[67] An author known for his geopolitical theses in the years of fascism,[68] D'Agostino Orsini referred to 'complementarity' between Europe and Africa not only in the anti-communist sense but also with regard to containment of the American superpower. And in extolling the tutelary action of Europe, he argued in opposition to American anti-colonialism. The notion of the West as an anti-communist barrier raised the question of relations with the political and cultural models of the English-speaking world, and that of the function of the empires as embodiments of an entire cycle of European civilization, and as political and symbolic ramparts in the new global conflict.

Europe and the ideology of the West

The anonymous author of an important essay published in France in May 1953 investigated the effective existence of an 'Atlantic spirit' by considering the strategic and ideal resources that cemented the various components of the alliance together.[69] Besides the bond created by a shared danger, also important was 'The friendship of an alliance cemented in blood during two world wars of common struggle against tyranny'. 'Sentimental bonds' 'built on the blood of the shared battles' that tied France and the Western countries together in an experience marked by the war against Germany. Apart from the differing perception of the German danger, among the factors that could undermine Atlantic cohesion was also a neutralism which was non-instrumental and pro-Soviet but concretely rooted in Europe and the tragic experience of the war: an attitude wary of subordination to the policies of the United States, come 'too young' to the role of great power.

The author posed the question of Europe's role in the new Western framework and with regard to the Anglo-American bloc: the ongoing processes of continental integration were a betrayal of Europe itself and its homelands due to a total 'Americanization' viewed with absolute distrust:

> Is Europe, the cradle of the main currents of civilization [...] called upon to play the role of a satellite or, on the contrary, to overcome its rivalries and act as the vanguard of the Atlantic community of free nations?[70]

'Americanization' consisted not only in the adoption of culture and customs but also in a different perception of the role of the empires and overseas territories that formed an integral part of national policies.

In an article published in those same months, General Bethouart discussed the implications of the EDC. He provided an optimistic analysis in which the ties between France and its overseas territories were recognized as a resource by the Europe under construction:

> We will be the only one of the signatory powers that disposes of overseas territories and resources without the support and use of which Europe cannot be defended. In the future, the defence of Europe will have to be [...] necessarily based on Africa and, in particular, on French Africa [...]. The links between overseas and metropolitan France are important for both France and the others, and as such they will be easily recognized.[71]

Not all commentators were so optimistic about the potential conflict between imperial interests and harmonious European integration.

Among others, it was an officer in the Navy – which was excluded from the integration of the EDC, primarily centred on land and air forces – who emphasised this conflict and, with it, denounced the short-sightedness of the American ideology that threatened to damage the interests and the very soul of the West. In the spring of 1952, Captain Maggiar wrote thus: 'Only the *Union Française* with its vast resources of men and materials, its geographical importance, and its future potential, guarantees France's capacity to balance German power in Europe and to maintain its rank in the world'. Having been crushed by two dreadful wars, France risked disappearing as an 'independent and sovereign nation', perhaps submerged 'in a vague European community'.[72]

The blindness of the alliance loomed large: 'Whilst the entire free world is committed to the defence of Europe, it seems unperturbed by the threats which undermine, from within and without, the capacity to survive of the *Union Française*', which was more important than Europe itself for the future of France.

> It is therefore essential to seek all the means possible to associate metropolitan France more closely with its *Union Française* [...Of these] North Africa is the most important and the most vulnerable. It is the strategic hinterland not only of France but also of Europe and the entire free world [...] even though the United States, tied by its origins to an anti-colonialist ideology, is not yet ready to accept the French point of view.[73]

The disastrous outcome of the Indochina campaign and French isolation anticipated the even more profound crisis caused by the defeat in Algeria, as a consequence of which these issues forcefully returned to oppose a certain view of Europe and the West against the forces – the United States, and de Gaulle himself – that had betrayed the genuine sense of the Western mission.[74]

The partisans of French Algeria maintained that both Europe and the Atlantic Community should come to the rescue of their cause by recognizing it as their own.[75] Thus, according to the spokesman of a strong faction in the army, General Valluy, the autonomy envisaged for Algeria inevitably opened 'a door [...] for infiltration by Moscow'. 'France does not have the right to run this risk. Therefore nor does Europe – I say Europe, not just its Mediterranean part – have the right to make France run that risk'. The solution could only spring from '250 million Western Europeans', or '400 million people of the Atlantic'.[76]

The withdrawal into the French motherland opened new roads for politics, but it definitively brought a century to its close, and with it the idea of a European civilization of whites still able to dominate a scenario by now organized around the East–West polarity.

Notes

1 La Gorge 1967, 450.
2 Cerquetti 1975; Nuti 1989; Ilari 1994; Labanca 2009. On the economic aspects of rearmament and italo–american relations see Selva 2009.
3 For an overview see Heller and Gillingham 1992; also Giauque 2004.
4 Milward *et al.* 1993.
5 Exemplary are the ethical doubts that emerged from the interviews conducted on a sample of French officers by the journal *Esprit* (Catholic and leftist) in the late 1940s. The prestige of the profession of arms entered a crisis because its patriotic foundation had been eroded: war was now civil war:

> You are not absolutely convinced that you are the invincible soldier of a great nation [....] We are no longer entirely sure that we must defend strictly national interests. Today it seems that one must kill only in the name of ideas.
>
> (La Gorge 1967, 481)

6 Lowe 2015.
7 Romero 2009, 41.
8 Heller and Gillingham 1992; Pach 1991; Giovagnoli and Tosi 2003. For Cold War studies see Freedman 2001; Johnston 2001. For a broader view see Morgan, 2003. For the ideology of the West see Jackson 2003.
9 Beginning with Elgey 1965. See Imlay 2009. For the military see Bodin 1992; Fouquet Lapar 1998; Irondelle 2008. On France and NATO see Trachtenberg 2011; Raflik 2011.
10 See note 2 and also Nuti 1992; De Leonardis 2011.
11 Howorth and Keeler 2003, Mérand 2003, Eichemberg 2003, Howorth 2014.
12 Mérand 2003.
13 Mérand's essay reports that, at the Academy of Saint Cyr, officers belonging to corps with traditional 'combat' functions (infantry and cavalry) were more reluctant than technical corps to accept the idea of a European army. On the continuity of national identity and perspective see also Howorth and Menon 1997; Foster 2006. On the European Officer profile: Caforio 2000. On the construction of a transnational military identity see Haine 2001; Carey 2002.
14 Varsori 1988.
15 Romero 2009, 41.
16 Acanfora 2013.
17 At that time and for long afterwards, there was strong continuity, and consequently backwardness, in the policy of the Italian army commanders. They preferred a

loose-knit army, were little interested in technological advances and were loath to accept the new prospect of nuclear weapons with their various uses. On this see Labanca 2009.

18 Molazza 1947.
19 Zanussi 1947.
20 Fioravanzo 1948. See also Di Giamberardino 1948.
21 A theorist of air power, from the 1930s onwards he waged an authoritative polemic against the positions, of international scope, taken up by Giulio Douhet.
22 Mecozzi 1950, 450. Other articles of a certain importance stigmatized Anglo-American positions oriented to peripheral defence. See Roluti 1949; Di Giamberardino 1950.
23 Orlando 1949a, 223.
24 Varsori 1998; Nuti 1989.
25 Filostrato, 1949, 387.
26 'Il Consiglio d'Europa'. 1949. *Rivista militare italiana.* 8–9: 873–4.
27 Orlando 1949b, 923–5.
28 In general, see Di Giovanni 2005. A positive view of these processes in Sorrentino 1953.
29 'Difesa atlantica' 1950. On this distinction between the European and Atlantic-American plans see Nuti 2008, 161. In general see Del Pero 2001.
30 Monaco, 1951.
31 Guillen 1986.
32 Guillen 1986, 83.
33 Guillen 1986, 79.
34 Guillen 1986, 84.
35 Guillen 1983.
36 Guillen 1983, 8.
37 Aron 1956.
38 For an overview see Clesse 1989; Bertozzi 2003; Preda 1990.
39 Rioux 1984.
40 Guillen 1986.
41 Acanfora 2013, 219.
42 Stanley Hoffmann closed his essay by referring to a substantial three-way division of the French, some of whom considered the German problem in terms of the 'bloody past' (Hoffman 1956, 86).
43 Rioux 1984, 52.
44 Rioux 1984, 39.
45 Quagliariello 2004, 109.
46 Béthouart 1953.
47 Guillen 1983, 27.
48 Rioux 1984.
49 Barriéty 1993.
50 Barriéty 1993, 377.
51 Buton 2003, 34.
52 On minister Pacciardi's ambitions to modernize the army see Labanca 2009.
53 A detachment also to be found in journals not analysed here. When General Giovanni Messe, senator of the *Movimento Sociale Italiano* but also a figure of prestige in the Italian army during the Second World War and the transition, addressed the Senate about the prospects for the national defence, he spoke mainly in Atlantic terms, referring to the EDC as a 'European matter' that would entail 'substantial, very substantial, changes to existing national structures': Messe 1953, 4.
54 Conti 1953, 631. Moreover, in his booklet on EDC-oriented government policies, Lamberti Sorrentino had treated the reluctance to break with tradition benevolently. An unidentified general argued: 'In my brigade there is a flag, the Italian one; a tradition, the Italian one; and – let me say – a fatherland, the Italian one': Sorrentino 1953, 48.

55 Acanfora 2013, 103.
56 Broggi 1953, 1009 and 1011.
57 Navarca 1948.
58 Fioravanzo 1948.
59 Altair 1949.
60 Bernardi 1949, Micali 1950.
61 'L'Armée Européenne'. *Rivista militare italiana*, 1953, n. 1 (p. 66), unsigned review of the book by General E. De Larminat. The book was published in France under the urging of the government in a failed attempt to create a reference point for a recalcitrant military staff.
62 Bernardi 1953, 22.
63 Di Giovanni 2005.
64 Issue no. 7–8 of August 1954, of the *Rivista Militare Italiana* published an article by Ferdinando Di Lauro, *La situazione militare terrestre nel quadro del Patto Atlantico*, which entirely ignored the potential presence of a continental organization, albeit within NATO.
65 Carboni 1954. The theme of damage to national independence had been a pillar of the left's opposition to NATO membership. See Cerquetti 1975 and Guiso 2006.
66 Carboni closed with a chapter dedicated to 'The flag of the homeland'. He railed against the deceptive policy of those who 'believe and would have us believe in the military efficacy of an amalgam-army mixing soldiers from six different countries, with different languages, different temperaments, […] soldiers from six countries that share only ancient and recent rivalries, grudges, and hatreds': Carboni 1954, 72.
67 D'Agostino Orsini 1953.
68 Sinibaldi 2010.
69 'Un esprit atlantique est-il possible?' 1953.
70 'Un esprit atlantique est–il possible?' 1953, 546.
71 Bethouart 1953, 140.
72 Maggiar 1952, 628.
73 Maggiar 1952, 633.
74 Galli 1962; La Gorge 1967; Bozo 1996.
75 La Gorge 1967, 661.
76 La Gorge 1967, 675.

Bibliography

Acanfora, Paolo. 2013. *Miti e ideologia nella politica estera DC Nazione, Europa e Comunità atlantica (1943–1954)*. Bologna: Il Mulino.

Altair. 1949. 'La Federazione europea e le sue forze armate'. *Rivista Marittima* 1: 28–38.

Aron, Raymond. 1956. 'Esquisse historique d'une grande querelle idéologique'. In *La querelle de la CED: essais d'analise sociologique*, edited by Raymond Aron and Daniel Lerner, 1–19. Paris: Colin.

Aron, Raymond, and Lerner, Daniel, eds. 1956. *La querelle de la CED: essais d'analise sociologique*. Paris: Colin.

Barriéty, Jacques. 1993. 'La décision de réarmer l'Allemagne, l'echec de la Communauté Europeenne de Défense et les accords de Paris du 23 octobre 1954 vue du coté français'. *Revue Belge de Philologie et Histoire* 1: 354–83.

Bernardi, G. 1949. 'Reti di alleanze sull'Europa'. *Rivista Marittima* 5: 396–409.

Bernardi, G. 1953. 'La C.E.D. Sue origini e suoi aspetti politici'. *Rivista Militare Italiana* 4: 17–33.

Bertozzi, Stefano. 2003. *La comunità europea di difesa. Profili storici, istituzionali e giuridici*. Torino: Giappichelli.

Béthouart, Antoine. 1953. 'Réflexions sur la Communauté européenne de Défense'. *Révue de la Défense Nationale* 2: 131–41.

Bodin, Jerome. 1992. *Les officers français: grandeur et misères: 1936–1991*. Paris: Perin.

Bozo, Frederic. 1996. *Deux strategies pour l'Europe: De Gaulle, les Etats-Unis et l'Alliance atlantique, 1958–1969*. Paris: Plon – Fondation Charles de Gaulle.

Broggi, Giovanni. 1953. 'Che cosa significa C.E.D'. *Rivista Militare Italiana* 10: 1007–13.

Buton, Philippe. 2003. 'La CED: l'affaire Dreyfuss della IV Repubblica?' In *Atlantismo ed europeismo*, edited by Piero Craveri and Gaetano Quagliariello, 21–50. Soveria Mannelli: Rubettino.

Caforio, Giuseppe. 2000. *The European Officer: a Comparative View on Selection and Education*. Pisa: Ets.

Carboni, Giacomo. 1954. *L'Italia nella politica militare mondiale: Eisenhower e l'irredentismo germanico*. Firenze: Parenti.

Carey, Sean. 2002. 'Undivided Loyalties: is National Identity an Obstacle to European Integration?'. *European Union Politics* 3: 387–413.

Cerquetti, Enea. 1975. *Le forze armate italiane dal 1945 al 1975*. Milano: Feltrinelli.

Chiarini, Roberto. 2003. 'Atlantismo, americanismo, europeismo e destra italiana'. In *Atlantismo ed europeismo*, edited by Piero Craveri and Gaetano Quagliariello, 487–520. Soveria Mannelli: Rubettino.

Clementi Marco. 2004. *L'Europa e il mondo. La politica estera, di sicurezza e di difesa europea*. Bologna: Il mulino.

Clesse, Armand. 1989. *Le projet de C.E.D. du Plan Pleven au 'crime' du 30 aout: histoire d'un malentendu européen*. Baden Baden: Nomos.

'Consiglio d'Europa'. 1949. *Rivista Militare Italiana*. 8–9: 873–6.

Conti, Mario. 1953. 'Che cosa è la C.E.D'. *Rivista Militare Italiana* 1: 625–35

Craveri, Piero, and Quagliariello, Gaetano, eds. 2003. *Atlantismo ed europeismo*. Soveria Mannelli: Rubettino.

Cyril, Buffet. 1991. *Mourir pour Berlin. La France e l'Allemagne 1945–1949*, Paris: Colin.

D'Agostino Orsini, Paolo. 1953. 'Eurafrica, Terza Forza Mondiale'. *Rivista Marittima* 10: 46–56.

De Larminat, Olivier, and Manet, Olivier. 1953. 'La Communauté Européenne de Défense'. *Politique Étrangère* 18, 2–3: 149–68.

De Leonardis, Massimo. 2011. 'Italy's Atlanticism between Foreign and Internal Politics'. *UNISCI Discussion Papers* 25: 17–40.

Delmas, Jean. 1989. 'A la recherche des signes de la puissance: l'Armée entre l'Algérie et la bombe A'. *Relations Internationales*: 77–87.

Del Pero, Mario. 2001. *L'alleato scomodo. Gli USA e la DC negli anni del centrismo (1948–1955)*. Roma: Carocci.

'Difesa atlantica'. 1950. *Rivista Militare Italiana* 1: 84.

Di Giamberardino, Oscar. 1948. 'Strategia dei grandi spazi'. *Rivista Marittima* 4: 5–11.

Di Giamberardino, Oscar. 1950. 'Il problema militare del patto atlantico'. *Rivista Aeronautica* 3: 28–36.

Di Giovanni, Marco. 2005. 'Ufficiali comandanti o tecnocrati? La formazione dei quadri della Marina militare italiana nel secondo dopoguerra'. In *Politiche scientifiche e strategie d'impresa: le culture olivettiane e i loro contesti*, edited by Giuliana Gemelli, 215–55. Roma: Fondazione Adriano Olivetti.

Di Nolfo, Ennio, Romain, Rainero and Brunello, Vigezzi, eds. 1992. *L'Italia e la politica di potenza in Europa (1950–60)*. Milano: Marzorati.

Eichenberg, R., 2003. 'Having It Both Ways: European Defense Integration and the Commitment to NATO'. *Public Opinion Quarterly* 67, 4: 627–59.

Elgey, Georgette. 1965. *La République des illusions*. Paris: Fayard.

Filostrato. 1949. 'Il Patto Atlantico'. *Rivista Militare Italiana* 4: 387.

Fioravanzo, Giuseppe, 1948. 'Filosofia strategica degli spazi crescenti'. *Rivista Marittima* 12: 463–82.

Foster, Antony. 2006. *Armed Forces and Society in Europe*. Basingtoke and New York: Palgrave Macmillan.

Fouquet Lapar, Philippe. 1998. *Histoire de l'armée française*. Paris: PUF.

Freedman, Lawrence. 2001. *Cold War. A Military History*. London: Cassell.

Galli, Giorgio. 1962. *I colonnelli della guerra rivoluzionaria*. Bologna: Il Mulino.

Gemelli, Giuliana. 2005. *Politiche scientifiche e strategie d'impresa: le culture olivettiane e i loro contesti*. Roma: Fondazione Adriano Olivetti.

Gerardot, Paul. 1951. 'Guerres européennes et guerres asiatiques'. *Révue de la Défense Nationale* 6: 638–54.

Giauque, Jeffrey. 2004. 'Adjusting to the Post War World: Europe after 1945'. *International History Review* 26, 2: 331–48.

Giovagnoli, Agostino, and Tosi, Luciano, eds. 2003. *Un ponte sull'Atlantico: l'alleanza occidentale 1949–1999*. Milano: Guerini.

Guillen, Pierre. 1983. 'Les chefs militaires français, le réarmement de l'Allemagne et la CED (1950-1954)'. *Revue d'histoire de la seconde guerre mondiale et des conflits contemporains* 129: 3–33.

Guillen, Pierre. 1986. 'La France et la question de la défense de l'Europe occidentale, du Pacte de Bruxelles (mars 1948) au Plan Pleven (octobre 1950)'. *Révue d'histoire de la Deuxième Guerre mondiale ed des conflits, contemporains* 144: 79–98.

Guillen, Pierre. 1990. 'La France et l'intégration de la RFA dans l'OTAN'. *Guerres mondiales et conflicts contemporains* 159: 73–91.

Guiso, Andrea 2006. *La colomba e la spada. Lotta per la pace e antiamericanismo nella politica del partito comunista italiano (1949–1954)*. Soveria Mannelli: Rubettino.

Haine, Jean Yves. 2001. 'L'Eurocorps: processus de socialisation et construction d'une identité transnationale'. *Les documents du C2SD*. Paris: Centre d'études en sciences sociales de la Défense.

Heller, Francis H., and Gillingham, John R., eds. 1992. *NATO: the Founding of the Atlantic Alliance and the Integration of Europe*. London: Macmillan.

Hoffman, Stanley. 1956. 'Les oraisons funèbres. Du vote du 30 aout au vote du 30 décembre 1954'. In *La querelle de la CED: essais d'analise sociologique*, edited by Raymond Aron and Daniel Lerner, 59–87. Paris: Colin.

Howorth, Jolyon. 2014. *Security and Defence Policy in the European Union*. Basingstoke: Palgrave Macmillan.

Howorth, Jolyon, and Keeler, John, eds. 2003. *Defending Europe: The EU, NATO and the Quest for European Autonomy*. New York: Palgrave Macmillan.

Howorth, Jolyon, and Menon, Anand. 1997. *The European Union and National Defence Policy*. London and New York: Routledge.

Ilari, Virgilio. 1994. *Storia militare della prima repubblica*. Ancona: Nuove ricerche.

Imlay, Talbot. 2009. 'A Success Story? The Foreign Policies of France's Fourth Republic'. *Contemporary European History* 18, 4: 499–519.

Irondelle, Bastien. 2008. 'L'horizon européen de l'armée Française'. *Pouvoirs: Revue d'Etudes Constitutionnelles et Politiques* 125, 2: 69–79.

Jackson, Patrick. 2003. 'Defending the West: Occidentalism and the Formation of NATO'. *Journal of Political Philosophy* 1, 3: 223–52.

Johnston, Andrew. 2001. 'The Construction of NATO's Medium Term Defence Plan and the Diplomacy of Conventional Strategy 1948–1950'. *Diplomacy and Statecraft* 12 2: 79–124.

Labanca, Nicola. 2009. 'La politica militare della Repubblica. Cornici e quadri'. In *Le armi della Repubblica: dalla Liberazione a oggi*, edited by Mario Isnenghi, 66–154. Torino: UTET.

La Gorge, Paul Marie de. 1967. *Le armi e il potere: l'esercito francese da Sédan all'Algeria.* Milano: Il Saggiatore.

Lowe, Keith. 2015. *Il continente selvaggio. L'Europa alla fine della seconda guerra mondiale.* Roma–Bari: Laterza.

Maggiar, Raymond. 1951. 'Force combinée mobile dans la stratégie Européenne et française'. *Rèvue de la défence nationale* 4: 391–404.

Maggiar, Raymond. 1952. 'Armée européenne et responsabilités Françaises'. *Rèvue de la défence nationale* 6: 627–33.

Massigli, Rene. 1978. *Une Comédie des erreurs, 1943–1956. Souvenirs et réflections sur une étape de la construction européenne.* Paris: Plon.

Mecozzi, Amedeo. 1950. 'Il secondo tempo della terza guerra mondiale'. *Rivista Marittima* 12: 445–50.

Mérand, Frédéric. 2003. 'Dying for the Union? Military Officers and the Creation of a European Defence Force'. *European Societies* 3: 253–82.

Messe, Giovanni. 1953. *Il problema della difesa nazionale: discorso pronunciato al Senato della Repubblica nella seduta del 19 ottobre 1953.* Roma: Tipografia del Senato.

Micali, F. 1950. 'Note sull'organizzazione e sui compiti delle FFAA italiane'. *Rivista Militare Italiana* 1: 569–80.

Milward, Alan S., Lynch, Frances M. B., Sorensen, Vibeke, Romano, Federico and Ranieri, Ruggero, eds. 1993. *The Frontier of National Sovereignity.* London: Routledge.

Molazza, Alfio. (pseudonym of Mecozzi, Amedeo) 1947. 'Sistemi di cobelligeranza'. *Rivista aeronautica* 3: 42–9.

Monaco, Fausto. 1951. 'Gli aspetti della guerra moderna e il problema organizzativo della difesa nazionale'. *Rivista Militare Italiana* 8–9: 951–86.

Morgan, Patrick. 2003. 'NATO and the European Security: The Creative Use of an International Organization'. *Journal of Strategic Studies* 9: 49–74.

Navarca. 1948. 'Crescente antieconomicità della guerra'. *Rivista Marittima* 4: 5–11.

Nuti, Leopoldo. 1989. *L'esercito italiano nel secondo dopoguerra, 1945–1950: la sua ricostruzione e l'assistenza militare alleata.* Roma: Stato maggiore esercito, Ufficio storico.

Nuti, Leopoldo. 1992. 'Appunti per una storia della politica di difesa in Italia nella prima metà degli anni cinquanta'. In *L'Italia e la politica di potenza in Europa (1950–60)*, edited by Ennio di Nolfo, 625–96. Roma: Fondazione Adriano Olivetti.

Orlando, Taddeo. 1949a. 'Salviamo l'Europa'. *Rivista Militare Italiana* 3: 223–7.

Orlando, Taddeo. 1949b. 'Italia e colonie'. *Rivista Militare Italiana* 10: 923–5.

Pach, Chester. 1991. *Arming the Free World: The Origins of the United States Military Assistance Program, 1945–1950.* Chapel Hill, NC: University of North Carolina Press.

Preda, Daniela. 1990. *Storia di una speranza: la battaglia per la CED e la Federazione Europea nelle carte della delegazione italiana (1950–1952).* Milano: Jaka Books.

Quagliariello, Gaetano. 2004. 'Prospettiva atlantica e prospettiva europea nel pensiero e nell'azione di Charles de Gaulle'. In *Atlantismo ed europeismo*, edited by Piero Craveri and Gaetano Quagliariello, 95–134. Soveria Mannelli: Rubettino.

Raflik, Jenny. 2011. 'The Fourth Republic and NATO, 1946–1958: Alliance, Partnership or Idiosyncratic Nationalism?'. *Journal of Transatlantic Studies* 9, 3: 207–19.

Rioux, Jean Pierre. 1984. 'L'opinion publique française et la Communauté européenne de Défense: querelle partisane ou bataille de la mémoire?'. *Relations Internationales* 37: 37–53.

Roluti, Francesco. 1949. 'Atomica Europa Italia'. *Rivista Aeronautica* 9: 36–42.

Romero, Federico. 2009. *Storia della guerra fredda. L'ultimo conflitto per l'Europa.* Torino: Einaudi.

Selva, Simone. 2009. *Integrazione internazionale e sviluppo interno. Stati Uniti e Italia nei programmi di riarmo del blocco atlantico (1945–1955).* Roma: Carocci.

Sinibaldi Giulio. 2010. *La geopolitica in Italia (1939–1942).* Padova: Libreriauniversitaria.it.

Sorrentino, Lamberti. 1953. *Io soldato d'Europa.* Roma: Il tempo.

Trachtenberg, Marc. 2011. 'France and NATO 1949–1991'. *Journal of Transatlantic Studies* 9, 3: 184–94.

'Un esprit atlantique est-il possible?'. 1953. *Rèvue de la défence nationale* 5: 544–54.

Varsori, Antonio. 1988. *Il patto di Bruxelles, 1948: tra integrazione europea e alleanza atlantica.* Roma: Bonacci.

Varsori, Antonio. 1998. *L'Italia nelle relazioni internazionali dal 1943 al 1992.* Roma–Bari: Laterza.

Zanussi, Giacomo. 1947 'Qualche ipotesi sopra un conflitto tra Occidente e Oriente'. *Rivista Militare Italiana* 1: 7–15.

5 Nuclear Europe

Technoscientific modernity and European integration in Euratom's early discourse

Barbara Curli

Introduction: nuclear energy and the languages of technoscientific Europe

The European Union has recently launched its *2030 Energy Strategy*, intended to achieve a substantial cut in greenhouse gas emissions and an increase in renewable energy consumption and energy savings. The Strategy integrates and adds to the Commission's *Energy Roadmap 2050* and to the *Green Paper on a 2030 Framework for Climate and Energy Policies*.[1] These documents make only occasional and very cautious reference to nuclear power. Although it accounts today for around 25 per cent of the energy produced in the EU, and although it is bound to continue to play a major role in Europe's energy scenarios if the Strategy's ambitious goals are to be attained, nuclear power seems to have virtually disappeared from the EU 'energy discourse'. After its long neglect following the 1986 Chernobyl accident, nuclear power progressively re-entered the language of Europe's energy policies during the 2004–2010 so-called 'nuclear renaissance',[2] which also marked the passage towards a discursive construction of nuclear energy as a green, sustainable energy source in accordance with the new vocabulary of 'ecological modernity'.[3] The 2006 *Green Paper on a European Strategy for Sustainable, Competitive and Secure Energy* listed nuclear power as one of the six 'priority areas' to be pursued, and included it among the energy sources bound to balance 'sustainable development, competitiveness and security of supply'. Nuclear power was deemed to be an essential component of energy diversification if the EU were to deal with increasing energy prices, import dependence, and ageing infrastructures, and also as a way to 'tackle climate change'.[4]

However, the 2011 nuclear accident at Fukushima, the current downward trend in oil prices, and the debate on energy transition and nuclear 'phase-out' have again prompted a more cautious linguistic approach to nuclear power on the part of the European institutions, probably as a way to pre-empt criticism by public opinion. Whereas a 2006 Eurobarometer recorded an overall favourable assessment of nuclear power as helping to reduce Europe's energy dependence (69 per cent of interviewees) and global warming (49 per cent),[5] today's attitudes may have changed as a result of recent events.[6] Whatever the case may be, it is evident that the present Energy Strategy is also the outcome of one of the recurrent 'linguistic adjustments' characterizing the history of European energy policies.[7]

While being removed from the forefront of the energy discourse, however, nuclear energy is attracting renewed interest in historical studies.[8] In particular, historiography is reassessing the nuclear experience with regard to the role that science and technology have played in European modernization, and to the current debates on the relaunching of the European Union's infrastructures of growth in such diverse fields as transport, communications, energy, 'big science' projects (e.g. the European Space Agency, ITER on nuclear fusion), and strategies of technological improvement in order to face international competition. Recent research on 'infrastructural Europeanism' has highlighted the role of technological networks, transnational systems of knowledge, and scientific expertise in the making of Europe in a long-term perspective, and it has emphasized the 'integrative effects' of large technical systems and infrastructures.[9]

Such research has stressed the need to rethink traditional periodizations and methodological approaches to the relationship between European integration and modernization through scientific and technological collaboration. In the nineteenth and twentieth centuries, Europe's 'material integration' and the building of technoscientific networks contributed to the definition of a transnational European 'identity' and 'common civilization', which are to be seen not in opposition, but rather in a complementary and dynamic relationship with the economic and political development of nation-states, and the connection of Europe to the rest of the world.[10] As recently argued, scientific and technical internationalism was 'a predominantly European project' interconnected with the development of knowledge-based national economies and the formation of transnational technocratic elites devoted to a European vision of growth, while at the same time pursuing national priorities of modernization.[11]

Post-1945 European technoscientific regionalism should therefore be appraised within the framework of long-term material and political transformations. At the same time, it exhibits some specificities related to: (1) the new postwar institutional framework of European integration, which provided for the redefinition of a regional identity, in particular vis-à-vis the United States; (2) the evolution of the state as a 'technoscientific entrepreneur', as emerged from the wartime experience[12]; (3) the ways in which the Cold War affected the politics and economics of scientific research and international transfers of technology, at both the national and international levels. This is particularly evident with regard to 'big science' projects which epitomized both national ideologies of growth rooted in 'golden age' optimism and the emergence of modern technocratic elites, as well as new dynamics of international cooperation and competition in advanced technologies.[13] In this regard, the Cold War was a new chapter in the long history of the 'stormy marriage between science and government',[14] at both the national and international levels.

If set against this interpretive background, the discursive dimension of post-1945 technoscientific Europe exhibits a peculiar combination of themes and references borrowed from different, albeit intersecting, languages: the language of modernization and public policy (the new role of the post-1945 'scientific state' in fostering well-being and growth); the rhetoric of science (science as a social activity overcoming political boundaries and providing the material basis for the promotion of peace and prosperity; 'men of science' as an epistemic community at the service of mankind regardless of political affiliation and nationality); the jargon of European integration, with its emphasis on the incapacity of individual European nation-states to face international competition in advanced technologies, and on the role that science- and technology-based modernization could play in remedying their structural weaknesses, thus making Europe as a whole once again able to compete on a world scale and in particular with the US.

Post-1945 discourses on technoscientific Europe thus resumed the traditional jargon of 'scientific internationalism' dating back to the nineteenth century, but now reduced on a regional scale and embedded in the rhetoric of European integration. Nineteenth-century scientific internationalism had emphasized the politically unifying features of science and infrastructures and their capacity to generate material and social exchange, and ultimately peace. Such beliefs were shattered by the experience of the two world wars, when science (and men of science) had placed themselves in the service of warfare according to political-military allegiances – a 'German', then a 'Nazi', science, and an 'Allied' science.[15] The internationalist discourse was then revisited and applied on a regional scale within the framework of European integration (science as overcoming intra-European boundaries and providing an instrument of integration and peace) in the larger context of the Cold War cleavage (a 'Western' and a 'Soviet' science) and competition within the West itself (Europe and the US).

An analysis of the languages and discourses of European technoscientific integration may contribute to better understanding of the ways in which a rhetoric of Europe and of European institutional regionalism was built after 1945. It may provide a telling example of what has been called 'the relationship between the rhetoric of the public sphere and the rhetoric of science',[16] in particular when related to the early construction of a supranational European 'public sphere' in the 1950s and 1960s.

This conceptual framework applies particularly to large technical systems and *big science* projects, given their high and politically sensitive investment costs and the significant involvement of public resources:[17]

> The twentieth-century phenomenon known as 'big science' provides an important domain for rhetorical analysis. Big science involves the motivation and coordination of large numbers of people; the legitimation of, and advocacy for, substantial public funding; and the transformation of contestable knowledge claims into accepted facts through persuasive argumentation within extended scientific communities.[18]

Big science provides a fruitful standpoint from which to investigate the 'rhetoric of public science policy'.[19] Its regional/European dimension may thus afford further insights into the elusive concept of a European public science policy.

Nuclear Europe and its rhetoric

Nuclear energy may provide a significant case-study on the language of big science and technoscientific European integration.

After the Second World War, the development of nuclear power for electricity production was associated with the modernity of advanced technologies and with science-led economic growth. The peaceful atom, as the epitome of progress, would enable the emancipation of mankind from the physical scarcity of resources. As a sector characterized from the outset by massive state intervention and technocratic cultures and values, nuclear energy reflected – even typified – the changing nature of the postwar public hand. The new 'nuclear state' embodied the most advanced version of the postwar 'scientific state'.[20] At the same time, the launching of national nuclear power programmes was affected in various ways by the military origin of atomic research and by the 'atomic rivalries' between the superpowers and within the West itself.[21] The 'centrality of the nuclear' in the postwar emergence of science and technology was thus a political 'affair of the state' and a key element in international relations.[22]

Moreover, nuclear scientists exemplified an epistemic community of 'men of science' who had 'lost their innocence' during the war by participating in the most destructive scientific experiment in the history of mankind. However, their postwar 'conversion' to the peaceful atom for electricity production also showed that modern science could once again place itself in the service of peace and economic progress – although always along the lines of Cold War divisions and international rivalries.[23]

In postwar Europe, in particular, and during the 1950s and 1960s, national governments and new European institutions, as well as different political, economic, scientific, and societal actors, shared a widespread confidence that nuclear power could become the main source of energy and contribute to Europe's technological rebirth. The nuclear vision embodied in Europe's golden age in fact resumed ideas on progress and on the role of science that dated back to the nineteenth century and that were redefined in the framework of Cold War policies and explicitly or tacitly related to US (political, technological, and economic) dominance (e.g. the Atoms for Peace programme), mass consumption, and social change.

The discourse surrounding the launching of nuclear energy programmes drew extensively on the rhetoric of Europe's industrial past and former primacy. It also pointed out the promises of modernity brought about by the economic miracle of the 1950s and embodied in the 'energy of the future'. In particular, as an advanced research-intensive sector, the nuclear industry would have restored Europe's capacity to compete with the United States. As a result, discourses on nuclear power mirrored more profound tensions within postwar European culture concerning modern economic growth and scientific and technological change, visions of society and utopias, and Europe's role in international relations.

The origin of Euratom was thus framed in a discursive construct intended to legitimize the development of a politically sensitive and capital-intensive industrial sector embodying both the fears and the promises of modernity.[24] The distinctive features of the nuclear industry (its military origin, high investment costs, security issues, the role of the state in financing and control, the leading role of the United States in the international market of nuclear technologies) required specific institutional arrangements and new strategies of communication and legitimation.

In effect, nuclear energy has played an unusual role in the history of European institutions and infrastructures of growth: it is the only realm of European scientific collaboration dealt with in a specific treaty: the 1957 Treaty establishing the European Atomic Energy Community (Euratom), which still today regulates atomic energy production in the EU and most activities connected to it (from uranium supply to safety measures), and enjoys separate legal status under the governance of the EU's institutions. These peculiarities are related precisely to the politically sensitive nature of the nuclear industry and the need to regulate security and non-proliferation. Such specific arrangements are rooted in the long-term Cold War institutional dynamics of international control, and in the contested schemes for European cooperation in R&D-intensive industrial sectors and common research policies.[25]

Euratom can thus be seen as representing the new supranational dimension of the postwar modern European 'scientific state' as the promoter of science-based modernity – a new supranational version of 'technoscientific governance'[26] – and hence as exemplifying 'the emergence of a new structure and a potent source of funding and of legitimation for expensive fields of scientific research and technical development' on a European scale.[27]

The following sections will present some features and themes of the discursive framework of Euratom's early activity. They will focus mainly on official documentation produced by the Euratom Commission under the Presidency of Etienne Hirsch (1959–1962) when the European atomic project was actually launched.[28] Whereas the social, cultural, and communication features of the nuclear age are attracting increasing scholarly interest,[29] to date very little research has been done on the ways in which such features contributed to a definition of 'Europe' as both a new regional institutional framework and a project of modernity.

'Not the Europe of Charlemagne, but that of the twentieth century': Euratom and the discourse on European modernity

The first recurrent theme that emerged during the negotiations following the Conference of Messina of June 1955 was the need for Europe to develop a nuclear industry as a response to its new condition of energy dependence, which was putting European modernization at risk, and as a way to counteract Europe's relative decline. After the Second World War and during the 1950s, as a consequence of reconstruction and the onset of the economic miracle, Europe underwent what is traditionally termed the 'energy transition' from coal to oil, which gave rise to a dramatic geopolitical change in its dependence on foreign energy sources.[30]

The energy dependence argument – and the question of the geopolitical shift in Europe's role in the world economy – was put forward by Jean Monnet himself and his entourage at the High Authority of the European Coal and Steel Community during the negotiations on the Spaak Report. Their support for the original idea of extending the competences of the ECSC to atomic energy – the energy of the future – was motivated by 'the risks involved in Europe's growing dependence on foreign sources of energy'. The development of a nuclear energy capacity required a strategic, long-term approach: thus, action was deemed urgent, since 'energy is rare and expensive in Europe'.[31]

This argument was central to the Euratom's Three Wise Men Report of February 1957. The Report was released just before the signature of the Rome Treaty, and it had been written in the last phases of the Brussels negotiations, after the Suez crisis, and after the visit by the Three Wise Men to the US in order to lay the bases for what would shortly become the first US–Euratom agreement.[32] The Three Wise Men (Louis Armand, Franz Etzel, and Francesco Giordani)[33] had been asked to report 'on the amount of atomic energy which can be produced in the near future in the six countries, and the means to be employed for this purpose'. In the Report, which took the form of a letter addressed to the six ministers of Foreign Affairs, the authors stated: 'While endeavouring to define this objective, we have been aware of the unique chance which the advent of nuclear energy offers our countries'. The Report thus returned to the nineteenth century, when Europe had enjoyed the abundance of coal which had been the basis of its industrial primacy; and it underlined the shift that had taken place in the immediate postwar years:

> On the eve of the second world war, our six countries' energy imports were only five per cent of total requirements. During the postwar recovery they began to rise steeply. This was generally assumed to be temporary, while European coal production got back on its feet. And, indeed, in 1950 something like the pre-war equilibrium seemed to be within reach. But now, after the growth of the last seven years, it is clear that the demand in industry and transport, in the home and in agriculture is rapidly outrunning internal supply. Europe has lost its independence in energy.

The development of a nuclear energy infrastructure was thus considered to be a way to address this new geopolitical condition, which would otherwise entail Europe's loss of its political role in the world:

> Europe's energy imports would rise to intolerable heights without nuclear power. Today already the six countries import nearly a quarter of their energy supplies, the equivalent of 100 million tons of coal, most of which is oil from the Middle East. The Suez Crisis has shown how precarious these supplies are. [...] These enormous figures in fact call in question the whole future of Europe's economic growth, and even of its political security in the world.[34]

Although nuclear energy was more costly than conventional sources, its role had to be assessed in political-strategic terms rather than in purely economic ones, in particular as a consequence of the redefinition of world power brought about by decolonization and the Cold War. In any case, although oil would provide 'cheap energy', especially after the discovery of new oilfields in the Sahara in 1959 and the consequent fall in oil prices, imports would place an unbearable burden on Europe's external balance of payments.

The second recurrent discursive theme ensued directly from this strategic argument. The 'new industrial revolution' brought about by nuclear energy would allow for Europe's 'technological renaissance', closely connected to the regional European political project. As the President of the EAEC (Euratom) Commission Etienne Hirsch stated during the visit by the three Communities' presidents to the United States in June 1959:

> Euratom's very name is significant, for it couples in a single word two of the revolutionary changes brought about in the 20th century. The first is the new industrial revolution unleashed by the peaceful application of nuclear energy. The second is the economic and political revolution that is leading toward the unity of Europe.[35]

Among the three Communities, and (unlike the Coal and Steel Community) as the Community in charge of a modern advanced industrial sector, Euratom would be the leader in this endeavour.

Indeed, no individual European state was in a position to pursue these ambitious goals. Euratom was designed precisely to provide Europe with a new institutional structure allowing for implementation of the nuclear revolution. As Hirsch himself explained to an audience of American journalists when recalling the decision to establish an Atomic Community:

> It was felt that the future of Europe was directly linked to the development which was offered by the nuclear reactions. It was felt that this could not be tackled by the countries working individually, and so my own Commission is in charge of promoting research and development in the nuclear field.[36]

As an advanced and sensitive sector, atomic research would foster Europe's institutional and bureaucratic modernisation, and supranational integration:

> The process started off by the implementation of the treaties is a revolutionary one. Our countries, our governments and our civil service bodies are anchored in century-old traditions, and it is not surprising that the entry into force of the treaties is not in itself sufficient to counteract the inertia of such traditions and habits.[37]

Two bodies in particular distinguished Euratom from the other two Communities, and they were particularly suited to pursuing these ambitious goals: the

Scientific and Technical Committee and the Joint Research Centre. The Scientific and Technical Committee, whose members were appointed by the Member States from among scientists, engineers, and experts, would provide the specific expertise required for the development of the new – and still largely unexplored – nuclear sector. They would represent a new technoscientific epistemic community translating to a supranational European level the task that 'men of science' were assigned in the modern state. They would help rebuild an enlightened *Europe des savants*, and Euratom would perform a leadership role among the three Communities as the heir to Europe's past technological primacy and, at the same time, as a means to project Europe towards the future. As Hirsch explained before the Parliamentary Assembly in April 1959, the purpose of establishing Euratom's Scientific and Technical Committee was to 'involve the most qualified scientists in the governance of the Community' on the example of 'large modern states' which 'seek and utilize their best wise men and scientists'.[38]

The establishment of a Joint Research Centre would attract and help create the 'best European technical teams': since Europe had 'brains', but not enough technical personnel, a new generation of technicians, scientists, and engineers had to be trained and increased in number and qualification.[39] As a result, the Atomic Energy Community would be 'the pioneer of large-scale achievements in Europe'.[40] As the Community in charge of a technologically advanced industrial sector, Euratom would lead Europe towards modernity. Following Euratom's 'dynamism' and 'imaginative' example, and 'new style', the European Communities would be able to achieve 'not the Europe of Charlemagne but that of the twentieth century', aware of its responsibility towards the rest of the world.[41]

'On behalf of the Europe of tomorrow': nuclear research and European unity

In fact, the atom had been a 'European' scientific achievement. However, Europe had been outpaced in its capacity to develop the industrial applications of the nuclear revolution, and it needed to re-create a viable environment for research and development. Given the resources required for this purpose, that environment had to be built on a regional continental scale, especially since Europe had to compete with countries much more advanced in the nuclear field. As one of the Euratom Commissioners told an audience of American and European students in 1959:

> While it is true that the discoveries of European scientists such as Planck, Einstein, Curie, Fermi and Hahn – to mention only a few of the early pioneers – provided the scientific basis for subsequent developments in this field, it is obvious that the United States, Great Britain and the Soviet Union are way ahead of the countries of continental Europe in the field of technological development.

Therefore European countries had to make 'every effort to develop and increase their own contribution in the field of science and research', as foreseen by the authors of the Treaty.[42]

This same approach and purpose had inspired the establishment of CERN, the European Organisation for Nuclear Research, officially inaugurated in June 1955 with the aim of constructing and operating a European laboratory for research on high energy physics. As recalled in the first CERN Report,

> In 1951, a number of European scientists and statesmen came to the conclusion that only by combining the efforts and resources of their respective countries would it be possible to establish a laboratory, for research relating to high energy particles, that would rank among the foremost in the world and participate, on behalf of the Europe of tomorrow, in the most advanced work in this field.[43]

These activities marked

> the emergence of CERN as a major international centre for nuclear research and studies at high energies, a status which, without drawing any odious comparisons, now approaches that of parity with the major centres in the United States and Russia and thus justifies the original conception of the potential value of CERN to Western Europe.[44]

The atom was a driver of Europe's modernisation and a way to counteract Europe's decline.

> If Europe wishes to maintain its rightful position in the vanguard of scientific and technical progress, it must follow through with the efforts which it has been making to smooth the way for its imminent breakthrough into the industrial stage of the nuclear era.[45]

Europe had especial responsibility in the new Cold War competition between a Communist and a Western science.

> It is now clearer than ever that, acting in isolation, our countries can never hope to play an effective part in guiding the destinies of the world in the presence of the two giant powers of East and West whose very size has given them a predominant voice in world affairs. In the economic and technical fields, only a really large-scale market and the pooling of our human and material resources will enable us to make headway at a speed comparable to that of states with vast territories and considerable resources at their disposal.[46]

The competition in science and technology was a kind of peaceful competition that Europe could not afford to lose: 'I need hardly remind you', Hirsch told the Parliamentary Assembly in 1960, of the spectacular results that have been achieved in the Soviet Union in the field of applied science by a vast concentration of resources and at a speed which has impressed even American competitors. If we are to forge ahead economically fast enough to prevent ourselves from being distanced by the undeniable advances being achieved by the Soviet Union, and if we are to prevent a regime and a philosophy very different from our own from being credited with successes which are largely due to the existence of these immense resources within a single context, we must make unreserved and undivided use of all the means at our disposal. If this is done and if we are clearly aware of what this peaceful competition, which we cannot afford to lose, involves, we shall be in a position to make the effort and the sacrifices required to reach an objective of this kind.[47]

Euratom's research centres could become truly transnational places where a new European identity would take shape.

By our day-to-day activities in the tasks mapped out for us by the Treaty, we not only endeavour to attain that nuclear competence which is indispensable for economic progress and for improving the standard of living of our peoples, but we also seek to bring about the creation of a European spirit, without which all our efforts would be in vain. In our administration, in our research centres, in the teams which we are sending to participate in activities under the system of associations and contracts, we are developing European cells widely distributed over the whole territory of the Community. The nationals of our six countries are acquiring the habit of working together, of getting to know each other, of overcoming prejudices, and of appreciating and respecting each other's qualities. In this connection, I can bear witness to the fact that in our day-to-day work, despite language problems, no difficulty has arisen to hamper useful cooperation. On the contrary, on the basis of the spontaneous emulation which results, as well as of the complementary character of the different educational backgrounds and mental approaches it is possible to achieve a degree of efficiency which would be inconceivable in a group formed of nationals of a single country.[48]

Thanks to the development of a new technoscientific sector where no previous vested interests or working habits were involved, atomic modernity would take advantage of Europe's cultural diversity while at the same time fostering the unitary European identity of the future.

Conclusion

The discourse surrounding Euratom's early phase was meant to legitimize the launching and development of a very costly, technically complex, and politically demanding new technoscientific sector, with the aim of creating a European nuclear industry. The task was difficult and ambitious, and it would encounter a series of economic and political difficulties: competition from cheap oil; de Gaulle's return to power, the launching of France's *force de frappe* and Hirsch's failed re-appointment by the French government; the US's aloof support for Euratom and the priorities of non-proliferation policies, intended to avoid the spread of nuclear technological capacity outside American political control. Moreover, the development of national nuclear research programmes and centres would contribute to the early demise of the Joint Research Centre, which was entrusted with second-rank research projects; while the troublesome development of a complex and still little-known technology would prevent the nuclear industry from attaining competitive prices as compared to conventional sources. All this would soon trigger a crisis of the European nuclear project and ultimately lead to a restructuring and redistribution of Euratom's competences as a result of the Merger of the Executives in 1967.

Euratom is still in need of historical appraisal (and reappraisal), and its discursive dimension should thus be assessed in a larger interpretive framework. However, a few concluding remarks on its early discursive construction may furnish a grounding for more general considerations. The nuclear rhetoric that underlay the launching of the Euratom project was part of a redefinition of postwar European modernity in the new Cold War setting: it was consistent with the golden age optimism of the time, and with a view of European integration as a means to rescue Europe's competitive position in the world economy vis-à-vis both the United States and the Eastern bloc. It was embedded in a technocratic vision of the future that marked the first step in the long history of the European energy discourse and of its periodically recurrent linguistic adjustments according to the role that the nuclear option would subsequently play in relation to domestic and international circumstances, technological constraints, and shifts in public opinion. The nuclear rhetoric of the 1950s, as much as the absence today of nuclear power from the language of energy strategy, is revealing of the political economic and societal constraints involved in the construction of a supranational 'European public hand' in advanced strategic sectors.

Notes

1 European Commission 2011, European Commission 2013.
2 Stulberg and Fuhrmann 2013.
3 Hajer 1995. On this passage see also Topçu 2013 on the French case, and Pestre 2014.
4 European Commission 2007.
5 European Commission, Special Eurobarometer 2007.
6 Even though Fukushima does not seem to have substantially altered public opinion, which in Europe traditionally varied (and continues to vary) according to established national attitudes. See, for example, UK Energy Research Council 2013.
7 On the more general transformation taking place in the EU language related to the environment and climate change, see for example Krzyżanowski 2015.
8 For a discussion of the present 'nuclear renaissance' in historical studies see Bini and Londero 2015.
9 Schipper and Schot 2011; Högselius *et al.* 2013. For a review of other literature on the subject see Kleinschmidt 2010.

10 Van der Vleuten and Kaijser 2006; Schot *et al.* 2005; Van der Vleuten *et al.* 2007; Grande and Peschke 1999.

11 Kohlrausch and Trischler 2014, 4–5; Badenoch and Fickers 2010.

12 Edgerton 2015; Carson 2015; Dahan and Pestre 2004.

13 Westfall 2013; Krige 2006; McDougall 2000.

14 McDougall 2000, 117.

15 Forman 1973; McLeod 2014.

16 Ceccarelli *et al.* 1996, 7.

17 On 'big science' Weinberg 1968, Galison and Hevly 1992, and for recent discussion on the concept and its uses Westfall 2013.

18 Kinsella 1996, 65.

19 Kinsella 1996, 65.

20 Among the many titles, see the classic studies by Gilpin 1968 and Jungk 1979.

21 Goldschmidt 1962; Goldschmidt 1967; Goldschmidt 1980.

22 Krige and Barth 2006, 1.

23 Among the various studies on this subject, see Kohlrausch and Trischler 2014; Welsh 2000.

24 On the history of Euratom, see Pirotte 1988; Dumoulin *et al.* 1994.

25 Hallonsten 2012; Krige 2006; Guzzetti 1995; Guzzetti and Krige 1997; Guzzetti 2000.

26 Pestre 2014.

27 Krige 2003, 897.

28 The first presidency of Louis Armand lasted only a few months. Most of the documentation, when not otherwise stated, is available online at the University of Pittsburgh Archive of European Integration, http://aei.pitt.edu.

29 See for example Van Lente 2012.

30 Clark 1990; Hassan and Duncan 1989; Hassan and Duncan 1994.

31 Historical Archives of the EU, Florence, Fonds Pierre Uri (PU), d.53/3 e 53/4, Haute Autorité de la Ceca, Division Economique *Note pour le Groupe de Travail 'Messine'*, Luxembourg, 29 October 1955; Comité intergouvernemental créé par la Conférence de Messine, Commission du marché commun, des investissements et des problèmes sociaux *Note sur l'intégration économique générale d'après l'expérience de la CECA presentée par le représentant de la Haute Autorité* (Pierre Uri), Bruxelles, 27 July 1955.

32 On early US–Euratom relations see Skogmar 2004.

33 On Armand and Giordani as representative of that first postwar generation of nuclear technocrats whose experience was rooted in the long-term search for new technoscientific infrastructures of growth dating back to the 1930s, see Curli 2000, Curli 2009.

34 Armand *et al.* 1957.

35 Finet *et al.* 1959; Three Presidents 1959.

36 Finet *et al.* 1959; Three Presidents 1959.

37 Hirsch 1960.

38 Hirsch 1959.

39 Hirsch 1959.

40 Euratom 1958, 14. On the history of the JRC, see Dumoulin 1997; Jourdain 1995; Ippolito 1989.

41 Hirsch 1959.

42 Krekeler 1959.

43 CERN 1955. CERN founding members were Belgium, Denmark, France, German Federal Republic, Greece, Italy, the Netherlands, Norway, Sweden, Switzerland, United Kingdom, Yugoslavia. On CERN early history, see Brown 1989; Amaldi 1989; Krige 1986; Hermann, Krige, Mersits, and Pestre 1987–90. CERN Annual Reports can be found online at http://cds.cern.ch/.

44 CERN 1958.
45 Euratom 1962.
46 Hirsch 1960.
47 Hirsch 1960.
48 Hirsch 1961.

References

Amaldi, Edoardo. 1989. 'The History of CERN during the Early 1950s'. In *Pions to Quarks. Particle Physics in the 1950's*, edited by Laurie M. Brown, Max Dresden, and Lillian Hoddeson, 508–518. Cambridge: Cambridge University Press.

Armand, Louis, Franz Etzel, and Francesco Giordani. 1957. *A Target for Euratom.* Report, Bruxelles.

Badenoch, Alexander, and Andreas Fickers. 2010. *Materializing Europe: Transnational Infrastructures and the Project of Europe.* New York: Palgrave Macmillan.

Bini, Elisabetta, and Igor Londero, eds. 2015. 'Nuclear Energy in the Twentieth Century: New International Approaches'. Forum Discussion, *Contemporanea*, XVIII, 4: 615–650.

Brown, Laurie M., Max Dresden and Lillian Hoddeson, (eds). 1989. *Pions to Quarks. Particle Physics in the 1950s.* Cambridge: Cambridge University Press.

Carson, Cathryn. 2015. 'Towards a New Technological Age: Technoscience from the 1930s to the 1950s'. In *The Cambridge History of the Second World War*, Volume 3. *Total War: Economy, Society and Culture*, edited by Michael Geyer and Adam Tooze, 196–219. Cambridge: Cambridge University Press.

Ceccarelli, Leah, Richard Doyle, and Jack Selzer. 1996. 'Introduction. The Rhetoric of Science'. *Rhetoric Society Quarterly* 26, 4: 7–12.

CERN, 1955. *First Annual Report of the European Organisation for Nuclear Research.* CERN: Geneva.

CERN 1958. *Fourth Annual Report of the European Organisation for Nuclear Research.* CERN: Geneva.

Clark, John G. 1990. *The Political Economy of World Energy. A Twentieth-Century Perspective.* New York: Harvester Wheatsheaf.

Curli, Barbara. 2000. *Il progetto nucleare italiano, 1952–1964. Conversazioni con Felice Ippolito.* Soveria Mannelli: Rubbettino.

Curli, Barbara. 2009. 'L'esperienza dell'Euratom e l'Italia. Storiografia e prospettive di ricerca'. In *L'Italia nella costruzione europea. Un bilancio storico (1957–2007)*, edited by Piero Craveri and Antonio Varsori, 211–229. Milano: FrancoAngeli.

Dahan, Amy, and Dominique Pestre, eds. 2004. *Les sciences pour la guerre. 1940–1960.* Paris: Éditions de l'École des hautes études en sciences sociales.

Dumoulin, Michel. 1997. 'The Joint Research Center'. In *History of European Scientific and Technological Cooperation*, edited by John Krige and Luca Guzzetti, 241–256. Luxembourg: Oopec.

Dumoulin, Michel, Pierre Guillen, and Maurice Vaïsse, eds. 1994. *L'energie nucléaire en Europe. Des origines à Euratom.* Berne: Peter Lang.

Edgerton, David. 2015. 'L'Etat entrepreneur de science'. In *Histoire des sciences et des savoirs*, edited by Dominique Pestre and Christophe Bonneuil, t. 3, *Le siècle des technosciences.* Paris: Seuil.

Euratom 1958, European Atomic Energy Commission, Euratom, *First General Report on the Activities of the Community (January 1958 to September 1958)*, 21 September.

Euratom 1962, European Atomic Energy Commission, Euratom, *Fifth General Report on the Activities of the Community (April 1961 to March 1962)*.

European Commission 2007. Communication from the Commission to the Council and the European Parliament, *Nuclear Illustrative Programme*, Brussels, 10 January, COM (2006) 844 final.

European Commission 2011. *Energy Roadmap 2050*, COM (2011) 885.

European Commission 2013, *Green Paper on a 2030 Framework for climate and energy policies*, COM (2013) 169. http://ec.europa.eu/energy/en/topics/energy-strategy/2030-energy-strategy. Accessed 11 December 2015.

European Commission, Special Eurobarometer 2007, n. 271, *Europeans and Nuclear Safety*, October–November 2006 (Publication February 2007).

Finet, Paul, Etienne Hirsch, and Walter Hallstein. 1959. *Interview of Three European Community Presidents, President Paul Finet [High Authority of the ECSC], President Etienne Hirsch [Commission of Euratom], and President Walter Hallstein [Commission of the European Economic Community]*. National Press Club. Washington DC, 11 June 1959.

Forman, Paul. 1973. 'Scientific Internationalism and the Weimar Physicists: The Ideology and Its Manipulation in Germany after World War I'. *Isis* 64, 2: 150–180.

Galison, Peter, and Bruce Hevly, eds. 1992. *Big Science: The Growth of Large-Scale Research*, Palo Alto, CA: Stanford University Press.

Gilpin, Robert. 1968. *France in the Age of the Scientific Estate*. Princeton, NJ: Princeton University Press.

Goldschmidt, Bertrand. 1962. *L'aventure atomique. Ses aspects politiques et techniques*. Paris: Fayard.

Goldschmidt, Bertrand. 1967. *Les rivalités atomiques, 1939–1966*. Paris: Fayard.

Goldschmidt, Bertrand. 1980. *Le complexe atomique. Histoire politique de l'énergie nucléaire*. Paris: Fayard.

Grande, Edgar, and Anke Peschke. 1999. 'Transnational Cooperation and Policy Networks in European Science Policy-making'. *Research Policy* 28: 43–61.

Guzzetti, Luca. 1995. *A Brief History of European Union Research Policy*, European Commission, DG XII, Luxembourg.

Guzzetti, Luca, ed. 2000. *Science and Power: the Historical Foundations of Research Policies in Europe*. Luxembourg: Office for Official Publications of the European Communities.

Guzzetti, Luca, and John Krige. 1997. *History of European Scientific and Technological Collaboration*. Luxembourg: OOPEC.

Hallonsten, Olof. 2012. 'Continuity and Change in the Politics of European Scientific Collaboration'. *Journal of Contemporary European Research* 8, 3: 300–319.

Hajer, Maarten A. 1995. *The Politics of Environmental Discourse: Ecological Modernization and the Policy Process*. Oxford: Clarendon Press; New York: Oxford University Press.

Hassan, John A., and Alan Duncan. 1989. 'The Role of Energy Supplies during Western Europe's Golden Age, 1950–1972'. *The Journal of European Economic History* 18, 3: 479–508.

Hassan, John A., and Alan Duncan. 1994. 'Integrating Energy: the Problems of Developing an Energy Policy in the European Communities, 1945–1980'. *The Journal of European Economic History* 23, 1: 159–176.

Hermann, Armin, John Krige, Ulrike Mersits, and Dominique Pestre. 1987–1990. *History of Cern*, 2 vol., Amsterdam: North Holland.

Hirsch, Etienne. 1959. *Sommaire du discours de M. E. Hirsch devant l'Assemblée parlementaire, 9 avril 1959.* EUR/C/709/59 (our translation).

Hirsch, Etienne. 1960. *Speech [on the 3rd General Report] delivered to the European Parliament by Mr. Etienne Hirsch, President of the Euratom Commission. Strasbourg, May 1960.*

Hirsch, Etienne. 1961. *Speech [on the annual report of the European Atomic Energy Community] delivered to the European Parliament by Mr. Etienne Hirsch, President of the Euratom Commission. Strasbourg, 29 June 1961.*

Högselius, Per, Anique Hommels, Arne Kaijser, and Erik Van der Vleuten, eds. 2013. *The Making of Europe's Critical Infrastructure: Common Connections and Shared Vulnerabilities.* New York: Palgrave.

Ippolito, Felice. 1989. *Un progetto incompiuto. La ricerca comune europea, 1958–1988.* Bari: Dedalo.

Jourdain, Louis. 1995. *Recherche scientifique et construction européenne.* Paris: L'Harmattan.

Jungk, Robert. 1979. *The Nuclear State.* London: John Calder.

Kinsella, William J. 1996. 'A "Fusion" of Interests: Big Science, Government, and Rhetorical Practice in Nuclear Fusion Research'. *Rhetoric Society Quarterly* 26, 4: 65–81.

Kleinschmidt, Christian. 2010. 'Infrastructure, Networks, (Large) Technical Systems: The "Hidden Integration" of Europe'. *Contemporary European History* 19, 3: 275–284.

Kohlrausch, Martin, and Helmuth Trischler. 2014. *Building Europe on Expertise. Innovators, Organizers, Networkers.* London: Palgrave Macmillan.

Krekeler, Hans. 1959. *Euratom and the Regional Problem of Atomic Energy.* Draft speech delivered at the Bologna Center of the School of International Advanced Studies of the Johns Hopkins University, 16 March, given by Hans L. Krekeler, member of the Commission of the European Atomic Energy Community.

Krige, John. 1986. 'La naissance du Cern. Le comment et le pourquoi'. *Relations Internationales* 46: 209–226.

Krige, John. 2003. 'The Politics of European Scientific Cooperation'. In *Companion to Science in the Twentieth Century*, edited by John Krige and Dominique Pestre, 897–917. Amsterdam and Abingdon: Routledge.

Krige, John. 2006. *American Hegemony and the Postwar Reconstruction of Science in Europe.* Cambridge, MA: MIT Press.

Krige, John, and Kai-Henrik Barth, eds. 2006. 'Introduction. Science, Technology, and International Relations'. *Osiris* 21: 1–21.

Krzyżanowski, Michał. 2015. 'International Leadership Re-constructed?: Ambivalence and Heterogeneity of Identity Discourses in European Union's Policy on Climate Change'. *Journal of Language and Politics* 14, 1: 110–133.

McDougall, Willliam. 2000. 'The Cold War Excursion of Science'. *Diplomatic History* 24, 1: 117–127.

McLeod, Roy. 2014. 'Scientists'. In *The Cambridge History of the First World War*, vol. 2, *The State*, edited by Jay Winter, 434–459. Cambridge: Cambridge University Press.

Pestre, Dominique, ed. 2014, *Le gouvernement des technosciences: gouverner le progrès et ses dégâts depuis 1945.* Paris: La Découverte.

Pirotte, Olivier. 1988. *Trente ans d'expérience Euratom. La naissance d'une Europe nucléaire.* Bruxelles: Bruylant.

Schipper, Frank, and Johan Schot. 2011. 'Infrastructural Europeanism, or the Project of Building Europe on Infrastructures: An Introduction'. *History and Technology* 27, 3: 245–264.

Schot, Johan, Thomas J. Misa, and Ruth Oldenziel, eds. 2005. 'Tensions of Europe: The Role of Technology in the Making of Europe'. *History and Technology*, Special issue, 21, 1.

Skogmar, Gunnar. 2004, *The United States and the Nuclear Dimension of European Integration*, Houndmills, Basingstoke, and New York: Palgrave Macmillan.

Stulberg, Adam N., and Matthew Fuhrmann, eds. 2013. *The Nuclear Renaissance and International Security*. Stanford, CA: Stanford University Press.

Topçu, Sezin. 2013, *La France nucléaire. L'art de gouverner une technologie contestée*. Paris: Seuil.

Three Presidents. 1959. 'Three Presidents on official visit to the U.S'. EC Information Service, *Bulletin from the European Community* Special issue, Washington, D.C.

UK Energy Research Council. 2013. *Public Attitudes to Nuclear Power and Climate Change in Britain Two Years after the Fukushima Accident: Summary Findings of a Survey conducted in March 2013*, Working Paper UKERC, WP/ES/2013/006, 19 September 2013.

Van der Vleuten, Erik, and Arne Kaijser, eds. 2006. *Networking Europe. Transnational Infrastructures and the Shaping of Europe, 1850–2000*. Sagamore Beach: Science History Publications.

Van der Vleuten, Erik, Irene Anastasiadou, Vincent Lagenduk, and Frank Schipper. 2007. 'Europe's System Builders: The Contested Shaping of Transnational Road, Electricity and Rail Networks'. *Contemporary European History* 16: 321–347.

Van Lente, Dick, ed. 2012. *The Nuclear Age in Popular Media: A Transnational History, 1945–1965*. New York: Palgrave Macmillan.

Weinberg, Alvin B. 1968. *Reflections on Big Science*. Cambridge, MA: MIT Press.

Welsh, Ian. 2000. *Mobilising Modernity. The Nuclear Moment*. London, New York: Routledge.

Westfall, Catherine. 2013. 'Rethinking Big Science'. In *Science and the American Century. Perspectives on Science, Technology and Medicine. Readings from 'Isis'*, edited by Sally Gregory Kohlstedt and David Kaiser, 269–298. Chicago, IL: University of Chicago Press.

6 Parliamentary groups and political traditions in the debates on EU institutional reform (1979–1999)

Paolo Caraffini and Filippo Maria Giordano

The European People's Party and Socialist parliamentary groups in the European Parliament from 1979 to 1999: a comparison of two processes

This chapter wishes to examine the discursive practices of the European Parliament (EP) and verify if a 'political rhetoric' exists, in a period particularly significant in the history of this European institution. By analysing the parliamentary records, and, more specifically, the speeches delivered during the plenary sessions, this chapter aims at examining the positions expressed by the two main political groups in the European Parliament, the European People's Party (EPP) and the Socialist Group, on several specific steps in terms of institutional reform of the European Community/Union, focussing in particular on those MEPs (Members of the European Parliament) whose discursive practices seemed to express their personal political positions and that of their parliamentary groups more clearly.

The focus of the analysis will be on the political language in parliamentary speeches, in order to understand how the use of a certain semantic may have helped to define or to manifest the position of the main political groups regarding the idea of Europe and the degree of consensus on its integration.[1]

The phase under consideration extends over four parliamentary terms, from the first direct elections to the EP, in June 1979, to the Amsterdam Treaty, at a time, therefore, during which the EP was searching for a different and stronger legitimation, after its direct election. It was also a time of intense transformation and great initiatives, such as the Spinelli Project, the reforms initiated by Jacques Delors, the Single European Act, the Maastricht Treaty and the monetary union, the strengthening of the EP's role, also through the co-decision procedure, the collapse of the Soviet bloc and the opening up of the prospective eastward expansion.

In this framework, the Socialist Group tends to show, progressively, a greater degree of cohesion on the institutional issues, overcoming, at least in part, the initial attitude of Euro-sceptic sectors of the French[2] and Dutch socialism, of the Danish Social Democrats, the Greek *Pasok*, and of numerous British Labour MEPs still critical towards the Community institutions in the Seventies and the early Eighties. This was also favoured by the entrance, first, of the Socialists from the Spanish PSOE (*Partido Socialista Obrero Español*) and from Portugal, and later of those from the former Italian Communist Party, that became the Democratic Party of the Left (PDS, *Partito Democratico della Sinistra*).

It should be remembered that at the European elections of 1979 the Socialist parties had not managed to agree on a shared programme, but only on an 'Appeal to the voters', the outcome of which, incidentally, did not reveal a cohesive orientation. The SPD had judged it too lopsided to the left; some of the Dutch socialists, regarding the Community as an instrument of international corporations, had even called for abstention; and Labour had presented a manifesto of its own in which they were anticipating a British withdrawal from the EEC.[3]

In contrast, the EPP Group, whose original nucleus was made up of parties with a Christian-democratic background, tends to blur the original European federalism, as well as the reference to a social market economy and, for the Catholic MEPs, to the social doctrine of the Catholic Church, all elements still detectable, for example, in the EPP programme for the elections in June 1979, but also those in 1989, which speaks of the 'United States of Europe'[4] objective. This takes place with the establishment, between the end of the Eighties and the early Nineties, of the strategy of opening up the parliamentary group to the conservative parties, in order to avoid the Socialists becoming the dominant group in the EP, contrasted by the Italian *Democrazia Cristiana* (DC) and the Christian Democrat parties in Benelux and France. This strategy was supported by the CDU (*Christlich Demokratische Union*) and by the Bavarian CSU (*Christlich-Soziale Union*) and was consolidated with the entry, at first, of the Spanish *Partido Popular* and, then, of the British and the Danish Conservatives. In the following years other parties, such as the Austrian ÖVP (*Österreichische Volkspartei*), the Swedish and Finnish conservative parties, the Portuguese *Partido social democrata*, *Forza Italia* and the French neo-Gaullists,[5] entered the group.

'The cart before the horse'? The Colombo–Genscher Declaration and the Spinelli Plan

In the first European elections of 1979, the citizens of the nine Member States elected 410 members of parliament: the result of the vote was the dominance of the two major political groups, the Socialist and EPP, with 113 and 107 seats respectively.[6]

The differences between the positions more oriented to supranational integration of the EPP and the more tepid ones on the Socialist side are evident in the first elected legislature. Re-reading the minutes of the parliamentary sessions, the dichotomy appears already in the discussions following the inauguration of the new EP, even during the debate between the two presidents of the Socialist Group, the Belgian Ernest Glinne, and the EPP Group, the leader of the CDU Egon A. Klepsch,[7] on the election and the role of the President of the EP.[8]

The French liberal Simone Veil was appointed president. In her inaugural speech she called for cohesion of the different political forces in order to enhance the role of the EP and to avoid 'the error of turning the [...]. Assembly into a forum for rivalry and dissent'. For Veil, all Member States were faced with three great challenges: peace, freedom and prosperity: in her view 'they can only be met through the European dimension'.[9]

The vision and the integration model described by Veil did not vary much from those imagined by the EPP Group. The EP had the moral and political task of completing the project of the founding fathers by promoting 'an ever-closer union between the peoples of Europe'. The Belgian Christian Democrat Leo Tindemans insisted on this point, calling for an evolution of the Community into a Union. He referred to the prospects of deeper integration that had been hypothetically put forward already at the Paris Summit of 1974: hypotheses which were then reinforced by the political outcome of the elections of 1979. On that occasion, the then President of the EPP and drafter of the eponymous Report reminded the EP of the three proposals implemented during the meeting between the European Heads of State and Government in the French capital. The first was addressed 'To transform the Summit Conference into a European Council; the second was to draft a report on European Union; and the third was to hold elections by direct universal suffrage to the European Parliament'. Tindemans concluded: 'It is my hope that the second proposal, involving progress towards a European Union, will not fall by the wayside and that suggestions for action in this area will be made in future'.[10]

In this sense, the EP elected by universal suffrage had 'a special responsibility'. Tindemans's words, connected perhaps to a strategy of political legitimacy of the EP after its election by direct universal suffrage, clearly demonstrate the EPP's European inclination. During the first Parliamentary term, the Christian Democrats tapped into the ongoing project of the founding fathers – reference to whom is frequent in MEPs' discourse and rhetoric in this political area – and leveraged the new role of the EP that should have acted 'as a more effective motive force in European integration'.

Even the president of the European Commission, British Labour Roy Jenkins, acknowledged the success of the first universal suffrage elections to the EP in his speech and he enthusiastically greeted the prospects that this event was opening for the future of Europe.[11] He called for the cooperation between institutions, as a means to search for the common interest: 'we – whether Parliament, Council or Commission – shall need all our combined strength and inherent unity';[12] and he indicated the supranational way as the route to take 'to sustain the impetus of the European ideal, to withstand the deep-seated problems which now confront us'.[13] Finally, addressing the debating chamber, and rebuking the attitude of his own country, he recalled that the Parliament's concern and opportunity 'are to ensure that Community issues, not the narrow lines of national politics, [must] dominate the discussion'.[14] That said, Jenkins acknowledged the difficult economic situation and reiterated the responsibility and the role that the Community would have had in the economic policies to counter recession, inflation and unemployment:

> What is absolutely clear – said the President of the European Commission – is that the ability of the Community to survive and to prosper depends on our joint determination to preserve what we have already achieved, to build on this, and, above all, to keep a vision and commitment to make progress towards a greater European unity.[15]

If for Jenkins, as much as for the Socialist MEPs, the Community had a duty to concentrate its political resources on economic and social policies, the EPP Group was more keen on the 'structural' and institutional aspects of the European construction. In fact, if we wanted to find the *leitmotiv* on European integration in the parliamentary speeches of the Christian Democrats in the first parliamentary term, we could summarize it in three words that clearly give the political direction of the PPE with respect to their expectations on the Community. First, the EPP Group refers to *solidarity* among member countries and between the peoples of Europe, not to mention the political *independence* of the Community from the superpowers, especially in some key areas, and of the EP from the other Community institutions, in its actions in favour of the integration process. Finally, they often reiterate the idea of *cooperation* both with third countries and with other international organizations. The EPP Group discourse in favour of Europe revolved around these terms, which clearly have a general scope and a tactical political essence. We must also add the expression 'European Union', which entailed the long term political and strategic objective shared by all the EPP MEPs in this first phase of the new EP's life. 'European Union', an expression with a double meaning, because unifying both in the discursive use and in the political objective.

In this respect, we must not forget the so called 'Genscher-Colombo Plan' in which this expression was brought up again. The initiative started off in 1981 thanks to the action of the then Italian Foreign Minister, the Christian Democrat Emilio Colombo, and his German counterpart, the Liberal Democrat Hans-Dietrich Genscher. After the German Minister's presentation of the Plan to the EP, there is a clear consonance of views by the Christian Democrat representatives in the EP, who are compactly aligned in favour of the reform project. This consonance is also apparent at a political language level: the terms of the German and Italian ministers are similar to those found in the speeches of the EPP Group members that take the floor and, as mentioned, words like 'solidarity', 'independence', 'cooperation' and 'unity' stand out. These terms, after all, reveal the remarkable convergence of purpose regarding a certain idea of European integration both within the EPP and among EPP members and Liberals covering national political appointments.[16] Genscher and Colombo shared the idea that 'only by standing together will this Europe have the strength needed to put these aims and values to good effect'.[17] The Christian Democrat MEPs agreed on this, being largely geared towards the promotion of an institutional reform and the support of the Community's transformation into a Union. The Greek members of the group also supported the prospect of political union, as revealed in the speech by Konstantinos Kallias, who, with a note of optimism, said that despite the 'long experience of the reservations and national egoism which still affect the relations between cooperating countries' the 'expectation that Europe is progressing, even though slowly, towards political union'[18] had not entirely disappeared.

The Plan was discussed in Parliament during the session of 19 November 1981, and won the support of large sections of the EP, albeit with exceptions and with some suspicion on the Socialist side. The Socialists judged the Plan as both too liberal and too cautious in terms of institutional reform prospects. The Dutch Socialist Doeke Eisma, who had gradually come closer to Altiero Spinelli's position, would push the integration process 'further by reinforcing what already exists and extending the integration process to cover new sectors', strengthening the democratic control of the Parliament, thus abolishing 'the practice of unanimity and introducing, instead, majority decisions in the Council'[19] and extending the Community's competence in the field of political cooperation.

Eisma's position, however, remained in the minority within his group; the Socialists raised, indeed, a number of concerns about the European Union project designed by Genscher and Colombo, especially in terms of economic and social outlook that any deepening of integration would have entailed. In fact, as pointed out by Glinne, for the Socialists the 'social justice inside the Community [was] a much more urgent imperative than any diplomatic breakthrough or institutional success, however impressive'.[20] However, they:

> take heart from the fact that Mr Colombo [...] laid great stress on the need to strengthen common economic policy by greater convergence and the need for instruments to correct the imbalances and contradictions which, unfortunately, still persist throughout the Community.[21]

The Socialists indeed had the tendency to steer attention towards the issues of unemployment, labour, economic recovery, dialogue and European social space; all of these, if unfulfilled, would have seriously risked compromising the credibility and the future of the Community, and on this axis the varied and mixed soul of the Socialist group was almost unanimously in agreement. In other words, European citizens, especially the unemployed, 'will judge the European Community on the practical steps it takes to improve employment and not on the measures we implement to reinforce our institutions'.[22]

Finally, worthy of notice is the Socialists' position, shared also by the EPP Group, regarding the need to push the integration process to a turning point through the EP, especially after the validation of the popular vote. Even in this case, however, the Socialists remained sceptical because they perceived the Community as an entity that was still distant from its citizens, subject to the continuous risk of bureaucratic involution. As Glinne explained in one of his speeches, referring to the Community's laborious system, the risk for the Community was to take up 'Byzantine ways'.[23] Indeed, he noted the lack of transparency of its institutions, reiterating that Europe 'has still not made a sufficient impression on its people; [...] Europe is too intermittent, too obscure to be understood and accepted by each and everyone of its citizens'.[24]

Therefore, if we want to summarize the substantial difference in position that emerged between the two groups with regards to the prospective deepening of European integration, the most evident contrast was the priority: the Socialists' emphasis was laid on the term 'social' reform, the EPP Group focussed on 'institutional' reform. This gap was partly filled by the compromise reached with the 'Spinelli Project', that, toward the end of the first parliamentary term, managed to concentrate the consensus of the two largest European parliamentary groups, albeit with obvious internal rifts.

The Draft Treaty of the European Union, promoted by Altiero Spinelli just after his election to the EP, was the most significant attempt to give a new constitutional arrangement to the Community, thus turning it into the European Union. As a matter of fact, from 1980 Spinelli had organized an action aimed at promoting the reform of the Treaties, first informally, with the meetings of the Crocodile Club, then through a parliamentary intergroup, made up of MEPs from different Member States and belonging to different political families. On 9 July 1981, after lengthy consultations and repeated debates, Spinelli was able to push through a resolution in the EP establishing the creation of an ad hoc Committee that, starting in 1982, was expected to produce a draft reform. On that occasion, and even more so during the final vote on the Spinelli Project, despite the strong differences in ideology and perspective, a forced convergence would be reached between the EPP Group and the Socialists, although deep concerns and obvious contrasts continued to persist between them. The project, approved by the MEPs in February 1984 with approximately 88 per cent of the votes, was still able to catalyse the consensus from more than 50 per cent of the Socialists, having been acknowledged as consistent and coherent even by its opponents. Amongst these one cannot ignore an important part coming right from the Socialist area. Nevertheless, we have to remember the efforts made by the Institutional Affairs Committee, chaired by Italian Socialist Mauro Ferri, in healing the Socialists' internal rift.

The work had been developed on the basis of the resolution dated 14 September 1983,[25] which had been reached with a strenuous compromise. The Socialists and the EPP Group had therefore reached an agreement in principle that was apparent from the official statements of their respective Presidents. Glinne, for example, regarded 'the preliminary draft treaty' as balanced and realistic, and expressed the hope that 'it should be the project of the whole Parliament and not only of the present majority'.[26] This did not prevent critical and contrary positions from emerging during the debate, highlighting the Euroscepticism of the Danish, British, Greek and French Socialists. All this is clear in the speeches during the Project's final presentation and voting session on 14 February 1984.

The critical stance inside the Socialist Group was once again dictated primarily by the concern of British Labour, which was rather Eurosceptic on economic issues and openly Euro-critical towards the Community system. Barbara

Castle, for instance, accused the report of putting 'the cart before the horse'.[27] Indeed, in the face of the economic crisis, Castle said that it 'would be absurd to strengthen the Community institutions so as to impose these disastrous policies as common ones'; and she concluded by stating that she would not be willing 'to subject Britain's vital interests or my own social and economic views to majority votes, either in this Parliament or in the Council of Ministers'.[28] The Dutch Socialist Robert Cohen, using the same metaphor, thought that promoting 'the institutional set-up of the European Union [was] rather like putting the cart before the horse',[29] regarding the possibility of the Community really being able to solve Europe's economic and social issues. That said, notwithstanding the reservations, Cohen confirmed his support of the project, also on behalf of his colleagues, but he explained how his vote in favour maintained a critical emphasis, 'in the awareness that the essential issue in Europe is not the institutions but a new policy. Institutions cannot be a substitute for a policy'.[30]

Conversely, the speeches of the EPP Group showed greater uniformity with regard to the Project. The Greek Konstantinos Kallias declared himself 'unreservedly and unequivocally in favour of the European Union'.[31] According to the Italian Pietro Adonnino:

> We of the Group of the European People's Party, who have contributed to the formulation of these proposals, appreciate their worth. And this appreciation is a contributory factor to our approval of the draft treaty that is before us, and for which we have fought with conviction.[32]

In conclusion, we can consider that beyond a strong internal discrepancy within the Socialist area, most of the group endorsed the project, supporting it during the vote. In any case, the divergence between the Socialist and the EPP Group remained obvious especially after examining the voters' data. Against the 237 votes in favour, twelve out of thirty-one who were not in favour were Socialist (four Danes, two Irish, six British), while thirty-four of the forty-three abstentions belonged to the Socialist area (five Germans, seven Greeks, eighteen French, one Dutch and three British).[33]

'*The mouse born of the Kirchberg mountain*': the Single European Act

The result of the European elections on 14–17 June 1984 did not produce substantial changes to the parliamentary balance of the EP. The Socialist Group was confirmed in first place with nearly 30 per cent of the seats. The EPP Group was the second group of the EP, with over 25 per cent of the seats. The gap would be widened, however, with the arrival of the Spanish and Portuguese delegations, who expanded the socialist ranks with as many as thirty-five members of parliament.[34]

This parliamentary term was characterized not only by the accession of Spain and Portugal, but also by the beginning, as of January 1985, of the mandate of the Commission chaired by Jacques Delors, and then by the White Paper on the completion of the internal market, by the Intergovernmental Conference (IGC) under the Luxembourg Presidency that would lead to the Single European Act (SEA), as a partial response of national governments to the already-mentioned Spinelli Project.

With respect to the institutional issues, there is still a substantial uniformity of the EPP Group, as there remains, in this parliamentary term, a prominent Christian Democrat tradition; and, conversely, there is still the persistence of divisions in the Socialist family, with conflicting positions of British, Danish and Greek MEPs – the latter, though, with usually more softened tones.

It should also be noted that, in view of the aforementioned European elections of June 1984, Labour and the Danish Social Democrats had not undersigned the part of the electoral Manifesto of the Confederation of Socialist parties of the European Community which supported the need for greater coordination within the framework of the European Monetary System (EMS) and for an increase of the EP's powers; moreover, they had not endorsed the report drawn up by the Institutional Committee of the Confederation, presided over by the German SPD member Helga Kohnen, with which an attempt was made to define a common position on the issue of institutional reforms.[35]

The Greek MEP, Spyridon Plaskovitis, in his speech in plenary on 9 July 1985, while making clear that there was no opposition by the *Pasok* 'to the idea of European Union', stressed that, in the absence of balance in the economic and social development of all Member States, stronger countries would have a chance to impose their policies.[36] On foreign policy issues, then, Greece was threatened by Turkey, according to Plaskovitis, who said

> So how can my country commit itself in advance to any foreign policy when nothing is forthcoming from the European Community towards a solution of those two most serious and outstanding problems, which concern vital Hellenistic interests? And how can we abandon the principle of unanimity when matters of such a kind and scale remain outstanding?[37]

And he added:

> With the Spinelli report, we have arrived at the point of being asked to accept formally the creation of a two-rate Europe in the name of European Union, and a repeal of the Treaties of Rome [...]. We are totally opposed to such solutions, which essentially lead not to progress, but to a backsliding of the Community to its early stages.[38]

The speech of the Italian Socialist Carlo Tognoli was very different. He sponsored the need to quickly reach a reform of the Treaties, with the strengthening of the Community institutions and a greater involvement of the European Parliament. He said: 'Variations can be considered; the road can be made wider or narrower, but the route is as indicated'.[39]

The leader of the EPP Group, Egon A. Klepsch, placed emphasis on the extension of a majority vote in the Council, with the use of vetoes only for valid and proven reasons, and the co-decision of the EP. Klepsch then declared:

> We hope that all twelve will follow this road together, but we cannot deny that we are a little tired of waiting for the slowest vehicle in the convoy, especially when its driver keeps claiming that [he] is not quite sure which way to go, whether the opposite direction is not perhaps the right one.[40]

Also during the plenary debate, the Italian Christian Democrat Roberto Formigoni, President of the Political Committee of the EP, expressed his satisfaction regarding the outcome of the European Council in Milan, which had been held a few days earlier, on 28 and 29 June 1985. The deferment to an IGC was fraught with dangers, however, as for the first time in its history the European Council had resorted to a majority vote. The EP should have demanded that it be involved in the work of the IGC and that the latter not degenerate into proposals of mere intergovernmental cooperation, pursuing the Spinelli Project instead. Formigoni was proposing then to ponder upon the idea of a referendum on a European scale, to ask citizens to express themselves on European integration.[41]

On 9 September 1985, opening day of the IGC in Luxembourg, the EP President, Pierre Pflimlin, read out a letter, during the session, addressed to the President-in-Office of the Council, Luxembourg's Foreign Minister, Jacques Poos, in which he called for a radical institutional reform with a strengthening of Parliament's powers, taking into account the aforementioned Spinelli Project.[42] Note that the Danish Social Democrat, Ove Fich, on behalf of his national delegation in the parliamentary group, expressed his disagreement with the content of the letter.[43]

Following the Luxembourg European Council on 2–3 December 1985, during the session on the 11th of the month, the British Labour Thomas Megahy declared that the results of the summit marked the end of the draft EP treaty, seeing the EP forced to accept a compromise, 'but we could have saved a lot of fine rhetoric over all these years'. This was to show 'the futility of all the time and energy that has been spent on talking about institutional reforms'.[44] He rejected the idea of monetary union, as it represented 'an undesirable path of the freedom of Member Governments to pursue their own policy'. Megahy then judged it utopian to think that the internal market would be beneficial, since it was impossible that it would actually work.[45]

A very critical judgment on the completion of the internal market was also expressed by another Labour MEP, George Robert Cryer, because in his view they were selling illusions: not only would the unemployment issue have not been settled, but, on the contrary, problems would have grown. With regards to the institutional issues, Cryer believed that States could only cooperate 'as equals, not in subjection to an appointed bureaucracy and certainly not subject to this place which cannot manage its own affairs very well, let alone taking over those of the Member States'.[46]

Another Labour MEP, Alfred Lomas, returned to economic issues, stressing that the major problems, crisis and unemployment, were not being tackled. There was a great deal of attention for the interests of business, but not of the workers. Moreover, he added that the Labour Party was not opposed to a reform of the Treaties, provided they were aimed at reducing 'the powers of those who seek to exploit working people in Europe', by rerouting competences to the national parliaments, 'where governments elected by the people can carry out the programmes on which they were elected. That is what we believe to be real democracy'. Regarding political union then, even though there was a clear need to act in a coordinated manner in some sectors, it was in his view 'an illusion to think that governments of quite different political natures can come together and start issuing common statements, particularly on world affairs'.[47]

A tough speech came from the Danish Socialdemocrat, Ejner Hovgård Christiansen, since he considered that the EP, in recent years, had negatively affected the European debate with 'ambitious plans', 'with its union plans, with the draft for the Spinelli Treaty'. It had, in fact, 'distorted the dialogue on the development of the cooperation'. He elicited an acknowledgement of the non-relevance of a treaty intended to create a European Union and that 'the ignition system for the union firework display no longer works' and that 'what has now come to us from the Intergovernmental Conference has nothing to do with the ambitious and fanciful institutional changes which the European Parliament wants and has committed itself to, but is concerned with the content of cooperation'.[48]

The German Social Democrat Gerd Walter, almost in response to his Danish colleague, claimed not to understand the motivations of Denmark's hostility to an extension of the EP's powers. The decisions taken in Luxembourg meant, in fact, greater tasks for the EEC and a minor influence of national parliaments, without an equivalent strengthening of the EP, which would serve to balance the powers lost by the national legislatures. This constituted, according to Walter, 'a dangerous way'.[49]

Once again on 11 December 1985, the Socialist leader, Rudi Arndt,[50] who was also a member of the SPD, acknowledged the rifts within the Socialist family. However, some progress had been made, even though not all expected decisions had sprung up from the Luxembourg Summit.[51] Even the French Socialist Georges Sutra de Germa believed that there had been 'real and definite progress'.[52]

This view was shared by several members of the EPP Group, such as the Luxembourger Nicolas Estgen, who, whilst describing unsatisfactory results, nevertheless emphasized that steps forward had been made.[53] The Frenchman Jacques Mallet certainly did not bestow upon the Luxembourg European Council the definition of 'historic event', adding that: 'We had dreamed of a cathedral and are being given a shack'. Nevertheless, the results were a starting point, had the EP used its power of influence with determination.[54] Along the same lines was the member of *Nea Dimokratia*, Panayotis Lambrias, who called for a constructive dialogue with the other Community institutions, most notably the Council of Ministers.[55]

It should be noted, though, that among the MEPs of the EPP there were quite a number of critical comments, dissatisfied with the inadequacy of the outcome of the IGC, such as in the cases of the vice president of the group, the Italian Christian Democrat Giovanni Giavazzi,[56] of the aforementioned Roberto Formigoni[57] or of the Dutch Bouke Beumer.[58]

Uncompromising was the comment by the *Democrazia Cristiana* MEP, Maria Luisa Cassanmagnago, who expressed deep disappointment at the outcome of the European Council on 2 and 3 December 1985, because of the inability of the governments to seize this 'historic opportunity', preferring a compromise that was creating 'nothing new' and, indeed, in some areas, was making steps backwards. There appeared to be no real strengthening of the EP and the Luxembourg compromise of 1966, which granted the Member States a right of veto, had not been abolished. The same goes for the European Political Cooperation.[59]

The Belgian Fernand Herman, of the French speaking *Parti Social-chrétien*, declared quite ironically in his speech:

> [...] the Community menagerie, which already contained a wealth of species, with the monetary snake, the kangaroo and crocodile, was joined a week ago by a new animal: the mouse born of the Kirchberg mountain. It really is a curious mouse that has been presented to the European Parliament, a variable geometry mouse. It could turn into a lion. The mouse that roars, as in the famous film, but presented before the Danish or British Parliament, it becomes a miserable shrew.
>
> Mrs Thatcher and Mr Schlüter said before their parliaments: this makes no difference, don't worry, don't lose any sleep, we are not losing any powers, there is no change.
>
> Here, on the other hand, it is viewed either as a new Messina or as a new departure towards a glorious European future.
>
> Well, such a difference of interpretation is evidence enough of poor drafting.[60]

'Are we building a Europe for the economy or are we building a Europe for its citizens?': the path from Maastricht to Amsterdam

During the third parliamentary term (1989–1994), the institutional issues were of great importance in view of the negotiations for the Treaty of Maastricht. In the EP, attention was therefore drawn on both IGCs, one on Economic and Monetary Union (EMU) and the other on political union, launched in Rome in December 1990 and that led to the signing of the Treaty on 7 February 1992.

In terms of the political groups, as was previously mentioned, this was the legislature which, as far as the EPP is concerned, gave way to the expansion strategy towards the conservative parties, which would then be achieved, in particular, with the accession of the former members of the European Democrats Group: first the *Partido Popular*, already in 1989; then, later, in May 1992, the

British and the Danish Conservatives.[61] The weight of these last two national political parties in the EPP parliamentary group was not yet felt in the debates held in plenary during the proceedings of the IGCs. The Spanish representatives, for their part, toed a line which was substantially aligned with the Christian Democrat one, in favour of the development of a supranational Europe.[62]

In the Socialist Group, there was the notable entrance of the Italian PDS in favour of a line of support for the process of European integration. The Labour Party under the leadership of Neil Kinnock was beginning a long march, partly because of the national election defeats,[63] which led, in 1994, to the rise of Tony Blair and to policies which were certainly more open on issues of European integration, as is already noticeable – it must be said – in the floor speeches of Labour MEPs during the drafting of the Maastricht Treaty.

In relation to this very phase, the representative of the Socialist Group, Vincenzo Mattina, holding his speech in plenary on 21 November 1990 just a few weeks before the opening of the IGC, wished for the creation of a European federation,[64] whilst, however, the leader of the same group, the Frenchman Jean-Pierre Cot, noted that a clear understanding of the architecture of the political union was lacking, and stressed the need to simplify, and not complicate things by, for example, proposals for a second Chamber. It was necessary to make Europe more legible to the citizens, hence the abolition of the right to veto and extending majority voting.[65]

In the EPP Group, Egon A. Klepsch, opposite Cot, argued for the need for a two-chamber system with one House as expression of the States and one directly elected by the citizens.[66] Marcelino Oreja Aguirre, member of the *Partido Popular*, declared on 12 June 1991 that the goal was indeed to be:

> A federal Europe, based on the principle of subsidiarity, which guarantees economic and social cohesion between the Member States and their regions [...] a Europe which is equipped with strong, democratic institutions, with a [...] a single currency and common foreign and defence policies.[67]

The British Labour MEP David Martin stressed the importance of achieving the EP co-decision, because otherwise the IGCs would have been a failure.[68] Even the Dutch Socialist Alman Metten, in a speech on 12 June 1991, during Luxembourg's final phase of the presidency, observed that a strengthening of the role of the Council of Ministers was springing up from the work of the two IGCs, but there needed to be a co-decision by the EP to provide a response to the issue of democratic deficit.[69]

A few days short of the Dutch Presidency's start, on 9 July 1991, the Italian MEP Antonio La Pergola was pushing to go beyond 'the mercantile, consumistic [*sic*] view of integration', overcoming the internal differences and speaking with one voice in foreign policy. The Italian MEP declared himself in favour of a Community that does not stifle the national State, since the political union was not intended as 'a superstate'.[70] His colleague, Cot, on 9 October 1991, emphasized the need for reform of the Treaties before further enlargements, so as not to risk a downgrade to a more confederal structure.[71] The following month he also expressed a critical opinion on the project submitted by the Netherlands, since the structure of the old Community did not appear substantially reformed, placing it, moreover, next to intergovernmental 'European unions' and added:

> In doing so, you are turning your back on the Single Act approach, you are proposing a Europe in separate compartments, you are exacerbating the democratic deficit.[72]

Among the members of the EPP, the Luxembourger Nicolas Estgen, on 9 July 1991, noted the need for practical solutions, since it was not possible to please 'all the ayatollahs of parliamentary federalism'.[73] In that same session, however, the vice president of the group, the Greek Georgios Saridakis, judged the recently ended Luxembourg presidency to be a lost opportunity. Transferring powers to the Community, without creating an effective legislative authority, reduced its democratic character. The EPP Group would continue to call for 'a greater remit for the Parliament, covering new areas such as foreign policy and security and defence, working towards greater federation'.[74] This was confirmed by Klepsch, on 20 November 1991, who stated that 'Christian Democrats as a whole both inside and outside this House are determined to see the European Community become a federation'. Regarding the often mentioned co-decision of the EP, Klepsch welcomed the idea of a gradual process, but ratifying the principle within the Treaties.[75]

Horst Langes, the vice president of the EPP Group, was rather harsh in his comment with respect to the work done by the Dutch presidency of his fellow countryman Klepsch. In fact, he declared:

> What your presidency is proposing amounts to dismantling the Treaty of Rome. It is a leap backwards rather than a leap forward and the Dutch Presidency has failed to provide a minimum level for genuine cooperation and dialogue between Parliament and the Council.[76]

The previous month, as a demonstration of the weight of national origins, the Dutch MEP Jean J. M. Penders, again in the EPP Group, had stressed that the EP had expressed two major objections to the proposal made by the Luxembourg Presidency: the little significance afforded to the role of the EP itself and, in addition, the pillar structure, because it would have formed an Intergovernmental Union next to the supranational Community. On the contrary, the Dutch Presidency's merit was that it had tried to avoid 'that mistake'.[77]

Another of the important issues discussed was that of the uniform electoral procedure – the French EPP MEP Jean-Louis Bourlanges, on 8 October 1991, commenting the De Gucht report[78] with critical tones, described how it could be defined as a result of disappointing outcomes, 'a "bladeless knife", one without a handle moreover, in other words no knife at all'. He furthermore reiterated his group's support on the principle of proportional representation.[79]

Astrid Lulling, of the Luxembourger *Parti Chrétien-social*, took the floor in the same session, stating that if the EP had not yet managed to give itself a uniform electoral procedure, this was due to the desire to push itself far beyond its competences and added:

> [...] it is attempting to interfere in the constitutional laws of the Member States [...].
>
> Insofar as sovereign states exist, it is up to them to decide whether or not to change their constitutions in order to grant non-nationals the right to vote [...]
>
> To our minds, the right to vote and stand for election is linked to nationality.[80]

In some speeches the emphasis was placed on the relationship between the EP and national parliaments. On 9 October 1991, the Portuguese Socialist MEP João Cravinho, commenting the report on this matter by Maurice Duverger, on behalf of the Institutional Affairs Committee, stressed the need for an involvement of national parliaments in the Community process, in a complementary role to the EP.[81]

Maria Luisa Cassanmagnago observed that the parliaments of the Member States had to make an effort in the supervision and management activity of their respective governments on the positions to be taken in the Council of Ministers. At a Community level, it was necessary to ensure the EP's full participation in the decision-making processes, with a close cooperation with the national assemblies, even through the parliamentary groups' action.[82]

Regarding the relationship between the national and European dimensions, one must reiterate the change in attitude of many British Labour MEPs, compared to the previous term. Indeed, on 12 June 1991, Alan John Donnelly, apart from stressing the importance of the Economic and Monetary Union, declared:

> What the people of the United Kingdom want to see is not for Britain to be in a second-class carriage in a two-speed Europe. We want to be in the centre of the argument. [...]
>
> Please do not relegate the United Kingdom to some sort of second-class carriage in a two-speed Europe. The people of the United Kingdom do not want that.[83]

On 20 November of that year, another British member, Glyn Ford, declared that Labour had become aware that the internal market would require a single currency as well as common standards in environmental and social issues. And he added:

> We want a European Community and not just a common market.
>
> Without majority voting, Community standards will end up being those of the lowest common denominator [...] we will have a distorted, crippled

Community, [...]. The Labour Party recognizes in our external relations that the economic and political potential in the Community is enormous. [...]. a wider Community and a deeper Community are inseparable. We in the Labour Party recognize that if the Community is to have such important responsibilities then the issue of democratic accountability is fundamental. That is why the Labour Party Conference approved the principle of co-decision powers for the European Parliament.[84]

The Danish Socialdemocrat Ejner Hovgård Christiansen, although with obvious caution, judged the Economic and Monetary Union as a natural extension of the creation of the internal market. However, he was remarking that it should be the politicians elected by the people in the Council of Ministers and EP who managed the economic cooperation and not the Executive Board of a European central bank or the European Commission.[85]

There were frequent speeches in which it was pointed out that a deeper economic and social 'cohesion' would constitute the *sine qua non* of economic and monetary union. The aforementioned João Cravinho argued that one could decide to set up a definitive transfer of sovereignty to the European institutions only in the presence of a true sense of solidarity.[86] In the same direction went the speeches of the group colleagues, including the Greek Christos Papoutsis[87] and the Dutch *Partij van de Arbeid* MEP, Win van Velzen.[88] The Belgian Raymonde Dury stated her fear that Europe, devoid of a social dimension and 'characterized by premeditated social dumping', would charge the less fortunate not only with the implementation of the monetary union, but also with the political one. Dury brought up the example of a greater strictness and the adoption of a majority vote procedure in the Council, in the event of failure to comply with the budget deficit limits, while on the subject of tax harmonization decisions would be taken unanimously, and concluded: 'Are we building a Europe for the economy or are we building a Europe for its citizens?'.[89] Also in the EPP Group, MEPs John Walls Cushnahan,[90] of the Irish Fine Gael, and Ioannis Pesmazoglou, of *Nea Dimokratia*, both emphasized the importance of economic and social cohesion.[91]

In the next parliamentary term (1994–1999), the reform process consolidated in the Treaty of Amsterdam and, while there was a growing Eurocriticism in the EPP Group, because of the aforementioned opening to the Conservative parties, the heterogeneity of the internal positions within the Socialist group decreased.

In the session on 13 December 1995, ahead of the Madrid European Council which led to the IGC in Turin in March 1996, the discussion of the programme, by the Reflection Group, headed by the Spaniard Carlos Westendorp, on the hypotheses of reform, revealed no overt internal rifts or conflicts between the two biggest European political groups.[92] This derived from the fact that, within the Reflection Group, the EP was represented by the German Christian Democrat Elmar Brok and the French Socialist Élisabeth Guigou.

Even the British Labour and Scandinavian Socialists now seemed more inclined to accept a reform of the Treaties that would go in the direction of further integration, including issues of social policy, that were always high on the Socialist's agenda. The Briton Stephen Hughes urged both for an employment plan and an institutional reform to ensure its implementation[93] and the Finn, Ulpu Iivari, alongside reflections on the Common Foreign and Security Policy, emphasized the urgent need to move towards the Economic and Monetary Union to fight unemployment.[94]

In the session dated 13 March 1996, during the debate on the report by the Institutional Affairs Committee regarding the political priorities of the EP in the IGC in Turin, Labour was united in favour of the reform guidelines drawn by the French Socialist, Raymonde Dury, and the Dutch Hanja Maij-Weggen, member of the EPP Group. Dury's perspective was clear on the political priorities: social justice, citizenship, fundamental rights, internal and external security, solidarity, development of the social and ecological dimensions, employment policy and economic and social cohesion.[95] The position of the British representatives was clear when the Labour MEP Pauline Green stated that 'the Socialist Group overwhelmingly endorse[ed] the Dury/Maij-Weggen report',[96] since the document 'defend[ed] and extend[ed] the desires of [the] group' to see Europe based 'on the principles of clarity, openness, democracy and effectiveness'.[97] Wayne David also welcomed the proposals in the report, especially with regards to a 'simplification of the [...] legislative procedures and more powers for the European Parliament in relation to both the Commission and the Council',[98] thus upholding the reverse of Labour's tendency to always oppose the strengthening of supranational institutions. British Labour's approval echoed that of the Scandinavian socialists, from Swedish Maj-Lis Lööw to the Finn Iivari.[99]

In the EPP Group, the conservative Dane, Poul Schlüter, had sided in favour of a simplification of the Community, agreeing with the Socialists on the need to change 'our institutions, so that they can continue to be effective',[100] in view of future openings. The Swedish colleague Charlotte Cederschiöld, of the *Moderata Samlingspartiet*, clarified the ways in which the EU should proceed on reforms: 'Europe must be modernised but cannot be involved in everything'.[101]

However, the clearest idea on the positions of the Conservatives, who had entered the EPP Group, was given by the Tory MEP Brendan Donnelly, who recalled how the British Conservatives had 'always supported the opt-out of the social chapter'.[102] He also rejected the hypothesis of a 'fusion of the pillars established in the Maastricht Treaty'.[103] From his point of view, to expect governments to abandon 'intergovernmentalism [was], as we say in English, to tilt at windmills'.[104]

Returning to the Socialist Group, the shift of the British and the Scandinavians to more favourable positions on European integration is also apparent in the disappointment with which some MEPs received the report by the Dutch State Secretary for Foreign Affairs, Michiel Patijn, on the results of the informal European Council in Noordwijk on 23 May 1997, which led to the signing of the Treaty of Amsterdam.[105] Green expressed pessimism on the agreements reached at the Summit because they disregarded many aspects considered vital by the Socialist Group, including social and environmental policies, as well as a substantial reform of the treaty going in the direction of more democracy and functionality of the institutional system. In fact it was the British Labour MEP's opinion that it was now 'an imperative to prepare the Union for enlargement'.[106]

Conclusions

A dialectical relationship between conservatism and change is evident in the activities of the European Parliament. The polarization reversal among the EPP Group and the Socialists is confirmed after the examination of the parliamentary acts. In the Socialist Group, a significant division switches to greater cohesion, starting in the late Eighties and early Nineties; while the opposite occurs in the EPP Group, with the emergence of critical positions towards the European integration process, especially as a result of the accession of the British and the Scandinavian Conservatives. Starting from 1992, it is possible to detect on certain issues how a greater convergence is registered between much of the Socialist Group and the traditional Christian Democrat part of the EPP than within the latter, more precisely between the original nucleus and the other conservative parties that later entered the group.[107]

This convergence proceeded in line with the beginning of a new phase in the European integration process, in which, as a result of the crises of the Nineties, a profound change in the European social and institutional order was noticed. The historical change marked by the fall of the Berlin Wall and the dissolution of the Soviet Empire helped to close the gap among the main political forces in the European Parliament, often leading them to support common positions and to defend the prerogatives of the supranational institution. Consequently, the European Parliament has experienced a slow process of politicization.

It should also be noted in this regard that the position of the MEPs within their parliamentary group was characterized by greater autonomy and less internal discipline than one can observe in the national parliaments.[108] The selections for the candidatures at the elections are still responsibility of the national parties, not of the Europarties, so leading to a strong loyalty to the national constituency. Regarding the specific instance of the EPP Group, it should also be added that, at the time of their entry into the parliamentary group, the Conservative MEPs obtained the right to vote differently from the group,[109] noting that their political line was not comparable to the founding nucleus of the parliamentary group and the European party, so sacrificing a more rigorous programmatic convergence, but with the aim, as we said, of an enlargement strategy competing with the Socialist Group. We have also to consider that the British Conservative delegation within the EPP Group contained a significantly higher proportion of pro-Europeans than the rest of the national party, but their number diminished over time.[110]

However, as stated by Matthew Gabel and Simon Hix, 'the Socialists became more pro-European as they began to endorse regulatory capitalism at the European and national levels (instead of welfare capitalism at the domestic level)', while, on the contrary, 'the EEP became more anti-European as they began to advocate neoliberal economic policies'.[111] In effect, some sectors of the EPP originally linked to the core Christian Democrat foundation became critical towards a role considered too interventionist of the common institutions, especially in the economic, social and civil liberties.

Among the Socialists, on the contrary, considering the economic globalization and taking note of the difficulty in offering answers with economic policies hinged on national bases, more attention on the European dimension as a resource, as a possible response to the economic issues, spread gradually, even in those areas of the group that were at the beginning critical or at least suspicious.[112]

Finally, in the discursive use of some Socialist MEPs we can also observe that the emphasis laid on the term 'social' reform, in the first term that we have examined, gave place to the adjective 'institutional', revealing a growing attention to the reform of the European institutions.

Notes

1 See Bostanci 2013, 172–84.
2 Reference is made in particular to the CERES (Centre d'Études, de Recherches et d'Éducation Socialiste). On issues of European integration closer to the Communists and, in contrast, in the French Socialist Party, with Michel Rocard's most pro-European wing, see Delwit 1995, 93; Pasquinucci and Verzichelli 2004, 139–40.
3 See Pasquinucci and Verzichelli 2004, 114–16.
4 See Gabel and Hix 2002, 949–50; Hanley 2004, 254.
5 It should be considered that, with the accession of the United Kingdom, Denmark and Ireland, there had been a widening of the Socialist parliamentary group in the EP (Labour, however, had appointed its deputies only in 1975); while the centre-right parties of the new Member States, the conservative non Christian Democrat ones, had not joined the EPP Group, but had given birth to an independent parliamentary group. See Van Hecke 2006, 154–56; Wintoniak 2006, 173–76; Delwit 2004, 140–41, 144–46. The implosion of the DC (*Democrazia Cristiana*) and the electoral weakening of the Benelux Christian Democrat political parties favoured the rise of the CDU-CSU line, see Delwit 2004, 147; Hix and Lesse 2002, 76.
6 See Parlement Européen 2009; Pasquinucci and Verzichelli 2004; Judge and Earnshaw 2003; Kreppel 2002.
7 Egon A. Klepsch was chairman of the EPP Group in the years 1977–1982 and 1984–1992. He was President of the EP from 1992 to 1994.
8 See Official Journal of the European Communities (henceforth OJEC), Debates of the European Parliament (henceforth DEP), n. 244, 1979, 12ff.
9 Ibid., 20–24.
10 Ibid., 31.
11 Ibid., 27–29.
12 Ibid, 27.
13 Ibid, 27.
14 Ibid., 28.
15 Ibid., 28.
16 See OJEC, DEP, n.1–277, 1981, 215ff.
17 Ibid., 219.
18 Ibid., 233.
19 Ibid., 234–35.
20 Ibid., 223.
21 Ibid., 223.

22 Ibid., 223.
23 See OJEC, DEP, n. 244, 1979, 30.
24 Ibid., 29.
25 See OJEC, DEP, n. 1–303, 1983, 27–198.
26 See OJEC, DEP, n. 1–309, 1984, 36.
27 Ibid., 98.
28 Ibid., 98.
29 Ibid., 79.
30 Ibid., 79
31 Ibid., 80.
32 Ibid., 83.
33 Lodge 1984, 396.
34 See Pasquinucci and Verzichelli 2004, 141–45.
35 See Hix and Lesse 2002, 38–40.
36 See OJEC, DEP, n. 2–328, 1985, 55.
37 Ibid., 55.
38 Ibid., 55
39 Ibid., 66–67.
40 Ibid., 50.
41 Ibid., 60–61.
42 See OJEC, DEP, n. 2–329, 1985, 2.
43 Ibid., 2.
44 See OJEC, DEP, n. 2–333, 1985, 165–66.
45 Ibid., 165–66.
46 Ibid., 176.
47 Ibid., 157–58.
48 Ibid., 163–64.
49 Ibid.,161–62. This position was shared by Mark Clinton, member of the Fine Gael in the EPP Group, see ibid., 170–71.
50 Rudi Arndt was the Socialist leader in the EP from 1984 to 1989.
51 Ibid., 128–29.
52 Ibid., 148–49.
53 Ibid., 159–60.
54 Ibid., 162–63.
55 Ibid., 168–69.
56 Ibid., 154–55.
57 Incidentally, Formigoni supported the necessity of a new IGC by 1987. See Ibid., 171.
58 Ibid., 164–65.
59 Ibid., 167.
60 Ibid., 171–72.
61 See Delwit 2004, 144–45.
62 See Samaniego Boneu 2004, 365–70, 380–93; Delwit 2004, 144–45.
63 It should be noted that, after its defeat in the general elections of May 1979, Labour toed a line which was markedly socialist and national. The manifesto for the general election of 1983 promised the United Kingdom's exit from the EEC in the case of victory. The electoral defeats, both in 1983 and in 1987, forced the party to review its position on this and other issues. During the European elections of 1989, the Labour Party gained forty-five of the eighty-one British seats and, also, since then the party was strongly attracted to the social aspects of the internal market and understood that the EU could safeguard some civil and social rights from the policies of the Conservatives. Worth noting is the party's acceptance of the Economic and Monetary Union project, during the summit of the European Socialist leaders held in Paris on 29 June 1989. See Bideleux 2004, 229–31; Hix and Lesse 2002, 46.

64 See OJEC, DEP, n. 3–396, 1990, 162.
65 Ibid., 152–54.
66 See OJEC, DEP, n. 3–396, 1990, 162, 154–55.
67 See OJEC, DEP, n. 3–406, 1991, 151.
68 See OJEC, DEP, n. 3–398, 1991, 123.
69 See OJEC, DEP, n. 3–406, 1991, 136–37.
70 See OJEC, DEP, n. 3–407, 1991, 63–64.
71 See OJEC, DEP, n. 3–409, 1991, 136–37.
72 See OJEC, DEP, n. 3–411, 1991, 127.
73 See OJEC, DEP, n. 3–407, 1991, 56.
74 Ibid., 62–63.
75 See OJEC, DEP, n. 3–411, 1991, 128–29.
76 Ibid., 143.
77 See OJEC, DEP, n. 3–409, 1991, 143. Penders reiterated this concept on 20 November 1991, stating: '[…] it is absolutely essential that the federal idea […] should be retained in the Treaty'. See OJEC, DEP, n. 3–411, 1991, 137–38.
78 The Flemish Liberal, Karel De Gucht, on behalf of the Committee on Institutional Affairs, had submitted a resolution which established the guidelines of the EP on the uniform electoral procedure. See Pasquinucci and Verzichelli 2004, 67–68.
79 See OJEC, DEP, n. 3–409, 1991, 80–81.
80 Ibid., 101–02.
81 Ibid., 108–09.
82 Ibid., 109.
83 See OJEC, DEP, n. 3–406, 1991, 148.
84 See OJEC, DEP, n. 3–411, 1991, 142–43.
85 See OJEC, DEP, n. 3–406, 1991, 150.
86 See OJEC, DEP, n. 3–398, 1991, 120–21.
87 See OJEC, DEP, n. 3–407, 1991, 99.
88 Ibid., 100.
89 See OJEC, DEP, n. 3–411, 1991, 145–46.
90 See OJEC, DEP, n. 3–406, 1991, 148.
91 See OJEC, DEP, n. 3–407, 1991, 101.
92 See OJEC, DEP, n. 4–462, 1996, 169ff.
93 Ibid., 189.
94 Ibid., 190.
95 See OJEC, DEP, n. 4–478, 1997, 94.
96 Ibid., 103.
97 Ibid., 104.
98 Ibid., 122.
99 Ibid., 120–21.
100 Ibid., 118.
101 Ibid., 118–19.
102 Ibid., 121.
103 Ibid., 121.
104 Ibid., 121.
105 See OJEC, DEP, n. 4–501, 1998, 15ff.
106 Ibid., 19.
107 Hanley 2004, 256.
108 Viviani 2009, 145–47.
109 Lynch and Whitaker 2008, 33.
110 Ibid., 37.
111 Gabel and Hix 2002, 951.
112 See Grazi 2015, 81.

Bibliography

Bideleux, Robert. 2004. 'Dall'Impero all'Unione: l'evoluzione dell'atteggiamento inglese verso l'integrazione europea'. In *Idee d'Europa e integrazione europea*, edited by Ariane Landuyt, 181–234. Bologna: Il Mulino.

Bonfreschi, Lucia, Giovanni Orsina and Antonio Varsori, eds. 2015. *European Parties and the European Integration Process, 1945–1992*. Bruxelles, Bern, Berlin, Frankfurt am Main, New York, Oxford and Wien: Peter Lang.

Bostanci, S. Anne. 2013. 'Making the Mythical European: Elucidating the EU's Powerful Integration Instrument of Discursive Identity Construction'. *Perspectives on European Politics and Society* 14 (2): 172–84.

'Debates of the European Parliament' (DEP). 1979–1999. *Official Journal of the European Communities*.

Delwit, Pascal. 1995. *Les partis socialistes face à l'intégration européenne (France, Grande Bretagne, Belgique)*. Bruxelles: Editions de l'Université libre de Bruxelles (ULB).

Delwit, Pascal. 2004. 'The European People's Party: Stages and Analysis of a Transformation'. In *The Europarties. Organisation and Influence*, edited by Pascal Delwit, Erol Külahci and Cédric Van de Walle, 135–55. Brussels: Centre d'étude de la vie politique, Editions de l'Université de Bruxelles.

Gabel, Matthew, and Simon Hix. 2002. 'Defining the EU Political Space: An Empirical Study of the European Elections Manifestos, 1979–1999'. *Comparative Political Studies* 35(8): 934–64.

Grazi, Laura. 2015. 'Il partito del socialismo europeo. Evoluzione, struttura e priorità politiche'. In *Unione politica in progress. Partiti e gruppi parlamentari europei (1953–2014)*, edited by Guido Levi and Fabio Sozzi, 73–90. Padova: CEDAM.

Hanley, David. 2004. 'At the Heart of the Decision-making Process? The European People's Party in the European Union'. In *The Europarties. Organisation and Influence*, edited by Pascal Delwit, Erol Külahci and Cédric Van de Walle, 243–61. Brussels: Centre d'étude de la vie politique, Editions de l'Université de Bruxelles.

Hix, Simon, and Urs Lesse. 2002. *Shaping a Vision. A History of the Party of European Socialists 1957–2002*. Brussels: Party of European Socialists.

Judge, David, and David Earnshaw. 2003. *The European Parliament*. Basingstoke: Palgrave Macmillan.

Kreppel, Amie. 2002. *The European Parliament and the Supranational Party System: A Study in Institutional Development*. Cambridge: Cambridge University Press.

Lodge, Juliet. 1984. 'European Union and the First Elected Parliament: The Spinelli Initiative'. *Journal of Common Market Studies*, XXII (4): 377–402.

Lynch, Philip, and Richard Whitaker. 2008. 'A Loveless Marriage: The Conservatives and the European People's Party'. *Parliamentary Affairs* 61 (1): 31–51.

Parlement Européen. 2009. *La construction d'un Parlement. 50 ans d'histoire du Parlement Européen 1958–2008*. Luxembourg: Publications Office of the European Union.

Pasquinucci, Daniele. 2013. *Uniti dal voto? Storia delle elezioni europee 1948–2009*. Milano: Franco Angeli.

Pasquinucci, Daniele, and Luca Verzichelli. 2004. *Elezioni europee e classe politica sovranazionale, 1979–2004*. Bologna: Il Mulino.

Samaniego Boneu, Mercedes. 2004. 'Prospettiva storica dell'integrazione ispano-comunitaria: un gioco di interessi politici ed economici'. In *Idee d'Europa e integrazione europea*, edited by Ariane Landuyt, 343–93. Bologna: Il Mulino.

Van Hecke, Steven. 2006. 'On the Road towards Transnational Parties in Europe: Why and How the European People's Party Was Founded'. *European View* 3: 153–60.

Viviani, Lorenzo. 2009. *L'Europa dei partiti. Per una sociologia dei partiti politici nel processo di integrazione europea.* Firenze: Firenze University Press.

Wintoniak, Alexis. 2006. 'Uniting the Centre-right of Europe: The Result of Historical Developments and Political Leadership'. *European View* 3: 173–78.

7 The political groups of the European Parliament in the face of Yugoslavia's disintegration and the discursive framing of EU foreign policy (1991–1995)

Giovanni Finizio and Umberto Morelli[1]

Introduction

The disintegration of Yugoslavia was one of the milestones in the construction of European Community/Union (EC/EU) foreign policy. The EU made use of a variety of instruments of intervention, but showed all the political and institutional limits of a player that, with the end of the Cold War and its involvement in the resolution of that crisis, would have wanted to revitalize its international role and show that it could take on increasing responsibility in the management of world peace. Just the acknowledgement of these limits gave the EU the impetus, at the end of the 1990s, to develop a European Security and Defence Policy (ESDP), questioning, among other things, the relations between Europe and the United States in the management of peace and international security.

Literature has extensively analysed the participation of the EU and its Member States in the Yugoslav crisis, highlighting their difficulties and their failure (Lucarelli 2000; Biermann 2004; Glaurdić 2011). This chapter, however, aims to analyse the contribution of the European Parliament (EP) to this participation, through the study of parliamentary debates between 1991 and 1995, that is, between the outbreak of the crisis and the Dayton agreement which marked the end of the war in Bosnia-Herzegovina. Through the study of the minutes of the parliamentary sessions published in the Official Journal of the European Communities, we will examine the positions adopted and the proposals that emerged from the parliamentary groups, and the political culture that inspired them at the sight of the dissolution of a European multi-ethnic state, the reappearance of war in Europe for the first time since 1945 and the recurrence of the 'Balkan issue'. We will also be able to characterize the EP's contribution to the European effort in managing the crisis and to the understanding and overcoming of the limits shown by the EU in this context.

The first part of the chapter looks, from the EP's point of view, at the EC's response to the crisis outbreak and to Slovenia and Croatia's proclamation of independence. Pivotal will be the debates within the EP relating to the principle of self-determination. The second part will focus on the role of the EC/EU in the management of the war in Bosnia-Herzegovina and on the construction of parliamentary groups' political positions regarding the diplomatic resolution of the conflict, the military intervention and the role of the EU and the United States.

The political groups of the EP and the outbreak of the Yugoslav crisis

The historical context of the Yugoslav crisis

In the south-eastern countries of Europe, the fall of the communist regimes and the loss of the binding force represented by the common ideology had awakened an unbridled nationalism and ambition to exploit their own minorities living in the neighbouring countries to implement an expansionary policy and a modification of boundaries to bring together, in a basically mono-ethnic single State, all members of the same ethnic group.

This policy revealed itself in an exaggerated form in Milošević and Tuđman's plans to create a Greater Serbia and a Greater Croatia. A stop to this policy had to be represented by the Helsinki Final Act (1975) and the Charter of Paris for a New Europe (1990), which reaffirmed the principles of the inviolability of borders and minority rights. The Western countries feared that territorial upheavals in the Balkans, especially if involving the use of force, could cause unpredictable effects in Turkey (Kurdistan) and in the USSR, where the centrifugal forces of independence movements and nationalism had already triggered a break-up process.

The Yugoslav problem broke out in an intense period of international crises (the fall of the Berlin Wall and of the communist regimes, the end of the Cold War, the Gulf War, the implosion of the USSR, the Nuclear Disarmament Negotiations and the START I treaty) monopolizing the attention of the chancelleries. In addition, the EC was focussed on domestic concerns (German reunification) and important objectives to be achieved (single market, negotiations for the new treaty, monetary union). During the initial phase these events distracted the EC's attention from the Yugoslav crisis.

The hour of Europe: the EC's initial response

Despite the strategic and economic interest in Yugoslavia (guarantee of the geopolitical balance in the Balkans, an important trading partner, an overland link between Greece and other member countries), the EC initially underestimated the gravity of the situation, and was convinced that the crisis could be confined internally and briefly resolved by the federal government. According to the position of the Commission and the Council it was necessary to: maintain the unity and territorial integrity of the country, in compliance with the same EC model in which different peoples lived in peace; not internationalize the crisis; strive to ensure stability in negotiating with the federal government; not suspend aid and encourage the process of political and economic reforms. The EC did not immediately sense the danger of an explosion of the virulent ethnic nationalism and the determination of Milošević to create the Greater Serbia and of the breakaway republics to gain independence.

After Slovenia's declaration of independence, a division emerged within the EC, between Germany (and Austria) – in favour of recognition of the new

Mitteleuropean State, formerly part of the Austro-Hungarian empire, open to trade with the German area – and other Member States, opposed to it for fear of the refugee flow, the secessionist contagion within them (especially in the United Kingdom, France, Spain) and in the USSR, the expansion of united Germany's influence in the Balkans, and the formation of a new area of instability. The European countries were split between supporters of territorial integrity, and consequently of the federal government as a stabilizing factor in the region, and the supporters of the principle of self-determination. The division among the Member States made it difficult to develop a common European policy and an effective solution to the crisis.

With the worsening of the situation and the display of the breakaway republics' determination in pursuing secession and the inability of the federal government to find a solution, it became apparent that the EC had to take on the problem. The President of the Council of Foreign Affairs, Jacques Poos, said optimistically in May 1991: 'This is the hour of Europe. It is not the hour of the Americans' an assertion which was met by a wide consensus from international diplomacy and the US itself.

The failure of the EC

The reality was quite different. The crisis was resolved after four years and with the political and military intervention of other players: the United Nations, the USA, NATO, the USSR, the Contact Group, who all ended up marginalizing the EC.

The various initiatives taken by the EC since mid-1991 did not succeed in saving the territorial integrity of Yugoslavia nor did they prevent the ethnic cleansing. On the contrary these initiatives showed:

- the EC's inability to adequately analyse the crisis, to understand how deeply the separatist will was rooted and how delusive the federal government's role as stabilizer was;
- the shallowness of certain decisions, such as the embargo of arms sales to all the former Yugoslav republics, which in fact favoured the federal army which had recently been received up-to-date equipment from Russia: a decision that was taken without considering the consequences;
- the lack of an effective common policy due to internal divisions. Germany asymmetrically assigned the responsibility of the conflict, by identifying the aggressor in Serbia and the victim in the breakaway republics, who demanded the right to self-determination against the Serbian expansionism. France and the UK judged the adversaries equally responsible for the rebirth of opposing nationalisms, arising from ancestral hatreds, only temporarily frozen during the Tito government;
- the EC's inertia in the face of the ethnic cleansing, the inability to enforce the countless ceasefires and the lack of willingness to use military force;

- the inability to take decisions, which resulted in the usual declaratory diplomacy and postponement of decisions, as in the case of the three-month freeze on the recognition of the independence of the breakaway republics.

The European economic giant once again proved to be politically, diplomatically and militarily weak.

The crisis showed that the EC did not have an effective foreign and security policy; hence the emergence of the negative consequences deriving from the decision, taken after the fall of the European Defence Community in 1954, to further develop the economic integration, while delegating defence to NATO, and then to the US. When the Yugoslav crisis broke out, the EC found itself devoid of political and military tools and experienced staff capable of managing it effectively. Member States were divided by conflicting interests and lacked a shared political will. Failing to set up a European military intervention force, the EC lost the opportunity to use the Yugoslav crisis to strengthen integration in security and defence. The crisis also brought about a change in the power relations within the EC. Germany had imposed the recognition of the breakaway republics; France and the United Kingdom could only take note of the hegemonic role that unified Germany was acquiring.

Rhetoric and illusions in the EP speeches

The EP dedicated great attention to the Yugoslav crisis; since 1991 the issue was addressed in almost all sessions with particularly heated debates. The crisis happened unexpectedly both for Members of the European Parliament (MEPs) and for the Community institutions. In 1989–1990 probably no MEP imagined that peace in Europe was in danger and that Yugoslavia was on the brink of civil war. At the beginning of the crisis, it was common belief that the problem was a matter to be solved on the spot, as it was later common admission that the gravity of the problem had been perceived too late, when the crisis had become international and had taken worrisome proportions. The speeches were focused in particular on the right to self-determination, on the recognition of the breakaway republics, on the desirability of a dismemberment, on the suspension of EC aid, on sanctions and on the role of the EC.

The principle of self-determination and recognition of breakaway republics were closely related issues as the legitimacy of the latter was based on the application of the principle. The debate fired up starting from 1991, when the prospect of the dismemberment of Yugoslavia became clear, and a contradiction emerged in some MEP speeches between the acceptance of the principle of self-determination and rejection of the recognition of the republics' independence. Although in some cases concerns about the application of self-determination did surface, no one was opposed to the principle, because it was considered a fundamental element of freedom of the people (and sure enough reference was made to Wilson's *Fourteen Points*). Regarding the recognition of the breakaway republics, instead, at first there was a rift between the left groups (generally against) and the right groups (generally in favour). The contradiction between the acceptance of self-determination and rejection of secession could have been overcome, as we will see in the next section, by proposing self-government, to which no one, however, made any reference. The division between the right- and left-wing parliamentary groups, however, subsided with the worsening of the crisis, when all the groups agreed not only on the right to self-determination, but also on the recognition of the breakaway republics, as long as the secession were decided at the negotiating table and not with weapons.

The Socialist Group (S), while endorsing the principle of self-determination and the reasons of the breakaway republics, was concerned about the consequences of secession, which could reach the point of breakup for Yugoslavia that was considered a stabilizing factor in a delicate area of Europe. The feared dangers were instability, virulence of nationalism, widening of the conflict, violent changes of borders, risks for the rights of minorities and separatist contagion both in neighbouring countries and within the EC. The Socialist Group opted for the unity of the country and for the beginning of the democratization process.

The stronger opposition to the recognition of the breakaway republics came from the far left, particularly the Left Unity Group (CG),[2] which was very ideological in its speeches, and denounced foreign interference aimed at causing the dismemberment of Yugoslavia. It wondered whether the obsession with independence was simply due to causes typically endogenous of the Balkans, or whether, on the contrary, it was encouraged by certain EC countries in order to expand their political, strategic and economic influence. The Greek MEP Dimitrios Dessylas, after defining self-determination a 'sacred right of the peoples of Yugoslavia', denounced in July 1991:

> the demagoguery of fascist circles in Slovenia and Croatia and elsewhere; the forces that served the Third Reich so willingly and will serve the emerging Fourth Reich; the plans of the ruling circles in Germany for a German EC, for a German Europe from the Adriatic to the Baltic States which posed a serious danger for the peoples of Europe including the Germans themselves; Bush's machinations for a post-cold war new order in the Balkans dictated by America; imperialistic rivalries between the USA and Germany and between Germany and Italy over economic and political and military control and hegemony in the Balkans; the smuggling of weapons into Slovenia and Croatia by the USA, Italy and Germany.[3]

The reference to American imperial machinations sounded rather curious, and ideological, given the initial American disengagement from Balkan affairs; the hour of Europe had been well received by the US, who were inclined to leave to the Europeans the task of untangling the Balkan quagmire. They decided to intervene only after Europe's failure. The fear of a German Europe had deep roots (it had been evoked by Sartre in 1977, with an article in the 10 February edition of *Le Monde* against the German-American Europe of capital) and had been rekindled by the recent reunification, which had awakened in many countries, especially France and the UK, ancestral fears of the return of hegemonic ambitions. On the subject of pressure from EC countries interested in the dismemberment as an opportunity to expand their influence, some MEPs of the Socialist Group and the European Unitarian Left (GUE) Group also intervened, albeit with more muted tones than the CG's and without specifically mentioning Germany. The fear of a Fourth Reich extending from the Baltic to the Adriatic, so blatantly evoked by the Greek MEP, was cleverly exploited by the Serbian propaganda.

In conclusion, the CG Group, while recognizing the inalienable right to self-determination, accused certain EC countries of having aggravated the tensions and nationalistic spirit to favour special interests.

The GUE Group took an intermediate position between that of the Socialist and the CG Groups. The preference was for the maintenance of some form of Yugoslav unity, but its dissolution was judged unavoidable. The GUE Group was in favour of the principle of self-determination, but it should not translate into the creation of homogeneous national microstates based on the expulsion of minorities. Contemporaneously to the recognition of the republics' sovereignty, it was necessary that the Yugoslav peoples find a new constitutional arrangement which would safeguard the independence of the republics, democracy, the rights of minorities and the maintenance of some kind of union that would allow the country to present itself as an internationally single subject and the different nationalities to live together peacefully. In October 1991 the MEP Giorgio Rossetti, during one of the few problematic speeches on the principle of self-determination, posed a question that touched on the legitimacy of self-determination, without, however, drawing the consequences: who had the right to self-determination? What was the nature of the frontiers of the republics which had declared themselves independent?[4]

This position of the leftist groups coincided with the initial policy of the Council and the Commission, which were reluctant regarding a hasty recognition of Slovenia and Croatia. Both the Socialist and the GUE Groups warned that the division of the country would not occur peacefully and observed that the establishment of new small states was against the political trend taking place in Europe: they demanded that the EC strive to ensure that the republics, after the possible secession, continue to cooperate with each other.

The Socialist Group's position changed after Slovenia and Croatia's declarations of independence. It was noted that Yugoslavia no longer existed and that people who had decided to separate through democratic referendums could not be forced to remain united. The Socialist Group hoped that the separation would take place peacefully, through negotiation and in compliance with the rights of minorities, that the secessionists would try to maintain the unity of the market and a minimum of political cooperation and that the EC would facilitate the establishment of new common institutional structures. However, within the Socialist Group there still remained critical voices on self-determination. The Greek MEP Paraskevas Avgerinos, in May 1992, complained that the EC rushed headlong into recognising republics which declared independence without first solving institutional problems, without reaching agreements with the interested parties, without ensuring minority rights, without examining whether the newly independent states could survive, without looking into the question of economic cooperation between them.

Avgerinos lastly put forward an embarrassing and disquieting question: to what extent would the recognitions of independence be pushed? Once the fragmentation in the Balkans was recognized, what would the EC respond to similar requests from the minorities of Member States?[5]

Even the speeches of the European People's Party (PPE) group dealt extensively with self-determination. The PPE recognized that Yugoslavia had been a stabilizing factor in the Balkans and did not hide its worries regarding its dismemberment; it judged the independence declarations, approved without assessing the consequences, as hasty. However, the PPE acknowledged that international democracy meant self-determination. The independence of Slovenia, Croatia, as well as Bosnia and Macedonia, had to be recognized because it had freely been decided by their peoples. Their recognition as sovereign states would allow the internationalization of the conflict, switching it from civil war to a war between states, and hence the achievement of a better protection of the victims by the international community. Self-determination, however, did not have to mean disintegration, nationalism, ethnocentrism, but growth of new democratic nations, which would push forms of economic integration and political union, following the example of European integration itself. Even within the PPE voices rose to criticize the right to self-determination. The British MEP Derek Prag, in June 1992, declared that

> the war had been caused by the wrong principle on which the EC got itself hooked, the principle of self-determination, without any clear definition of what self-determination was to be, how big were the units to be, who was to be entitled to self-determination.

At the same time, however, he complained that the EC had based the self-determination on the frontiers established by the Croatian Tito in 1945 with the intention of weakening the Serbs, the largest ethnic group. Those borders were no longer valid because 'you could not force onto people frontiers that they did not want and to live in a State that they did not want to live in'; so it was necessary to change the boundaries.[6]

The Green Group (V) was strongly in favour of self-determination, considered as a value to be supported all over Europe, including the Western part (Basques, Scots, etc.). Its assertion, however, should not lead to ethnic incompatibility, separations, boundary changes or lead to the Balkanization of Europe. The EC should promote those democratic reforms that implied respect for minority rights in the prospect of a multinational Yugoslavia included in Europe.

Even the Liberal and Democratic Reformist (LDR) Group declared itself in favour of immediate recognition of the republics, while hoping they would maintain some form of relationship, because some tasks were better fulfilled by large units rather than by fragmented States. In his long speech in October 1991, Alain Lamassoure complained that the EC still endorsed the unity of Yugoslavia, when Slovenia and Croatia had already severed ties with the federation and the Federal President, Stjepan Mesić, had confessed that the state he was leading no longer existed. It was wrong to maintain an attitude of neutrality when it was clear, by now, who the aggressor and the victims were:

> the EC claimed it was pitting Right against might; three months on, the unpunished aggressor had achieved most of his military objectives; worse, he was invited to the negotiating table on the same footing as his victims. This was another blatant Munich.

For Lamassoure recognition of the independence of Slovenia and Croatia was the only way of obtaining the application of chapter VII of the UN Charter from the Security Council.[7]

The Greek MEP Dimitrios Nianias repeatedly spoke for the European Democratic Alliance (RDE)[8] Group in favour of maintaining the unity of Yugoslavia. The main objective of his speeches was Macedonia, whose declaration of independence was unacceptable to the Greeks. The country was described as the totalitarian state of Skopje, a secessionist force that used the name Macedonia, but there was no Macedonian nation; according to Nianias, independence had been proclaimed following a referendum that was a parody because none of the rules of democratic elections had been followed.[9]

A part of the European Democratic (ED) Group[10] and the Technical Group of the European Right (DR, whose speeches were characterized by a pronounced anti-communist ideological approach) were in favour of the recognition, because they were convinced that Yugoslavia was a historical error and that the democratically elected authorities in the republics had the right to change the constitutional order. The DR Group clearly saw the anti-communist will of the breakaway republics manifested in the independence referendums, the need to modify the boundaries, arbitrarily established by Tito, in order to bring ethnic factors and geo-politics into line, and the will of the Slovene and Croat peoples to become independent partners in a future Europe of nations.[11]

Even The Rainbow Group (ARC), a regionalist group, and the Non-attached (NI) were in favour of the recognition of the breakaway republics and the right to self-determination for all peoples, including those oppressed within the EC (Irish, Basque, Corsican, etc.). According to NI the ambition of a people's and national identity was making its way everywhere and it was necessary to associate the Europe of regions to the Europe of nations.[12]

In the parliamentary groups there was widespread belief that the EC bore some responsibility for the outbreak of the conflict because of the uncertainty shown in the management of the crisis, due to concerns about the possible repercussions on separatist movements within some Member States and about the rifts inside the EC itself. The level of responsibility held against the Commission and the Council, which were in favour of preserving Yugoslav unity, depended on the position that the group had adopted on self-determination. The Socialist Group supported the Community policy in principle, judging the efforts made to reach a negotiated settlement positively. This did not in any case prevent them from observing the limitations – notably an underestimation, especially at the beginning, of the gravity of the crisis, the delay in taking the initiatives and the stubborn propensity to legitimize the federal central power in the illusion that it might represent an element of stability. Even for the GUE Group it was necessary to support the community effort undertaken with The Hague Peace Conference, which opened in September 1991 and was chaired by Lord Carrington.

Expressions of appreciation for the mediation efforts of the EC, for the troika's efforts for trying to save the integrity of the federation, and for convening the Peace Conference also came from the ED Group.[13]

Decidedly critical of Community action was the CG group, which accused the EC of having contributed to the dissolution of a stabilizing factor like the Yugoslav federation, of not admitting that the responsibility for the crisis fell on both sides, and of recognizing too hastily the independence of the breakaway republics.

The PPE, the Green Group, and the right-wing groups in general did not spare criticism of the work of the Commission and Council, which they blamed on the one hand for the waiting and neutral attitude towards the democratic republics, and the nationalist and authoritarian Serbia on the other, for the delay in recognizing the dissolution of the country, for the failure of the Brioni Agreement (the first attempt of the EC to settle the crisis in July 1991) and the Peace Conference, for the failure to swiftly recognize the right to self-determination, and for the defence of the Yugoslav federation, a factor that had provided an inadvertent cover for the Serbian aggression. The PPE Group called on the EC to be more active, not only to deliver statements which were never followed by facts, thus losing credibility.

Particularly harsh were the speeches of Marco Pannella (NI) in October 1991 and April 1992. Pannella accused the EP itself of expressing

> every so often good intentions for the future, but then regularly refrained from any serious initiative thanks to party and clan solidarity, to the depreciation of ideals, to the feelings of solidarity with Internationals, which were all accomplices of the powers, starting with the Social-Democratic International.

In front of the attitude of the Serbs and the federal army violence, the EC's policy of remaining neutral between the two sides, the Munich-style policy, was a deranged policy of complicity, which created counterproductive repercussions in other geographical areas.[14]

The debate on the Yugoslav crisis unfolded simultaneously with the negotiations and ratification of the Maastricht Treaty, which was not mentioned in the speeches on Yugoslavia. However, the failure of the EC first to prevent and then to put out the Balkan fires led some MEPs to a critical re-examination of the Community's powerlessness and to the appeal for the strengthening of its institutional structures. The Socialist, Green, PPE and LDR Groups observed that the EC, a major economic power, lacked political unity and adequate policy instruments in foreign and security policy; so its initiatives met great difficulties. The Spanish Socialist MEP Manuel Medina Ortega clearly declared, in May 1992, that the EC could not carry out the tasks that it was expected to, simply because it did not have the necessary powers; in the face of crisis, the Commission and the Council were powerless.[15]

These speeches, however, had no effect on the Maastricht Treaty, which despite the improvements in the area of foreign policy and security did not put the EC in a position to speak with a single and effective voice on the international scene.

The contradictions of the principle of self-determination and the powerlessness of the EC

A vast consensus had therefore collected around the principle of self-determination, sanctioned by the March 1991 resolution, thanks to the role played by the MEP Otto von Habsburg (PPE), while many European governments, the Commission and the Council were still insisting on Yugoslavia's integrity. The right to self-determination was considered by the EP a vital element of democracy. But no critical reflection was made on the principle, except for the occasional speech by some MEPs about the ownership of this right: a reflection that would have been useful to extricate a dramatic situation like the Yugoslav one. Self-determination, whose objective is the protection of national identity, is based on the coincidence of State and nation: to every nation must correspond an independent State. The ultimate consequence is the mono-ethnic state. Humanity, however, is not separated into national groups, but in any area there is a mixture of ethnic, linguistic, and religious groups. The aberrant conclusion is that homogeneity can only be achieved with ethnic cleansing.

Some MEPs wondered who had the ownership of self-determination; an essential question, because the outcome of a possible referendum on the subject depends on this identification. But also the definition of nation is controversial. The borders of states are not natural (nature has no boundaries), but historically defined (usually after a war on the basis of strategic needs). If self-determination applies to individuals residing within a certain territory, why not apply it to the minorities living within that same territory? If the Croats have the right to self-determination, why not also include minorities living in Croatia (Serbs, Bosnians, Italians, Hungarians etc.)? And so on, up to where? Can you imagine a world fragmented into innumerable and infinitesimal mono-ethnic microstates? Let's not also forget the inconsistency of the principle of self-determination, invoked in certain cases, but denied in others (for example, the territorial integrity of Turkey prevails on the self-determination of the Kurds).

Finally, fragmentation is contradictory with the growing interdependence that at present characterizes human relations and economic and political organization. The right to self-determination therefore ends up exerting a regressive function, disintegrating rather than integrating.

More than self-determination, it would be useful to recall the concept of self-government as a suitable principle to solve the problems of coexistence between different groups, a democratic principle that can be practised within a state that is multi-ethnical and decentralized on the basis of the principle of subsidiarity.

Avoiding the dissolution of Yugoslavia and the civil war would have required prompt and effective action by the EC at a political level (facilitating the implementation of self-government instead of self-determination) and at an economic level (massive financial aid to tackle the economic crisis in the country). This calls into question the role played by the EC in the Yugoslav crisis. Many speeches in the EP deplored the Community's shortcomings, but knew better than to indicate the causes. The push for nationalism and disintegration that emerged after 1989 derived from the power vacuum left by the dissolution of the communist bloc and the USSR. This power vacuum was not filled by the EC, which had reached an advanced economic integration, but without political institutions capable of allowing it to carry out a proper foreign policy. So the EC, with its economic development, exerted a strong pull on non-member European countries, but without having the political instruments to adequately respond to their problems. Yugoslavia should immediately have been offered the assurance of accession to the EC in a short time, subject to achieving specific objectives and pinpointed by well-defined stages, and a plan to accompany it in the process of economic conversion, democratization and preservation of unity of the State, relying on the democratic forces in Ljubljana, Zagreb and Belgrade. With Balkan Europe, the EC did not enter into any agreement similar to the Europe Agreements signed with the Eastern European countries since 1991 to pave the way for their accession. Only after the Kosovo war did the EC finally initiate a policy of stabilization and pre-accession, first with the Stability Pact and later with the Stabilisation and Association Process, which defines financial assistance programmes and binding obligations in the field of political, economic and human rights reforms, modelled after the Europe Agreements, to join the EC.

Without the prospect of certain accession, the reform process in Yugoslavia was blocked by authoritarian and conservative forces. This in turn triggered the separatist process in Slovenia and Croatia (the most developed republics), who saw the secession as the only way, on one side, to hook up with Europe, particularly Germany, Austria and Italy with whom they had strong trade links, and, on the other, to end the flow of resources to the federal capital and the less developed republics. To legitimize secession, Slovenia and Croatia exacerbated ethnic-regional nationalism, in turn reinforcing the ambitions for a Greater Serbia in Belgrade, thus triggering the downward spiral of opposing nationalisms. Without denying the serious Serbian responsibility in the Yugoslav tragedy, it must be remembered that Slovenia and Croatia's separatism found its drive in nationalism and in the rejection of solidarity with the less developed regions, not in opposition to the authoritarian and communist-nationalist regime of Milošević, as alleged in the interventions of the right-wing parliamentary groups. Such a regime could have best been fought by a coalition of all democratic forces in Yugoslavia, rather than by secession and the ensuing civil war. And on this fact the EC carries a part of the responsibility which is not clearly highlighted in the debates in the EP, which were all focused on the uncritical support of the right to self-determination as a resolving element of the crisis.

The lack of a single European strategy on the Balkans allowed each Member State to pursue its own plans and deepened the division within the EC. Germany pursued its plan on recognition of independence of the breakaway republics, fuelling the other states' fears of its Balkan policy. Whoever complained within the EP about the German (real or alleged) hegemonic ambitions should also have asked themselves why Germany could pursue a policy independent from EC.

In the face of the inability of politics and diplomacy to prevent ethnic cleansing, the use of force seemed inevitable. The EC showed an unwillingness to use force, as was condemned in some speeches in the EP. The reason that the EC did not resort to the use of force was expressed in October 1991 by Piet Dankert, President of European Political Cooperation, with disarming clarity: the recognition of the republics by the EC in no way ensures greater security for the people in Croatia, in Bosnia or in other regions of the former Yugoslavia for the simple reason that we do not have the right tools.[16] The Community powerlessness was confirmed by João de Deus Pinheiro, President-in-Office of the Council, in May 1992:

> The Community does not in fact have the necessary instruments and I am the first to admit it. After the Gulf War we found that we did not have the basic elements of security and defence.... The only thing we did not do was intervene militarily. And let us say it here and now: we are not prepared to do so.[17]

Upon the outbreak of the Yugoslav crisis, the EC found itself unprepared to deal with it, lacking a foreign and security policy, but with an evanescent European Political Cooperation. The Community powerlessness, acknowledged at the highest European levels, found no response in the Maastricht Treaty. The foreign and security policy continued to be conditioned by the unanimity required for decisions. As morally authoritative as they were, European actions continued to have little effect on the political level, not to mention on the military. Again, it would have been useful to express greater awareness, depth of analysis, a proactive approach in speeches at the EP, but they were however limited to a generic appeal to strengthen the capacity of action of EC. The Yugoslav crisis should have pushed the member States to provide the EC with the political tools to enable it to play in the international arena, and used the democratic means of dialogue and negotiation to resolve disputes. The opportunity was lost.

In conclusion, the Nation-State culture exerted a strong conditioning on the debate about the Yugoslav crisis. The MEPs found no other option but to resort to the principle of self-determination and did not clearly address the fundamental issue of the EC's inability to act on the international level, namely the lack of a single foreign, security and defence policy. A single policy in this area would in fact require a transfer of sovereignty to the EC that the MEPs, tied to the Nation-State culture, did not intend to consider.

The political groups of the European Parliament and the crisis in Bosnia-Herzegovina

The EU and the management of the crisis in Bosnia-Herzegovina

The war in Bosnia-Herzegovina, which broke out on 6 April 1992, has been defined as the worst crisis in Europe since the Second World War, and it struck global consciousness more than any other war in the 1990s. Moreover, it produced a huge international effort involving major countries and many international organizations, inducing the redefinition of their roles and positions in the post-Cold War era.

The crisis was the extension of the conflicts in Slovenia and Croatia (which would continue with the war in Kosovo in 1999), reiterating their causes and underlying logic. Therefore, it did not come as unexpected, and it should not have caught the EC unprepared. Instead the Community showed its limits just as in previous months, causing increasing irritation, frustration, discouragement and even ridicule in political circles and among the European and non-European observers. However, the complexity and implications of the war in Bosnia-Herzegovina had no equal in the earlier post-Cold War crises (Iraq–Kuwait, or even the previous stages of the Yugoslav crisis), as it was the archetype of a new kind of war that challenged the traditional beliefs of the international community about the nature of war and the maintaining of peace and security (Kaldor 2013). So, in addition to its usual problems of cohesion, the EC also faced the challenge of a paradigmatic shift of its external action that would then lead to the development of specific tools and approaches in the management of crises.

Among the republics of former Yugoslavia, Bosnia-Herzegovina was the most diverse in terms of ethnicity, with a population that in 1991 was made up mostly of Muslims (43.7 per cent), Orthodox Serbs (31.4 per cent) and Catholic Croats (17.3 per cent). About one quarter of the people lived in mixed marriages, and in the urban areas there was a flourishing secular and pluralist culture that made the country one of the peaceful coexistence models in Europe.

At the root of the conflict was the political attempt of the Bosnian Serbs and Croats to complete the establishment of ethnically homogeneous territories that could become part of Serbia and Croatia from which they received support, and split the mixed area of Bosnia-Herzegovina into a Serbian part and a Croatian part. In contrast, the Bosnian government, controlled by the Muslims, had the objective of maintaining the territorial integrity of the country, where they were the majority. Ethnic nationalism, that everyone in the EC (except the radical right political groups in the EP) considered the trigger of the conflict, was actually seconded by the approach of the Europeans who, after Slovenia and Croatia's recognition, also recognized Bosnia (15 October 1991) on the basis of an undefined principle of self-determination, the same principle with which the war leaders' rhetoric and language were imbued.

The response of the Europeans, who initially had the responsibility of managing the crisis, suffered at least three major limitations: (1) the lack of preparation in interpreting a war that was not a clash between states, but a transnational conflict in which the ethnic cleansing and violence against the civilian population were both the instrument and the main objective; (2) the institutional inadequacy of the EC in the area of foreign policy, despite the innovations of the Maastricht Treaty; (3) the lack of adequate military capabilities for crisis management. In these conditions, the EC, rather than acting immediately for the protection of civilians, using force if necessary (possibly making use of organizations such as WEU, UN and CSCE), put in place a multi-faced strategy: statements of condemnation or support for one side or the other (declaratory foreign policy); the guarantee of humanitarian aid to Bosnia, to refugees and displaced persons, managed directly by the European Commission; the dispatch of observers to monitor the evolution of events and the respect of the agreements reached; the attempt, by the European Political Cooperation (EPC) before and the EU after, to manage the crisis diplomatically, even by promoting peace tables and conferences; the threat or the imposition of sanctions to induce the warring forces to sit down at the negotiating table.

The weakness of this strategy became evident very soon, up to the point of damaging the EU's legitimacy as an international player. Indeed, the excessive use of statements, firm condemnations or threats, with no subsequent actions, damaged its credibility; the increased allocation of resources for humanitarian aid offered relief to recipients, but was affected by the inability to ensure that such aid would reach its destination and not be 'taxed' or diverted by the warring parties; the EC/EU observers played an important role, but the impossibility of ensuring security on the field exposed them to occasional, even deadly, attacks; the increasingly strict sanctions were violated with impunity by several European countries (Greece in particular). Meanwhile the arms embargo harmed Serbia just a little, as it had inherited the Yugoslav army, but Bosnian Muslims very much, as they suffered for the Croatian and Serbian actions.

As for diplomatic initiatives, several peace plans were proposed over time and subject to negotiations: first by Lord Carrington[18] (March 1992), who proposed the division of Bosnia into three parts; then by Cyrus Vance and David Owen (January 1993),[19] who called for its division into ten autonomous cantons, nine of which were based on the predominance of one of the different ethnic groups; and finally, that promoted by the US envoy in Yugoslavia, Richard Holbrooke, and accepted by the parties with the Dayton agreements (October 1995), which provided for a solution that was not very different from Carrington's plan.

These instruments, aimed at bringing the war to an end as soon as possible by finding a compromise between the various leaders, had the shortcoming of assigning to these the standing of representatives of the Bosnian population and of basing the search for an agreement on the territorial division along ethnic lines. Given the inability of the EC/EU and the international community to impose the acceptance of these plans, and to stop the aggressive intentions of the warring parties, these divisions could only reflect the balance of power developed on the field. According to some, the Dayton agreements were signed because the ethnic cleansing plans at this point had already been accomplished (Hassner 1995).

The ineffectiveness of the tools and approaches used was in addition to the traditional difficulties the Europeans experienced in reaching common positions, due not only to the priority granted to national interests, but also to the unanimity required in the decision-making processes of the EPC/CFSP. This at times prevented the EC/EU from taking decisions, and most of the time it only allowed for belated and weak decisions dictated by the lowest common denominator. These structural difficulties legitimized some countries in breaking forward, undermining the group solidarity. French President Mitterrand, for example, on 28 June 1992, unilaterally made a surprise visit to Sarajevo, and only consulted, at short notice, the Portuguese and German Prime Ministers, Mario Soares and Helmut Kohl. He justified his action by stating that 'international institutions are very slow monuments to move. Therefore, I believe in the symbolic force of acts' (quoted in Lucarelli 2000, 34). Ultimately, the same problems, together with the lack of a single and stable reference figure for the EC/EU[20] led the US to prefer a direct relationship with a restricted number of European countries rather than with the EC. This was the case of the 'Contact Group', requested by Washington in April 1994 and consisting of France, Germany and the UK, USA and Russia.

The ineffectiveness of the EC/EU action, the worsening of the fighting and the brutal human rights violations against the civilian population, brought the Europeans first to seek a burden-sharing with the United Nations, both in political (replacement of Lord Carrington with Cyrus Vance and David Owen) and military (UNPROFOR peacekeeping operation) terms. Then, once they realized that the UN action was completely inadequate, they relied on NATO air strikes and on the US, which led to the Dayton agreements in October 1995 but deprived the EU of any autonomy and de facto marginalised it from the political process, by involving only a few member countries in the management of the crisis.

'It's the hour of the US, not of Europeans', was the epilogue of the crisis in Bosnia-Herzegovina.

The debates at the European Parliament on the crisis in Bosnia-Herzegovina: general characteristics

The political groups had already seen the signs of war in Bosnia-Herzegovina before the recognition of Slovenia and Croatia, and the way they read the events was in line with their interpretation of the broader Yugoslav crisis. Each one, from its perspective, warned 'the House', the public opinion and the states that if the mechanisms of the previous months were not stopped the crisis would spread to Bosnia-Herzegovina and then to Macedonia and Kosovo. So, when the war broke out, its severity and risks for the region, for Europe and for the EC – that was in the middle of the Maastricht Treaty ratification process – were immediately clear. Not surprisingly, for more than four years, until the Dayton agreements, the conflict was discussed and dealt with in almost all EP sessions, with regular reports by the Presidency of the Council and by the Commission, followed closely by debates in the plenary and by presentations of resolutions by one or more political groups. Then, after discussions, these generally gave rise to compromise resolutions common at least to the major groups (Socialists, EPP, LDR and Greens, often joined by RDE) with the clear and explicit[21] objective of maximizing the impact of the EP on the external environment (public and third party actors) and the Council.[22] From the debates on the crisis in Bosnia, it is clear that the discourse dynamics developed on two different and interconnected levels: on one side the dialectic between the groups and within them, on the other side the sometimes fired-up confrontation with the Council, the main player within the EPC/CFSP. This phenomenon is typical of an institutional system in which the EP has the weakest position, and is thus brought to develop a diverse rhetoric on the substance of the issues, but a convergent rhetoric (we might say, of frustration) of the groups towards the Council, aiming to claim a greater role in foreign policy decision-making, proportionate to its democratic legitimacy (see further, 'The "guilt" and the debates on the military solution of the conflict', below).

The debates on the political solution of the conflict: the inevitable partition?

In the initial phase of the conflict, the expectations of a European-led political solution were relatively high and the debates mainly concerned how this could be achieved, the players to be involved and the quality of the final outcome. The different positions within the EP were closely connected with the interpretation of the war and its causes. The outbreak of war had in fact taken place concurrently with the recognition of Bosnia-Herzegovina as an independent state by the Europeans. While on the intergovernmental side this decision had been taken without the vivid confrontations which occurred in the cases of Slovenia and Croatia, on the parliamentary side, on the contrary, this wasn't the case.

For the DR radical right-wing group, the causes of the Bosnian crisis were to be found on the one hand in the inevitability of the collapse of an artificial entity like the Yugoslav communist state and, on the other hand, in the federalist ideology pervading the EC, that in their view would have induced it to support the Yugoslav integrity preventing the self-determination process and encouraging the chauvinistic imperialism typical of Serbian communism and the invasion of Croatia and Bosnia by Belgrade.[23] The tragedy in Bosnia was the demonstration that 'attempting to build utopian, multi-ethnic societies is a fatal mistake',[24] and a future of this kind for the country would be neither desirable nor possible. While condemning war, the group sponsored, rather, its partition into ethnically homogeneous territories.

RDE's position was different. This group, while not appearing to be a supporter of multiculturalism, was firmly opposed to the disintegration of the states (Bosnia, in particular) in favour of unsustainable statelets, which would fight among themselves and within which there would be nationalities and minorities fighting each other, in the grip of adventurers, demagogues of the nationalistic type, and ambitious career soldiers.[25] Bosnia's unity would have to be preserved, therefore, in the peace negotiations.

The EPP, contrary to RDE, was very much in favour of Bosnia's recognition, since it had determined itself through a referendum on inter-ethnic bases,[26] but was against its territorial partition along ethnic lines because Bosnian society was mixed, multi-cultural and multi-ethnic, and in all municipalities of the country there were significant minorities.[27] There were exceptions within the group, however: the British Conservative Derek Prag, for example, noted how it was natural for Bosnian Serbs and Croats to want to live in Serbia and Croatia, and one could not expect to force people to live within established and immutable boundaries. He therefore proposed the establishment of a frontier commission (albeit without specifying in what institutional context) to resolve the issue of minorities, of borders, of human rights and avoid unsustainable situations in the region.[28]

The leftist groups, on the contrary, criticized the recognition believing that it would cause instability and further fragmentation within Bosnia and the region. The Socialist group challenged the recognition of Bosnia because, while it had taken place on the basis of a referendum requested by the EC, it had been hastily granted by the Europeans, without first creating the political conditions to stabilize the country: 'We were told to rush into recognition of Bosnia in order to avert civil war. [...] Yet by recognising it without preparing for peace a terrible civil war broke out'.[29]

Even more radical – and ideologically characterized – were the positions of the groups more to the left of the Socialists, like CG. It considered the recognition of Bosnia a tool of Western imperialism to encourage the fragmentation of the region into statelets functional to political, economic and military influence of this or that state, and harbingers of further conflict.[30]

These general considerations were decisive in the positions taken by the groups on the solution of the crisis. Everyone, at least in the early stages of the conflict, put trust in a political solution. However, the approach adopted by the negotiators – previously Lord Carrington, then Vance and Owen – and endorsed by the Council gradually stimulated the opposition of most of the groups. David Owen, nominated by the EC itself, actually had to resign because of the EP's pressure, accused of having taken a position that was favourable to the Bosnian Serbs and awarded their territorial conquests.[31] The speeches of the majority of MEPs in the EP (except the DR group) expressed strong criticism against the structure of the negotiations that they called unfair, because the acceptance of the territorial division between the parties along ethnic lines as the only possible solution, legitimized the *fait accompli* and the logic of 'might makes right', encouraged the continuation of ethnic cleansing and destroyed ethnic coexistence in Bosnia-Herzegovina.[32] The weak point of these speeches was, however, the lack of alternative proposals. The exception were the Greens, who right from the beginning had shown themselves to be the most coherent group involved in the battle against any ethnic connotation of the future Bosnian arrangement. Led by the charismatic South Tyrolean Alexander Langer,[33] who imparted the group with a markedly multi-ethnic orientation (Grimaldi 2005), they expressed a rhetoric based on a 'bottom-up' logic: the peace process, rather than relying on the leadership of the war criminals driving the warring parties, would have to involve civil society and all the democratic forces in Bosnia, in particular those sectors – be they Serb, Croat or Muslims – in favour of a multi-cultural, multi-ethnic, peaceful Bosnia-Herzegovina, that could help a reconciliation from below.[34]

The increasingly obvious failure of the diplomatic initiatives seemed to confirm these criticisms, which, however, softened in the final stages of the conflict, when the final solution led by the US became real and inevitable, although inspired by criteria that were not any different from the past.

The 'guilt' and the debates on the military solution of the conflict

As months and years passed by, featuring a persistent fruitlessness of negotiations and a worsening of violence especially by the Serbs, the EP matured what we might call 'the rhetoric of frustration and guilt'. The MEPs felt a general 'sense of guilt' regarding the Bosnian population, both as members of a Community that could not bear up to its responsibility and put an end to the conflict, and as members of a body that could not affect the Council adequately.[35] Most of the MEPs felt it a duty to open up their speeches with a 'mea culpa' that, in a repetitive and almost sickening way, was regularly repeated until the end of the conflict:

> I truly believe that we in this Parliament are guilty today of well-intentioned complacency and European governments are guilty of total hypocrisy, in that they do not see their national interests served by involving themselves any further in halting the bloodbath and slaughter of innocent women and children in former Yugoslavia. [...] How, Madam President, will we explain this to our grandchildren when they ask: 'What did you do to stop the massacre of the Bosnian Muslims?'[36]

At the same time, the rhetoric of frustration caused increasing friction with the Presidencies of the Council. Several MEPs challenged the Council's weak or damaging policy choices, and accused it of not appropriately taking into account the EP and its positions, up to the point of repeatedly summoning the attention of the distracted President-in-Office in the plenary.[37] On the other side, the Council deplored the EP for never producing concrete proposals and alternatives.[38]

Simultaneously, the debate began to consider the possibility of the use of coercive force to protect civilians, stop the violence of Croatian and Serbs against Muslims and force the parties to sit down seriously at the negotiations table. For many MEPs, military intervention would permit a resolution not only of the conflict, but their own sense of guilt and frustration too. The matter, however, was particularly divisive and even the positions of those in favour (DR, EPP, LDR, Greens) were quite varied and their discourses rather vague and confused: about the authority delegated to use force (EC, CSCE, UN, WEU, NATO); the possible methods of its use (strengthened peacekeeping, UN contingent self-defence, air strikes or intervention by NATO ground troops) and objectives (protection of human rights of civilians, protection of humanitarian convoys or peacekeepers themselves, enforcement of no-fly zones, 'defeat' of the Serbian front equated to an aggressor army, enforcement of peace plans).

After arranging an arms embargo on Yugoslavia, upon the EC's request, in February 1992, the UN Security Council had decided (Res. No. 743) on the deployment in the region of UNPROFOR, the second largest UN peacekeeping force ever authorized. UNPROFOR was sent to Bosnia-Herzegovina in June 1992, and its task was not peace-making, but surveillance and support to humanitarian aid convoys, without giving the blue helmets even a chance to respond to fire with fire. The embargo was placed under the supervision (but not enforcement) of a WEU-NATO mission in the Adriatic Sea. The EC, for its part, had unarmed observers on the ground to monitor the development of the situation. As early as June 1992 requests by the Bosnian government called for military intervention of the WEU, CSCE and UN (Lucarelli 2000, 33–4).

In the face of violence against civilians by the Serbs, that was beginning to target Sarajevo and many villages in Bosnia-Herzegovina, the EP found itself discussing an amendment of the EPP to a widely shared resolution proposal, which proposed a military intervention in the country. After calling for 'more UN' in the preceding months ('the European observers and the UN troops must be present anywhere they can prevent or halt conflict'),[39] Oostlander with his amendment was now calling for more EC 'to take measures, whether in the framework of the WEU or the CSCE and preferably with the consent of the United Nations, to undertake a limited military intervention to secure the airspace and the sea off Yugoslavia'. However, the amendment did not specify the concept of 'military intervention' and skirted the issue of EC's ability to use force. This position was supported by the LDR Group, which assigned its preference to the WEU, but was immediately challenged by the RDE and the Socialists, who criticized the EPP also for not subordinating the use of force to the Security Council. CG was clearly opposed (once again, ideologically) to the same amendment, because:

> War is unacceptable and if there is a force, purely European, it must have two aims: firstly, to keep the peace and, secondly, to keep the Balkans out of the grasp of America and its policies. Even then, I would not be willing to back the Oostlander amendment.[40]

In a general conceptual and terminological confusion, thus emerged the positions of the main political groups, which would be replicated and developed – but not clarified enough – in the following months and years. First, there was the confirmation of what we might call the rhetoric of 'EC first and then UN' that expressed the absolute preference for European solutions, with the leadership of the EC, and subordinately for the UN.[41] The limits of the first option were soon perceived but not adequately understood by the political forces, so that the Council, after reaffirming the unpreparedness of the EC/EU to intervene militarily, felt compelled to make clear what it could or could not do:

> It would also be appropriate if we had some idea of the difference between *peace-keeping* and *peace-making*. The Community has advocated peace-keeping, it has made itself available for peace-keeping. But it has not made itself available for peace-making. Nevertheless, there are international bodies which have the authority and the power to decide on the question of peace-making, and they are not the Community or the CSCE, but the United Nations Security Council.[42]

As for the UN, the UNPROFOR operation, after some initial successes, proved all its ineffectiveness as the Serb and Croat assaults intensified against the civilian population, the humanitarian convoys, the EC observers and even the peace-keepers themselves, who were effectively defined as 'eunuchs at the orgy' (Kaldor 2013, 61).[43] Consequently, especially in the EPP and LDR groups, the rhetoric of 'more UNPROFOR' consolidated, calling for the strengthening of the operation so that the troops could at least defend themselves, and for the creation of no-fly zones[44] that were later established but not enforced. LDR, in particular, understood the basic problem in the use of a 'light' tool such as peace-keeping in the context of these new wars:

> We can wave goodbye to the Union's foreign and security policy if we are unwilling to grant UNPROFOR a new mandate, giving it the role of a 'peace-making' force, because peace cannot be 'kept' where there is war. A new mandate would enable UNPROFOR to actively intervene to protect the so-called 'safe areas', whose lack of safety puts the Union to shame.[45]

'Peace-making' (or 'peace-enforcement'), although necessarily implying the use of military force is very different from 'war-making'. The Greens, who were basically non-violent, understood this, and according to them force should have been used only as a last resort, under the UN aegis and hence with precise limitations: not to wage war on Serbia, but to end aggression and bring the parties back to the negotiating table, to impose demilitarization and to effectively protect the humanitarian convoys.[46] This very misunderstanding seemed to be partially responsible for the Socialists' opposition to military intervention:

I hope and pray that the proposal for military intervention will come to nothing – I have no idea who favours such ideas – as these are paranoid, irresponsible notions. How can anyone suggest such a thing: make war when we should be making peace? Peace is not made through warfare, ladies and gentlemen, peace is not made through warfare...[47]

The Socialists believed instead that the only hope for resolving the conflict were the diplomatic solution and the sanctions, given that the military intervention (especially by air) would have caused further losses of human lives and the taking of UN Blue Helmets as hostages, which would then need to be liberated with ground troops, exposing the contingents to further losses.[48]

At the same time, in the eyes of many in the EP the attack on the safe areas, including Gorazde and Srebrenica, made it all the more evident that the only protection for Muslims could have come from their army, since they could not count on the international community. For this reason, the EPP and LDR repeatedly attempted to exert pressure on the Presidency of the Council to ensure that the arms embargo be withdrawn,[49] since the Bosnian Serbs still received weapons from Serbia, and the peace process needed restoration of the balance of military power between the contenders.[50] The Socialists and CG, for their part, refused even this road in the belief that only a negotiated solution was possible and acceptable.

The majority of MEPs, even those who invoked the use of force, rarely explicitly mentioned their hope of NATO involvement,[51] probably because it would have implied calling for the US' centrality. It was NATO, however, that despite delays and indecision, began the effective implementation of the no-fly zones and the restoration of the balance of power invoked by the EPP, with the establishment of a Rapid Reaction Force and air strikes to liberate cities conquered by Serbs. The NATO air strikes were therefore openly (or silently) welcomed by the political forces in favour of military intervention, even if the taking of hundreds of blue helmets as hostages by the Serbs, in retaliation for the intervention, seemed to confirm the proposition 'violence calls violence' opposed by the Socialists.

Forget and start over, as soon as possible

The growing and decisive centrality acquired by the United States in the political and military handling of the conflict caused different reactions in the EP. In general, except for the right-wing and radical leftist groups, Washington's involvement was welcomed, given the acknowledged failure of the EU, which the innovations introduced by the Maastricht Treaty had not been able to correct. The awareness was spreading that the US had succeeded where the EU (and the UN) had failed miserably.[52] Its dependence on the US fuelled the EP's will to revive the common foreign and security policy. The issue of relations with the US had always constituted a fundamental rift in Europe, both on the intergovernmental (Atlanticism vs. Europeism) and on the parliamentary front. In the case of Bosnia-Herzegovina and Yugoslavia in general, the various groups had developed very different discourses on the subject. While the EPP was rather in favour of a US involvement and called for a unity of purpose with the EU, the CG group called the US an 'imperialist player' responsible for the conflict together with 'German imperialism', while the RDE believed that Washington should be absolutely kept out of the crisis, which was a European affair;[53] the RD group remarked that the US was to blame even more than the EU because of their historical experience according to which federalism had caused a civil war 'which resulted, let us not forget, in six hundred thousand deaths'.[54] The Socialists indeed believed that the US should be 'counterbalanced' by a naturally wiser Europe,[55] and the Europeans would have to avoid applying the muscular policy typical of the 'American Rambo'.[56]

The contingent impulse to rethink the EU instruments and its relations with the US was offered on 11 November 1994 by President Clinton who, under pressure from the Republican majority in Congress, unilaterally decided to establish the US withdrawal from monitoring the embargo on the Bosnian government, in order to facilitate the Muslim resistance to the Serb–Croat aggression. The decision raised a general objection by the EP that defined it as 'unilateral' and therefore 'irresponsible'[57] and 'unfair', taken without any consideration of the country's commitments to its allies and the UN. The episode was also interpreted as a signal of the European need to finally develop autonomy from Washington, and to therefore relaunch the architecture of the EU foreign policy and rethink the relationship between the EU, WEU and NATO. It was mostly the Socialist group that felt this necessity and set out to make a contribution to this process in view of the Intergovernmental Conference that would lead to the Treaty of Amsterdam (1997).[58]

The other reaction in the EP to the leadership of the US and to the end of the war was the need to overcome a painful and unpleasant experience. The speeches in the plenary immediately after the Dayton agreements indeed clearly expressed the wish that the EU look beyond the proven limits and regain a prominent role, dedicating itself to something that it could do far better than the US: rebuild.[59]

After a bad nightmare and a sigh of relief, it was necessary to turn the page and start again.[60]

Conclusions

The parliamentary debates on the outbreak of the Yugoslav crisis and the war in Bosnia-Herzegovina have shown that:

1   The analysis of the political phenomena by MEPs, with some exceptions, did not prove to be sufficiently thorough. For example, the use of the concept of self-determination and its implications – crucial to propose appropriate actions and solutions to the Yugoslav crisis – remained too vague in the EP speeches. Similarly, the rather nonchalant use of the rhetoric 'EC first and more UN' shows that MEPs had not matured solid and adequate categories to address issues such as military intervention in the new context deriving from the end

of bipolar confrontation and from globalization. Probably, this was also due to the marginality to which the EP is still relegated in the CFSP decision-making, thus diluting the MEPs' responsibility and encouraging the lack of concreteness in their speeches. As if to justify the marginalization, the Council repeatedly criticized the MEPs for these limits, from which, moreover, governments themselves were not exempt.

2   The end of the Cold War had brought a certain euphoria among the MEPs, who, just like the governments, believed that the EC not only should, but could, take charge of continental security. The 'EC first' rhetoric clearly showed excessive confidence in the ability of the EC/EU, which was necessarily followed by a profound disillusionment, a sense of helplessness and, above all, a sense of guilt that, however, seems excessive: the reiterated condemnation by the MEPs of the EC and even of the EP for their ineptitude should have taken into greater consideration the institutional limits of the EU's external action (and the EP's role in this area), to which the Maastricht Treaty had not made any real improvement. A thorough critique of these limits took place in the debates too timidly and too late, only in the last years of the conflict in Bosnia-Herzegovina. The target of criticism, in other words, was partly wrong: rather than repeatedly challenging the EC (which could not offer much more than sanctions and an attempt at diplomatic solution) for its inaction, the rhetoric of the MEPs should have been directed more against the governments for the priority given to their national interests, and the weakness of the institutional reforms of the Maastricht Treaty.

3   Instead, the powerlessness of the EC and the EP, which understood it was not able to influence the Council, led the different parliamentary groups to accept its effects on the evolution of the crisis. For example, even the groups originally opposed to the principle of self-determination and the recognition of Slovenia and Croatia ended up accepting them, apparently after it became clear that the EC could never prevent their independence and guarantee the unity of Yugoslavia. Similarly, many MEPs who declared themselves opposed to the approach adopted at the negotiating tables on Bosnia-Herzegovina, based on territorial and ethnic division, ended up accepting it when it became clear that it was the only possible solution left. And even those groups who wanted a European or UN solution to the conflict, to prevent heavy operations like air strikes and Washington's political and military involvement, ended up welcoming them both when they realized that only the European dependence on the US would solve the crisis.[61]

4   The EP, with an approach that gave priority to the production of broadly shared (although often minimalist) resolutions, managed to get some results, such as the replacement of the negotiator David Owen, considered too much in favour of the Bosnian Serbs and of the legitimacy of the *fait accompli* in terms of territorial conquests. It was, however, a matter of Pyrrhic victories: the successors, Carl Bildt and then Richard Holbrooke, were unable to take very different approaches. The EP remained a weak body in a weak EU, and the discourses in the EP could not but recognize it.

Notes

1 Section 1 by G. Finizio and U. Morelli; section 2 by U. Morelli, sections 3 and 4 by G. Finizio.
2 The CG group comprised MEPs of the Communist parties in France, Greece, Portugal and Ireland. The acronym of the parliamentary groups is French (*Coalition des Gauches*), as indicated in the Official Journal of the EC.
3 Debates of the European Parliament (DEP) 1991, n. 3–407,167.
4 DEP 1991, n. 3–409, 169.
5 DEP 1992, n. 3–48, 73.
6 DEP 1992, n. 3–419, 60. Prag had already expressed his doubts on self-determination in July 1991 when, as ED Group member, he wondered what it would have meant to recognize secession when faced with similar requests that could be advanced by Wales, Scotland, Corsica, South Tyrol and the Shetlands. See DEP 1991, n. 3–407, 167.
7 DEP 1991, n. 3–409, 166.
8 RDE was a heterogeneous centre-right group consisting, at least in the first phase, mostly of MPs of the French Gaullist Rally for the Republic (RPR) and colleagues from Fianna Fáil, the Irish Conservative party.
9 DEP 1991, n. 3–403, 225; n. 3–408, 91; n. 3–409, 170.
10 The ED Group, largely formed by British Conservatives, joined the PPE on 1 May 1992.
11 DEP 1991, n. 3–403, 218 and 1992, n. 3–421, 113.
12 DEP 1991, n. 3–401, 272. The regionalists, with their passion for independence, did not realize the paradox that was inherent in their claims: how could the Europe of regions, made up of hundreds of local authorities, work without a highly centralized European institutional apparatus, and therefore contrary to their independence ambitions?
13 Referring to the Common Foreign and Security Policy and before the Treaty of Amsterdam, the Troika was a group composed of the Foreign Minister of the Member State holding the rotating Presidency of the European Council of Foreign Ministers and their immediate predecessor and successor.
14 DEP 1991, n. 3–409, 170–1; 1992, n. 3–417, 274–5.
15 DEP 1992, n. 3–418, 76.
16 DEP 1991, n. 3–410.
17 DEP 1992, n. 3–418, 77–8.
18 Lord Carrington, former NATO Secretary-General, presided over the Peace Conference sponsored entirely by the EC to prevent the escalation of the conflict in Yugoslavia. The plan is also known as the Carrington-Cutileiro Plan, named after the Portuguese ambassador who negotiated it.
19 Appointed as negotiators respectively by the EC and the UN, David Owen was a former Foreign Minister and leader of Britain's Social Democratic Party; Cyrus Vance was former US Secretary of State and envoy of the UN Secretary-General in Yugoslavia.
20 The CFSP High Representative would be established only by the Amsterdam Treaty in 1997.
21 The impossibility, in certain circumstances, of reaching common resolutions led to regrets and reprimands by some leaders who urged their colleagues to avoid compromising the unity of the EP before the Council: see for example J. W. Bertens (ELDR), DEP 4–451, 226.
22 Added to this are the question times, with frequent questions addressed by MEPs to the EPC, the Council and the Commission.
23 B. Antony (DR), DEP 1992, n. 3–418, 72–3; K. C. Dillen (DR), DEP 1992, n. 3–418, 236–7. In particular, Antony repeatedly lashed out at the President of the European Commission Jacques Delors, who in the throes of a pro-Soviet fanaticism would have guiltily tried everything to keep the Soviet Union and Yugoslavia united: B. Antony (DR), DEP 1992, n. 3–419, 57–8 and DEP 1993, n. 3–426, 135; M. Lehideux (DR), DEP 1993, n. 3–427, 172–3.

24 M. Lehideux (DR), DEP 1993, n. 3–430, 291.
25 D. Nianias (RDE), DEP 1992, n. 3–419, 56–7.
26 A referendum that showed the will of the population in favour of independence was proposed as a condition for the recognition of Bosnia-Herzegovina by the Arbitration Commission of the Conference on Yugoslavia (the Badinter Commission), set up by the EC as legal support to the European mediator Lord Carrington. The referendum was held, with favourable results, between 29 February and 1 March 1992.
27 For example, A. M. Oostlander (PPE), DEP 1992, n. 3–416, 89.
28 D. Prag (PPE), DEP 1992, n. 3–419, 60.
29 P. Avgerinos (S), DEP 1992, n. 3–418, 73.
30 V. Ephremidis (CG), DEP 1992, 3–418, 75; A. Alavanos (CG), DEP 1992, n. 3–419, 281.
31 For example A. M. Oostlander (PPE), DEP 1994, 3–447, 131.
32 Despite the opposition of most of the groups to the underlying approach of the Vance-Owen Plan, it was widely supported by them, at least in the initial phase of the conflict, because in the face of the increasing violence it was the only and concretely discussed solution on the table. But although, for example, the Socialist Group was officially in favour of the plan, within it the reserves had always been strong: E. P. Woltjer (S), DEP 1993, n. 3–430, 93. Similarly, the EPP positions were heterogeneous: see for P. Sarlis (EPP), DEP 1993, n. 3–430, 129–30; against D. Pack (PSE), DEP 1993, n. 3–427, 174.
33 Langer committed suicide on July 3, 1995, before the end of the conflict.
34 For example A. Langer (V), DEP 1994, n. 3–442, 127.
35 For example A.M. Oostlander (PPE)

> It is not the European Union which is to blame for any of this, but the Council and the Council alone [...]. The Council has completely ruined its reputation through its policy on former Yugoslavia, and the fact that this is painfully clear is no reason for pity, since it has brought it all on its own head.
>
> (DEP 1995, n. 4–467, 124)

36 C.M. Crawley (S), DEP 1993, n. 3–430, 290–1.
37 A. Langer (V) and A.M. Oostlander (PPE), DEP 1994, n. 3–447, 130–1.
38 See for example W. Claes, of the Belgian Presidency:

> This House too is manifestly very good at precise and correct diagnosis. But I am sure you will not take it amiss if I say that I have not heard any suggestions from you either for an alternative, effective and feasible remedy, none at all.
>
> (DEP 1993, n. 3–434, 77)

39 A.M. Oostlander (PPE), DEP 1992, n. 3–417, 274.
40 A.M. Oostlander (PPE), E. Mcmillan-Scott (PPE), J.W. Bertens (LDR), E.P. Woltjer (S) and D. Nianias (RDE), DEP 1992, n. 3–419, 52–7.
41 For example Habsburg (PPE):

> The reference to the UN is nothing more than an excuse. We should in fact be saying to ourselves that this is primarily a European problem. We must take the initiative so that the responsibility may again rest where it actually belongs.

See also M. von Alemann (LDR): '...this is our task as Europeans and that we should not be relying entirely on the United Nations', DEP 1992, n. 3–419, 58, 59; J.W. Bertens (LDR):

> We must do something effective and for that we need real intervention. The Community must take the lead here. If that can be done under the auspices of the CSCE then so much the better. But if that proves impossible then the Community must act independently.
>
> (DEP 1992, n. 3–418, 74)

42 J. de Deus Pinheiro, President-in-Office of the Council, DEP 1992, n. 3–418, 78.
43 See, among others, S. Guillaume (RDE), DEP 1993, n. 3–421, 72.
44 J.W. Bertens (LDE), DEP 1992, 3–421, 111.
45 J.W. Bertens (LDE), DEP 1994, n. 3–441, 206.
46 A. Langer (V), DEP 1992, n. 3–420, 79.
47 P. Avgerinos (S), DEP 1992, n. 3–419, 58.
48 J. Sakellariou (PSE, former S), DEP 1994, n. 3–441, 207. The contradictions were, however, frequent in the group: Woltjer, for example,

> it now needs to say quite clearly to the parties involved: either you accept a peace plan, or you will have to deal with a determined coalition, in the form of Western Europe and the United States, which is prepared – and mandated by the UN – to enforce that peace plan, using all possible means if necessary.
> (DEP 1993, n. 3–427, 277; see also Woltjer, DEP 1993, n. 3–431, 300)

49 The presidency opposed the reasoning that a) the revocation of any embargo could only be decided by the Security Council, and not by the EC; b) the increase in insecurity determined by the withdrawal of the embargo would result in the withdrawal of peace-keeping troops and, consequently, the suspension of humanitarian aid with serious repercussions on the population: U. Seiler-Albring, President-in-office of the Council, DEP 1994, 4–453, 71–2.
50 P. Avgerinos (S), DEP 1992, n. 3–419, 58.
51 For instance, albeit without mentioning NATO, some MEPs openly called for 'violence' ('Violent men understand nothing except violence') and the bombing of the Serbs, an operation obviously more suitable to that organization than to the UN: D. Pack (EPP), DEP 1994, n. 3–442, 252–3; DEP 1993, n. 3–426, 136–7.
52 For example, M. Hoff (PSE), DEP 1995, n. 4–467, 120. On the part of a few, this awareness gave rise to a new criticism towards the Council, which would be compromising Europe's reputation far more than other institutions. The lines of conduct proposed in the past by the Commission and EP, ignored by the Council, had been finally adopted by the US, solving the crisis at Europe's expense: Oostlander (EPP) and G. La Malfa (EDLE), DEP 1995, n. 4–467, 124. Incredibly, the Council contended that once the war was over it would be realized that the success was mostly European: C. Westendorp, President-in-Office of the Council, DEP 1995 4–467, 129.
53 D. Nianias (RDE), DEP 1992, 3–419, 56–7.
54 Y.M. Blot (DR), DEP 1992, 3–421, 113.
55 G.R.P. Fuchs (S), DEP 1992, 3–420, 81.
56 C. Papoutsis (S), DEP 1992, 3–420, 85.
57 A.J. Puerta (GUE), DEP 1994, 4–453, 74.
58 Among the first to express this need was P. Green (PSE), DEP 1994, n. 4–453, 72. Green interpreted this event as a deliberate warning by the US to the Europeans, that they would have to take charge of their responsibilities effectively. For British Labour, careful observers of US moods, this awareness would have been one of the main drivers of Tony Blair's decision to propose the creation of the ESDP, in 1998 (Howorth 2014, 22).
59 For example L. Caligaris (UPE), M. Rocard (PSE) and L. Van der Waal (EDN), DEP 1995, n. 4–467, 121; 126–7; 123.
60 E. Rehn (ELDR), DEP 1995, n. 4–469, 147.
61 J.M. Wiersma (PSE), DEP 1995, 4–463, 235.

Bibliography

Biermann, Rafael. 2004. 'Back to the Roots. The European Community and the Dissolution of Yugoslavia – Policies under the Impact of Global Sea-Change'. *Journal of European Integration History* 10, 1: 29–50.

'Debates of the European Parliament' (DEP). 1991–1995. *Official Journal of the European Communities.*

Glaurdić, Josip. 2011. *The Hour of Europe: Western Powers and the Breakup of Yugoslavia.* New Haven, CT and London: Yale University Press.

Gnesotto, Nicole. 1994. *Lessons of Yugoslavia.* Paris: Institute for Security Studies.

Grimaldi, Giorgio. 2005. *Federalismo, ecologia politica e partiti verdi.* Milan: Giuffé.

Hassner, Pierre. 1995. 'Ex-Yougoslavie: le tournant?' *Politique Internationale* 69 (Autumn): 205–15.

Howorth, Jolyon. 2014. *Security and Defence Policy of the European Union.* 2nd edn. Houndmills: Palgrave Macmillan.

Kaldor, Mary. 2013. *New and Old Wars: Organized Violence in a Global Era.* 3rd edn. Cambridge: Polity Press.

Klemencic, Matjaž. 2011. 'The International Community's Response to the Yugoslav Crisis: 1989–1995'. www.wilsoncenter.org/publication/320-the-international-communitys-response-to-the-yugoslav-crisis-1989-1995. Accessed November 2015.

Lucarelli, Sonia. 2000. *Europe and the Breakup of Yugoslavia.* The Hague: Kluwer Law International.

Marolov, Dejan. 2012. 'The Policy of the USA and EU towards the Disintegration of Yugoslavia'. *International Journal of Social Science Tomorrow* 1 (2): 1–16. https://eprints.ugd.edu.mk/1224/1/276.pdf.

Privitera, Francesco. 2004. 'The Relationship between the Dismemberment of Yugoslavia and European Integration'. In *Reflections on the Balkan Wars*, edited by Jeffrey S. Morton, R. Craig Nation, Paul Forage and Stefano Bianchini, 35–53. Basingstoke: Palgrave Macmillan.

Rupnik, Jacques, ed. 2011. *The Western Balkans and the EU: 'The Hour of Europe'.* Paris: Institute for Security Studies.

Sibian, Ionut Eugen. *The EU Policy Concerning the Disintegration of Former Yugoslavia Cases: Slovenia, Croatia,* FYROM. http://ebooks.unibuc.ro/StiintePOL/EuroAtlantic Studies/11.htm.

Sierp, Aline. 2015. *Democratic Change in Central and Eastern Europe 1989–90. The European Parliament and the End of the Cold War.* Luxembourg: European Parliamentary Research Service.

Part III
Communicating Europe

Introduction to Part III

Communicating Europe

Europe's current crisis is not only political and economic: it is also a crisis of discursive narratives. If the 'language' of Europe seems unable to provide institutional legitimacy and policy guidance, recent events have also shown the dangers of rhetorical simplification and the need for new narratives aimed at addressing emerging social issues and changes in the stakeholders of public discourse. Part III of this volume contains a selection of case studies on discourses and counter-discourses that contribute to the definition of a European 'public sphere'. These are discussed from a multidisciplinary perspective, involving linguistics, sociology and political science specialists, and making extensive use of language analysis and representations.

A common thread running through the chapters is the way that they highlight narratives of Europe that fall outside established traditional or mainstream models, while not concentrating exclusively on offering critiques of those models. Instead, the chapters focus on 'side issues' by adopting a counter-intuitive approach. While Chapters 8 and 9 look at discursive practices taking place 'inside' Europe, Chapters 10 and 11 concentrate on languages of Europe as seen from the 'outside'.

Chapter 8 observes the effects of alter-globalist counter-discourses, as set out by the ATTAC association, on reports on women's rights issued by the European Parliament between 2004 and 2012. Discourse analysts usually describe international discourse as neutral and void of conflict, which from a European perspective would mean that counter-discourses about EU politics, society and identity are neutral. However, a close study of the available data reveals a complex relationship between discourse and counter-discourse. In the case of women's rights, one can observe how the ATTAC counter-discourse has influenced the rhetoric of the European Parliament and how the effect of this influence is different in the English and French versions of EU reports. The chapter thus looks at this influence from the perspective of discourse and translation theory and practice.

The media are central actors in the European integration process, as they influence the cognitive environment in which public opinion develops. In the attempt to reduce perception of the so-called democratic deficit, EU institutions have paid increasing attention to communication policies and to defining a European communication strategy, which has recently been oriented towards strengthening relations with local media and taking advantage of opportunities provided by social media. Despite this extensive institutional effort, when one looks at the discursive outcomes one realizes that 'Europe' is paradoxically less present where one would expect to find it most, and vice versa. Chapter 9 explains the attitudes of the Italian media regarding public discourses about Europe. It analyses the issues that recur most frequently and looks at a range of media settings, as well as using data collected to study the dominant representation of Europe in a variety of media, such as newspapers, news broadcasts and Twitter. The main focus of the chapter is on the recent EU Parliamentary election. The analysis of the language of the Italian campaign for the European elections shows that Europe is mostly absent from political and party discourse, which continues to be mainly dominated by domestic issues and confrontation between national parties. Moreover, old media, where Europe still occupies a niche, remain more attentive to European issues than new media.

But how is Europe communicated when seen from the outside? Chapters 10 and 11 show that Europe can be perceived both as a large, weak entity whose identity is diluted into a more general 'West', yet at the same time also as a reliable – even strong and attractive – partner and actor within the international system.

Chapter 10 discusses ISIS' communicative strategies as a memetic activity, where terminologies, discourses and narratives of the 'enemy', i.e. the West and Europe, are re-appropriated and spun in order to satisfy the organization's own needs. Analysts agree that ISIS demonstrates specific skills in managing different media and that it can articulate message production with a distinctive 'western' style, supporting the impression that its public diplomacy follows memetic criteria. The chapter carries out a comparative analysis of ISIS publications (in particular *Dabiq* magazine, published in English) as compared to the NATO doctrine, in order to show how the memetic process can be reversed and to pose the question of who learns from whom in this game of mirrors, in which codes are re-appropriated and legitimized. Dabiq's discourses on Europe's portray it as having a marginal influence in NATO, seeing it only as an enemy or ally of the US, and therefore the target of an asymmetrical narrative that rests on Europe's political weaknesses.

On the other hand, Chapter 11 looks at how Europe is represented and understood in negotiation processes between the EU and non-member states. By virtue of its long-lasting relationship with the EU and its member states, Tunisia before and after the 'Jasmine revolution' is used as a case study to shed light on the role of perceptions in shaping and (re-)framing the relationship in the context of pivotal policy areas such as that of migration and mobility. The findings suggest new ways of looking at EU foreign policies and Euro–Mediterranean relations, thus filling the gap in a debate on the external image of the EU that so far has mainly been focused on the internal impact of outward perceptions.

8 The alter-globalist counter-discourse in European rhetoric and translation

Women's rights at the European Parliament

Maria Cristina Caimotto and Rachele Raus[1]

Introduction

It is a shared opinion amongst many linguists[2] that the language employed by international institutions and organisations tends to be deprived of all kinds of positioning and bias up to the point of becoming a 'cotton language', a language made less effective by the removal of internal discussion.[3] This appears to be in contrast with the widespread perception that the European Union is unable to speak with a single voice as a unitary actor (see also Chapters 9 and 11). Our hypothesis is twofold: the conflict among multiple voices may be due to the presence of counter-discourse and/or to the translation from one official language into another – notably processes that are present within the European Parliament (henceforth EP). Analysing the communication of the EU from the point of view of Discourse Studies and Translation Studies thus proves particularly relevant.

Hence our research aims to investigate whether it is possible to identify traces of counter-discourse coming from the alter-globalist ATTAC association in the EP reports.[4] Our observation starts from the French versions, as ATTAC France is the main source of the counter-discourse. We shall then move to the comparative analysis of the EP English and French texts in order to observe the effects of translation on discourse. The multilingual versions available on the official EP websites are the results of processes of translation and editing. In 'Translators and translation' we explain why, together with Translation Studies scholars,[5] we prefer to use the term 'translation' to refer to these texts.

The reason for choosing parliamentary reports is that, as a genre, they do not possess binding value, thus they encourage the deployment of a discourse that is not yet institutive,[6] and allow polyphony and co-discursive openness towards other discourses, such as the counter-discourses. Such openness should not be envisaged as a lack of legitimation or pragmatic weakness, as the reports actually contribute to the circulation of the European Union's ideas and values. According to Judge and Earnshow[7] and taking into account the enlargement policy, Aydin-Düzgit highlights 'the important degree of discursive power' of the EP.[8]

The corpus

The corpus under investigation consists of texts published between 2004 and 2012 by the Committee on Women's Rights and Equal Opportunities (5th legislature) and the Committee on Women's Rights and Gender Equality (6th and 7th legislature). We analysed legislative and non-legislative final reports, which are normed by the EP Regulations and were written between 2004 and 2012. Following Maingueneau, these documents can be labelled as '*routinier*'[9] as they reproduce the same textual, discursive and lexical structure. The space allowed for variation, even if wider in comparison with binding legal texts, remains limited to specific sections. Moreover, such documents are heterogeneous from the constitutive point of view,[10] written in one of the EU official languages or one of the working languages, and later amended and translated into the various languages (see 'Translators and translations').

For the alter-globalist counter-discourse, we consulted the articles concerning M/W equality from 2002 to 2012 on the ATTAC France website.[11] These texts are usually authored either by a plurality of writers or presented as the common production of the association (*Lignes d'ATTAC France*). We have also taken into account the printed publications concerning the subject. Counter-discourse belonging to this specific association was chosen because ATTAC explicitly positions itself on an international level and in relation with the EU. In fact it differentiates itself from other similar associations through its willingness to create structured relations amongst directors, adherents, social movements, unions and press agencies. ATTAC presents the EU as the driving engine of globalisation, that is the '*mondialisation liberale*'.[12] Its criticism is directed at European institutions including the EP,[13] which is considered one of the actors of liberalisation policies.

Analysis method

In order to analyse the corpus, our approach blends the French approach to discourse analysis (henceforth DA) with the school known as Critical Discourse Analysis (henceforth CDA) and more specifically Discourse Historical Analysis[14] (henceforth DHA). We believe that these two approaches are strongly correlated and share an interest in focusing on the relationships linking words to ideology and society – notably on enunciators, their position and their point of view – and focusing also on the notions of inter-discourse and inter-text.[15]

We thus envisage our work as inscribed within the research domain recently labelled as *Discourse Studies*:[16]

> Since the 1960s a new field of research has emerged around the concept of *discourse*, known as Discourse Analysis or – more recently – Discourse Studies. [...] Discourse studies (abbreviated as DS) is, we believe, the result of the convergence of a number of theoretical and methodological currents originating in various countries (above all in Europe and North America)

and in different disciplines of the social sciences and the humanities [...] Discourse Studies could be considered as not only a trans-disciplinary or even post-disciplinary project but rather one which runs counter to the division of knowledge into specialized disciplines and sub-disciplines.

Overcoming the differences of their various approaches, Angermuller, Maingueneau and Wodak point out that:[17]

> The common denominator of the many strands in Discourse Studies is that they consider meaning as a product of social practices. Meaning [...] results from the use that is made of language in specific context. [...] Discourse Studies, with its many approaches, schools and developments, is now emerging as a new and fully-fledged field in which a number of currents meet – from structuralism to symbolic interactionism, from poststructuralism to problem-oriented strands like Critical Discourse Analysis.

In his works, Teun van Dijk also highlighted a certain level of convergence and transversality of approaches, at least on the level of CDA methods. In his own words:[18]

> [T]here is not 'a' or 'one' method of CDA [Critical Discourse Analysis], but many. Hence, I recommend to use the term *Critical Discourse Studies* for the theories, methods, analyses, applications and other practices of critical discourse analysts, and to forget about the confusing term 'CDA'. So, please, no more 'I am going to apply CDA' because it does not make sense.

The presence of a real 'cluster' of European researchers working around CDA[19] makes further synergies possible, together with the cross-influence of similar approaches. In this sense, as Angermuller points out,[20] the name of Foucault represents a point of reference. To this, we should add that of Althusser, whose notion of ideology is central for CDA as well as for the French discourse analysts, from which stems the interest towards political discourse especially at the beginning of DA. Thanks to the choice of putting the notion of inter-text and inter-discourse at the centre of the debate, the recent conception of *Discourse Historical Analysis* favours the rapprochement between CDA and DA even more, as these two analytical categories are at the very heart of the enunciation configurations in which the French discourse analysts are interested.

Translators and translations

Given the nature of the EP reports that comprise our corpus, a reflection on the use of labels is not a futile academic exercise. The reports under scrutiny are often drafted by several authors, using more than one language; the texts are later transformed into monolingual texts and translated again in a number of languages; to obtain parallel texts with the same status, the notion of 'original' and derivative texts is explicitly avoided. The individuals who draft the texts tend to be highly skilled from the linguistic point of view, so that the notion of first, second and foreign language proves somewhat inappropriate to describe their language proficiency. As a consequence, it would be misleading to use widespread terminology such as 'source' and 'target' texts, as the translation processes these texts undergo is often more intertextual than would be expected.

This high level of manipulation, editing and rewriting recalls the translation process observed in News Translation.[21] The labelling of translation procedures represents one of the thorniest terminological issues within Translation Studies.[22] Together with Schäffner we believe it is more appropriate to simply refer to the complex array of linguistic transformations as 'translation' – thus avoiding the risk of perpetuating the diminishing conception of translation as a word-to-word transfer process.[23]

As for the role played by translators working on these documents, again the situation appears complex and, as Cosmai explains:[24]

> It makes little sense to provide an abstract and generalised definition of EU translators, not least because the officials of the EU institutions' language services originate from a very wide variety of training and working paths, and their qualifications and skills cannot be reduced simply to knowledge of one or more foreign languages.

Hence, we shall simply state that what Cosmai points out concerning the translation of EU political documents[25] certainly includes the EP reports.

The counter-discourse of ATTAC France

ATTAC's counter-discourse often marks their alternative positioning:[26]

> Dès sa fondation en 1998, ATTAC a identifié les politiques néolibérales menées partout dans le monde, et particulièrement en Europe et en France (quels que soient les gouvernements), comme la cause principale de la montée des inégalités […]. [*gloss translation*: Ever since its foundation in 1998, ATTAC has recognised the neoliberal policies implemented all over the world, and notably in Europe and in France (prescinding from the governmental political position), as the main cause for the growth of inequalities].

As a consequence, members of the association distance themselves from the International and European lexis and discourse through antonymic comments, marking their choices through a process of polemical over-statement (*sur-énonciation*):[27]

> Défini par l'Union européenne comme «une forme d'emploi caractérisé par une durée inférieure à la durée légale, conventionnelle ou usuelle», le temps partiel regroupe en réalité des pratiques et des logiques sociales opposées.

[…] Qu'il soit «choisi sous contrainte» ou «subi», le temps partiel concerne essentiellement les femmes. Dans l'Europe des Quinze, le taux de féminisation du temps partiel atteint 81%. [*gloss translation*: Defined by the EU as a 'kind of employment characterised by a duration inferior to the legal, conventional or usual one', part-time work actually comprises contrasting social practices and logics. […] Whether it is 'chosen under constraints' or 'suffered', part-time work concerns women mainly. In the Europe of the Fifteen, the rate of feminization of part-time work reached 81%].[28]

Le terme d'«équité», abondamment ressassé, a précisément pour fonction de ne pas parler de lutte véritable contre les inégalités. A aucun moment bien sûr, il n'est question de remettre en cause la division sexuelle du travail […]. [*gloss translation*: The term 'equity', abundantly over-employed, helps avoiding the discussion of a proper war at inequalities. Of course, the sharing of burdens between the sexes is never questioned […].[29]

As far as prostitution is concerned, denunciations are even more precise and address the EP, among others:

Une offensive internationale contre la Convention de 1949 est menée par les pays réglementaristes qui introduisent la notion de prostitution forcée par opposition à celle de «prostitution libre». [*gloss translation*: An international attack against the 1949 Convention is driven by the pro-regulation countries that introduce the notion of forced prostitution as opposed to that of 'free prostitution'][30]

Dans ce débat [entre pays réglementaristes et abolitionnistes], non seulement tous les mots sont piégés, mais aussi les concepts: «droit», «libre choix», ou encore «travailleuse du sexe». [*gloss translation*: in this debate [between pro-regulation and pro-abolition countries], not only are all the words manipulative, but also the concepts: 'right', 'free choice', or also 'sex worker'].[31]

[…] au Parlement européen, certaines féministes, au nom du consentement, disent pouvoir distinguer de façon incontestable la prostitution «libre» de la prostitution «forcée». [*gloss translation*: in the European Parliament, some feminists, in the name of consent, declare that they can incontestably distinguish between 'free' prostitution and 'forced' prostitution].[32]

The embedding of ATTAC's words in EP discourse after the 'crisis'

Given the wide diachronic space under scrutiny, it is possible to observe the presence of at least one event that influences both discourse and counter-discourse,[33] i.e. the 'crisis' – first financial, in 2007, and later economic, starting from 2008 – which questions the (classic) liberal model of development. From the lexical viewpoint, EP reports show the embedding of the event through the increased frequency of the French word '*crise*' which imposes itself from 2010 substituting the more generic 'crisis' employed in previous texts (see Figure 8.1). The official translations are reported here simply to help English-speaking readers, their analysis can be found in 'The effects of translation'.

From a rhetorical viewpoint, the crisis becomes a paradigmatic commonplace and is inscribed in the EP reports:

> Tarabella (2010: 8) observe que la crise économique, sociale et financière peut représenter une opportunité pour faire de l'Union une économie plus productive et innovante et une société prenant davantage en compte l'égalité entre les femmes et les hommes, si les politiques et les mesures adéquates étaient adoptées.

> Tarabella (2010: 8) points out that the economic, social and financial crisis might offer an opportunity to make the Union, as an economy, more productive and innovative and, as a society, more mindful of gender equality, if the right policies and measures were to be put into effect.

> Romeva i Rueda (2010: 19) Les réponses à la récession à l'échelle européenne et au niveau des États représentent également une opportunité et œuvrent une période de transformation visant à promouvoir l'égalité des sexes; la crise économique et financière fournit ainsi une opportunité pour élaborer des réponses, dessiner des perspectives et identifier les espaces politiques d'intervention.

> Romeva i Rueda (2010: 18) The responses to the recession at the European and national levels also represent an opportunity and transformational

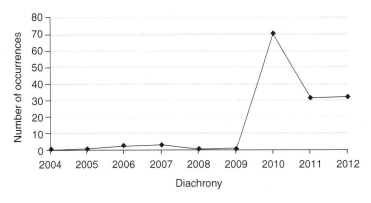

Figure 8.1 '*Crise*' (crisis) frequency in the French version of the EP reports (2004–2012). Results roughly correspond when investigating the English versions for the word 'crisis'.

moment to promote gender equality, the financial and economic crisis also provides us with an opportunity to develop responses and perspectives and identify policy spaces for intervention and alternative solutions.

Nedelcheva (2011: 9) la crise économique et financière doit être envisagée comme une occasion de faire des propositions nouvelles et innovantes [...]

Nedelcheva (2011: 10) the economic and financial crisis should be seen as a chance to put forward new and innovative proposals [...]

This commonplace statement tries to posit the crisis as legitimating an EU revival through new policies while it presents the advantage of bringing together the EP discourse and the alter-globalist counter-discourse.[34] In fact, the ATTAC slogan '*Un autre monde est possible*' ('Another world is possible') starts being embedded in the EP texts after the introduction of the 'crisis'. Still, such inclusion is implemented through a co-discursive mechanism of 'silencing'[35] through the paradigm of stating 'x' instead of 'y'. Here is an extract to exemplify the way in which the alter-globalist paradigm becomes embedded in EP texts:

Tarabella (2010: 14) La crise économique, financière et sociale qui secoue l'Union européenne et le monde a un impact sur les femmes [...] Cependant, la crise recèle également un énorme potentiel: les gouvernements et l'Union européenne doivent revoir la façon dont ils élaborent leurs politiques. **Une nouvelle société est possible**,[36] portée par un idéal d'égalité réelle.

Tarabella (2010: 13) The economic, financial and social crisis that is destabilising the European Union and the rest of the world is having a definite impact on women [...]. At the same time, however, the crisis offers tremendous potential, as governments and the Union must rethink their approach to policy making. A new society, underpinned by an ideal of genuine quality [*sic*], could conceivably emerge.

The comparison reveals two differences: '*nouvelle*' (new) substitutes '*autre*' (another) and the focus is on society ('*société*') rather than world ('*monde*'). The former is part of the novelty paradigm which is spread in discourse through the phrase '*nouveau*+X / X+*nouveau*':[37]

Tarabella (2010: 8) il faut davantage d'actions concrètes et de **nouvelles politiques**.

Tarabella (2010: 8) the need for further practical action and new policies.

Figueiredo (2010: 6) considérant que nous ne pouvons rester attachés à des modèles économiques vidés de leurs substances [...] que nous avons besoin d'un **nouveau modèle** basé sur la croissance et l'innovation.[38]

Figueiredo (2010: 6) whereas we cannot continue to be tied to worn-out, environmentally unsustainable economic models [...] whereas we need a new and socially sustainable model based on knowledge[39] and innovation.

Nedelcheva (2011: 9) la crise économique et financière doit être envisagée comme une occasion de faire des **propositions nouvelles** et innovantes.[40]

Nedelcheva (2011: 10) the economic and financial crisis should be seen as a chance to put forward new and innovative proposals [...]

Novelty reminds us both of something added to what exists and the presence of innovation, which can also rise on the discursive surface in various forms such as '*innovation*' '*innovantes*' (innovative).

The substitution of the notion of otherness with that of novelty allows us to:

1   avoid delegitimising the previous policies, as the notion of alternative implies that the previous dominant model failed. Moreover, the EU does not give up on their development policies;
2   avoid altering the positive idea of progress, notably in the phrase 'X+ *nouveau*', which links novelty to innovation;
3   inscribe and align to the 'cotton language' usually found in EU documents and statements (New Lisbon Strategy,[41] New strategy for equality between men and women...).

As for the need for novelty, in 2012 the novelty paradigm becomes saturated by the green economy, as the crisis becomes the pretence for legitimising an economy trying to balance growth and environmental sustainability:

Gustafsson (2012: 7) souligne la nécessité de convertir la société à un **modèle d'économie verte** [...14] Dans une économie verte, le développement économique s'inscrit dans le cadre de ce que la nature supporte et il garantit une distribution équitable des ressources entre les individus, entre les hommes et les femmes, ainsi qu'entre les générations.[42]

Gustafsson (2012: 6) supports the need to move society towards a green economy [...13] Economic development in a green economy therefore takes place within the context of what nature can tolerate, and ensures a fair distribution of resources between people, between men and women and between generations.

With the aim of legitimating the new economic model in the era of globalisation, the EP discourse draws from the general European discourse strategies:[43]

In the situation of globalisation and the prolonged global crisis as well as increased public mistrust towards the EU, the EU policy discourse apparently cannot only resort to describing policy and implementation paths as such but must also provide relevant modes of legitimation of the policies in question.

Coming back to the reformulation of the alter-globalist slogan, it is worth pointing out that the use of society (*'société'*) by the EP is certainly due to a co-discursive strategy aimed at the adaptation of the other's discourse into one's own discursive and ethical realm, which also allows the institution to occupy its place and positioning. Even if often contested, the 'European social model'[44] is a pivotal element of the EP discourse and of the EU in general, which employs it to underline the importance that Europe attributes to social aspects.

A different case study: the notion of 'patriarchy'

ATTAC has been aligned with feminists in the struggle against patriarchy ever since the first contestations of the world social forums:[45]

> Le mouvement des femmes est un puissant vecteur qui lutte contre la mondialisation libérale avec des moyens naturellement alternatifs en raison même de la situation des femmes dans la société patriarcale. [*gloss translation*: The women's movement is a powerful vector to fight liberal globalisation with naturally alternative methods as a consequence of the situation of women in a patriarchal society.]

The 2012 Brussels call, proposed by the European Women's Lobby and signed, among others, by ATTAC, shows their convergence concerning patriarchy: '*La prostitution s'inscrit dans la longue tradition patriarcale de mise à disposition du corps des femmes au profit des hommes*' ('Prostitution is inscribed in the long patriarchal tradition of making women's bodies available for men'). As a form of domination of men over women, patriarchy creates unequal power relationships between sexes from the structural point of view, which is why it is criticised.

From the point of view of co-discourse, we want to investigate whether the criticisms towards patriarchy are embedded in the EP discourse and, if so, how. Here are some excerpts from the texts under scrutiny concerning 'patriarchy':

> Valenciano Martínez-Orozco (2004: 17) Le peuple rom repose sur une **tradition patriarcale** très ancrée. [...] Elles [les femmes rom] se trouvent au croisement entre la culture traditionnelle et la modernité et sont confrontées aux valeurs de leurs familles et au poids culturel du patriarcat [...].

> Valenciano Martínez-Orozco (2004: 15–16) there is a very strong patriarchal tradition among the Roma [...]. They [Roma women] must come to terms with their system of family values and the cultural burden of patriarchy as well as racist attitudes towards their people from the rest of society.

Karamanou (2004: 7) invite les gouvernements de l'Europe du Sud-Est, à la lumière de l'accroissement du fondamentalisme religieux et de retour au **patriarcat** dans les sociétés, à garantir les libertés fondamentales [...].

Karamanou (2004: 7) invites the governments of South-East Europe, in the light of increasing religious fundamentalism and the re-patriarchalisation of societies, to guarantee fundamental freedoms and respect for human rights [...].

Bozkurt (2005: 5) considérant que le sous-développement économique et social dans certaines zones urbaines et rurales en général et dans certaines régions défavorisées de Turquie [...] aggravent les problèmes des femmes dans ces régions et affaiblissent leur position, qui est aussi fragilisée par des **structures sociales patriarcales** dominantes [...].

Bozkurt (2005: 5) whereas economic and social underdevelopment in some urban and rural areas in general and in disadvantaged regions of Turkey [...] aggravate the problems of women in those regions and undermine their position, which is also hampered by prevailing patriarchal social structures [...].

Járóka (2006: 4) considérant qu'il semblerait que, en raison de **traditions patriarcales**, beaucoup de femmes – notamment des femmes et des filles roms – ne bénéficient pas du respect total de leur liberté de choix [...].

Járóka (2006: 4) whereas there are indications that, as a result of patriarchal traditions, many women – including Romani women and girls – do not enjoy full respect for their freedom of choice [...].

Romeva i Rueda (2007: 12) Le phénomène du féminicide [au Mexique] est à replacer dans un contexte social influencé par la **mentalité patriarcale** dans lequel les femmes supportent la majeure partie du travail domestique et procréatif [...].

Romeva i Rueda (2007: 11) Feminicide appears in a social context conditioned by a patriarchal mentality, where most domestic and reproductive labour is performed by women [...]

Parvanova (2010: 8) demande a la Commission et aux États membres, en collaboration avec les ONG, de réaliser des campagnes de sensibilisation ciblant les femmes appartenant à des minorités ainsi que le grand public et d'assurer la pleine mise en œuvre des dispositions pertinentes pour lutter contre les habitudes culturelles discriminatoires et les **modèles patriarcaux** [...].

Parvanova (2010: 7–8) calls on the Commission and the Member States, in collaboration with NGOs, to carry out awareness-raising campaigns aimed at ethnic minority women as well as the general public, and to ensure the full implementation of the relevant provisions in order to combat discriminatory cultural habits and patriarchal role models [...].

Gustaffson (2012: 12) demande à la Commission de prêter une attention particulière au fait que, dans de nombreux pays en développement, la possibilité pour les femmes d'embrasser une carrière dans l'économie verte est encore fortement limitée en raison **des systèmes patriarcaux** et des modèles sociaux [...].

Gustaffson (2012: 11) calls on the Commission to pay particular attention to the fact that in many developing countries, the opportunities for women to pursue careers in a green economy are still severely limited as a result of social conditioning and patriarchal patterns, and that women fail to gain access to the information, training and technologies needed to access this sector;

The EP discourse concerning patriarchy turns on 'other' contexts: patriarchy is an issue for minorities, notably Roma, and underdeveloped areas (Mexico, developing countries), that is, countries lacking modernity, which can also be due to Muslim religious traditions (Turkey). Differently from the ATTAC discourse, patriarchy is not an issue for developed countries (i.e. the EU), but it is presented as exclusively attached to other cultures as part of tradition. Discriminations that women suffer within 'modern' Europe are rather presented as the consequence of stereotypes that justify unequal power relationships, which are reinforced by the media and school books:

Svensson (2008: 4) La publicité véhiculant des stéréotypes de genre se fait l'écho d'un rapport de force inégal [...].

Svensson (2008: 4) whereas gender stereotyping in advertising thus echoes the unequal distribution of gender power [...].

Liotard (2012: 4) considérant que les stéréotypes persistent à tous les niveaux de la société [et qu'ils] perpétuent des rapports de force latents; [...] les enfants sont confrontés aux stéréotypes liés au genre dès leur plus jeune âge par le biais des modèles mis en valeur dans les séries et les émissions télévisées, les débats, les jeux, les jeux vidéos, les publicités, les manuels et les programmes scolaires, les attitudes à l'école, dans la famille et la société, ce qui retentit sur leur perception du comportement que devraient adopter les hommes et les femmes et a des implications sur le reste de leur vie et sur leurs aspirations futures.

Liotard (2012: 4) whereas stereotypes still exist at all levels of society and in all age groups [and they] perpetuate underlying power relations; [...] children are confronted with gender stereotypes at a very young age through role models promoted by television series and programmes, discussions, games, video games and advertisements, study materials and educational programmes, attitudes in schools, the family and society, which influence their perception of how men and women should behave and which have implications for the rest of their lives and their future aspirations.

Counter-discourse is thus 'silenced'[46] and reframed through a discourse revolving around the opposition between tradition (others) and modernity (European developed countries). Silencing represents a co-discursive mechanism that EU discourse produces through the reframing of counter-discourse. In this sense, co-discursive mechanisms of appropriation and reframing contribute to the European rhetoric of identity-building and internal values as opposed to exterior cultures (see also the notion of '*narrative against*' in Chapter 10). This kind of rhetoric was analysed in the speeches of individual European actors (for instance interviews or speeches delivered by official representatives of national governments), where the opposition between the EU and the rest is expressed through the use of pronouns 'we' 'them', as argued by Attila Kriszan or Caterina Carta.[47]

In the EP reports, the use of impersonal formulae – which are typical of this genre – do not allow the use of first and second personal pronouns, and the lack of deixis makes the contrast us–them even more effective through assertiveness and assumptions. Contributing to what Guilbert calls the '*effet d'évidence*' (evidence effect),[48] the intertextual repetition contributes to the growing validation of these discursive strategies, which at the same time naturalise the identification of patriarchy and otherness and the link connecting patriarchy and the lack of women's emancipation (access to fundamental liberties, safety, career…).

Járóka[49] remains an exception, as she employs an alethic modality ('can contribute', '*peut contribuer*') to talk about patriarchy as a potential, hence not certain, cause of violence.

> Járóka (2006: 11) Romani women often live within traditional patriarchal communities, which can contribute to the violence against them and denies them basic freedoms of choice.

> (*Idem*) Les femmes roms vivent souvent dans des communautés patriarcales traditionnelles. Cette situation peut contribuer à la violence dont elles sont victimes et à l'absence de libertés de choix fondamentales.

This is not the only case in which she distances herself from the typical discourse strategies of the genre. In the explanatory statement, she uses the first person pronoun, which, by contrast, is never found in the report:

> Járóka (2006: 11) While preparing the draft of my report, I have had discussions with both public and private parties in the European Union. […] As a woman of Roma origin, I have experienced first hand much of the same discrimination that faces Romani women across Europe.

In fact, even if the explanatory statement is the freest part of this textual genre (Raus 2010: 117), most authors still avoid the use of first person pronouns and translators intervene to remove such pronouns if they are found – it is usual for translators to intervene when there is a problem with the drafting.[50] Moreover, in the following part of the English version, Járóka herself will go back to the impersonal reference to herself ('the rapporteur') but only after having legitimised her words by telling about her own personal experience.

These othering discourse strategies – breaking the expected discursive constraints – can be explained by the fact the author herself is of Roma origin. Her rhetoric thus distances itself form the usual European discourse – which is why the latter is then internally modified.

The effects of translation

Given the peculiar nature of Járóka's text, as explained above, the translation of her writing shows significant transformations that deserve closer observation. This French version shows the removal of the first person, as explained above:

> Járóka (2006: 11) Lors de l'élaboration du présent projet de rapport, votre rapporteur a eu des discussions avec des organes publics et privés de l'Union européenne. […] en tant que femme d'origine rom, votre rapporteur a elle-même subi une grande part des discriminations dont sont victimes les femmes roms de toute l'Europe.

As is often the case, the translator transedits and normalises some language choices that deviate from standard English:

> Járóka (2006: 11) some criteria **have be borne in mind** when analysing the problems faced by Romani women.

> (*Idem*) certains critères **ont été appliqués** à l'analyse des problèmes des femmes roms.

> Járóka (2006: 11) There is a **cry** of minority and **in special** Romani women to find themselves in the policies and actions of the member states as well as European Union's Institutions when addressing both gender equality and racial and ethnic discrimination.

> (*Idem*) Parmi les minorités et **en particulier** les Roms, les femmes **souhaitent être prises en compte** dans les politiques et actions des États membres et des institutions de l'Union européenne en matière d'égalité hommes–femmes et de discrimination raciale et ethnique.

In both cases, we notice how what appeared to be non-idiomatic in standard English has been rendered with ordinary French Eurospeak.[51] At the same time, what we could label as 'interlingual revision',[52] has altered the meaning that could be reasonably understood from the English version notwithstanding the 'errors'. In the first case, the expression – which was probably intended to be 'have to be borne in mind' – sounds like a caveat for the recipients, warning them of the necessity to remember the underlying difference that characterises the situation of the two groups described. The French translation glosses over the imperative meaning of the direct addressing and refers to criteria that 'have been applied', which leaves the French reader unsure of who has applied what.

Something similar happens in the second case, where the non-idiomatic expression 'in special' is rendered with the French 'en particulier' but the strength of the lexical choice 'a cry' is weakened in translation with the verb '*souhaitent*'. We can perhaps dare to hypothesise what happened in the cognitive process of the translator, whose attention was focused on normalising the 'mistake' in the English text – solved by removing the existential phrase 'there is' – and then weakening the strong lexical choice in a process of normalisation.

The case of Járóka shows changes that appear to be part of a process of adaptation to render the translated text in line with French Eurospeak, while at the same time glossing over the points that rendered the text effective in its dis-cursive choices. This form of normalisation is of course ideological in itself as it weakens the author's performativity. This ideological normalisation can also be observed in the translation of texts that do not bear non-idiomatic choices that might need 'correction', and it is possible to notice that these kind of changes are introduced as part of the translation process exactly where the effect of counter discourse (ATTAC's in our case) could be observed in the first place.

If we look at the following example – which was already discussed above in 'The embedding of ATTAC's words' – we notice a discrepancy between the English and the French versions, French most probably being the language in which the Belgian Tarabella wrote the text.

> Tarabella (2010: 14) Une nouvelle société est possible, portée par un idéal d'égalité réelle.

> Tarabella (2010: 13) A new society, underpinned by an ideal of genuine quality [*sic*], could conceivably emerge.

We see how the English version adds distance and the process of creating this new society by guaranteeing genuine equality appears as something natural that 'could emerge' spontaneously and not as a consequence of the work carried out by the EU and the governments. By shifting the ideal of genuine equality and introducing it between commas after 'society' the English version cancels the performativity implied in the French text as '*portée par un idéal d'égalité réelle*' is referred to the possibility of making it real and not to the society itself. The introduction of the metaphorical verb 'emerge' in English to substitute the existential '*est possible*' not only distances the action and backgrounds the role of those who are expected to make this possibility real, but also contributes to the removal of the intertextual reference that in the French version clearly reminds the recipients of ATTAC's motto. From the point of view of modality, the French '*est possible*' is more assertive compared to 'could', which introduces doubt and contributes to the lack of certainty expressed through the lexical choice of 'conceivably'. Moreover, the typographic error that turns 'equality' into 'quality' also adds to a form of distortion and silencing; for example someone searching automatically for the word 'equality' would miss that passage.

The changes in meaning that these aspects bring to the English text when compared to the French one prove even more significant when we compare the same sentence across other European versions. All the versions checked retain the structure of the French version, which also confirms our hypothesis that at least this passage was originally written in French. Some of the other languages use a strategy of explicitation and reveal more clearly what the French version implies, that is '*it is possible hence we should make sure it happens by promoting genuine equality*'.

> Tarabella (2010: 13) Una nuova società è possibile, a patto che sia ispirata a un ideale di reale uguaglianza.

> Tarabella (2010: 14) Es posible construir una nueva sociedad, basada en un ideal de verdadera igualdad.

> Tarabella (2010: 14) Este posibilă crearea unei noi societăţi, animată de idealul unei egalităţi reale.

> Tarabella (2010: 14) Uma nova sociedade é possível, animada por um ideal de igualdade real.

> Tarabella (2010: 15) Eine neue Gesellschaftsordnung ist möglich, getragen von der Idealvorstellung einer echten Gleichberechtigung.

The Italian sentence introduces the expression '*a patto che*' (providing that, only if) while the Spanish and the Romanian versions introduce the verbs '*construir*' and '*crearea*' foregrounding that this new society needs actions in order to become real and will not simply 'emerge' on its own. Even if the EU declaredly promotes the equal importance of all the European languages, it is not hard to imagine that the English version had much wider diffusion compared to the other languages reported. Thus the effect of a change in meaning in the translation process when translating into English is likely to cause powerful effects.

Conclusions

The examples reported in this chapter illustrate the kind of transformation EP texts undergo both in the process of drafting, with the embedding of counter-discourse – in a process that often reveals strategies of silencing and normalisation – and in the process of translation. The examples illustrated here may appear very subtle and could be ruled out as insignificant discrepancies in the overall process of communication that is carried out in the EP everyday activities. Nevertheless, in our view the sum of all these subtle discrepancies, both between the counter-discourses and the EP reports and between the various parallel versions produced by the EP, altogether contribute to a co-discursive rewriting process that tends towards a normalisation and a taming of the messages.

Of course the balance is a difficult one, as the translated texts require a process of explicitation, but at the same time it is important that the message of the text to be translated is rendered fully without adding or removing references and implicatures. Hence the translator, when adding or removing the mentioned features introduces a form of positioning that doubles the enunciative instance. Thus, we need to bear in mind that both neutralising and adding performativity through different discourse strategies are potentially ideological operations. Moreover it could be argued that some texts are created through a self-translation process even when they are drafted, as their authors may be writing in a language different from their native one and may thus be translating in their mind or anyway creating a text which is influenced by the structures of a different language. In the case of Járóka we can observe a diastratic effect, as her English is not idiomatic, the register is not appropriate and these aspects weaken the effectiveness of her message both in the English text and in the translated version analysed. This weakening is also consequence of an attempt to normalise her text and adapt it to the necessities of the genre, but at the same time, it appears ideological in the way it tames the spontaneous and sincere ring of the English version, in particular in its axiological aspects, i.e. 'cry'.

In conclusion, we can state that in the cases analysed we have observed some strategies of normalisation that appear ideological. Counter-discourse is embedded within the official discourse in ways that gradually weaken its effectiveness through the various passages that texts undergo, through intertextual references that distort and silence the original message and through the translation process. Moreover, in the cases observed during this study, the co-discursive processes that allow intertextuality and interdiscursivity are more productive when translating towards French while counter-discourse is silenced when translating towards English. This may explain the apparent paradox presented in the introduction, i.e. the internal rhetorical cohesion of what we called 'cotton language' versus the 'lack of a common language' that results in an EU perceived as not really united. Our findings appear to highlight how the process of embedding counter-discourse silences and normalises the reports while the process of translation may reintroduce disalignments. Further research could investigate the way in which different languages and translators affect discourse in the translation process.

Notes

1 This chapter is a joint production and reflects the views of both authors. All the paragraphs referring to the French texts were written by Raus and those referring to the English texts were written by Caimotto.

2 See for example Gobin and Deroubaix 2010.

3 The expression 'cotton language', introduced by François-Bernard Huyghe in 1991, indicates the kind of language and consensual rhetoric based on an empty and naturalising logic which is typical of the current institutional language, among others. See Rist 2002.

4 The association was born in France in 1998 as a reaction to financial globalisation and is now one of the main associations opposing neo-liberalism on a global scale (see also their international website: https://www.attac.org/en). The acronym stays for 'Association for the Taxation of financial Transactions and to Aid to Citizens'. For an historical overview, see ATTAC 2002, 10–21.

5 See Bassnett 2014.

6 Oger and Ollivier-Yanniv 2003, 3.

7 Judge and Earnshow 2003.

8 Aydin-Düzgit 2015, 155.

9 Maingueneau 2007, 30.

10 Raus 2010, 122.

11 See https://france.attac.org.

12 ATTAC 2002, 36.

13 ATTAC 2002, 37.

14 For an introduction to CDA, see Wodak and Meyer 2009, 1–33.

15 Even if they may appear similar, there are differences between these two notions, see Paveau 2010, 93–105.

16 Angermuller *et al.* 2014, 1.

17 Angermuller *et al.* 2014, 3.

18 Teun van Dijk 2013, 1.

19 Angermuller 2007, 12.

20 Angermuller 2007, 17.

21 Bielsa and Bassnett 2009.

22 Van Doorslaer, 2010, 179.

23 Schäffner 2012, 881.

24 Cosmai 2014, 111.

25 Cosmai 2014: 115.

26 ATTAC 2007, 8.

27 See Rabatel 2005.

28 ATTAC 2003, 67.

29 ATTAC 2003, 115.

30 ATTAC 2003, 139.

31 ATTAC 2008, 75.

32 ATTAC 2008, 35.

33 Concerning the impact of historical events on discourse see also the effects of the last European elections in Chapter 9 and the Arab uprisings in Chapter 11.

34 This coming together is certainly fostered by the intermediary role played by the European Women's Lobby who, in the meantime, had got closer to ATTAC itself (Raus 2015).

35 Puccinelli-Orlandi 1996, 62.

36 As Marc Tarabella is Belgian, we suppose he produced his text in French. Bold type added.

37 In French, adjectives can be positioned before or after the noun.

38 The expression is part of the Spanish amendement suggested by Garcia Perez: «*considerando que necessitamos un nuevo modelo basado en el conocimiento y la innovaciòn*».

39 The translation of *croissance* (growth) as 'knowledge' clearly appears to be a mistake and does not seem to have any potential ideological explanation. We believe it might be the consequence of using translation memories, i.e. segments of texts stored by Computer Aided Translation tools to databases that translators can use to speed up the translation process.

40 Nedelchova is Bulgarian and often employs French, hence her version was probably either in French or in Bulgarian.
41 There are other translations of this expression ('Renewed/Revised Lisbon Strategy'). See also IATE site.
42 The expression is the result of a manipulation of the French text to improve readability. The French report project simply read '*une économie verte*'. The English version was not modified: 'Supports the need to move society towards a green economy in which ecological considerations go hand in hand with social sustainability, e.g. greater equality and greater social justice'.
43 Michał Krzyzanowski 2014, 111.
44 Jonckheer 2006.
45 Marty *et al.* 2002.
46 Puccinelli-Orlandi 1996.
47 Kriszan 2011; Carta 2014.
48 Guilbert 2015, 88.
49 Járóka wrote the amendments to this report in English, which led us to reasonably establish that English was her own language of choice when writing the first version of the text.
50 This process can be observed in the other translations of this document, where the first person pronoun was rendered in French as '*votre rapporteure*', in Italian as '*la relatrice*', in Spanish as '*la ponente*', in Portuguese as '*a relatora*'.
51 The translated sentences are not particularly idiomatic in French either, as the translated version is closer to French Eurospeak rather than the everyday French used in France. This European variant of French (cf. Raus 2014, 386–388 and 391) is characterised by the influence of the translation process over lexical choices and over the sentence and discourse structure of the target language – French in this case – which sometimes results in discrepancies if compared to standard French. Still, differently from the French version, Járóka's English is at times ungrammatical and distant from the formal register required by this textual genre. In fact her English shows a positioning that results from her personal experience and tends to connote the discourse.
52 Drawing on Jakobson 1959.

References

Angermuller, Johannes. 2007. 'L'analyse du discours en Europe'. In *Analyse du discours et sciences humaines et sociales*, edited by Simone Bonnafous and Malika Temmar, 9–22. Paris: Ophrys.

Angermuller, Johannes, Dominique Maingueneau and Ruth Wodak. 2014. 'The Discourse Studies Reader. An Introduction'. In *The Discourse Studies Reader. The Main Currents in Theory and Analysis*, edited by Johannes Angermuller, Dominique Maingueneau and Ruth Wodak, 1–14. Amsterdam: John Benjamins Publishing Company.

Aydin-Düzgit, Senem. 2015. 'European Parliament "Doing" Europe. Unravelling the Right-wing Culturalist Discourse on Turkey's Accession to the EU'. *Journal of Language and Politics* 14/1: 154–174.

Bassnett, Susan. 2014. *Translation Studies*. Oxon and New York: Routledge, 4th Edition.

Bielsa, Esperança, and Susan Bassnett. 2009. *Translation in Global News*. London and New York: Routledge.

Carta, Caterina. 2015. 'The Swinging "We". Framing the European Union International Discourse'. *Journal of Language and Politics* 14/1: 65–86.

Cosmai, Domenico. 2014. *The Language of Europe. Multilingualism and Translation in the EU Institutions: Practice, Problems and Perspectives*. Brussels: Editions de l'Université de Bruxelles.

European Women's Lobby. 2012. *Brussels' Call 'Together for a Europe Free from Prostitution'*. www.womenlobby.org/spip.php?article5270&lang=en. Accessed 26 September 2016.

Gobin, Corinne and Jean-Claude Deroubaix (eds). 2010. *Mots. Les langages du politique* 94.

Guilbert, Thierry. 2015. 'Autorité et évidence discursives. Autovalidation dans les éditoriaux et chroniques du *Point*'. *Mots. Les langages du politique* 107: 85–99.

Jakobson, Roman. 1959. 'On Linguistic Aspects of Translation'. In *On Translation*, edited by Reuben A. Brower, 144–151. Cambridge, MA: Harvard University Press.

Jonckheer, Pierre. 2006. '"L'Europe sociale" ou le "modèle social européen" plus qu'un slogan?' *Revue parlementaire* 891.

Judge, David, and David Earnshow. 2003. *The European Parliament*. Basingstoke: Palgrave.

Kriszan, Attila. 2011. *'The EU is not them, but us'. The First Person Plural and the Articulation of Collective Identities in European Political Discourse*. Newcastle: Cambridge Scholars Publishing.

Krzyzanowski, Michał. 2015. 'International Leadership Re-/constructed? Ambivalence and Heterogeneity of Identity Discourses in European Union's Policy on Climate Change'. *Journal of Language and Politics* 14/1: 110–133.

Maingueneau, Dominique. 2007. 'Genres de discours et modes de généricité'. *Le français d'aujourd'hui* 159: 29–35.

Oger, Claire, and Caroline Ollivier-Yanniv. 2003. *Du discours de l'institution aux discours institutionnels: vers la constitution de corpus hétérogènes*. http://archivesic.ccsd.cnrs.fr/sic_00000717/document. Accessed 26 September 2016.

Paveau, Marie-Anne. 2010. 'Interdiscours et intertexte. Généalogie scientifique d'une paire de faux jumeaux'. In *Linguistique et littérature: Cluny, 40 ans après*, 93–105. Besançon: PUFC. http://f.hypotheses.org/wp-content/blogs.dir/246/files/2010/07/Paveau-Cluny-2008.pdf. Accessed 26 September 2016.

Puccinelli-Orlandi, Eni. 1996. *Les Formes du Silence dans le mouvement du sens*. Paris: Editions de Cendres.

Rabatel, Alain. 2005. 'Les postures énonciatives dans la co-construction dialogique des points de vue: co-énonciation, sur-énonciation, sous-énonciation'. In *Dialogisme et polyphonie*, edited by Jacques Brès, Pierre-Patrick Haillet, S. Mellet, Laurence Rosier and Nolke Henning, 95–110. Brussels: De Boeck.

Raus, Rachele. 2010. 'Terminologia comunitaria e di settore nelle relazioni parlamentari'. In *Multilinguismo e terminologia nell'Unione europea. Problematiche e prospettive*, edited by Rachele Raus, 115–156. Milan: Hoepli.

Raus, Rachele. 2014. 'L'Eurojargon et sa variante française'. *Argotica* 1/2: 383–394. http://cis01.central.ucv.ro/litere/argotica/Argotica_Fr.html. Accessed 26 September 2016.

Raus, Rachele. 2015. 'Types de contre-discours et remaniements "codiscursifs": l'inscription du dit d'ATTAC et du LEF dans les rapports du Parlement européen sur les femmes (2004–2012)'. *Semen* 39: 115–134.

Rist, Gilbert (ed.). 2002. *Les mots du pouvoir. Sens et non-sens de la rhétorique international*. Paris: Presses Universitaires de France.

Schäffner, Christina. 2012. 'Rethinking transediting'. *Meta* 57/4: 866–883.

Van Dijk, Teun A. 2013. *News as Discourse*. London: Routledge.

Van Doorslaer, Luc. 2010. 'The Double Extension of Translation in the Journalistic Field'. *Across Languages and Cultures* 11/2: 175–188.

Wodak, Ruth, and Michael Meyer (eds). 2009. *Methods of Critical Discourse Analysis*. London: Sage, 2nd edition.

Sources

ATTAC. 2002. *Tout sur ATTAC 2002.* Paris: Mille et une Nuits.

ATTAC. 2003. *Quand les femmes se heurtent à la mondialisation.* Paris: Mille et une Nuits.

ATTAC. 2007. *Manifeste altermondialiste.* Paris: Mille et une Nuits.

ATTAC. 2008. *Mondialisation de la prostitution, atteinte globale à la dignité humaine.* Paris: Mille et une Nuits.

Bozkurt, Emine. 2005. *Report on the Role of Women in Turkey in Social, Economic and Political Life/Rapportsur le rôle des femmes en Turquie dans la vie sociale, économique et politique.* PE 355.812v03–00.

Figueiredo, Ilda. 2010. *Report on Assessment of the Results of the 2006–2010 Roadmap for Equality between Women and Men, and Forward-looking Recommendations/Rapport sur l'évaluation de la feuille de route pour l'égalité entre les femmes et les hommes 2006–2010 et les recommandations pour l'avenir.* PE439.237v02–00.

Gustafsson, Mikael. 2012. *Report on the Role of Women in the Green Economy/Rapport sur le rôle de la femme dans l'économie verte.* PE487.914v02–00.

Járóka, Lívia. 2006. *Report on the Situation of Roma Women in the European Union/ Rapport sur la situation des femmes roms dans l'Union européenne.* PE 370.154v02–00.

Liotard Kartika, Tamara. 2012. *Report on Eliminating Gender Stereotypes in the EU/ Rapport sur l'élimination des stéréotypes liés au genre dans l'Union.* PE491.091v02–00.

Marty, Christiane, Claude Piganiol-Jacquet and Evelyne Rochedereux. 2002. *Problématique genre et mondialisation.* www.france.attac.org/archives/spip.php?article1180. Accessed 26 September 2016.

Nedelcheva, Mariya. 2011. *Report on Equality between Women and Men in the European Union – 2010/Rapport sur l'égalité entre les femmes et les hommes dans l'Union européenne – 2010.* PE450.870v02–00.

Parvanova, Antonyia. 2010. *Report on the Social Integration of Women Belonging to Ethnic Minority Groups/Rapport sur l'insertion sociale des femmes appartenant a des groupes ethniques minoritaires.* PE440.992v02–00.

Romeva i Rueda, Raül. 2007. *Report on the Murders of Women (feminicides) in Central America and Mexico and the Role of the European Union in Fighting this Phenomenon/ Rapport sur les meurtres de femmes (féminicides) en Amérique centrale et au Mexique et le rôle de l'Union européenne dans la lutte contre ce phénomène.* PE388.414v03–00.

Romeva i Rueda, Raül. 2010. *Report on Gender Aspects of the Economic downturn and Financial Crisis/Rapport sur les aspects relatifs à l'égalité entre les femmes et les hommes dans le contexte de la récession économique et de la crise financière.* PE439.236v02–00.

Svensson, Eva-Britt. 2008. *Report on how Marketing and Advertising affect Equality between Women and Men/Rapport sur l'impact du marketing et de la publicité sur l'égalité entre les hommes et les femmes.* PE404.565v02–00.

Tarabella, Marc. 2010. *Report on Equality between Women and Men in the European Union/Rapport sur l'égalité entre les femmes et les hommes au sein de l'Union européenne.* PE429.680v02.00.

Valenciano Martínez-Orozco, Elena. 2004. *Report on the Situation of Women from Minority Groups in the European Union/Rapport sur la situation des femmes issues de groupes minoritaires dans l'Union européenne.* PE337.818.

9 Europe in the media space

The construction of the EU public sphere in Italy

Marinella Belluati and Cristopher Cepernich

European culture has always been a polycentric and polymorphous space composed of a wide range of cultural and religious, geographic and political realities.[1] For this reason, the creation of a European identity often resembles a 'tumultuous disorder'[2] rather than a smoothly accomplished project. Our aim is to analyse the presence of Europe as a horizon of social and political consciousness and to reflect on how the media and communication channels are acting in the construction of a European public sphere. We will show how and to what extent the Italian media on the one hand, and the political parties' communications machines on the other, are (or are not) contributing to that construction. We will throw light on the more recurrent narratives and on the main players. Finally, we will consider whether the social media are indeed covering new ground for the development of a progressively Europeanized public sphere.

The Italian public sphere

According to Jürgen Habermas's theory of normative cosmopolitanism, the European integration process should not be based on the search for supposed common roots, because to do so risks reigniting traditional ethnic and territorial conflicts. Nor will an effective Union be brought about by philosophical considerations or economic rationality. The solution suggested by Habermas is instead the construction, however difficult and complex, of a public sphere that can create the prerequisites for equal access to rights for the different social and cultural identities that make up the current European mosaic. This is a space in which the main actors –both public and private – that contribute to the process of integration can initiate public discourses oriented towards integrating different values into a common political culture.

Accepting Habermas's arguments, this chapter will examine the ways in which different social organizations – beginning with the media and political institutions – take part in the forming of a common public space that provides greater opportunities for reciprocal exchanges between heterogeneous communities.[3] From this standpoint, multiculturalism and the pluralization of the public sphere[4] represent the most important challenge to the process of integration. This challenge, expressed in terms of communicative action, highlights the need for increased opportunities and forums for debate between European subjects as a determinant in the development of a common civil society.

More recently, Habermas's definition of a European public sphere has been enlarged in order to encompass processes of multi-level governance.[5] The deliberation process, which takes place at a local level around global questions, turns the European public sphere into a 'transit station' which, however, may alter the trajectory of the decision-making process and, therefore, the final outcome. One thinks, for example, of the lack of a European response to crucial issues such as the financial and economic crisis, the refugee emergency in the Mediterranean region, or the responses to climate change. It is quite clear, in these cases, that the object of policies is firmly anchored at the level of the nation state, and that the direction of the process concerns the whole world, but even so the interpretative frameworks that guide the decision-making process are formed at the level of the European public space, determining its direction. At the same time, however, an ever-growing body of empirical research on the transnational coverage of the great political and social crises demonstrates how these are things that contribute to the strengthening of the European public sphere in so far as they generate journalistic debates.[6]

Ultimately, the public sphere is the place in which societies redefine themselves. The process of modernization has seen the expansion and pluralization of dynamic worlds and social opportunities, which have entered into close relationships with one another and defined the new structure of the communication environment. In this respect the media today play a crucial role within the public sphere, as the main route by which institutions, political powers and organized citizens propagate information. While at one time a 'high quality' public sphere could – according to Habermas – rely on a mainstay of information released by the elite press,[7] much the same can be said about the pluralization of sources of communication and information. On the other hand, social and political systems are always broadly interested in an extended process of media coverage in which communication acquires political meaning.[8]

Moreover, the digital media, primarily the Internet, have profoundly transformed the communication and information landscape. The disintermediation of traditional information services provided by mainstream media has, in effect, shortened the distance between decision-makers and civil society, offering new opportunities for direct participation, bypassing intermediary networks.[9] The social media increasingly integrate social circles, and challenge the functions carried out by traditional intermediary bodies – first and foremost those of politicians and journalists.

According to Dahlgren, in the face of a growing demand for civic engagement the Internet has radically transformed forms of agency and demands for representation, to the point that it is no longer possible to see the public sphere as a totality.[10] Rather, it should be re-conceptualized as the coexistence of a variety of autonomous spaces of collective decision-making, partly able to challenge the agencies that have traditionally intermediated in socially significant matters.

Digital technologies are bringing profound change to the relations between power and the social base by enabling direct participation. Bernard Manin has described this burgeoning deliberative power as 'audience democracy'[11] while others have called it an 'unprecedented pre-eminence of communicative relations'.[12] Each of these definitions focusses on the fact that the public sphere has been re-conceived, redefined and pluralized thanks to the process of mediatization and the increase of communicative rationality, which sees the new technologies as the new mainstay of the public space.

In accordance with this theoretical framework, this chapter intends to investigate the methods and extent of the Europeanization of the public sphere in Italy. It will analyse media spaces, discussing, in the first instance, data on the representation of Europe by the old and new media, and showing how the Union has had an increasingly visible presence, even if in unexpected ways. Second, it will analyse the presence of Europe on the Internet, focussing on the European elections of 2014, with special attention to the presence of the frame 'Europe' in the electoral communications of the parties on Twitter.

The mediatization of Europe

In the 1993 'White Paper on Growth, Competitiveness and Employment' Jacques Delors estimated that in the following twenty years the rate by which European decisions influenced national policies would grow by 80 per cent. This is a prediction which is being proved broadly correct,[13] which means that issues relating to Europe are entering the public space and are no longer being framed neutrally. After a phase of 'permissive consensus',[14] Europe has moved into a new era, marked more and more by disagreements and conflicts between member states, and in particular one in which citizens are increasingly urged to take an active part and to adopt a disenchanted stance towards the opportunities and limits of the European project.

Authors who defend the need for more 'constraining dissensus' share this attitude,[15] as do those who interpret growing criticism of Europe as a form of enlargement of the public and political sphere and of cognitive involvement on the part of civil society. According to this argument, dynamics of conflict and differences of opinion are inevitable in a properly functioning public sphere, and internal controversy concerning the political system can only strengthen the common project.[16] Within the public sphere, conflict is a sign of the good health and dynamism that has accompanied the renewal of all political and social phases, as Charles Tilly and Sidney Tarrow explain by means of their concept of 'contentious politics'.[17] Although usually deemed negative, the expression of sceptical or critical sentiments within the European public sphere can even be considered evidence of vitality in the building of the common project. The risk is that, if not managed, these sentiments can produce unexpected outcomes.

European political institutions have always been aware that the integration process is mainly a communicative undertaking and that cultural, economic and political disparities must be overcome.[18] Indeed, the first provisions for a

European communications and transparency policy date back to the Commission chaired by Jacques Delors (1985–1995), and were included in the Maastricht Treaty (Final declaration, right of access to information). Since then, the attention paid by European institutions to communications policies has steadily increased. In 1995 the PRINCE programme launched the first communication strategy of the European Parliament and Commission aimed at the wider public, with the cooperation of the mainstream media; in 1998 the 'Green Paper on Public Sector Information in the Information Society' introduced the use of IT as a facilitator of information access. The Prodi Commission (1999–2004) provided further impetus in the 'White Paper on European Governance'.

It was, however, during the Barroso Commission (2004–2014) that the most important directives were issued: the 'Plan D' (2005); the 'White Paper on a European Communication Policy' and the 'Green Paper on the European Transparency Initiative' (2006); and a series of more or less structured measures for regulation of the Internet and social media. In 2007, the European Commission's 'Communicating about Europe via the Internet' laid the foundations for the organization of an online strategy of the Union. In 2010 it was the turn of the European Parliament, through resolution (2008/C 211/22) dealing with the role of journalism and new media in the consolidation of the European public space. Also in 2010, the European Commission presented its 'Digital Agenda', one of the seven initiatives of the Europe 2020 strategy aimed at better exploiting the potential of Information and Communication Technology (COM/2010/245). Finally, in 2014 the Commission issued a document (COM/2014/72) on the governance of the Internet. The Junker Commission, in office since November 2014, has so far followed the main European policy guidelines, concentrating resources on the reorganization of internal communication.

Despite many regulatory efforts, Europe's communication plans have struggled to take off. The biggest obstacle remains the lack of a common language, which stands in the way of joint broadcasting. Attempts have been made to resolve this problem, but with scant success. Such initiatives include the TV news channel 'Euronews' and other centralized products that had little impact. The main challenge, however, has always been that of persuading member states to open themselves up to the communication channels of Europe, but this has suffered countless setbacks. News emanating from European institutions has for a long time been placed in the 'foreign' sections of the press and news bulletins, and today the correspondents from Brussels still find it difficult to pass news to editors of national media,[19] thereby increasing the information deficit. Indeed, the most recent Eurobarometer on the relations between the EU and media channels (no. 76/2011) shows that 76 per cent of Italians believe information on Europe to be scarce. This statistic is broadly in line with the European average, but very far from the more positive results of North European countries. Television remains the medium most used to obtain information on Europe, although use of the Internet is rising (33 per cent of the survey).[20] Undoubtedly, when the process of European unification accelerates, the demand for information becomes urgent.

For a long time the public representation of Europe was conveyed by national media mainly in a generic and celebratory way.[21] Despite the fact that important treaties, such as Schengen and Maastricht, had come into force, the opportunity to make the European project a topic of public debate was lost. Thereafter a highly centralized approach continued to make Europe an object of discussion rather than a narrative subject. From the early 1990s to the economic crisis of 2008, one can still speak of a Europeanized national public sphere, as European issues, while present in political agendas and in national media, remained highly dependent on the orientation of the governments in office.[22] Europe became the justification for unpopular decisions and a positioning strategy aimed at developing internal political consensus.[23] Only in recent years, under the influence of globalization and the effects of the economic crisis, did the institutional relevance of Europe become more relevant, and thus the public debate on Europe has changed. Indeed, the Europeanization of the public sphere can be a sign that the process of integration is working.[24] National public figures are increasingly obliged to act within an operating range that is Europeanized and more connected globally.[25]

Two aspects are considered crucial to the assertion of a new European identity. The first is the persistence of a democratic deficit and strong internal inequalities in the European Union. The second relates to the cognitive tools that may allow European citizens to fully grasp the scope of the integration process.[26] Paradoxically, it was the strong oppositions to the integration project, made by politicians in recent years, that revealed the presence of a European public space more central to the life of member countries. For many, the upsurge of conflicts within the Union is seen as a positive development, in that it displays the vitality of the European public sphere, made possible in part by the refashioning of the communication space as a digital ecosystem.[27] Others, however, have insisted that the operating logic of social media – which constitute a significant part of the everyday communication and information practices of a large part of European citizens – clearly favours the circulation online of Eurosceptic views and claims.[28]

The major investment by European institutions in innovative communication policies, even if often accompanied by a technocratic vision and overly pedagogical aims, can be considered a positive attempt to activate the European public sphere and facilitate civic engagement. In times of advanced media coverage,[29] hybridization of media systems[30] and of new media cultures,[31] communication and information on Europe still gives evidence of contradictory outcomes, which will be analysed below.

Europeanization or domestication? An analysis of mainstream Italian media

The situation in Italy falls within this general picture, while some specificities relate to the national situation and its media system. The way in which mainstream Italian media represent Europe has been brought to light by various studies which, beginning from the early 1990s, have tried to identify the main trends. Research on Italian press and television has drawn the same conclusions for at least the past twenty years: Europe, as represented by the media, has been more of a hope than a fact,[32] more an externalization than a thematization,[33] more a constraint than an opportunity.[34]

For a long time, the main Italian media position towards Europe has often been aligned with that of the government in office. After a long phase preconceptionally in favour of the European Union, the past twenty years have been characterized by uncertain and inconsistent Europeanism, especially on the part of government ministers.[35] The news cycle on Europe has passed through a time of permissive consensus, or rather of uncritical support for the European project, to one of populist Euroscepticism in which Europe is used as a scapegoat for controversial political decisions ('Europe made us do it!'). Recent studies, however, have revealed a discrepancy between the main political discourse about Europe and the actual feelings of Italians. A 'liquid consensus' has emerged, in which negative images of Europe in the media and in the political debate are matched by contrasting expressions of confidence and critical awareness of the opportunities that Europe might offer.

Some data on the media's coverage of Europe help depicting this trend. On the whole, the evening news provided by TG1 – the prime service with the highest ratings – has moved much more in this general direction (Figure 9.1). Considering that television remains the main source of information on Europe (Eub 76/2011), in the past few years the general public has been offered a greater amount of information. The qualitative analysis of the data confirms that, as in the past, the most common kind of narrative is that in which Europe, as a topic of discussion, usually plays second fiddle to the national government. Furthermore, whenever Europe plays an autonomous role, its actions are described in negative or critical terms, and yet, for all that, the Italians' confidence in the European Union remains undiminished.[36]

The greater weight being given to Europe in media debates in Italy has been evident in moments of special importance, namely the general political elections,

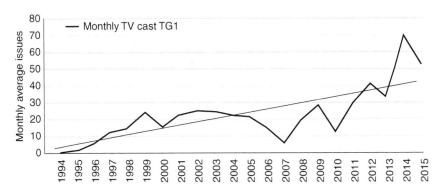

Figure 9.1 The incidence of features on Europe in news programs (monthly average 1994–2015, TG1).

in particular since the late 1990s. The first political programme to have expressly focused on Europe in order to capture votes was Romano Prodi's in 1996. From 2008 onwards, however, with differences of orientation, Europe has been an item on the manifestos issued by all political parties.[37]

In the elections of 2013, however, something novel occurred. For the first time Europe featured in the campaign for votes not only as a manifesto item, but as an out-and-out form of political action. Research data on the front pages of the five leading national dailies (*Il Corriere della Sera*, *La Repubblica*, *La Stampa*, *Il Giornale* and *Il Sole 24 Ore*) confirmed that European institutions were a central issue of the national public debate. Almost all the newspapers devoted a front page to election news that referred explicitly to Europe.[38] But it is noteworthy that in the same election Mario Monti's candidacy for Prime Minister was strongly supported by Europe, and yet was ultimately unsuccessful: while staying true to their European credentials, Italian voters refused to let these influence their choice of political leader.[39]

Another moment in which the influence of Europe was felt strongly in the Italian political debate was the European elections, although many political analysts concur in defining these elections as secondary and subordinate to national elections because they are less relevant to the internal political balance, and dominated by a kind of 'domestic' narrative which tends to address the question of Europe from a national standpoint.[40] Even so, the European election, and EU leaders and institutions are now being given a much higher profile,[41] a sure sign that the Italian public sphere is slowly being Europeanized.[42]

Studies on the visibility of European elections in Italy have confirmed this trend. Interest in Europe was already on the rise in 2009, and in 2014 research by the Observatory on Communication and Public Policy of Turin verified that the data had stabilized.[43] This development was validated by the visibility barometer, a research instrument which demonstrated that overall, compared to 2009, attention paid to European elections had increased substantially (Figure 9.2). In fact, in the week before the 2014 vote, the value registered was almost equal to that of the general elections of 2013, which were used as a point of comparison. It should be said, however, that in 2014 mostly national issues were at stake in the elections, for Prime minister Matteo Renzi used them as a test of his leadership, as he had not come to power by being elected but after formally being charged with forming a new government by the President following the resignation of Enrico Letta (former prime Minister). The European elections bore all the marks of a national event closely followed by the media, and this was reflected in the high voter turnout (57 per cent compared to the European average of 43).

The 2014 European elections were unusual for a number of other reasons. The first was that they were the first to take place after the Treaty of Lisbon and the European Constitution had come into force. The second was that for the first time the electorate could not only choose a party, but also the leader of the coalition who, in the event of victory, would become the President of the European Commission. The third novelty was that the European Parliament gave

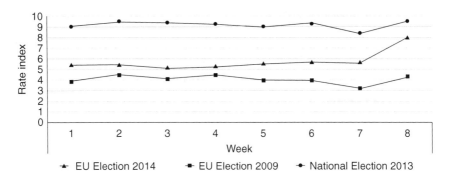

Figure 9.2 Visibility barometer of the EU elections.

specific voting recommendations to national political parties. The final difference was the political campaign strategy of the European institutions which, compared to the past, was devised centrally. Most efforts were based on finding common narrative formulas, beginning with the slogan 'Act, react, impact', and on experimenting with more personalized communication formats, such as televised head-to-heads between different leaders broadcast concurrently in all the countries of the Union. And not to be forgotten was the massive EU investment in web campaigning, particularly in the social media, seen as a means of stimulating participation and active involvement on the part of citizens.

The detailed analysis of the 2014 election campaign, carried out on 885 articles, has confirmed two things (Table 9.1). The first is that the general backdrop to the debate continues to be negative, so that during the campaigns Europe was discussed mostly in critical and controversial terms that implicitly supported Eurosceptic positions. The second relates to the fact that the key to understanding the European elections was national, whereas the majority of the campaign's themes addressed questions more closely linked to Europe as a supranational institution and to its influence on national public spaces. Although displaying characteristics typical of a second order election campaign, the political and electoral discourses are assuming an increasingly Europeanized form, moving towards interdependence between the European and domestic public spheres.

Another noteworthy finding concerns the politicians involved in the 2014 campaign. The results of the various parties exhibit a typically Italian political geography which reproduces the traditional political spectrum. Certain aspects should, however, be highlighted. The first is that in electoral campaign the voices 'against' Europe in Italy had more visibility (Table 9.2). Taken as a whole, the Eurosceptics parties – the centre-right coalition, the Movimento 5 Stelle (populist movement), Lega Nord and Fratelli d'Italia (extreme Right and chauvinist parties) – outnumber the pro-European ones, namely the centre-left coalition. The second aspect relates instead to the presence of leading Europeans in the media's campaign coverage. Eleven per cent of the time was devoted to

Table 9.1 Campaign issues (domestic vs European) and tonality (855 articles)

	Positive (%)	Negative (%)	No. articles (N)
Domestic issues			*470*
Party lists, candidacies and coalitions	32	68	195
Internal politics	38	62	55
Scandals	35	65	153
Post-electoral scenarios	30	70	5
Electoral law	29	71	62
European issues			*415*
Campaign events	24	76	127
Euroscepticism	29	71	39
EU and other European countries	22	78	46
Electoral manifestos (programmes)	50	50	4
Opinion polls	13	87	30
Abstentionism	21	79	19
Equal conditions/information	16	84	25
European coalition leaders	34	66	29
Gender	25	75	24
Endorsements	47	53	15
Other	33	67	57

candidates for the leadership of the Commission, and 4 per cent of the time to European heads of government (primarily Angela Merkel) whose public pronouncements and positions were absorbed into the Italian electoral campaign narrative. Here, then, is further confirmation of the fact that the 2014 campaign took place in a context that was both contentious and Europeanized to a greater degree: a small sign, at least in Italy, of growing political interdependence within the Union.

A further issue related to the visibility of the political actors concerns the issue of gender, as the European parliament had issued explicit recommendations calling for a balance between male and female candidates. In total, there were 227 candidates, but only 23 per cent were women: in Italy, as in other countries, the recommendations were not respected. The sole exception was that

Table 9.2 Politicians (%)

	Total mentions (1,763)
Politicians from the centre-right coalition	23
Politicians from the centre-left coalition	19
Politicians from the Movimento 5 Stelle	15
European leaders and actors	11
Eurosceptic front	9
European heads of state	4
Other political actors	19

Table 9.3 Female politicians (multi-response) (%)

Female centre-left candidates	55
Marine Le Pen	52
Angela Merkel	45
Female centre-right candidates	38
Total citations (N)	65

of the Partito Democratico (centre-left party) which put forward five women at the head of their party lists in the electoral constituencies, but this was hardly mentioned in the media coverage of the campaign. As a direct consequence of the focus on women, the centre-left coalition candidates, many of whom were women, attracted more attention than did those of the centre-right, not to mention the Movimento 5 Stelle which did not field any female candidates. Overall, however, the most interesting outcome was the presence of two women: Angela Merkel and Marine Le Pen. Although polar opposites in style and political persuasion, both were important, not least for their high profiles. The role of these women leaders was not only transnational, but was also presented without gender connotations, a sign of the fact that equalization may yet be achievable.

A final point (Figure 9.3) deals with the general thematic content of the election campaign. A lexicological analysis (which can only be carried out on Italian text and hence is untranslatable) reveals the semantic sphere clearly showing two polarities. The first relates to a structure of debate (horizontal axis) that distinguishes the European narrative plan (right-hand quadrant) from that of Italy (left quadrant). The second polarity is more central to the European debate (vertical axis) and denotes a split between the institutional dimension (bottom left quadrant) and the political-electoral dimension (top left quadrant). The data unmistakably reveals that even on the level of discourse these two planes appear as separate arguments, implicitly confirming that the causes of the European crisis reside in the lack of integration between the institutional and political levels. With regard to the quadrant denoting the Italian political dimension, we see that the debate is linked more to the electoral narrative plan. The interesting point is that the semantic spaces occupied by Matteo Renzi (in favour of Europe) and Beppe Grillo (leader of the Movimento 5 Stelle and openly opposed to Europe) are more closely connected compared to that of Silvio Berlusconi (coalition of the centre, with its openly right-wing and anti-European positions). The conclusions that can be drawn from this are that the first two were the real frontrunners of this electoral cycle while the third seemed to be chasing the political debate. In all probability the general pro-European/anti-European alignment does not explain the victory of the centre-left, but the fact remains that this political argument was used and partly worked as symbolic politics.

The conclusion that can be drawn from this series of data is that Europe is certainly present in the traditional media's public discourse, but it has not by any means become a general discussion. Despite certain more positive signs, Italian

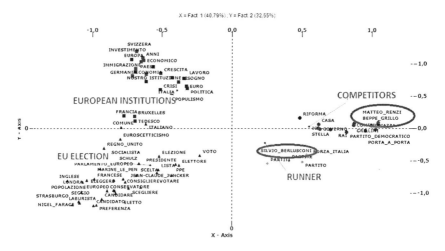

Figure 9.3 Thematic context of the EU electoral campaign.[44]

politics remains the dominant theme, even during electoral campaigns about shaping the future of Europe. European politics and institutions still remain very separate spaces, even if their interdependence is slowly but surely being strengthened and enhanced.

The European digital public sphere: Europe in the Italian social media

To what extent, however, has the online public sphere in Italy been Europeanized? And to what degree can European public discussions within the national debate be promoted through the Internet? The following survey of the Europeanization of the online public sphere in Italy is conducted on the basis of restricted criteria since the arena of the web is in fact too wide-ranging for detailed analysis. Our observations therefore focus on the communications of the political parties during the 2014 European elections, keeping the following considerations in mind. First of all, the communications of the principal players, which is to say the political parties. They are in fact among the main actors – together with the institutions of the Community and the media – that can contribute the most to the construction of a Europe-wide public sphere.[45] Second, the specific timeframe of the European elections, because the actual casting of votes constitutes one of the events that most attracts the attention of the national media to the Union and European themes and protagonists,[46] thereby promoting Europe as a framework of public debate.[47]

Third, the social media, because these have taken on a fundamental strategic function within election communication systems, and are able to bypass the traditional mediation of journalism. There exists a broad range of literature, as the previous section of this chapter showed, relating to how the Union and European issues struggle to raise their profile in the Italian national media. The Union is frequently presented in a negative way that benefits anti-Europeanism and Euroscepticism and sows doubts about supranational organizations. As a result, European themes are seldom featured in a constructive way, if at all, within the public debate.[48] At the same time, however, the social media claim to be proponents of a new, second-level communicative reintermediation carried out by people who exert interpersonal influence within the leading social circuits.

And, finally, Twitter, because this online networking site is ideally suited to serve as a forum for politicians and journalists. In certain contexts, therefore, it functions as an effective press office tool. Twitter presents itself as the privileged 'third place' of political communication and information.[49] It is a space that generates new and plural interpretative communities in which news is published, knowledge and information shared, and discussions conducted via short messages. In Italy, in particular, Twitter is gradually establishing itself as an electoral space where politicians can reorganize relations with journalists – thanks to the immediacy of their reactions – and with informed citizens, through the consolidation of relationships of trust and community.

Moreover, the particular architecture of the Twitter platform makes it more compelling than others in the specialized field of political-electoral communication and information: through the use of hashtags, users can intervene in the structuring of the flow of tweets that are being posted and read, thus guiding the development of conversations.

We should, however, distinguish the instrumental role of hashtags from their communicative ones. Primarily, hashtags are indispensable keywords that help users to search for and organize interconnected content and to trace discussions, but in this context also to identify and select the most discussed topics in a particular timeframe: so-called trending topics. As a result, hashtags establish a foundational hierarchy of content as a product of collective participation.

Secondarily, however, hashtags discharge more complex communicative functions linked to the structure of the cognitive domain of their users: above all, they define and promote frames around which the contents of communication are organized and developed. This is of crucial importance, because the choice of frames (that is of hashtags) essentially implies selection and salience and may affect meanings and interpretations. The framing selects certain aspects of a perceived reality and may promote a particular definition of the problem, causal interpretation, moral judgment and/or indication of the treatment of the element described.[50] Furthermore, the possible development of themes that a discussion moves towards is dependent on the choice of hashtags: in other words, both the ability to engage in a conversation related to the public being addressed and the outcomes of the discussion derive, to a certain extent, from this choice: for example, whether this will be conducted through dialogue or controversy and polarization.[51]

In short, the selection of Twitter hashtags is part of the strategic action of an electoral campaign that cannot be ignored. Just as happens in the information coverage of the mainstream media, in fact, it is pivotal to the outcome if, and to what extent, communication is oriented more towards the promotion of thematic frames (issues), game frames, or strategy frames.[52]

Following on from these considerations, we shall examine and evaluate the communication stream produced by the parties in the European elections of 2014 on Twitter in order to see how and to what extent they contributed to the Europeanisation of the electoral debate. We shall study if and how communication from the parties aimed to overcome the chronic difficulties of spreading news on Europe by circumventing, as far as possible, the traditional media through the tactical use of Twitter. Or, if not, to Europeanize the agenda by making good use of the relational capital with journalists, which Twitter offers.[53] This analysis will centre on the forms taken by the frame 'Europe' in party communications during the 2014 European elections, and on the hashtags used in the flow of communication produced by the parties' official Twitter profiles.

The analysis will monitor the communication stream on Twitter of the supranational[54] and national[55] parties from 14 April to 25 May 2014, thereby reviewing a pre-campaign week and the entire month-long campaign. Afterwards, it will present an account, albeit brief,[56] of the results of the research with the aim of illustrating the importance of the Twittersphere for the national and supranational arenas respectively. Overall, the number of tweets[57] – measured weekly – posted by the European parties is higher than those of the national ones, in particular the major ones (Figure 9.4). This, however, appears disconnected from the dynamics of the electoral campaign, where for the most part we find that the national parties have the greater agency within their own territory.

The only significant spike in movement and attention can be seen in the first televised debate between the candidates for the Presidency of the European Commission, broadcast live in all member states on 29 April 2014. The participants were Jean-Claude Juncker (EPP), Martin Schulz (PES), Guy Verhofstadt (ALDE) and Ska Keller (Greens).

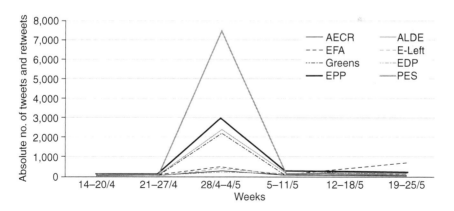

Figure 9.4 The volume of information flow from the European parties (absolute numbers of tweets and retweets).

On the one hand, this fact demonstrates a typical operation of Twitter, which is able to boost the volume of interactions in response to high-visibility events on traditional media (especially television) and, to a lesser extent, in response to events on the ground.[58] On the other hand, it represents how a single event of the campaign (but not so much in the case of the second debate broadcast on 15 May) was capable – at least potentially – of generating international attention and of creating an arena for supranational debates that would unify national public opinions.

The most structured parties – namely the PES and EPP – produced the most constant flow of communication by volume: the PES with an average of 1,386 tweets per week, double the EPP's average of 672. ALDE came next with 500, then the Greens with 494. Nevertheless, high output does not per se connote efficient use of the medium. In fact, the best indicators of diffusion and engagement in the discussion are very low, considering the vastness of the available audience: the PES, by far the most active party, obtained an average of 4,777 retweets per week, followed by the EFA with 3,510, the EPP with 3,361, the Greens with 2,133 and ALDE with 1,451. The data is even lower in relation to mentions, which are the best indicator of 'engagement' in a discussion and therefore of interaction with followers: we find a weekly average of 456 for the EFA, 384 for the PSE, 359 for the EPP, 260 for the Greens, and 242 for ALDE.

The larger parties, who carried out the most sustained live tweeting during the two televised debates by the presidential candidates (first the PES and EPP, but also ALDE and the Greens) tweeted, as might be expected, on the official hashtags of the debate: #EUdebate2014 for the first (despite its length) and #TellEurope for the second. Of particular significance was the fact that, vice versa, the live tweeting posted by the Italian parties on the same televised event (actually, not much of an 'event', given the low number of shares) operated alternative hashtags with the strategic intent of hijacking conversations in the Italian media arena by writing in Italian. This seemed to say: the elections may be European, but the electoral campaign, and therefore the construction of consensus, is an Italian affair. This is surely an indication of the current feebleness of efforts to Europeanize communication in the context of elections, which, it should be said, is partly due to the meagre mediating potential of an event that puts on stage political figures not directly elected by the people and who are running for a non-elective office, that of the President of the Commission.

On the whole, the weekly flow of tweets from the Italian parties evidenced an approach notably more connected to the dynamics of media coverage and the traditional scanning of media and territorial events characteristic of an election campaign (Figure 9.5).

The significantly highest flow of tweets was produced by Forza Italia (centre-right party with a weekly average of 1,003), followed by Nuovo Centrodestra (centre-right party 400), Lega Nord (339), Fratelli d'Italia (338), Sinistra Ecologia e Libertà (left party 299), Partito Democratico (264), L'Altra Europa per Tsipras (left party 193), Movimento 5 Stelle (147), Scelta Europea (centre party 102). The only parties writing fewer than 100 tweets per weeks were Italia dei Valori and Unione di Centro (both centre-right parties).

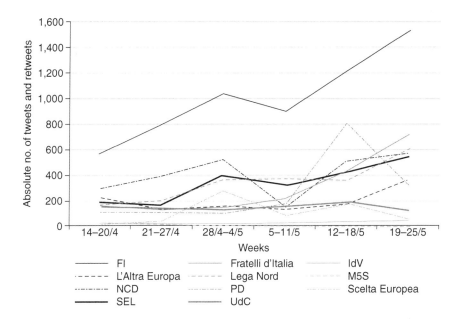

Figure 9.5 The volume of the communication flow from the Italian parties (absolute numbers of tweets and retweets).

Ultimately, the majority of relational activity in terms of dissemination of content and volume of interaction coalesces around the tweeting of the Italian parties. Measurements of circulation thus confirm that, on Twitter, the main arena in which the election game is played is the national one, the home ground. These indices of the dissemination of content are led by the Lega Nord with its 26,473 average weekly retweets from its followers.[59] Behind them come the Partito Democratico (10,403), Forza Italia (10,322), Fratelli d'Italia (8,682), Sinistra Ecologia e Libertà (5,747), L'Altra Europa per Tsipras (3,777), Movimento 5 Stelle (2,658), Scelta Europea (848), Italia dei Valori (115) and Unione di Centro (92). These rates of interaction are much higher than those of the European parties in absolute terms and especially with regard to the sheer scale of the audience being targeted: the most potentially interactive party was Forza Italia, with 1,130 average mentions per week, followed by Nuovo Centrodestra (995), Fratelli d'Italia (656), Partito Democratico (508), Sinistra Ecologia e Libertà (440), L'Altra Europa per Tsipras (229), Scelta Europea (167), Lega Nord (ninety-nine) and Unione di Centro (thirty-six).

In conclusion, the system of the supranational parties has shown an ability to produce content whose total volume exceeds the 14.4 per cent produced by the system of the national parties. Nevertheless, the low level of dissemination of content in the form of number of retweets obtained (–330.7 per cent of the national parties) and the equally limited level of interactions achieved (–128.4 per cent)

– which leads one to hypothesize a similar level of engagement in conversations – reaffirms the central role played by the national dimension of campaigning and the concomitant marginality of the supranational one. In making this analysis of framing we have concentrated exclusively on content published on Twitter by the national parties.

The low correlation of the tweeting of the European parties with the dynamics of national campaigning clearly suggests the presence of two arenas of discursive production and public debate, barely interconnected with one another: the supranational and the national. This is an indicator of the paucity of the Europeanization of the public sphere during the electoral campaign.

From here on the analysis of the frames launched in the debate through Twitter hashtags contained within the original tweets of the Italian parties may help us to answer to the following research questions: how much of Europe and, then, which Europe, has been communicated by the parties in the European election campaign of 2014? By disintermediation of the journalistic apparatus made possible by Twitter (and keeping in mind that the literature sees the media as one of the main causes of the inconspicuousness of European themes in the public debate) have the parties been active in directly promoting the European frame? Have they worked towards Europeanizing the agenda of the mainstream media, however unresponsive it may be?

The principal aim of this analysis[60] was to investigate the saliency and relevance[61] inherent in the use of hashtags concerning particular European events, actors and themes: (a) saliency is measured by the number of 'European' hashtags used by the party in public discussions in ratio to the total numbers of tweets posted by them in the period under review; (b) the relevance of 'European' hashtags is measured through the frequency of their use in ratio to the frequency of the party's total use of hashtags in the same monitored period.

The data (Table 9.4) show, above all, the low number of 'European' hashtags in the communications of the three major parties: for Forza Italia they were only 6 per cent of the total hashtags used, with a frequency of only 1 per cent. The

Table 9.4 Saliency and relevance of the European dimension in the hashtags used by the parties (absolute numbers in brackets)

	No. #	EU (%)	Mistakes	Frequency of use	EU (%)
Forza Italia	46	6 (3)	1	4,449	1 (57)
Fratelli d'Italia	406	8 (34)	21	4,477	8 (369)
L'Altra Europa	79	18 (14)	0	441	32 (141)
Lega Nord	43	5 (2)	0	742	17 (128)
Movimento 5 Stelle	2	0	0	12	0
Nuovo Centrodestra	12	17 (2)	0	122	29 (35)
Partito Democratico	85	10 (8)	0	543	8 (44)
Scelta Europea	23	65 (15)	2	268	86 (230)
Sinistra Ecologia e Libertà	125	10 (12)	1	413	19 (77)
Unione di Centro	99	11 (11)	0	223	25 (56)

statistics of the Democrats is only slightly higher with 10 per cent of the hashtags used by them during the campaign making reference to Europe, with an 8 per cent frequency of total tweeting. The Movimento 5 Stelle, on the other hand, only used hashtags twice, in neither case referring to EU matters.[62]

In the second instance, the rates of Europeanization of the electoral message are inevitably greater for the two blocs founded in occasion of the continental consultation as aggregations of parties at risk of failing to meet the electoral threshold: Scelta Europea and L'Altra Europa per Tsipras. These alliances, obviously, were open to the European dimension from their very start, as their names imply. Scelta Europea is the one whose flow of communication used European frames more than any others, with 65 per cent of its hashtags and 86 per cent frequency of use within its overall tweeting stream. L'Altra Europa follows with 18 per cent of European hashtags and 32 per cent frequency of use.

Finally, the strategic use of Twitter by the remaining small parties is varied. The Lega Nord, despite a flow of tweets whose volume – as we have seen – is considerable, launched only two hashtags referring to Europe out of the forty-three used during its election campaign (that is, 5 per cent), albeit with a 17 per cent frequency of use, which is by no means one of the lowest. The position of Fratelli d'Italia, on the other hand, is paradigmatic in other ways: this right-wing party, in fact, makes an anomalous use of hashtags, in terms of both quantity and modality. Indeed, it used a full 406 during the period reviewed, of which only 8 per cent referred to Europe, and its 8 per cent frequency of use further suggests that the use of European frames is not strategic in the social communication of the group but is, at most, tactical.

In short, taking into consideration the remaining minor parties and with the exception of Scelta Europea, Table 9.4 presents a picture of low salience and relevance (in the case of Movimento 5 Stelle it was in fact nil) by the parties, events, participants and themes that identified with the European frame.

Having established that the parties displayed very little inclination to practice framing on Europe in their election campaign tweets, it is necessary to investigate which 'Europe' they sought to communicate instead. Which hashtags and, consequently, which frames did they insert in the public discourse, thus trying to influence the agendas of the media and of receptive sections of public opinion.

The importance of the strategic game of establishing frames most suited and therefore more advantageous to the parties during election campaigns and, following from this, to the electorate's interests has already been underscored.[63] Naturally, Twitter, it should be remembered, is only one of the instruments – and certainly not the foremost – through which this 'battle' for the definition of reality is conducted by the parties' electoral communication machines.

The key reference for formulating an analysis of the types of hashtag that support a European frame is that of Aalberg, Strömbäck and de Vreese.[64] This theoretical model, created for the analysis of media coverage, has been adapted here to the field of political communication. The analysis is based on the distinction between three types of hashtag that correspond to the three basic dimensions of strategic game frames identified in the literature, starting with the three authors cited above. These are: (a) hashtags that relate to the political game (game frame), which refer to and are centred on the representation of elections as competitions. They include accounts of who is winning or losing in the battle for consensus, in parliamentary debates or in the political domain in general; surveys of the orientation of public opinion (polls or mere hearsay); the pronouncements and positions of all interest groups; the prediction of the outcome of the consultation, of the consequences of adopting certain policies or choosing certain coalition partners; (b) hashtags that refer to the strategies and tactics which the party or its candidates deploy in pursuit of their electoral and political objectives, the methods of campaigning, and whatever else concerns the life and the leadership of the party, its internal cohesion, and personalized communication formats; (c) hashtags that relate to the issues of the campaign.

So, then, which Europe appears in the hashtags of the Italian political parties in the 2014 European elections? Table 9.5 underlines again, in its first column, how, in the total flow of electoral tweets, the number of European hashtags is somewhat restricted in terms of salience and relevance. Moreover, the investigation reveals a use of hashtags that is no more than moderately innovative, to say the least.

The first general evidence is that the parties' communications favoured the hashtags (and therefore the frames) that refer to the political-electoral game, and this appears to confirm an adherence to the proven logic of journalistic news.

As for the major parties, Forza Italia focused all three of its hashtags on the game dimension: #Europee2014, #Europee, #Gheitner, with a frequency of use in the entire campaign of forty-nine, eight and three respectively. In contrast, the Partito Democratico employed a greater range in its eight hashtags (50 per cent game, 25 per cent strategy, and 25 per cent issues), but the frequency of use of issue hashtags was only 9 per cent of the total, while game hashtags represented 57 per cent. The three hashtags most often used by the Democrats were: #SoU2014 (thirtcen), #Europee2014 (ten), #Eurock (eight).

The Nuovo Centrodestra concentrated its restricted use of European hashtags (two) on the game dimension: #Europee (thirty-five) and #Europee14 (just one). The party which, against the norm, most directed its communications at issues was Fratelli d'Italia (which used them 45 per cent of the time), showing at the same time scant interest in the strategy hashtags (5 per cent use). The game dimension nevertheless remained prevalent, totalling 41 per cent of the thirty-four 'European' hashtags used during the electoral campaign. The top three hashtags used by Fratelli d'Italia and their relative frequency of use were: #Europee2014 (seventy-three), #Ue (sixty-four), #Europa (forty).

Even the production of hashtags by Unione di Centro shows a certain inclination towards the proposition of European issues: six of the eleven hashtags use (55 per cent) related to themes, with a 27 per cent frequency of use of the total number, although the use of game hashtags was much higher (71 per cent), of which the most used, #Europee, had thirty-five total uses. This was followed by #Ue (six) and #Europa (five).

Table 9.5 Types of hashtags and their use in party tweeting (percentage in brackets)

	No. # used	Game # (%)	Use frequency (%)	Strategy # (%)	Use frequency (%)	Issue # (%)	Use frequency (%)
Forza Italia	3	100 (3)	100 (60)	0	0	0	0
Fratelli d'Italia[65]	34	41 (14)	47 (172)	9 (3)	5 (20)	32 (11)	45 (165)
L'Altra Europa	13	23 (3)	35 (47)	62 (8)	61 (82)	15 (2)	4 (6)
Lega Nord	2	0	0	100 (2)	100 (128)	0	0
Movimento 5 Stelle	0	0	0	0	0	0	0
Nuovo Centrodestra	2	100 (2)	100 (36)	0	0	0	0
Partito Democratico	8	50 (4)	57 (25)	25 (2)	34 (15)	25 (2)	9 (4)
Scelta Europea	15	40 (6)	50 (115)	47 (7)	49 (112)	13 (2)	1 (3)
Sinistra Ecologia e Libertà	11	36 (4)	29 (22)	36 (4)	66 (51)	28 (3)	5 (4)
Unione di Centro	11	36 (4)	71 (40)	9 (1)	2 (1)	55 (6)	27 (15)

The other parties displayed a preference for the strategy type. The Lega Nord, in fact, used only one European hashtag, #bastaeuro, which was identified with the party throughout its election campaign, being used 127 times. L'Altra Europa per Tsipras used eight of its thirteen European hashtags for strategic purposes (62 per cent) with a frequency of use of over 60 per cent. This trend is confirmed by the party's top three hashtags: #TsiprasInItalia (used thirty-four times), #TellEurope (thirty-one), the only one of the top three of the game type, and #IoVotoTsipras (twenty-eight). Sinistra Ecologia e Libertà divided its use of hashtags between game and strategy, with emphasis on the strategic approach (66 per cent frequency of use). The most used, not by chance, was #Tsipras (forty-five times), followed by #Europee (ten) and #TellEurope (seven). Finally, balanced between game and strategy, was Scelta Europea: a little less than half of the fifteen hashtags it used during the campaign (seven) were of the strategy type and six were of the game. Its top European hashtag was #LEuropaCheScelgo (used in fifty-one tweets), followed by #EP2014 (forty-three) and #TellEurope (thirty-three).

Finally, our analysis allows a concluding reflection on the parties' reluctance to extend the discussion beyond the national media arena. The use of #EP2014, the official international hashtags launched by the European Parliament, played a marginal role in the Italian context, with the exception of the Sinistra Europea, which used it forty-three times. The only other parties to use it slightly more than occasionally were L'Altra Europa per Tsipras (fifteen) and Fratelli d'Italia (eight).

The parties' general disinclination to seize the opportunity to transnationalize their discussions was exhibited during the televised head-to-heads between the presidential candidates. The second of the two attracted more attention. TV leadership debates are generally a high point of any electoral contest,[66] and interest is now heightened by the dual-screening phenomenon which allows the audience to watch the debate on television while commenting on it via Twitter. Not all the Italian parties, however, took advantage of the communicative potential of the event by Europeanizing their campaign messages. Scelta Europea made intensive use of the official hashtags of the debate #TellEurope (twenty-two times) as well as the parallel hashtag #SoU2014 (twenty-four times); L'Altra Europa per Tsipras used the hashtag #TellEurope in its tweets thirty-one times during the debate, while its ally, the Sinistra Ecologia e Libertà bloc, limited itself to only seven times, and the Democratic Party focused its tweeting exclusively on #SoU2014 (thirteen times). On the other hand, the party bloc of the right and centre-right (as well as the Movimento 5 Stelle) avoided live tweeting on the event altogether.

Conclusions

The approach of the public sphere to the study of communication and information on Europe sometimes produces counterintuitive results. The analysis of institutional communication and coverage reserved by the mainstream media (particularly the press) towards Europe shows that the great investment of policy and cognitive pressures that reach into the globalized public space are improving this coverage. The discourse is still very fragmented and often barely capable of representing the complexity of Europe, but at least this is now on the agenda. In the last European elections, despite the continuing prevalence of a national outlook, the visibility of Europe and its main players was higher than ever before. The signs of Europeanization in the public sphere, at least in Italy, can now be seen and are clearly reflected in the mainstream media.

Paradoxically, however, where it would be reasonable to expect greater championing of the European dimension – that is, in the communications of politicians on Twitter during the European election campaign – this in fact continues to be woefully insufficient in terms of time and technique. The analysis of the campaign frames deployed through Twitter hashtags has demonstrated how the parties presented Europe only as a set of criteria on the margins of the electoral campaign, paying little attention to hashtags about events, themes and personages of continental importance. The data indicate how, in their paltry activity of European framing, the parties underused the dimension of issues in the production and diffusion of hashtags, preferring instead those of game and strategy. Political communication thus displays signs of dividing into two spaces that are only barely interconnected. There is an arena of supranational public debate, within which the European political 'families' operate and the production of European content has great significance: here, however, public discussion is meagre and inadequate. There is, in addition, an arena of national public discussion, within which the local political parties operate, and their capacity to intervene in the public debate is substantial. But the distance between the two arenas is such that one cannot yet imagine – at least for social communication circles – an enlarged European public sphere. Not even in the very special setting of an election campaign.

Notes

1 Norris and Inglehart 2006.
2 Morin 1987.
3 Habermas 1992, 2011.
4 Marini 2015.
5 Volkmer 2014.
6 Hepp *et al.* 2015.
7 Habermas 2011, 57–62.
8 Strömbäck 2008.
9 Grossi 2011.
10 Dahlgren 2009.
11 Manin 1997.
12 Bennet and Entman 2001.
13 Brouard, Costa and König 2012.
14 Brechou *et al.* 1995.
15 Down and Wilson 2008;
16 Risse and Börzel 2003.
17 Tilly and Tarrow 2006.
18 D'Ambrosi and Maresi 2013; Golding 2007.
19 Cornia 2010; Martins *et al.* 2012.

20 Eurobarometer 76/2011, related to the Internet, shows that institutional sites, on the other hand, attract 23 per cent of Italians interested in European news. Five per cent mostly use their blogs to inform themselves on European questions and another 4 per cent refer to video sharing platforms like YouTube. While still marginal, in particular among the less youthful population, the social media are gaining ground. Nine per cent of Italians and Europeans interviewed use sites like Facebook or Twitter as their main source of information on the European Union, a proportion that has surely grown during the passing of the years. This fact, however, relates to informational content strictly referring to the European dimension. Instead, in relation to overall information consumption, 49 per cent of Italians claim to use the Internet on a daily basis for news, and 14 per cent do so at least several times per week (a total of 63 per cent). Those who instead make use of social networks for news constitute 29 per cent, while 12 per cent do so several times per week (Demos and Pi, *Gli Italiani e l'informazione.* December 2015 – available at www.demos.it/a01201.php. Accessed 23 June 2016). It goes without saying that news sources not focused solely on Europe give some exposure to news about Europe.
21 Marletti and Mouchon 2005, 24.
22 Bindi 2011.
23 Belluati 2015.
24 Ladrech 2010; Della Porta and Caiani 2006; Graziano and Vink 2007.
25 Volkmer 2014.
26 Norris 1997.
27 Wodak and Koller 2008; Triandafyllidou *et al.* 2009.
28 de Wilde *et al.* 2013, 2014.
29 Lundby 2014; Strömbäck and Esser 2015.
30 Chadwick 2013.
31 Bondebjerg and Golding 2004.
32 Losito and Porro 1992; Grossi 1996.
33 Marini 2004; Marletti and Mouchon 2005.
34 Belluati 2012.
35 Bindi 2011.
36 Belluati and Serricchio 2014.
37 Bindi 2011.
38 Belluati and Serricchio 2013.
39 The Italian election of 2013 was narrowly won by the Partito Democratico (with 25.4 per cent of the vote, although the coalition of which they were the major party gained 29.5 per cent). This was led by Pierluigi Bersani, who was unable to form a government, following which the task was handed to Enrico Letta. The electoral surprise was the Movimento 5 Stelle which became the second party in terms of absolute vote share (25.6 per cent), while Berlusconi's party (Popolo della Libertà) was in third place with 21.6 per cent of the vote. Mario Monti's party, supported by Europe, achieved only 8.3 per cent.
40 Reif and Schmitt 1980.
41 Belluati 2015.
42 Della Porta and Caiani 2006.
43 The barometer is an overall index made up by a series of indicators that consider quantitative and qualitative elements: (a) the number of articles published in four important Italian newspapers chosen for their circulation and political orientation (*Il Corriere della sera, La Repubblica, La Stampa* and *Il Giornale*); (b) the degree of centrality of the electoral issue within the article; (c) the degree of depth of journalistic discussion; (d) the presence and space given to the article on the front page. The barometer's scale runs from 0 to 10 and has been measured in the weeks preceding the vote (Belluati and Bobba 2010). In the 2009 elections the articles included in the count were 1,167 and in 2014, 1,443. The choice of daily newspapers was made

following a mixed criteria: *Il Corriere della Sera* and *La Repubblica* for being the most popular; *La Stampa* for being most sympathetic to pro-European positions and *Il Giornale* for being anti-European.

44 This figure is an output from T-Lab, a software package system used for linguistic analysis. In this specific case, it processed a corpus of Italian newspaper articles about the 2014 European elections and the output is therefore in Italian. To facilitate understanding we have labelled the main thematic areas.

45 Cepernich 2015.

46 Boomgaarden *et al.* 2010.

47 de Vreese *et al.* 2006.

48 de Vreese *et al.* 2006; Maier and Tenscher 2006; Norris 2000.

49 Chadwick 2009.

50 There is an extensive literature on the concept of framing as an effect of the media. The key reference points for this research have been above all: Aalberg *et al.* 2011; Cappella and Jeamison 1997; Entman 1993; Iyengar 1991.

51 Cepernich 2009.

52 Aalberg *et al.* 2011; Cappella and Jamieson 1997.

53 With regards to this it must be remembered that, as the date of the election drew near, it was the European Parliamentary Research Service (EPRS) that advised the candidates of the importance of disintermediated communication, in other words communication directed directly towards citizens through the use of social networks. Starting from the assertion that it is difficult, during a European campaign, to mobilize the electorate 'because the work of the European Parliament rarely makes the news', the EPRS recommended an aware and appropriate presence on social media platforms because they 'allow candidates to communicate directly to citizens, to keep control over content, on the diffusion and timing of messages and because they reduce dependency on traditional intermediaries, above all journalists'. Further on in the briefing it is stated that 'social media can also serve to influence journalistic coverage. Journalists, in fact, in order to compete in an ever accelerating media environment, make ever greater use of blogs, Twitter conversations and multimedia content as sources for their stories'. See Ron Davies, *Social media in election campaigning*, 21 March 2014. The briefing is online at this address: www.europarl.europa.eu/Reg Data/bibliotheque/briefing/2014/140709/LDM_BRI(2014)140709_REV1_EN.pdf. Accesssed 23 June 2016.

54 The supranational parties observed were: AECR, ALDE, EFA, E-Left, Greens, PDE/ EDP, EPP, PSE.

55 The national parties observed were: Forza Italia, Fratelli d'Italia, Italia dei Valori, L'Altra Europa per Tsipras, Lega Nord, Movimento 5 Stelle, Nuovo Centrodestra, Partito Democratico, Scelta Europea, Sinistra Ecologia e Libertà, Unione di Centro.

56 The complete data presented in an extended format can be downloaded from the Observatory's website: do/homepl/view?doc=osservatoriocpp.html.

57 'Flow' is used in the sense of the sum of original tweets and retweets from the official party account.

58 Elmer 2013.

59 The Lega Nord, visibly higher than the standard registered, was supported by an application that automatically retweets tweets from the party in the profiles of its supporters. The practice is not illegal, but a similar application that generates 'likes' on Facebook has been blocked.

60 Italia dei Valori was excluded from this analysis because the almost residual volume of its tweeting activities and the discontinuities registered during the period monitored render any consideration on their specific case useless.

61 Shaw 1979.

62 By far the most widely used hashtag used throughout the electoral campaign by the Movimento 5 Stelle was the famous #vinciamonoi (that is #WeWiu).

63 Lang and Lang 1983.
64 Aalberg *et al.* 2011.
65 The datum relating to Fratelli d'Italia must be seen alongside the fact that there are four hashtags (of thirty-four) classified as 'mistakes' because they contain typos. They cannot be classified otherwise, since their errors remove all connected tweets from public discussions, and, due to their lack of clarity, they do not fit within the theoretical model adopted (#Dublino and #Versavia). They make up 2 per cent of the hashtags (that is, 6 per cent of the total).
66 Houston *et al.* 2013.

Bibliography

Aalberg, Toril, Jesper Strömbäck and Claes H. de Vreese. 2011. 'The framing of politics as strategy and game: a review of concepts, operationalizations and key findings'. *Journalism* 13(2):162–178.

Belluati, Marinella. 2012. 'The local communication flow as strategic resource in the construction of a European public sphere'. In *The European Public Sphere. From Critical Thinking to Responsible Action*, edited by Luciano Morganti and Léonce Bekemans, 197–210. Brussels: Peter Lang.

Belluati, Marinella. 2015. 'Europa Liquida. Contraddizioni e ri-orientamenti del processo di costruzione della sfera pubblica in Italia'. In *L'unione Europea tra istituzioni e opinione pubblica*, edited by Marinella Belluati and Paolo Caraffini, 179–192. Rome: Carocci.

Belluati, Marinella, and Giuliano Bobba. 2010. 'European elections in Italian media: between second order campaign and the construction of a European public sphere'. *CEU Political Science Journal* 5(2):160–186.

Belluati, Marinella, and Fabio Serricchio. 2013. 'Quale e quanta Europa in campagna elettorale e nel voto degli italiani'. In *Itanes Voto Amaro. Disincanto e crisi economica nelle elezioni*, 181–192. Bologna: il Mulino.

Belluati, Marinella, and Fabio Serricchio. 2014. 'L'Europa va in campagna (elettorale)'. *Comunicazione Politica* 15(1):133–151.

Bennet, W. Lance, and Robert Entman, eds. 2001. *Mediated Politics. Communication in the Future of Democracy*. Cambridge: Cambridge University Press.

Bindi, Federiga. 2011. *Italy and the European Union*. Washington, DC: Brookings Institution Press.

Bondebjerg, Ib, and Peter Golding, eds. 2004. *European Culture and the Media*. Portland: Intellect Books.

Boomgaarden, Hajo, Rens Vliegenthart, Claes H. de Vrees and Andreas R. T. Schuck. 2010. 'News on the move: exogenous events and news coverage of the European Union'. *Journal of European Public Policy* 17(4):506–526.

Bréchon, Pierre, Bruno Cautrès and Bernard Denni. 1995. 'L'évolution des attitudes à l'égard de l'Europe'. In *Le vote des Douze. Les élections européennes de juin 1994*, edited by Pascal Perrineau and Colette Ysmal, 203–228. Paris: Presses de Sciences.

Brouard, Sylvain, Olivier Costa and Thomas König, eds. 2012. *The Europeanization of Domestic Legislatures. The Empirical Implications of the Delors Myth in Nine Countries*. New York: Springer-Verlag.

Cappella, Joseph N., and Kathleen H. Jamieson. 1997. *Spiral of Cynicism. The Press and the Public Good*. New York: Oxford University Press.

Cepernich, Cristopher. 2009. 'The new technologies: the first Internet 2.0 elections'. In *The Italian General Election of 2008. Berlusconi Strikes Back*, edited by J. L. Newell, 171–189. Basingstoke: Palgrave Macmillan.

Cepernich, Cristopher. 2015. 'L'Europa nella comunicazione dei partiti su Twitter alle Europee 2014'. In *L'Unione Europea tra istituzioni ed opinione pubblica*, edited by Marinella Belluati and Paolo Caraffini, 256–270. Rome: Carocci.

Chadwick, Andrew. 2009. 'Web 2.0: new challenges for the study of e-democracy in an era of informational esuberance'. *I/S. A Journal of Law and Policy for the Information Society* 5(1):11–41.

Chadwick, Andrew. 2013. *The Hybrid Media System. Politics and Power*. Oxford and New York: Oxford University Press.

Cornia, Alessio. 2010. *Notizie da Bruxelles. Logiche e problemi della costruzione giornalistica dell'Unione europea*. Milan: Franco Angeli.

D'Ambrosi, Chiara, and Andrea Maresi, eds. 2013. *Communicating Europe in Italy. Shortcomings and opportunities*. Macerata: Eum.

Dahlgren, Peter. 2009. *Media and Political Engagement. Citizens, Communication and Democracy*. Cambridge: Cambridge University Press.

Della Porta, Donatella, and Manuela Caiani. 2006. *Quale Europa? Europeizzazione, identità e conflitti*. Bologna: il Mulino.

de Vreese, Claes H., Susan A. Banducci, Holli A. Semetko and Hajo G. Boomgaarden. 2006. 'The news coverage of the 2004 European parliamentary election campaign in 25 countries'. *European Union Politics* 7(4):477–504.

de Wilde, Pieter, Asimina Michailidou, and Hans-Jörg Trenz. 2013. *Contesting Europe Exploring Euroscepticism in Online Media Coverage*. Colchester: ECPR Press.

de Wilde, Pieter, Asimina Michailidou, and Hans-Jörg Trenz. 2014. 'Converging on euroscepticism: online polity contestation during European Parliament elections'. *European Journal of Political Research* 53(4):766–783.

Down, Ian, and Carole J. Wilson. 2008. 'From permissive consensus to constraining dissensus: a polarizing union?' *Acta Politica* 43:26–49.

Elmer, Greg. 2013. 'Live research: Twittering an election debate'. *New Media & Society* 15(1):18–30.

Entman, Robert. 1993. 'Framing: toward clarification of a fractured paradigm'. *Journal of Communication* 43(4):51–58.

Golding, Peter. 2007. 'Eurocrats, Technocrats and Democrats'. *European Societies*, 9(5):719–734.

Graziano, Paolo, and Maarten Vink, eds. 2007. *Europeanization: New Research Agendas*. Basingstoke: Palgrave.

Grossi, Giorgio. 1996. *L'Europa degli italiani, l'Italia degli europei: un mese di giornali e di televisioni: 1994–1995*. Rome: RAI-ERI.

Grossi, Giorgio. 2011. 'Sfera pubblica e flussi di comunicazione nell'epoca della rete'. In *Nuovi media, nuova politica? Partecipazione e mobilitazione online da MoveOn al Movimento 5 Stelle*, edited by Mosca Lorenzo and Cristian Vaccari, 35–62. Milan: Franco Angeli.

Habermas, Jürgen. 1992. 'Cittadinanza politica e identità nazionale. Riflessioni sul futuro dell'Europa'. In Jürgen Habermas, *Morale, diritto, politica*, 105–140. Turin: Einaudi.

Habermas, Jürgen. 2011. *Il ruolo dell'intellettuale e la causa dell'Europa*. Bari: Laterza.

Hepp, Andreas, Monica Elser, Swantje Lingenberg, Anne Mollen, Johanna Möller and Anke Offerhaus. 2015. *The Communicative Construction of Europe. Cultures of Political Discourse, Public Sphere and the Euro Crisis*. Basingstoke: Palgrave Macmillan.

Houston, Brian J., Mitchell S. McKinney, Joshua Hawthorne and Matthew L. Spialek. 2013. 'Frequency of tweeting during presidential debates: effect on debate attitudes and knowledge'. *Communication Studies* 64(5):548–560.

Iyengar, Shanto. 1991. *Is Anyone Responsible? How Television Frames Political Issue*. Chicago, IL: University of Chicago Press.

Ladrech, Robert. 2010. *Europeanization and National Politics*. Basingstoke: Palgrave Macmillan.

Lang, Gladys Engel, and Kur Lang. 1983. *The Battle for Public Opinion. The President, the Press and the Polls during Watergate*. New York: Columbia University Press.

Losito, Gianni, and Renato Porro. 1992. *Le rappresentazioni giornalistiche dell'Europa e del 1992: primi risultati di una ricerca pilota*. Rome: RAI VQPT.

Lundby, Knut, ed. 2014. *Mediatization of Communication*. Berlin and Boston: De Gruyter Mouton.

Maier, Michaela, and Jens Tenscher, eds. 2006. *Campaigning in Europe, Campaigning for Europe. Political Parties, Campaigns, Mass Media and the European Parliament Elections 2004*. Berlin: Lit Verlag.

Manin, Bernard. 1997. *The Principles of Representative Government*. Cambridge: Cambridge University Press.

Marini, Rolando, ed. 2004. *Comunicare l'Europa*. Perugia: Morlacchi.

Marini, Rolando. 2015. 'Concentrazione e distrazione: come i giornalismi nazionali rappresentano l'Unione Europea'. *Annali di Sociologia 2010–2012* 18:197–219.

Marletti, Carlo, and Jean Mouchon, eds. 2005. *La costruzione mediatica dell'Europa*. Milan: Franco Angeli.

Martins, Ana Isabel, Sophie Lecheler and Claes H. De Vreese. 2012. 'Information flow and communication deficit: perceptions of Brussels-Based correspondents and EU officials'. *Journal of European Integration* 34(4):305–322.

Morin, Edgar. 1987. *Penser l'Europe*. Paris: Gallimard.

Norris, Pippa. 1997. 'Representation and the democratic deficit'. *European Journal of Political Research* 32:273–282.

Norris, Pippa. 2000. *A Virtuous Circle. Political Communications in Postindustrial Societies*. Cambridge: Cambridge University Press.

Norris, Pippa and Ronald Inglehart. 2006. 'God, guns and gays: the supply and demand for religion in the US and Western Europe'. *Public Policy Research* 12(4):223–233.

Reif, Karlheinz and Hermann Schmitt. 1980. 'Nine second-order national elections: a conceptual frame-work for the analysis of European election results'. *European Journal of Political Research* 8(1):3–45.

Risse, Thomas and Tania A. Börzel. 2003. 'Conceptualizing the domestic impact of Europe'. In *The Politics of Europeanisation*, edited by K. Featherstone and C. Radaelli, 57–80. Oxford: Oxford University Press.

Shaw, Eugene F. 1979. 'Agenda-setting and mass communication theory'. *International Communication Gazette* 25(2):96–105.

Strömbäck, Jasper. 2008. 'Four phases of mediatization: an analysis of the mediatization of politics'. *The International Journal of Press/Politics* 13(3):228–246.

Strömbäck, Jasper and Frank Esser, eds. 2015. *Making Sense of Mediatized Politics. Theoretical and Empirical Perspectives*. London: Routledge.

Tilly, Charles, and Sidney Tarrow. 2006. *Contentious Politics*. Oxford: Oxford University Press.

Triandafyllidou, Anna, Ruth Wodak and Michal Krzyzanowski, eds. 2009. *The European Public. Sphere and the Media Europe in Crisis*. London: Palgrave Macmillan.

Volkmer, Ingrid. 2014. *The Global Public Sphere. Public Communication in the Age of Reflective Interdependence*. Cambridge: Polity Press.

Wodak, Ruth and Veronika Koller, eds. 2008. *Handbook of Communication in the Public Sphere*. Berlin: De Gruyter.

10 ISIS' *Dabiq* communicative strategies, NATO and Europe

Who is learning from whom?

Michelangelo Conoscenti

1 Introduction[1]

The paper discusses ISIS' communicative strategies as a memetic activity.[2] The term 'meme' was introduced by Dawkins and it is the cultural counterpart of a gene, representing a cultural unit – an idea, value, or behavioural pattern – that is passed from one person to another by non-genetic means such as imitation or repetition.[3] Examples of memes are tunes, ideas, catch-phrases and religions. Just as genes propagate themselves in the gene pool by leaping from body to body via sperms or eggs, so memes propagate themselves in the meme pool leaping from brain to brain via a process which, in the broad sense, can be called imitation.[4] 'Memes are sustainable information units that influence and form individual and collective systems and spread successfully within them'.[5] From an Information Operations (InfoOps) and Psychological Operations (PsyOps) perspective memes are the best active agents to be used because when your message/idea becomes a cultural unit passed between humans, you then have the opportunity to generate an 'awareness campaign' to drive actions, or to generate attitudes towards an issue – i.e. consensus.

In the case of ISIS, terminologies, 'discourses' and narratives of the 'enemy', i.e. the West and Europe, are re-appropriated and spun in order to satisfy the organisation's own needs. The eleven issues of *Dabiq* magazine, distributed online in English, make it possible for us to understand ISIS' communicative strategy first hand.[6] Analysts agree[7] that ISIS employs specific skills in managing the various media available and that it can articulate message production with a distinctive 'western' style. This supports the impression that its public diplomacy follows memetic criteria.[8]

The paper first carries out a quantitative analysis of *Dabiq*, then analyses the inconsistencies of its self-narrative compared with those of the addressees. Thus, it will be possible to reverse-engineer the memetic processes at work and to discover who learns from whom in this 'game of mirrors' where codes are appropriated and legitimised.[9] The present discussion, comparing the ISIS narrative to the specific NATO doctrine on InfoOps and PsyOps, claims the presence of exogenous elements in the structuring of the message. These generate an informative process that is neither a narrative nor a counter-narrative, but rather a narrative against a specific enemy: Europe. *Dabiq* discourses of/on Europe are thus marginalising where NATO is concerned. Furthermore, the old continent is considered as an enemy/ally of the USA, and thus the target of an asymmetrical narrative that leverages on continental political weaknesses and, in both cases, with a deep impact on European public opinion.

Given the nature of this research some confidential sources will be treated according to the Chatham House Rule (CHR):

> When a meeting, or part thereof, is held under the Chatham House Rule, participants are free to use the information received, but neither the identity nor the affiliation of the speaker(s), nor that of any other participant, may be revealed.

2 Review of the literature

Given the recent appearance of ISIS on the international scene most of the discussion can be found in specialised blogs or websites, although since 2015 some scientific contributions have been published. Ingram[10] offers a critical overview of recent papers and books on the topic. Stern and Berger, Hall and Weiss and Hassan[11] have specific sections on ISIS' media campaign. Maggioni and Magri[12] focus exclusively on ISIS' communication, within a sociology of communication framework. None of the items reviewed offers a specific linguistic or multimodal analysis of *Dabiq*. The works quoted above clearly attribute a military label to ISIS' communicative activities, i.e. InfoOps/PsyOps, thus framing the entire phenomenon in a specific context. Nonetheless, they do not explore the nature and the origins of this effective military approach to communication. This is the reason why throughout this chapter I will constantly refer to the ways military doctrine defines and describes these activities.

Furthermore, one cannot but note that journalists thus far have the lion's share in book publishing on ISIS. Hall, Weiss and Hassan are journalists and their works, albeit timely, are broad in scope with a tendency to generate analyses that are suitable for media venues but do not favour a critical analysis of the message. The consequence is that most of the narratives and perceptions available to the public are not generated by ISIS' media production, but rather by what analysts and the media report and interpret as being ISIS. This is so because journalists are always sensitive to maintaining an 'exchange relationship' with the institutions they depend on for getting news, given that 'news is what an authoritative source tells the journalist'.[13] Consequently, they prefer not to veer from the mainstream narratives. It will be shown, by means of a quantitative and multimodal analysis of the corpus, that several 'facts' reported about ISIS are not factual and have no statistical and informative relevance in its official publication. This effect has been achieved thanks to a strategy that is a blend of military InfoOps/PsyOps. Cheterian[14] maintains that:

> ISIS is not necessarily more violent than other warring factions in the conflicts of the Middle East today. What distinguishes the jihadi group is its

celebration and exhibition of violence, using it as a weapon with which to terrorise the population it aims to dominate, and to attract media attention. In order to be constantly on our screens, in competition with other violent groups, ISIS has escalated its violence: when beheadings became familiar, ISIS introduced a new, shocking form – placing a prisoner in a cage and burning him to death.

Rękawek[15] states that:

> ISIS is an organisation that is often misunderstood. Usually, it is seen as a barbaric and terrorist cult intent on acts of extreme violence, and an entity focused on achieving global objectives. At the same time, it presents itself as an opportunistic entity and is clearly telling us what its plans are.

This is one of the key and long-running elements prominent in ISIS's strategic narrative, i.e. the intention to inform the world of its future plans (*heavy boots* trampling the *idols*). This inconsistency of content and modality of the message is one of the first traces of an exogenous presence in its making. Further, openly informing the global audience of its priorities is a strategic mistake. Kingsley[16] warns that

> the fear about ISIS ... is borne out of their social media campaign, not reality ... ISIS's use of social media is so slick that it has made the group seem more powerful than it is.

Of course, if ISIS does that, the aim is to deceive the addressees, as described in doctrinal manuals on InfoOps/PsyOps and its *Dabiq* Issue #4. In fact, this operational attitude overlaps with the NATO and with the Anglo-American doctrine. It is interesting to note how journalists immediately labelled the process as military InfoOps, without detecting the inherent possibility of deception that the label entails.

If a detached stance from ISIS' media production is adopted, then the phenomenon, which is hard to understand if taken at face value, can be explained. *Dabiq* can be read at two levels. One is through its high quality graphics, as if it were a glossy magazine. 'It is the same phenomenon as advertising techniques that aim to endorse your choice of a product rather than inspire it'.[17] The other is to analyse the textual content with a corpus linguistics approach and let words speak for themselves, without any bias. The exogenous component will then become evident.

3 Corpus description and names of the entity

This chapter uses a combination of quantitative and qualitative analysis within the corpus linguistics framework. The corpus consists of the eleven issues of *Dabiq* published so far and it counts 277,856 tokens (words) and 13,224 types (unique word forms, or its vocabulary). They cover the July 2014–August 2015 time span. The software used for the quantitative analysis is WordSmith Tools. Before analysing corpus data it is important, for those unacquainted with Corpus Linguistics, to define some parameters that are used in the discussion.

Frequency is how many times a type repeats itself in the corpus. Normally it is also associated with its ranking in the list of words present in the corpus, but here the first value will suffice.

Distribution is important to see how and where the author disseminates meaning in the text. We will see how important this is for ISIS.

Collocates are the words which occur in the neighbourhood of a given key word. Collocates of *letter* might include *post, stamp, envelope*, etc. For computing collocation strength, we can use:

- the frequency with which two words are associated: how often they co-occur, which assumes we have an idea of the possible distance to count them as 'neighbours'. In our case we look five words to the left and five to the right of the key word;
- the frequency of the key word in the corpus;
- the frequency of the collocate in the corpus;
- the total number of running words in our corpus: total tokens.

The *statistical index* I use to measure the collocation is the *Z-score*. The higher the value, the higher the likelihood two words collocate not by chance, but because of the author's intention.

Thus, *types* (vocabulary), *tokens* (frequency), *collocations* (the Z-score) and *distribution* allow us to index and realise a four-dimensional matrix that maps the ways meaning is instantiated in a specific text and shapes reality.

To discuss the nature of ISIS' communicative strategy and narrative, a first methodological note must be made on the way to designate this entity. Currently several names are in use and the 13 November 2015 attacks in Paris have prompted a new debate.[18] These are: ISIS (Islamic State of Iraq and Syria), ISIL (Islamic State of Iraq and the Levant) and the more generic, all-including, IS (Islamic State). As I will discuss later, all of these acronyms imply a particular interpretation of the entity's narrative. Since this chapter adopts a corpus-based approach, I will use the acronym most frequent in *Dabiq*. The Discourse Analyst's approach, in fact, is to document a phenomenon as narrated by the informant, not as reported by others, in this case analysts, international actors and the media. *IS* is present 40 times and concentrated in the last issue. This parallels the use of *Daesh*, the Arabic version of the acronym, previously used with little or no success by the French President and now more frequent after the Paris attacks. It is often used by Arabic-speaking critics of ISIS because it sounds offensive. In fact, it is similar to the Arabic word *Dahes*, 'one who sows discord'. This is used five times, with negative connotations, four of them in the 11th issue. *ISIL* is used thirty-five times with a predominance in the 4th (16)[19] and 11th (9) issues. *ISIS* (96) is regularly distributed in all issues (it is absent in the third) with peaks in the 7th, 8th and 9th, with a decrease in the 10th and 11th due to the emergent use of *IS*. It must be noted that the expression *Islamic State* occurs 1,108 times and is regularly distributed, with peaks in the 9th, 10th and 11th issues. Nonetheless, this nominal group mainly refers to the theological implications of the rule of ISIS not to the geographical boundaries of the state they are aiming to establish.

4 The corpus linguistic analysis

In this section I address, by means of quantitative analysis, the gap between the narrative provided by ISIS and the one provided by the media on ISIS itself. The latter favours a distorted interpretation of the message by public opinion and is prone to ignore the warning signs that the message generates. In fact, the data presented below is surprising.

4.1 Who is the enemy?

The first most frequent word included in Table 10.1 is *Jihad*. I included it since it constitutes a benchmark for ISIS, or at least this is what we would expect. Actually, in spite of its high frequency the word does not generate collocations of statistical interest. This is a feature of all the words in the corpus that I will discuss below. Surprisingly, the key word collocates with *defensive* (9) and has a high Z-score. *Offensive* (3) has a lower Z-score. These are the most relevant collocations, but with a low informative impact, given their frequency. It must be considered that normally, for word patterns, the software has a threshold frequency of five and I have had to lower it to one in order to find any data. Thus, ISIS considers its position in defensive terms in order to maintain the status quo in the area under control. In fact, one of the most frequent clusters is *the jihad claimants* (33) always used in an argumentative way against those who would like to usurp the ISIS 'brand'. This would show, as we will discuss later, an inherent weakness in ISIS that could be well exploited by people outside the borders of this particular State. The only other regular locution is *Jihad Fi Sabilillah* (11) (Jihad in the cause of Allah). All in all, it would count for an average of one occurrence per issue, which is neither statistically nor analytically meaningful.

If we continue the analysis of the table we observe that the counter key word of *jihad*, namely *crusade*, has a low frequency (43) and the only repeated pattern is *crusade against the Islamic State* (7). The *NATO* and *American led crusade into/against Sham/Islam* patterns score only 1 each.

The next key word is linked to the opponents, i.e. the *Crusaders* (329). Although the frequency is high, no significant Z-scores or premodifications can be observed. There are only two meaningful patterns: *the Crusaders and their Apostate/Allies* (4) and *the allies of the crusaders and Jews in their war against the Muslims* (3). The distribution pattern confirms what will be discussed soon, i.e. a timely increase of the frequencies when the enemies, i.e. the West, are

Table 10.1 *Enemy* as a person or a religion

Key word	Frequency in corpus	Issue where the key word is present	Issues where the key word is peaking (or missing) and notes
Jihad	465	evenly distributed	7, 8, 9, 10, 11
Crusaders	329	evenly distributed	7, 9, 11
Crusader	214	evenly distributed	7, 8, 9, 10, 11
Kuffar (unbeliever, disbeliever, infidel)	178	6, 7, 8, 9, 10, 11	7, 8, 9, 10
Apostate	143	evenly distributed	9, 10, 11
Apostates	130	evenly distributed	6, 7, 8, 9, 10, 11
Murtadd (apostate)	120	evenly distributed	missing in 1, 2
Rafida (Shiites, rejectors, those who reject/refuse)	117	evenly distributed	6, 9, 11 Rejectors (0)
Jews	103	evenly distributed	5, 8, 9, 11 Jew (11) Jewish (40)
Murtaddin (apostate)	95	evenly distributed	5, 6, 7, 10
Mushrikun/kin (polytheists)	84	3, 4, 7, 8, 9, 10, 11	8, 10 Mushrik (24) Polytheists (2)
Rafidi (sing. of rafidah)	83	evenly distributed	6, 9, 11
Christians	59	evenly distributed	4, 9, 10 missing in 1, 2 Christian (19)
Kafir (sing. of Kuffar)	56	evenly distributed	7, 8, 9, 10 Kafirah (fem.) (0)
Disbelievers	49	evenly distributed	7 missing in 1 Disbeliever (10)
Crusade	43	evenly distributed	4 missing in 1, 2, 5, 8

facing difficulties in maintaining consensus: a counterproductive strategy, one could say, or a counterintelligence InfoOps/PsyOps operation.

Crusader (214) does not yield any interesting Z-scores, with the exception of *Britain* with five collocations in four issues. The most interesting use is as a premodifier of *army*, generating twenty patterns:

> The spark has been lit here in Iraq, and its heat will continue to intensify – by Allah's permission – until it burns the crusader armies in Dabiq.

It can be observed that the statement is generic and statistically insignificant, enough to allow for a free-hand manipulation by Western media.

Dabiq tends to determine the enemy categories linked with religion by means of an Arab word and sometimes offering, in a didactic manner, the English translation. The first most frequent category is *kuffar* (178), that accounts for unbelievers, disbelievers and infidels. One would expect a repertoire of words collocating with this enemy category but no meaningful clusters are recorded for the word. They have a low frequency, the highest is six, but the average is two. Among the latter *enslaving* has no statistical relevance. The tendency to repeat words without collocating them in a meaningful context is confirmed again, as well as a distribution peaking in the last issues. The equivalent English translation, *disbelievers* (49) peaks in issue seven but does not display any particularly interesting Z-scores or clusters. The singular, *unbeliever* and *infidel* both score 0. Searches for *kill/punish(ment)(of) disbelievers/ kuffar* returned 0. *Kill the disbeliever* (1) and *kill any disbeliever* (2) are the only two found. This is not surprising since the verb *kill* (106) only once generates a statement that cannot be considered against the West:

> With specific regards to the soldiers of Allah present in the lands of Kufr, the Islamic State took the occasion to renew its call to attack, kill, and terrorize the crusaders on their own streets.

The singular *kafir* (56) yields the same pattern. Z-scores show a tendency to collocate with a person's name, with *journalist* and with *humiliation* because they are associated with the images of executions.

Despite its civilian facade, Al-Baghdadi's organisation is a paramilitary organisation whose main job is fighting its real or imaginary enemies. These are flexible categories that can be extended, as ISIS is also prominently targeting the *apostates*, i.e. those who abandoned religion, or *disbelievers*. Nonetheless, throughout its history, and in its strategic narrative, ISIS has consistently demonstrated a preference for fighting 'local' battles, or for striking the 'near enemy' rather than the 'far enemy'. In fact, the theological category *apostate* (143) *murtadd* (120), *murtaddin* (95), if one adds all the variants in the corpus, would be the first enemy with a frequency of 488. Of all these key words only *murtadd* shows some relevant Z-score associated with names, the Jordanian *pilot* executed by burning alive, *Egypt* and *Sisi's*. Nonetheless, the generated clusters have a frequency of three or four.

Murtaddin generates twice a pattern with *PKK*, *Peshmerga* and *secularist*; known enemies to whom little discursive attention is given.

Apostate, peaking in the last four issues, collocates with the *Crusaders and their Allies* cluster (4), *Agents* (2) and *women* (2). The *jihad against the apostate regime* also scores two.

Apostates is only relevant with *Crusaders and Apostates* (11) and with fighting against the Nusayri apostates (5), i.e. the Syrians and *Assad* (34) who is never threatened with death.

Rafidah (117), i.e. Shiites, 'rejector/s' (0/0), 'those who reject' or 'those who refuse' are given particular attention in issues six, nine and eleven. Again, meaningful Z-scores have a low frequency (3) and generate only two patterns: *massacred Rafidah* and *filthy Rafidah*.

The singular form *Rafidi* (83) generates only one meaningful cluster: '*the Rafidi temple in Kuwait*' (2). Another possible singular *Rawafid* scores five.

Jews (103) confirms the trend observed so far. A few clusters score low, but above the average for this corpus with the following frequencies: *the Jews and (the) Christians* (17) and *the Jews and Crusaders* (8).

Mushrikun/kin (polytheists) (84), peaks in eight and ten. *Enslave muskrik women* (1) echoes a cluster that will be discussed and that was so popular with the press, in spite of its meaningless frequency. The other notable cluster is *kill the mushrikin wherever you find them* (5). This is one of the few strong and aggressive statements found in the corpus, although with a limited frequency.

It must be noted that *kill* (106) and *attack* (61) generate few 'strong' statements. Apart from the one discussed above, the other is *kill him/them* (4/4) both being supposed quotations/interpretations from the *Qur'an* (86).

As for *Christians* (59), the same meaningless patterns are observed as for *Jews*. The only noticeable cluster is *Roman Christians* (4), all in issue four, and linked to a specific explanation:

> Rome in the Arabic tongue of the Prophet (sallallahualayhi wa sallam) refers to the Christians of Europe and their colonies in Sham prior to the conquering of Sham at the hands of the Sahabah.

The next statement gives an example of the way words are used in an unrelated and decontextualised manner:

> He then warned against the propaganda of the crusaders by saying, 'America and its allies from amongst the Jews, Crusaders, Rafidah, secularists, atheists, and apostates claim that their coalition and war is to aid the weak and oppressed, help the poor, relieve the afflicted, liberate the enslaved, defend the innocent and peaceful, and prevent the shedding of their blood'.

The analysis now focuses on enemy states.

The outcome of the analysis for entities such as states, institutions and geopolitical blocks is substantially the same as for the previous section. Z-scores for

Table 10.2 Enemy as a state, city or organisation

Key word	Frequency in corpus	Issue where the key word is present	Issues where the key word is peaking (or missing) and notes
US	125	evenly distributed	3, 4
West	118	evenly distributed	7, 8, 9
			The West (72)
America	84	evenly distributed	4, 6, 9, 11 USA (2)
Iran	80	2, 3, 4, 6, 8, 9, 10, 11	6, 9, 11 (34)
Western	68	evenly distributed	missing in 1
Europe	42	4, 5, 7, 8, 9, 10, 11	
Rome	26	1, 2, 4, 5, 8, 9, 10, 11	4, Italy (7)
France	22	evenly distributed	7, 8, Paris (7)
NATO	18	4, 8, 10, 11	11
UK	6	4, 7, 10, 11	Britain (2), London (5)
Israel	6	3, 4, 8, 10	Israeli (9)

the key words, patterns and clusters offer little information in terms of statistical evidence. Nonetheless, it is interesting to note that the representation of *Europe* (42) is marginalised and diluted in other entities, such as a generic, but inclusive, *West* (118). The latter, together with the *US* (125), are indicated as the main enemies. As previously stated, *Europe* is associated with *Rome* (26) and its related symbolic meaning. In spite of this apparent disregard, it is *Europe* that has been frequently attacked and damaged by ISIS. As we will see in Section 6 below this could be considered a case of deception.

It is also worth mentioning the frequency of *Iran* (80) and *Israel* (6), respectively. *Iran* collocates with *Russia* and *Assad*, generating clusters with above average frequency.

5   A linguistic interpretation of *Dabiq*

A first consideration that can be drawn from the previous analysis is that ISIS propaganda has few explicit calls for attacks on the West and even less than would be expected on Israel, which the organisation should supposedly perceive as their 'natural enemy'. Rather, the enemies that significantly collocate and generate clusters are Iran, Russia[20] and Assad. Confirmed is the tendency in all ISIS' communicative output to promote its paramount goal: to secure the Islamic State. That could change overnight, and the Paris attacks would favour this inference, but the quantitative results would confirm what experts say: for now the securitisation of the Islamic state sharply distinguishes ISIS from Al Qaeda, which has long made attacks on the West its top priority. We must remember that the majority of the organisation's victims, so far, have been Muslims.

What we learn from the key words and from the tables is that the use of lexis in *Dabiq* is engineered in an unusual way. Words rarely produce relevant

0–10%	|	51	| ◎◎◎◎◎◎◎◎◎◎◎◎◎◎◎◎◎◎◎◎◎◎◎◎◎
10–20%	|	79	| ◎◎◎◎◎◎◎◎◎◎◎◎◎◎◎◎◎◎◎◎◎◎◎◎◎◎◎◎◎◎◎◎◎◎◎◎◎
20–30%	|	63	| ◎◎◎◎◎◎◎◎◎◎◎◎◎◎◎◎◎◎◎◎◎◎◎◎◎◎◎◎◎◎◎◎
30–40%	|	56	| ◎◎◎◎◎◎◎◎◎◎◎◎◎◎◎◎◎◎◎◎◎◎◎◎◎◎◎◎
40–50%	|	44	| ◎◎◎◎◎◎◎◎◎◎◎◎◎◎◎◎◎◎◎◎◎◎
50–60%	|	22	| ◎◎◎◎◎◎◎◎◎◎◎
60–70%	|	40	| ◎◎◎◎◎◎◎◎◎◎◎◎◎◎◎◎◎◎◎◎
70–80%	|	59	| ◎◎◎◎◎◎◎◎◎◎◎◎◎◎◎◎◎◎◎◎◎◎◎◎◎◎◎◎◎
80–90%	|	26	| ◎◎◎◎◎◎◎◎◎◎◎◎◎
90–100%	|	23	| ◎◎◎◎◎◎◎◎◎◎◎

◎ = 2, total: 463

Figure 10.1 Distribution of node *humanitarian* in the corpus of the Kosovo war NATO press conferences.

collocations, patterns or clusters. It is just a list of repeated key words apparently not generating a specific meaning or interpretation. This holds true especially if they are considered apart from the striking images accompanying them in the glossy magazine. In fifteen years of research in this field, I have never observed such a peculiar technique. Generally, repetitions are functional to the generation of meaning through collocations and patterns that draw the cognitive map discussed above. This process can be defined a case of flexible language engineering or generic reframing,[21] i.e. words are uttered in an apparently casual way just to resonate and have effects on the reader's previously established isotopies so that they can be manipulated by other entities such as spin doctors, analysts or journalists. This is confirmed by the distribution of the key words in *Dabiq* issues. Their peaks replicate a technique used by NATO spin doctors in times of crisis. In our case words tend to peak at regular intervals and in the latest issues. If we observe Figure 10.1, it displays the distribution of the key word *humanitarian* within the corpus of the Kosovo war NATO press conferences we note that its occurrences have a wave-like pattern.[22]

During the early days of war, when it was necessary to generate and build up consensus for the military initiative, this effect was achieved by summoning the possible association with *humanitarian*, as the intervals between 0 and 30 per cent show. One can state that the use of *humanitarian* increases whenever the need to reinforce public consensus on the conflict is perceived as necessary, for example after a critical event that endangers the mainstream narrative. Accordingly, the distribution of words, acronyms and topics shows that ISIS follows the same scheme. In other words, ISIS is not the trend setter or the spinner of its narrative, but rather the follower, which is unusual. The distribution of the key words thus follows a pattern which does not satisfy ISIS' needs, but rather those of western countries and media. This will be evident when we analyse the search trends for ISIS. In fact, they are in phase opposition to the distributions observed.

Thus, here an absolutisation of words is observed, in the sense they are rarely pre- or post-modified. Words exist on their own and do not establish relationships with the other words. It is a kind of unicist view that, in a way, would confirm ISIS' proclamations that there is 'no grey zone' in the conflict; it is purely a clash of black and white, a total war that is not feasible militarily. A by-product of this attitude is that the receiver of the message is free to interpret and manipulate meanings. Is this the case?

6 Deception, in *Dabiq* and in military doctrine

The military forces consider communication a way to control the environment of operations and establish supremacy over the enemy. Thus, Language Engineering[23] is a deceiving activity. Traditionally, in military doctrine, 'deception involves actions executed to deliberately mislead adversary military, paramilitary, or violent extremist organization decision-makers'.[24] Consequently, strategic informative deception can be divided into cover and disinformation. Cover induces the belief that something true is in fact false. Disinformation aims to produce the belief that something false is in fact true. In other words, cover conceals the truth while disinformation conveys false information. When the military disseminate false information, it is always intended to mislead. When the press, as an effect of language engineering processes, disseminates false information that helps keep classified information secret, the military have reached their main goal. This practice derives from the CIA protocols on TS/SCI, or top secret/sensitive compartmentalised information. This ensures that outsiders do not know what they do not need to know and insiders know only what they have a 'need-to-know'. In relation to this approach Jacobsen[25] quotes Churchill: 'I cannot forecast to you the action of Russia. It is a riddle wrapped in a mystery inside an enigma; but perhaps there is a key. That key is Russian national interest.'[26]

Dabiq's issue #4, page 14, devotes a detailed section to the topic 'War is Deception'. After a rhetorical start we read:

> The Prophet (sallallāhu 'alayhi wa sallam) said: war is deception. Al-Muhallab said, 'You must use deception in war, for it is more effective than reinforcements'.

Several methods of deception are discussed in the section. Definitions and suggestions show a deep knowledge of Allied InfoOps/PsyOps doctrines and overlap with them. There are several pages of good advice, for instance, the following:

> Feign an intent to attack an area other than the actual target.... Among the signs of a leader's experience and sophistication is that he takes advantage

of opportunities.... For unity during the course of battle is a predominant interest that cannot be superseded by anything else.... Don't be deceived by the ease of any Operation.

One cannot but note the total mastery of the principles of consensual ideology and deception techniques, normally only available to specialists or highly trained professionals. Furthermore, a proper and strategic use of different media is considered paramount to carry out a successful military strategy. In the section 'Ineffective Proxy Wars and Airstrikes', page 44, where the memetic use of military terminology is worth underlining, it is stated:

> It is important that the killing be attributed to patrons of the Islamic State who have obeyed its leadership. This can easily be done with anonymity. Otherwise, crusader media makes such attacks appear to be random killings.

7 Dabiq as Armageddon? A Western isotopy for a Western narrative trajectory

In order to discuss the complexity of the communicative system under scrutiny it is necessary to combine corpus linguistics with the concepts of isotopy and memetics.

In the first issue of *Dabiq* we read:

> As for the name of the magazine, it is taken from the area named Dabiq in the northern countryside of Halab (Aleppo) in Sham. This place was mentioned in a hadith describing some of the events of the Malahim (what is sometimes referred to as Armageddon in English). One of the greatest battles between the Muslims and the crusaders will take place near Dabiq.
>
> (*Dabiq* #1, 4)

Here the editors of the magazine start to activate the isotopy that will guide the western readers' interpretation of their communication. The complex process of isotopy generation was

> first introduced in an early work by A.J. Greimas. The notion of isotopy is now a key term of the Paris school approach and was included in Eco's taxonomy of interpretation strategies... Isotopy was originally said to consist in the *permanence* of contextual features ('classemes'), whose variations, instead of destroying the unity of the 'text', serve to *confirm* it. The features in question are thus redundant, in the sense of information theory, i.e. they are repeated all through the 'text', assuring its coherence, and, more in particular, a single interpretation.[27]

Even without reading the magazine, its title and especially its geographical localisation in English, *Armageddon*, is highly evocative and immediately echoes images of destruction and violence, which the 1998 Hollywood movie has generated in collective memory. The reader is thus forced into an interpretative framework pre-established by the authors, which will limit his/her ability to veer from the specific script. In this case, a situational framework with the title '*Islamic Terrorism*' is activated and determines the rules according to which we interpret and react in a determined situation. Tuastad[28] maintains that:

> Imaginaries of 'terrorism' and 'Arab mind' backwardness can be seen as closely connected: the latter explains the former as irrational – violence thus becomes the product of backward cultures. I regard this way of representing the violence of peripheralised peoples as a specific expression of symbolic violence: new barbarism ... and presents violence as a result of traits embedded in local cultures. New barbarism and neo-Orientalist imaginaries may serve as hegemonic strategies when the production of enemy imaginaries contributes to legitimise continuous colonial economic or political projects.

As a consequence, whole series of expectations with regards to the experience we are about to go through are also active. The expectations form part of the isotopy generated from the specific framework and it is the task of the latter, at cognitive level, to verify whether our expectations will be confirmed in what are defined as expected products. If this is not the case, it means that the other social actors involved in the communicative process do not know the rules of the framework and generate emerging products that must be accommodated within the current framework. Or they are deceiving us and are doing so on purpose. In this case it is evident that *Dabiq* is telling us what we have to expect from here on, i.e. a high level of threat from ISIS. It is a fact that from that moment on the emergent products we experience may cause strong and unpredictable emotional reactions, including the closing down of communicative channels, the wrong interpretation of the message, or, worse still, our decision to stop any attempt to perform critical analysis. These are the same processes boosted by fear. The only way to avoid entering the spiral of emotional reactions is to be flexible from a cognitive and emotive point of view and to activate a new isotopy which manages to follow the new emergent products, transforming them into expected products. Unfortunately, this ability is uncommon in standard or non-professional communicators/receivers. Moreover, such reactions happen even when we see pictures that we had understood in a receptive framework of a certain type. *Dabiq* images have such a strong impact that they completely divert our attention from the text they accompany; they work as distractors, neurolinguistically programming the reader. The quantitative analysis offers a typical example. In Table 10.2, I listed Rome and then Italy because the city is considered here as the symbol of Christianity. The peak is recorded in issue four, *The Failed Crusade*, with the front cover displaying St. Peter Square's obelisk with ISIS' black flag on top of it. Although the image can be of great impact, what is striking, from an informative point of view, is that the issue opens with a statement by az-Zarqāwī (the Emir of Al-Quaeda in Iraq and of the Mujahideen

Shura Council) that once more reflects the ambiguous nature of ISIS' communication: '*The spark has been lit here in Iraq, and its heat will continue to intensify – by Allah's permission – until it burns the crusader armies in Dābiq*'. The statement is interesting because it clearly displays ISIS' regional ambitions and it is repeated several times. Nonetheless, this issue became famous in western media for another statement: '*We will conquer your Rome, break your crosses, and enslave your women, by the permission of Allah, the Exalted*'. Beside the fact that, as we have seen, Rome is used in a symbolic way, the point is that the expression occurs just once in the corpus, together with *we will conquer your Rome* (4) and *enslave their women* (2 in issue seven). The same goes for *Islam is the religion of the sword, not pacifism* (1) and four repetitions as the heading of a page issue. Here we observe a common trait of western analysts and media reactions to *Dabiq*. They completely subscribe to the face value of the organisation's message, falling into the traps of deception as discussed earlier, even though, statistically, the message is not meaningful (Gambhir[29] is just one example). As a result, these statements made the headlines for several days and are now part of the collective knowledge on ISIS. Given the current financial constraints, journalists are less specialised and more prone to save time in using sources that are considered reliable. The military know this well and in recent years have increased the number of media officers. On the other hand, the same goes for intelligence services who are forced, in a competitive environment, to collect data from the open source and from 'rumours' with approaches to data mining techniques that sometimes veer from their original aim. The point here is the generation gap between old intelligence officers and new communicative tools that makes these officers easy to manipulate.[30] *Dabiq*, with its design, satisfies both needs: it is generic enough to fit in in the enemies' mental framework and their wishful thinking and it is delivered in a format that favours an acritical 'cut and paste' use. This also accounts for the existence of multinational/multilingual versions which enlarge the audience subject to deception. Again, an exemplary case in the best InfoOps/PsyOps tradition.

Creswell and Haykel[31] have pointed out the contrast between the carnage shown on ISIS' media production for the consumption of the West and the use of poetry as an internal propaganda tool, where the movement addresses itself: *it is in verse that militants most clearly articulate the fantasy life of jihad*. As a discourse analyst I cannot but agree with the authors. If we were to read and analyse *Dabiq* only through its words and not with the accompanying images, we would immediately realise the deceptive nature of its communication and its impact on military analysts and western journalists. By focusing on *Dabiq* they miss the point. They do not realise that the key to fighting the movement is its internal communication. It is as if professionals have forgotten that they are being exposed to propaganda. Thus, ISIS communicates with a modality that confirms the average western readers' isotopic expectations, namely, they confirm that the Islamic terrorists say what is expected of them by means of several memetic codes borrowed from these average readers' communicative registers. Readers are thus unable to spot possible inconsistencies in the message and confirm Tuastad's[32] hypothesis: 'imaginaries of "terrorism" and "Arab mind" backwardness can be seen as closely connected'. This is why a corpus linguistics approach, integrating the ideas of memetics,[33] can help to better understand the use of terminologies and narratives in *Dabiq* without applying any pre-determined and therefore interfering bias.

As anticipated, the combination of memes and isotopies allow us to explain certain characteristics of the communicative phenomenon we are observing. A typical effect of the memetic spread of ideas is the 'me too' effect. This is well known in marketing techniques where you replicate the salient characteristics of a successful product, frequently with a lower price. Thanks to the memetic process consumers transfer the properties of the original to the 'me too' follower. The best case in this area of studies, so far, is Al-Jazeera English (AJE). In 2005 the channel entered the market to provide either a regional voice or a global perspective for a potential world audience of over one billion English speakers who do not share the Anglo-American worldview. AJE positioned itself as the 'me too' of BBC World and CNN in terms of reliability of its information and sources. In order to achieve this it hired 13 former BBC journalists and a number of technicians. As a result, even the format of the video screen layout was exactly the same for the two stations and the musical breaks before the starting of the news were similar, just played with a few different notes and detuned.[34]

Al-Hayat Media Centre is the publisher of *Dabiq*. As it may be noted from the following pictures their logo is a memetic product of Al-Jazeera one.

The result is that readers, because of the memetic use of this logo, start to decode the message they are going to receive with a pre-activated isotopy that has set for them, beforehand, a specific interpretative path. Furthermore, most of the expected reactions to the communicative product have been already pre-selected by the sender, thus strongly influencing the outcome of the strategy and

Figure 10.2a Al-Hayat logo.

Figure 10.2b Al-Jazeera logo.

Figure 10.3 Network for the topic '#Syria'.
Source: Weng *et al*. 2012, 2.

pre-determining the ways physical and cognitive networks of meaning attribu-
tion will be generated. This is in line with the military approach to InfoOps/
PsyOps. Last but not least, this technical approach to communication guarantees,
in a world with limited attention and with but a few memes able to go viral, a
high chance of success for carefully engineered memes if combined with the
structure of specific social networks. *Dabiq* has these characteristics, as confirmed by Weng *et al* 2012.

   Figure 10.3 shows the visualisation of meme diffusion networks for the topic
'Syria', quite relevant for ISIS.

> Nodes represent Twitter users, and directed edges represent retweeted posts
> that carry the meme. The brightness of a node indicates the activity (number
> of retweets) of a user, and the weight of an edge reflects the number of
> retweets between two users ... #Syria display characteristic hub users and
> strong connections, respectively.[35]

   Further confirmation is provided by the two graphs below showing the trend
in Google Search for the words ISIS and ISIL. In January 2014, when ISIS
started to declare its intents with the new denomination, the organisation was

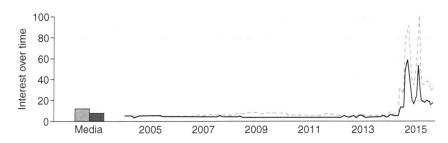

Figure 10.4 Trend for ISIL (dotted line) ISIS (continuous line) in Google Search.

Source: created by the author.

Note
Numbers represent search interest relative to the highest point on the chart for the given time. A value of 100 is the peak popularity for the term.

still not considered.[36] One can observe how quickly the searches have increased since July 2014, following *Dabiq*'s first issue.

> IS has had a meteoric rise in public consciousness since mid-2014 following its capture of Mosul and its subsequent series of videos featuring the beheading of several Western journalists and aid workers. IS's rise is even more remarkable given that it was almost wiped out in Iraq by the simultaneous Sunni 'Awakening' and US military surge in 2007–08.[37]

The graphs witness the success of InfoOps/PsyOps coordinated by Al-Hayat that follow the principle of Colonel P.J. Crowley, Spokesman National Security Council:

> How can you think to fight a war today without taking into account the media focus, which is a reality today, so you have to plan how to handle your media strategy, just as you plan your operation strategy, for any campaign.[38]

It is quite an achievement for a badly organised group of insurgents, as they were described by the press in the first instance. It is also important to note how the trend for 'Military Intervention against ISIS' replicates and overlaps with the trend for 'ISIS'. As we observed in the distribution patterns, this demonstrates the usefulness of the isotopies and memes which ISIS is able to propagate, albeit serving not its own goals but those of western spin-doctors and consensual ideologists. Berger, quoted by Brooking,[39] states:

> This is a combination of an extremely ambitious military campaign with an extremely ambitious PR campaign. Social media is most of that PR campaign.

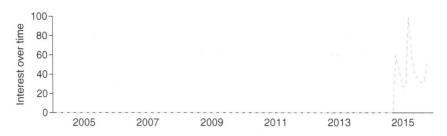

Figure 10.5 Trend for 'Military Intervention against ISIS' in Google Search.

Source: created by the author.

Note
Numbers represent search interest relative to the highest point on the chart for the given time. A value of 100 is the peak popularity for the term.

Brooking also points out:

> There are two observations to draw from IS' media presence. The first is that the individuals guiding the propaganda operations of the Islamic State have a highly sophisticated understanding of social media dynamics – better than many Western governments.

The point is: *many* western governments, but not just any. It seems that all the analysts and researchers implicitly get very close to the point, i.e. there are at least hints, not to mention evidence, that in ISIS' media production there are elements found in its narrative, skills and technological organisation that could be exogenous. It is as if analysts and researchers were reluctant to come to a logical conclusion, or at least to properly evaluate the salient aspects that characterise the problem. After the November 2015 attacks in Paris this much has become clear: the exogenous elements could be generated by some countries with a particular interest in the development of a situation in the Middle East in order to have consequences in/on Europe. Hence, this chapter will now focus on those salient aspects, apparently neglected but able to explain this paradoxical situation.

8 The narrative against Europe

Alastair Crooke, Director and Founder of Conflicts Forum, in the round table 'The War of Words', hosted by the ROME 2015 Mediterranean Dialogues on 10–12 December 2015, outlined the historical roots and interferences that have generated turmoil in ISIS' sphere of influence and the western role in them. These interferences have been clear since 1 June 2013 when, in a London court, the trial of a man accused of terrorism in Syria collapsed after

> it became clear British intelligence had been arming the same rebel groups the defendant was charged with supporting. The prosecution abandoned the

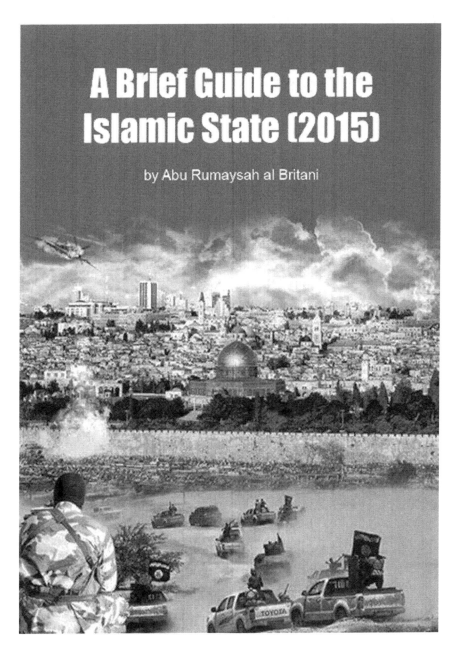

Figure 10.6 Cover of *A Brief Guide to the Islamic State* (2015).

Figure 10.7 Still from BBC documentary *World's Richest Terror Army.*

case, apparently to avoid embarrassing the intelligence services. The defence argued that going ahead with the trial would have been an 'affront to justice' when there was plenty of evidence the British state was itself providing 'extensive support' to the armed Syrian opposition. That didn't only include the 'non-lethal assistance' boasted of by the government (including body armour and military vehicles), but training, logistical support and the secret supply of 'arms on a massive scale'.[40]

My informed opinion, without downplaying the actions that this organisation has carried out, is that part of the assistance also included specific InfoOps/PsyOps personnel to help with the communicative processes and that some allied states surreptitiously support these activities. An interesting case is that of *A Brief Guide to the Islamic State* (the so-called *ISIS Tourist Guide*, Figure 10.6) by Abu Rumaysah al Britani. This was published on 18 May 2015.

Some visual elements are interesting, namely, the Jerusalem image and the Spitfire, the Battle of Britain's famous aeroplane, a symbol recently appropriated by UKIP. These elements could be easily accommodated within the memetic framework we have discussed, i.e. *Jerusalem* (6), a non-target, is transformed into a generic westernised outpost. Nonetheless, the lower part of the image is the most challenging one. Compare it to Figure 10.7.

This is taken from *The Richest Army in the World*, a BBC 2 documentary on ISIS aired on 22 April 2015. It is evident that we are observing the same image, but the point is that, apparently, the ISIS guide's author has obtained some footage that could be considered a kind of 'director's cut'. In fact, the BBC documentary only uses this frame for one second, while the guide's image is taken from a longer sequence of the same scene. While one cannot say who passed on these images to the author, this example reinforces the observation made by several analysts that the group also harbours trained designers and professional communicators.

> There are a lot of people in Isis who are good at Adobe applications – InDesign, Photoshop, you name it. There are people who have had a professional career in graphic design.[41]

These skills are such that they have produced the Dawn smartphone application, that is to say, the opportunity to keep up on the latest news about the jihadi group by relaying ISIS' messages via smart-phones. The point is that (a) you can easily generate deceiving messages with all the listed applications, (b) ISIS, beside its ideological message, must have other means to attract so many professionals to work in such an environment, (c) it should be understood how it is that Dawn was so easy to download from the AppStores until recently. According to *Mashable*, the third most important blog in the world, an employee with a major social media company confirmed that

> U.S. intelligence officials approached the company and asked that the ISIL accounts not be taken down, despite the often bloody and threatening content. The reason? American intelligence officials are monitoring the ISIL accounts, trying to glean information about the deadly group and its strengths, tactics and networks.[42]

The point is that this laissez faire could have favoured the perpetrators of the attacks in Paris. There are plenty of such incoherencies that I collected while carrying out research for this chapter,[43] but an analysis of the narrative itself will suffice to make the point.

From here on, I will frequently refer to the notion of 'narrative'. Several definitions are available, and Tanner[44] summarises those that could work for the Middle East. For Freedman,[45] narratives are 'compelling story lines which can explain events convincingly and from which inferences can be drawn'. The following one, from a document that could be incorporated into NATO's Strategic Communication Doctrine,[46] is suitable for our purposes:

> a coherent system of stories that creates a cause and effect relationship between an originating desire or conflict, and an actual or desired or implied resolution. In so doing, NARRATIVE has the capacity to express identity, values, moral basis, legitimacy and vision around [which] entities (organisations or activities) can unite.

Graphically, the above concept can be represented in Figure 10.8.

This definition fits in with the data we have discussed so far. Ingram[47] argues that the overarching purpose of ISIS' InfoOps/PsyOps campaign is 'to shape the

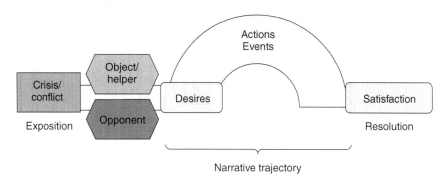

Figure 10.8 A narrative trajectory.

perceptions and polarise the support of audiences via messages that interweave appeals to pragmatic and perceptual factors'. This point is undeniable. In fact, a hallmark of ISIS' campaign has been the central role of InfoOps in its overall strategy. Consequently, it might be fruitful to consider who has mostly gained by the ISIS narrative. Kfir[48] has pointed out the problems NATO is facing:

> the vacillating commitment of alliance members who chose to address security issues through EU mechanisms or optional coalitions of the willing threatens NATO's relevance. If NATO's members are unclear about the alliance's agenda and identity, others cannot know what the alliance is willing to do to protect its interests.

Kfir points out that the Ukrainian issue is no longer sufficient to keep the alliance cohesive. ISIS is the other element that could foster consensus among the reluctant allies. The self-proclamation of the Caliphate in July 2014 was timely for a NATO that was facing a complex crisis and was going to the September 2014 summit in Swansea. There, President Obama began outlining a counter-offensive that was backed by Matt Olsen, director of the National Counterterrorism Center, who said

> the Islamic State operates the most significant global propaganda machine of any Islamist extremist group ... No group is as successful and effective as ISIL is at using propaganda, particularly social media.[49]

We must note the timing chosen when introducing the issue of ISIS into the NATO agenda and the American tentative extension of the memetic isotopy of the acronym. From ISIS, located in two specific states, to a more general *Levant* (ISIL), thus expanding the perceived threat to the Near East of the European allies. This marks the rise of a pro-NATO narrative in a moment in history when the Alliance was facing a consensual crisis on the European side.

Putin's threat in Ukraine and ISIS represent a narrative trajectory of needs and actions that satisfies the desired solution for the problem, i.e. Putin and ISIS must be stopped through a reinforcement of NATO itself. Recent events, i.e. the tentative alliance between France and Russia and the shooting of a Russian bomber by the Turks, have partially altered the desired trajectory but the essential characteristics are still at work. This narrative of fear that through ISIS has struck continental Europe is designed not as a *counter-narrative*, as the quantitative analysis has shown, but rather as a manipulative *narrative against* Europe that fits in with American plans, supported by the British, for a New Transatlantic Partnership. This would also explain the nature of an organisation that challenges the role of Iran and Russia in the area, destabilising it, and serving the Anglo-American and Israeli strategic agenda. This is a classic doctrinal case of red–red fight in military InfoOps/PsyOps, where decisive actions in dividing one or more enemy fields are necessary. In this case ISIS' narrative is used to leverage a Europe that is considered without a strategy,[50] with programmes that are too 'womanly'[51] and with the goal of obtaining consensus to operations that will favour the American disengagement from the continent.[52] This scenario is a replica of a 2005 case study of the US Joint Special Operation University, *Dividing Our Enemies*,[53] combined with what analysts have recognised:

> the media proficiency of the IS exists because of an extensive media infrastructure that allows it to produce high-quality, timely products in different languages to different audiences that fit the narrative that the group wishes to convey. In addition to the production side, the IS is also capable of pushing this narrative out along a number of mediums, to include the internet, broadcast airways, and traditional publications.[54]

The 13 November 2015 attacks in Paris have reignited a debate that is now candid[55] in acknowledging the role, since 2003, of covert US and British regional military intelligence strategy in empowering what today is known as ISIS and is now proving to be counter-productive to the narrative's master-minds. Waleed Aly, member of the Global Terrorism Research Centre at Monash University and anchorman in the *Project* TV programme, well aware of the deceptive nature of ISIS' communicative strategy, suggested that the attacks were not the work of ISIS, even though ISIS has taken responsibility for them, because of the question of deception discussed previously in this chapter. Apart from the unclassified documents that are emerging, my claim is supported by another element. In late April 2014,[56] while researching for another essay, I met an English speaking InfoOps/PsyOps officer, who claimed he had been involved in the events leading to the Arab Spring. He told me in an ironic tone that he was going to be sent to Saudi Arabia to improve his Arabic language in May 2014. This is where the media proficiency that Milton refers to could originate from. A Media Operation Centre can be set up in weeks and NATO has already directed propaganda against Europe in the past.[57]

Thus, exogenous agents could have exploited, as for Hezbollah,[58] the fact that ISIS 'is an opportunistic organisation that is keen on making the most of available opportunities'[59] to generate *Dabiq*. Thus, the 'local' ambitions of a group have been given resonance to promote another agenda. Consequently, ISIS master-minds are forced to devote an increasing amount of space to the 'global' in *Dabiq*'s narrative. Brooking[60] has noted that:

> the messaging tactics that have served IS so well ... made it exponentially harder for the organization to ever shift course.... Even if IS leaders did attempt to moderate their rhetoric in an effort to consolidate existing gains, how could they begin to rein in the vast social media network that now claims to speak for the organization?

The exogenous agents, with their own assistance and technical support, could have drafted and directed a narrative that frames ISIS in its role and is suitable to leverage European audiences shifting consensus in the shadow of fear. This is where the use of military InfoOps/PsyOps techniques of western origin is evident. At the tactical level, some events can be used to divert public opinion in times of crisis. The ISIS' blowing up of the Palmyra Arch of Triumph on 5 October 2015, while a heated debate was going on in Europe on NATO's credibility after its bombing of Kunduz's Doctors without Borders hospital on 3 October 2015, can be seen as a timely way out for the Alliance and an example of how certain events can be promptly spun.

Thus, at strategic level a grand narrative, *the fear of ISIS*, is used. This is functional at two levels: (a) it gives credibility and internal force to ISIS in its limited geographical sphere, (b) it allows generating consensus among its opponents and it legitimates military actions in a destabilised area. In this way internal divisions within the European Union are increased to the advantage of countries engaged in the *Great Game*,[61] namely the United States and those 'in the special relationship'.[62]

In May 2014, during one of the meetings I attended for research purposes, a Senior Officer showed the slide below, representing the narrative trajectory of the Ukrainian crisis.[63]

The presenting Officer and the audience, all NATO professionals in the field, had to recognise that this narrative, although a possible counter-narrative, a quasi-conspiratorial one, was extremely plausible in accounting for the present situation. In fact, the September 2014 NATO summit in Wales ratified a 'resolution' whose effect is close to the one shown above, with ISIS as an added new variable.

9   Conclusions

> In dealing with jihadism, the western narrative is part of the problem, not the solution.... The Neo-Cons said 'actually all those secular Arab States like Syria, Iraq, Egypt were just Soviet agents, they are part of the empire of

Figure 10.9 Narrative trajectory of the Ukranian crisis.

the evil.… This does not reflect the fact that actually we have been using these forces [the ones opposing the secular states] for our own purposes, because we are the forces of good'.

This is an excerpt from Crooke's speech[64] at the Rome 2015 Mediterranean Dialogues conference.[65] During this three-day high level meeting the main-stream nature of the ISIS narrative was challenged for the first time. It was recognised that it is important 'not to overreact, but to think first … because most of the attackers in Paris were Europeans'.[66] Participants also agreed that this threat to Europe comes during the continent's worst political and economic crisis and that the Mediterranean must again be 'an area of dialogue and great opportunities',[67] through a narrative that promotes the European continental and Mediterranean vision to counter the 'narrative against' discussed in Section 8 above. The Paris attacks, 'a political mistake of Daesh',[68] have proved to be the opportunity for continental Europe to critically react to this challenge. For the first time public opinion is also aware that some national interests are at work to create turmoil in European internal affairs, and that, given the off-the-record conflicting positions within NATO, a positive agenda must be sponsored. The example of France, a NATO country, seeking alliance with Russia is just the latest case which runs parallel to Russian Minister Lavrov's carefully engineered opening statement in Rome: 'All that is connected with the Mediterranean region strikes a special chord in the souls of Europeans and Russians are not an exception'.

'Europe is a distant place when seen from Washington'.[69] It is no coincidence that. using the pages of *Foreign Policy*, Walt[70] posed an interesting question: 'What should we do if the Islamic State wins?' His answer, 'Live with it', has little consequences for the USA and for Britain, the latter already considering its Brexit, but it would have great effects on continental Europe – the real one, not the narrated one. To paraphrase Churchill, the key is not ISIS' but someone else's national interest. Let a European narrative make these elements explicit, because 'we do not follow maps to buried *treasures* and X *never* ever marks the spot' (*Indiana Jones and the Last Crusade*).

Notes

1 I started research for this chapter in August 2014. While I was writing the final version, the Paris attacks of 13 November 2015 occurred. After a few days of reflection and observing the debate that developed on some of the issues addressed here, i.e. the presence of exogenous elements in ISIS communicative strategy and narrative, I decided to continue my work. It is my tribute to all the innocent victims of violent acts.
2 Conoscenti 2005.
3 My reformulation of Dawkins' (1976) key concepts.
4 Dawkins 1976, 192.
5 Vada 2008, www.slideshare.net/oyvindvada/making-memetics-a-science-10249035. Accessed 25 January 2016.
6 Ryan 2014.
7 Shane and Hubbard 2014.
8 Weng *et al.* 2012.
9 Conoscenti 2016b.
10 Ingram 2015.
11 Stern and Berger 2015: Hall 2015; Weiss and Hassan 2015.
12 Maggioni and Magri 2015.
13 Bell 1991, 191–192.
14 Cheterian 2015.
15 Rękawek 2015, 1.
16 Kingsley 2014.
17 Mullen and Todd 2014.
18 'What to Call the Islamic State?', *The Economist*, 15 November 2015. www. economist.com. Accessed 30 September 2016.
19 Henceforth, when an issue number or *key word* is followed by a number in brackets, this refers to its frequency, the number of times the word type is repeated.
20 'Russia is ISIS's new target' (Watts 2015).
21 Conoscenti 2011.
22 For a detailed analysis of the effect of this event on the media management and language engineering strategy, see Conoscenti 2004, 60–78.
23 Conoscenti 2004.
24 Field Manual 3–13, Inform and Influence Activities, Headquarters Department of the Army, Washington, DC, 2013, 28 and AJP-3.10 Allied Joint Doctrine For Information Operations, NATO HQs, Brussels, 2009, 0125–1–9.
25 Jacobsen 2011, 82.
26 www.churchill-society-london.org.uk/RusnEnig.html. Accessed 25 January 2016.
27 http://filserver.arthist.lu.se/kultsem/encyclo/isotopy.html. Accessed 25 January 2016.
28 Tuastad 2003, 591.
29 Gambhir 2014.
30 This issue has been addressed in the 2012 documentary *The Gatekeepers*. It tells the story of the Israeli domestic security service.
31 Creswell and Haykel 2015.
32 Tuastad 2003, 591.
33 Conoscenti 2016a.
34 Conoscenti 2005.
35 Weng *et al.* 2012, 2.
36 The few previous searches refer to ISIS Pharmaceuticals.

37 Gearan 2014.
38 Conoscenti 2004, 33.
39 Brooking 2014.
40 Milne 2015, courtesy of Guardian News and Media Ltd.
41 Kingsley 2014, courtesy of Guardian News and Media Ltd.
42 Daileda and Franceschi-Bicchierai 2014.
43 Owing to space constraints I have limited the amount of materials that support my claim. Readers interested in further evidence are invited to use my contact address, michelangelo.conoscenti@unito.it.
44 Tanner 2014.
45 Freedman 2006, 22.
46 The CHR applies here.
47 Ingram 2015.
48 Kfir 2015, 219.
49 Gearan 2014.
50 Holt 2015.
51 Kristol 2011.
52 Conoscenti 2015.
53 www.hoover.org/sites/default/files/uploads/inline/docs/dividingourenemies.pdf. Accessed 25 January 2016.
54 Milton 2014, 47.
55 In November and December 2015 even the most important Catholic weekly magazine *Famiglia Cristiana*, traditionally pro-NATO, published several challenging articles questioning the Anglo-American role in recent events.
56 The CHR applies here.
57 Conoscenti 2004, 21, 84–89.
58 Di Peri 2014.
59 Halverson *et al.* 2011, 184.
60 Brooking 2014.
61 Hopkirk 1990.
62 Colin Powell Memorandum to President Bush on the visit of pm Tony Blair 5–7 April 2002.
63 The CHR applies here. The slide is the original one, mistakes included.
64 www.youtube.com/watch?v=c-8cc9HnSxQ. Accessed 25 January 2016.
65 Henceforth quotations are from participants at the Conference.
66 Joost Hiltermann, Programme Director, Middle East and North Africa, International Crisis Group, Brussels.
67 Paolo Gentiloni, Italian Minister of Foreign Affairs.
68 Gilles Kepel, Professor, Sciences Po, Paris.
69 Alastair Crooke, Director and Founder, Conflicts Forum.
70 Walt 2015.

References

Bell, Allan. 1991. *Language of News Media*. Hoboken, NJ: Wiley-Blackwell.
Brooking, Emerson. 2014. 'The ISIS Propaganda Machine is Horrifying and Effective. How Does It Work?' *Council on Foreign Relations*, 21 August. http://blogs.cfr.org. Accessed 25 January 2016.
Cheterian, Vicken. 2015. 'ISIS and the Killing Fields of the Middle East'. *Survival: Global Politics and Strategy* 57:2, 105–118.
Conoscenti, Michelangelo. 2004. *Language Engineering and Media Strategies in Recent Wars*. Roma: Bulzoni.

Conoscenti, Michelangelo. 2005. *Media in the Mediterranean area: Communication Codes and Construction of Dialogue. Problems and Outlook*. La Valletta: Midsea Books.

Conoscenti, Michelangelo. 2011. *The Reframer: An Analysis of Barack Obama's Political Discourse (2004–2010)*. Roma: Bulzoni.

Conoscenti, Michelangelo. 2015. '"Europe with a View": How Communication Students and an Analyst of Media Discourse Understand and Narrate (Another?) Union'. In *(Mis)communicating Europe*, edited by Isabel Verdet, 27–38. Barcelona: CIDOB. www.cidob.org.

Conoscenti, Michelangelo. 2016a. 'In Transit between Two Wor(l)ds: NATO Military Discourse at a Turning Point'. In *'Languaging' In and Across Communities: New Voices, New Identities. Studies In Honour of Giuseppina Cortese*, edited by Sandra Campagna, Elana Ochse, Virginia Pulcini and Martin Solly, 427–452. Bern: Peter Lang.

Conoscenti, Michelangelo. 2016b. 'Para Bellum, or, the U.S. Department of State (DoS) "Pre-emptive Narrative" in the 1997–2001 Daily Press Briefings: A Multidisciplinary Corpus Approach'. In *The Construction of Us and Them in Relation to 9/11*, edited by Anna Gonerko-Frej and Malgorzata Sokol, Volume 2: Language Studies, 19–57. Newcastle: Cambridge Scholars Publishing.

Creswell, Robyn, and Bernard Hykel. 2015. 'Battle Lines. Want to Understand the Jihadis? Read Their Poetry'. *The New Yorker*, 8 June. www.newyorker.com. Accessed 25 January 2016.

Daileda, Colin, and Lorenzo Franceschi-Bicchierai. 2014. 'US Intelligence Officials Want ISIL Fighters to Keep Tweeting'. *Mashable*, 11 July. http://mashable.com. Accessed 25 January 2016.

Dawkins, Richard. 1976. *The Selfish Gene*. Oxford: Oxford University Press.

Di Peri, Rosita. 2014. 'Islamist Actors from an Anti-system Perspective: The Case of Hizbullah Politics'. *Religion & Ideology* 15:4, 487–503. DOI:10.1080/21567689.2014. 934360.

Freedman, Lawrence. 2006. *The Transformation of Strategic Affairs*. Abingdon: Routledge.

Gambhir, K. Harleen. 2014. 'Dabiq: the Strategic Messaging of the Islamic State'. The Institute for the Study of War. www.understandingwar.org. Accessed 25 January 2016.

Gearan, Anne. 2014. 'U.S. Attempts to Combat Islamic State Propaganda'. *Washington Post*, 7 September. www.washingtonpost.com. Accessed 25 January 2016.

Hall, Benjamin. 2015. *Inside ISIS: The Brutal Rise of a Terrorist Army*. New York: Center Street.

Halverson, Jeffrey R., Harold L. Goodall and Steven R. Corman Jr. 2011. *Master Narratives of Islamist Extremism*. New York: Palgrave Macmillan.

Holt, D. Blaine. 2015. 'Europe, Where Is Your Strategy?' *American Foreign Policy Interests* 37:3, 123–131. DOI: 10.1080/10803920.2015.1056676.

Hopkirk, Peter. 1990. *The Great Game: On Secret Service in High Asia*. London: John Murray Publishers.

Ingram, J. Haroro. 2015. 'The Strategic Logic of Islamic State Information Operations'. *Australian Journal of International Affairs*. DOI: 10.1080/10357718.2015.1059799.

Jacobsen, Annie. 2011. *Area 51. An Uncensored History of America's Top Secret Military Base*. New York: Little, Brown and Company.

Kfir, Isaac. 2015. 'NATO's Paradigm Shift: Searching for a Traditional Security–Human Security Nexus'. *Contemporary Security Policy* 36:2, 219–243. DOI: 10.1080/13523260.2015.1061766.

Kingsley, Patrick. 2014. 'Who is Behind ISIS's Terrifying Online Propaganda Operation?' *Guardian*, 23 June. www.theguardian.com. Accessed 25 January 2016.

Kristol, Irving. 2011. *The Neoconservative Persuasion: Selected Essays, 1942–2009*. New York: Basic Books.

Maggioni Monica, and Paolo Magri (eds). 2015. *Twitter and Jihad: the Communication Strategy of ISIS*. Milan: ISPI.

Milne, Seumas. 2015. 'Now the Truth Emerges: How the US Fuelled the Rise of ISIS in Syria and Iraq'. *Guardian*, 3 June. www.theguardian.com. Accessed 25 January 2016.

Milton, Daniel. 2014. 'The Islamic State: An Adaptive Organization Facing Increasing Challenges'. In *The Group That Calls Itself A State: Understanding the Evolution and Challenges of the Islamic State*, edited by Bryan Price, Daniel Milton, Muhammad al-'Ubaydi and Nelly Lahoud, 36–76. West Point, NY: Combating Terrorism Center.

Mullen, Jethro, and Brian Todd. 2014. 'Battling "Crusaders": ISIS Turns to Glossy Magazine for Propaganda'. CNN. http://edition.cnn.com/2014/09/17/world/meast/isis-magazine. Accessed 25 January 2016.

Rękawek, Kapcer. 2015, 'Ignore Them at Your Peril: The (Missing?) Strategic Narrative of ISIS'. *Strategic File*, 12(75), PISM.

Ryan, W.S. Michael. 2014. 'Dabiq: What Islamic State's New Magazine Tells us about their Strategic Direction, Recruitment Patterns and Guerrilla Doctrine'. *Terrorism Monitor*. www.jamestown.org/. Accessed 25 January 2016.

Shane, Scott, and Ben Hubbard. 2014. 'ISIS Displaying a Deft Command of Varied Media'. *New York Times*, 30 August. www.nytimes.com. Accessed 25 January 2016.

Stern, Jessica, and Jessica Berger. 2015. *ISIS: The State of Terror*. London: William Collins.

Tanner, Rolf. 2014. 'Narrative and Conflict in the Middle East'. *Survival*, 56:2, 89–108. DOI: 10.1080/00396338.2014.901735.

Tuastad, Dag. 2003. 'Neo-Orientalism and the New Barbarism Thesis: Aspects of Symbolic Violence in the Middle East Conflict(s)'. *Third World Quarterly* 24:4, 591–99.

Walt, Stephen M. 2015. 'What Should We Do if the Islamic State Wins?' *Foreign Policy*, 10 June. http://foreignpolicy.com. Accessed 25 January 2016.

Watts, Clint. 2015. 'Russia Returns as al Qaeda and the Islamic State's "Far Enemy"'. *Foreign Policy Research Institute*, 26 October. www.fpri.org. Accessed 25 January 2016.

Weiss, Michael, and Hassan Hassan. 2015. *ISIS: Inside the Army of Terror*. New York: Regan Arts.

Weng, Lee, Alessandro Flammini, Alessandro Vespignani and Filippo Menczer. 2012. 'Competition among memes in a world with limited attention'. *Scientific Reports* 2: 335. DOI: 10.1038/srep00335.

11 Changing perceptions of the European Union in the MENA region before and after the Arab uprisings

The case of Tunisia

Rosita Di Peri and Federica Zardo

Introduction

The legitimacy of the EU in the global arena has been historically questioned. From the outset, politicians, observers and scholars have criticized the supranational institutions for not having the capacity to develop an effective foreign action. This lack of confidence prompted a discourse on actorness, unity, coherence,[1] consistency, effectiveness and accountability of its external agency that informed both actions and perceptions, within and outside Europe.

As noted by Diez, the academic focus on discourses and foreign policy gradually shifted from exploring 'how "speaking Europe works in EU foreign policy"' to 'how others "speak Europe"'.[2] Between these two dimensions lies the issue of the outward perceptions of the EU.

External perceptions are a relevant source of knowledge about foreign policy. As Elgström shows in his study of the EU in international trade negotiations, they contribute to shaping identity and they are means of international accreditation and legitimacy.[3] Yet, not only scholars have so far overlooked image or role theory[4]; external perception studies have all concentrated on the EU identity and international agency rather than questioning specific cases.[5] Lucarelli, for example, evaluates how outsiders' perceptions influence the self-representation processes of actors.[6] Such a focus, though highly relevant, disregards the explanatory potential that perceptions may have when it comes to the impact of EU policies in the targeted countries and the quality of EU–third countries relations. In fact, as Mišík rightly argues, 'perceptions can be characterised as the individual attitudes of state actors (decision makers) not only towards other states, but also their own country'.[7]

This chapter contributes to this debate and to this book's interpretive framework by focusing on what discourses on Europe prevailed in Euro–Mediterranean relations before and after the Arab uprisings and how external perceptions of these discourses may affect dialogue and policy choices. Assuming that 'perceptions of the other' frame and inform decisions in international relations,[8] we argue that the outward image of the EU in the negotiation processes contradicts the widespread representation of the EU as fragmented and non-unitary actor.

The EU succeeded in conveying its discourse on coherence, effectiveness and unity even in highly fragmented policies. This affected the external perceptions influencing the outcome of bargaining.

Our study focuses on Tunisia, and on the pivotal policy arena of migration and mobility. The main reason accounting for this choice is that Tunisia and the EU have a long story of cooperation. Besides the colonial past and a relatively easy transition to independence, Tunisia was the first Middle Eastern and North African (MENA) country to sign a cooperation agreement with the EU in 1969 and an Association Agreement in 1995 following the launch of the Barcelona Process. Such a smooth relationship entailed by itself a discourse on partnership, effectiveness and success that became an additional part of the EU discourse towards the region. Tunisia, indeed, has been considered a 'bon élève' by the international institutions and this has had a strong impact on the way Tunisia has perceived EU discourse and EU–Med relations and vice versa. Moreover, in our analysis of changing perceptions, the 'Jasmine Revolution' is a critical incident to consider in evaluating whether or not the EU attempt to create its image influenced Tunisian cognitions.

When it comes to the selected policy, migration and mobility is not only a strategic issue-area for both the counterparts, but also a policy in the making, a characteristic that allows for easier analysis of perceptions. Its contentious development embeds many discursive struggles and two of them are particularly relevant for our purposes. The first is between member states and supranational actors in relation to the EU capacity to act effectively and as a unitary actor in this realm. The launch of the Global Approach to Migration and Mobility (GAMM) in 2005 and its renewal in 2011 provided the EU with an overarching framework for dealing with migratory issues and represented an attempt to overcome the security-led approach.[9] After a slow start in the implementation of the GAMM, Mobility Partnerships were signed with many countries, including Tunisia.[10] Nonetheless, when it comes to migration and mobility, scholars, practitioners and the European public opinion still represent the EU as a fragmented and ineffective actor.

The other involves the EU and third partner countries on the normative or hegemonic nature of the relationship.

Which notions of Europe prevailed during EU–Tunisia negotiations on migration? How have Tunisian perceptions of Europe affected bilateral dialogue?

By focusing on Tunisian perceptions in the process of negotiation of the migration dossier, this contribution adds a variable to the understanding of Euro-Mediterranean relations.

Overall, a choice is made here to concentrate predominantly on the elites' perceptions, because of the specific actors' landscape in Tunisia and the difficulty in collecting relevant data on public opinion's perceptions under the authoritarian rule and also in the chaotic post-uprising environment. Nonetheless, the literature on the EU external image suggests that the differences between these three groups are rather minor. And this holds true especially for the external perceptions of the EU, where public opinion is shaped by their very little knowledge of the European Union.[11] The joint policy-making process between the EU–Tunisia in this realm is the angle from which to observe how the EU discourse is perceived and then how this external perception affects policy choices.

The chapter proceeds as follows. In the first section we outline the literature on external perceptions of the EU and the EU's image to illustrate how the EU political discourse is built and conveyed with a particular attention to the Mediterranean region; in the second, an overview of the different phases of the cooperation between EU and Tunisia before and after the uprisings will be given; in the third section the chosen cooperation policy will be analysed, consulting original documents from EU institutions, and following a series of in-depth interviews carried out in Tunisia and Brussels,[12] in order to understand how this policy has contributed to shape the EU image in Tunisia and to what extent it has concurred to modify the EU–Tunisian relationship before and after Ben Ali's departure. In the conclusions these empirical findings will be analysed to understand whether and to what extent the Tunisian case is representative of the whole Mediterranean Southern Neighbourhood.

Europe as a global actor: discourses, perceptions and images

As the need for a reflection on the European Union arose, scholars and practitioners increasingly focused on the gap between reality and EU self-representation as part of both the prognosis and the treatment for the EU crisis. There is, indeed, substantial agreement on the impact that 'cognitive dissonances' may have on EU policy effectiveness, identity and legitimacy.[13] This holds true also in the realm of foreign policy, since discourses, perceptions and images shape the way in which other actors interact with the EU, and an understanding of changing perceptions may contribute to expectations and practices relating to the EU as a global actor.[14]

The literature on International Relations has been using perceptions in foreign policy analysis since the 1950s, through either image theory or role theory.[15] The former was developed in the framework of the Cold War to study policy choices according to the perceptions that the counterparts, namely the United States of America and the USSR, had of each other. This approach focussed on how the image that third parties have of a decision-maker may affect the decision-making process. The same approach was subsequently re-used to study the war against terrorism[16] or national security policy.[17] Role theory, instead, framed researches on actors' view of their own state and pointed to how material factors are perceived and mediated by the actors themselves.[18]

EU studies began dealing with external perceptions only in 2000, parallel to the growing interest in the specific nature and agency of this global actor. A first group of scholars focussed on the Asian Pacific region[19] and, by arguing that perceptions are both issue and region-specific, stimulated more and more research on others' views on the EU, especially those of African countries, either looking at multilateral[20] or bilateral arenas.[21] Overall, it is fair to say that, like many IR and EU studies, most of the literature concentrated on the difficulty for the EU of speaking with a single voice and be a unitary actor. Supranational actorness, legitimacy and EU identity were the main dependent variables observed.

Among the analysis of bilateral relations are those that investigate the perceptions of the EU by the countries in the immediate Neighbourhood. This group made up of 16 EU partners – covering the Eastern region (Ukraine, Moldova and Belarus), the Caucasus and the MENA area – have close connections to Europe through historical, geographical and cultural linkages and share, since 2004, the same policy framework, namely the European Neighbourhood Policy (ENP). Researches on EU–Neighbourhood relations produced the many labels such as that of normative power, hegemon or empire but, interestingly, most of them theoretically framed the EU as a global actor without thoroughly considering external perceptions.

Nonetheless, the Neighbourhood region is worthy of attention, not only in order to contribute to what is a somewhat overlooked case in the study of external perceptions, but also because the nature of the bilateral processes involving these countries makes them suitable cases for understanding the role of images in policy-making. In fact, according to the ENP strategy paper and its related communications,[22] these countries supposedly share with the EU 'everything but institutions'[23] and bilateral relations should be based on increasing joint-ownership. These characteristics approximate the new ENP decision-making practices to those that inform intra-EU dynamics, wherein behaviours are strongly influenced by the perceptions of the EU of the member states elites and public opinion.[24] Such a characteristic calls for a brief outline of the literature dealing with discourses, images and perceptions within the EU, which is far richer than that on external perceptions mentioned above.

In the field of integration studies, scholars were interested in dealing with elite, public and media perceptions of the European integration, exploring how perception shapes preferences of the member states and their influence at the EU level and understanding the effects of perceptions on different EU policies. Studies from the first group pointed to the many variables – sociological, historical, religious, but also time and context specific, as well as the level of trust – affecting perceptions of European integration and support for the integration project.[25] Overall, the legitimacy of European integration tends to be more a function of the perception of supranational effectiveness and convenience than that of its objective functioning.[26] Unlike the literature on the EU external perception, these researches focussed a lot on the image of the EU and its policies in the media[27] and foreign policy and enlargement as portrayed in the press were often among the main topics debated by academia.

Swinging between studies on external perceptions and internal perceptions of the EU in the international arena are recent analyses of diplomats' views of the EU and preference formation in the developing EU diplomatic institution,[28] aiming at understanding whether and to what extent the EU fragmented agency is a consequence of a still-missing EU diplomacy.

Moving on to the MENA region, the relevance of studying perceptions of the EU by Southern Mediterranean countries not only lies in the distinctiveness of decision-making processes but also in the symbolic potential of the region in terms of EU capacity to effectively adapt its discourse and practice to changing environments. Together with the financial crisis, indeed, events unfolding in the MENA countries fostered the need for new discourses and brought to light, more than any other foreign policy target, dissonances between reality and EU self-representation. Since discourse helps create an opening to policy change by altering actors' perceptions of the policy problems, policy legacies and fit,[29] a Neighbourhood case could contribute to assessing the potential for policy change of post-2011 EU discourses. In fact, as pointed out by Barbé and Herranz Surrallés with regard to the Neighbourhood policy, the process of convergence to EU rules is not only influenced by the structure of incentives offered to the counterpart, but also by mutual perception of legitimacy.[30]

Ultimately, the notion of perceptions was also useful in the literature in order to investigate the nature of states. As Jervis argues in 'Perceptions and Misperception in International Politics',[31] misperceptions can influence states' relations, since objective reality cannot alone explain behaviours.[32]

These approaches bring us to the core of our analysis of Euro–Mediterranean relations. Southern Mediterranean countries are small states, and relations between them and EU are mostly characterized by asymmetry. Nonetheless, researches on asymmetric interactions and on small countries highlight that 'whether a state behaves as a big or a small one depends on the way it is perceived by that state itself and by other actors'.[33] Hence, the behaviours and attitudes of Tunisia in its interactions with the EU are assumed to be, more than other big countries in the region, the reflection of the EU's image in Tunisian pivotal actors.

Framing the EU–Tunisia relationship before and after the Arab uprisings

EU–Tunisian relations, as a part of the broader relations between the EU and the Mediterranean neighbourhood countries, have been characterized by a deep asymmetry. This asymmetry dates back to the colonial period when an orientalist vision of the region prevailed.[34] According to this interpretive lens, the Southern bank of the Mediterranean Sea was marked by a historical backwardness that has cultural as well as socio-economic roots. This condition would lead the region to a sort of predestination towards authoritarianism and subalternity.[35] Moreover, the difficulties of the decolonization processes and the impact of Middle Eastern politics on North African countries have contributed to fuelling an image of the MENA region dominated by political and economic instability. This representation is also the result of a broader narrative that describes this region, as characterized by violence and permanent clashes.[36] All these aspects strengthened the asymmetry in the relations between the two shores of the Mediterranean, especially after the decolonization process, when 'privileged relations' were established between European countries and former colonies or former mandatory territories.[37] These 'privileged relations' have heavily favoured European countries in commercial and economic terms.[38]

Relations between, formerly, the European Economic Community (EEC) and, later, the EU towards the MENA region have been alimented by the above-mentioned representation of the region.[39] As a result cooperation policies (mainly at the economic level, at least initially) have been established, in order to contribute to the stabilization of the MENA region, to contain the forces that could lead to the destabilization of Europe (mainly immigration fluxes and terrorist attacks). As the main consequence, attention to security issues has become increasingly central for the EU over the years. This interpretation is crucial to understanding why, in the aftermath of the outbreak of the Arab uprisings, after a moment of euphoria for a transition of authoritarian long-term regimes towards democracy, as soon as it was clear that changes would not lead to democratic regimes in the short term, the EU strengthened the tools that went in the direction of greater protection of its security, both in terms of discourses and practices/policies.[40] As many scholars argue, especially in the aftermath of the Arab uprisings, EU policies towards the MENA region, including those related to the promotion of human rights and democracy, continue to be concentrated on security aims, especially in terms of containment of migration flows and defence against terrorist attacks.[41]

The consolidation of this attitude is particularly evident when looking at the transformation of the relations between the EU and Tunisia before the uprisings.[42] EU–Tunisia relations date back to March 1969 when a cooperation agreement (mainly trade-based) was signed between the EEC and Tunisia. During the 70s, a unitary approach to the issue of Euro-Mediterranean policy, the so-called Global Mediterranean Policy (GMP), emerged with the aim of improving export trade from North Africa to the EEC, to sustain economic, financial and technical co-operation, and to provide institutional assistance.[43] Within this framework, a new agreement between the two sides was signed in 1976. This agreement was then renewed in 1981 and 1986. After the signing of the Maastricht Treaty in 1992, the GMP was replaced by the Renovated Mediterranean Policy (RMP) and, according this new framework, a new set of agreements was negotiated between 1992 and 1996.[44] The RMP is part of an EU policy of 'proximity' towards the Mediterranean Basin focussing on commercial co-operation and on programmes of financial assistance (Med Programmes: MedCampus, MedInvest, MedUrb), but it does not provide any agreement on development; although it promotes a deeper general co-operation and reinforces the political dialogue in the region.[45] Since the Barcelona process (1995) that gave birth to the Euro–Mediterranean Partnership (EMP) EU commitment to the MENA Region has been driven by a policy framework that has foreseen different instruments and policies (EMP, European Neighbourhood Policy – ENP, National Plans, and Association Agreements). These instruments were differentiated according to the three main strands foreseen by the EMP: partnership in political affairs and security (first strand), in cultural and social affairs (second strand), or financial affairs (third strand). Regarding the first and the third strand, according to EMP principles, EU partners were asked to promote and strengthen practices of democratic government with ad hoc 'Association Agreements' with the aim of increasing political and economic stability. Within this general framework, Tunisia was, in 2004, the first country to sign a bilateral 'Action Plan' with the EU as a part of ENP.[46] The decision to sign the Action Plan was a reaction of the EU to September 11 and, more broadly, to security threats.[47] This is the last of a series of agreements that have shaped EU–Tunisia relations since 1998, the year when the first EU–Tunisia cooperation Agreement was signed (the first between the EU and a MENA country).

The attention to the economic dimension as a means to produce indirect effects on EU security is particularly evident in the case of Tunisia. As Van Hüllen rightly points out, if Tunisia has been a pioneer in promoting Euro–Mediterranean relations in terms of economic cooperation, the same cannot be said in the field of the promotion of democracy and human rights where relations between the two sides have been more problematic.[48] Even during the 80s Tunisian authorities mostly relied on socio-economic development to obtain popular support and compensate for a repressive strategy of exclusion.[49] This attitude, that Brumberg has termed 'survival strategy', has made Tunisia less open to blackmail in terms of negotiation, especially on the issue of human rights and democracy promotion:[50] as argued by Powel, promotion of democracy in Tunisia has been stifled by the need for stability.[51] It is in this context that relations between the EU and Tunisia have evolved over decades. The EU tools to enhance economic and financial cooperation were a direct consequence of the impossibility of using coercive tools in order to promote democracy. The creation of a business-friendly environment was seen by the EU as a means of maintaining stability and, the same time, safeguarding its interests. This strategy contributed, over the years, to increasing the asymmetry in the relations between EU and Tunisia, while enhancing the 'economic dossier' that is, indeed, the most advanced aspect of EU–Tunisian relations. The EU is the main commercial partner of Tunisia and trade relations between the two actors have increased since 2003. The EU accounts for the 74.1 per cent of Tunisian exports and for 66.9 per cent of Tunisian imports.[52] However, even if this strategy has had some positive effects on Tunisian macroeconomic indicators, it contributes, on the one hand, to making Tunisia more dependent on international aid and, on the other hand, to creating a myth of stability. This is, for example, the case of the tourism sector, a pivotal sector for the Tunisian economy.[53]

In hindsight, this approach has been strategic for the EU to maintain its goals of stability and security: in supporting the development of Tunisia, expanding its domestic market and including the country in a regional market, the EU has helped to finance the underdeveloped regions of the country, especially inland and in the south, thus indirectly trying to create an alternative to emigration. In other words, the EU has used financial and technical assistance and conditionality to protect its borders.

If, before the uprisings, Tunisia was considered the 'bon élève'[54] by foreign investors (IMF, the WB, and the EU), after the revolts, the Tunisian political instability, the crisis of strategic sectors such as tourism and the terrorist threats, have shown the weakness of this country, hidden by the rhetoric of change and stability under authoritarian rule.[55] This has resulted in the need to establish a new agenda of cooperation, as part of the privileged partnership, which led to the signing of a new action plan on 19 November 2012, focussed on issues of economic development and democratic transition. However, the EU has re-proposed old formulas where security priorities prevail in defining its external agency. This will increase the asymmetry in EU–Tunisia relations, a never-ending story of colonial penetration (subjection) of the EU in the Mediterranean region.[56]

Mapping perceptions within EU–Tunisia negotiations on migration

EU–Neighbourhood cooperation in the strategic realm of mobility and migration is taking place more actively than any other policy area.

The external dimension of the EU migration policy was officially embraced at the 1999 Tampere European Council, where the Heads of State and Government declared that

> the separate but closely related issues of asylum and migration call for the development of a common EU policy ... and a comprehensive approach to migration addressing political, human rights and development issues in countries and regions of origin and transit.[57]

Nonetheless, EU member states have so far resisted to the adoption of binding commitments in this area and focused on limiting the access of 'unwanted' third country nationals by stepping up controls at the external borders, tightening entry requirements and restricting visa policies.[58] Moreover, the share of competences included in the Treaties kept the management of migratory issues firmly in the hands of the member states. The increase in migration flows in the 1990s and the subsequent perception of the Mediterranean region as a threat to European security[59] led to the signature of, and the launch of negotiations on, readmission agreements, but these were bilateral alliances with individual members such as France, Italy, Malta, the United Kingdom and Bulgaria.[60] The Communication on the Global Approach to Migration[61] gradually shifted management responsibilities towards the development of an 'overarching framework of the EU external migration and asylum policy', but a strict mandate still binds the bargaining power of the European Commission.

When it comes to EU–Tunisia cooperation, activities started in 2003 with the Dialogue on Mediterranean Transit Migration, an informal consultative platform run by the International Centre for Migration Policy Development, up to the signature in 2014 of the Joint Declaration establishing a Mobility Partnership, which is the only formal – though not binding – thematic agreement on the issue.[62]

The Tunisian approach to migratory issues changed over time, following domestic constraints as well as international priorities. While in the late 1960s Tunisia started with the same sort of approach as Morocco, encouraging emigration in order to manage unemployment levels,[63] by 1974 the state had started supporting the return of its nationals. These attempts did not prevent 9 per cent of the population from living abroad,[64] through either regular or irregular migration channels.

Hence, from the 1990s until at least the first signs of discontent in 2008,[65] Tunisian migration policies were either focused on promoting legal migration through the signing of agreements with European countries and with countries outside Europe and strengthening links with Tunisian emigrants.

The hard development of a common migration policy and the still high institutional fragmentation highlighted above gave resonance to the intra-European discourse on the weak EU agency in this realm[66] and, by extension, to the ineffectiveness and lack of coherence of EU external action.[67] Yet, interestingly enough, such a puzzled actorness did not affect Tunisian perceptions of the EU during the negotiations. This holds particularly true along the bargaining process of the Mobility Partnership, when Tunisia felt 'powerless and small vis-à-vis the unshakeable EU machinery'.[68]

The signature of the Joint Declaration for a Mobility Partnership in 2014 between Tunisia, the European Union and the participant Member states was an important breakthrough in EU–Tunisia cooperation. After decades of stalemate and rather passive cooperation in this realm, the agreement seemingly sealed the mutual will to cooperate in a sensitive policy area. For a long time Ben Ali succeeded in exploiting the self-representation of Tunisia vis-à-vis the EU as a performing and receptive country pursuing a zero-sum bargain, aiming to protect the regime without external interferences.[69]

The 'Jasmine revolution' came to blur this picture and unveiled the 'myths' underlying the Tunisian rhetoric,[70] allowing the EU to reach its goal in a 'laggard policy-area'. The Tunisian interim government under Beji Caïd Essebsi had agreed to establish a dialogue on migration, mobility and security with the EU in October 2011. Nevertheless, following the elections of the Constituent Assembly, the launch of the constitution-making process and the political stalemate that led to the so-called *Dialogue National*, this dossier moved to the back burner. In addition, the political and societal crisis that accompanied the transition was exposing the government to the pressure of the public opinion – which was extremely critical of the Mobility Partnership – boosting dissent towards the Tunisian *troika* and destabilizing an already precarious situation. Civil society organisations had publicly condemned the proposal as a case of 'hidden externalization of European borders',[71] mentioning, in particular, the 'readmission of third country nationals' clause. In the absence of a Tunisian law on asylum and with no *ex-ante* conditionality on that matter, this provison questioned the respect of human rights.[72]

Whilst it is true that the volatility of the transition after the fall of Ben Ali's regime strongly limited Tunisian leeway,[73] the EU entered the latest round of negotiations under multiple pressures. On the one hand, the European Commission was prompted by the tragedies that, from October 2013 on, repeatedly occurred off the Italian and Libyan coasts. These events not only questioned the legitimacy of supranational institutions to act and react in the field of migration and border management, but also the capacity of the EU as a whole to withstand another crisis after the long-lasting economic turmoil. On the other, the Tunisian transition was the sole opportunity for the EU to prove its actorness in the MENA region after the Arab uprisings had taken Brussels and the member states by surprise.[74]

Against a challenging negotiation background, the EU promptly resorted to unprecedented political declarations pointing to the 'EU cohesion vis-à-vis the issue of migration',[75] the 'conditionality of the EU support on the efforts that Tunisia could make in the cooperation on migration'[76] and the 'EU determination to sign Mobility Partnerships with the MENA partners'.[77]

This narrative of 'coherent and effective actor' put forward by the European Commission tipped the scales in favour of the supranational discursive struggle and proved effective in shaping Tunisian perceptions during the negotiation phase. The EU discursive strategy overshadowed the impact of the migration crisis on EU legitimacy so much that, ultimately, the Tunisian government did not mention the signing of the agreement, either in public speeches or in official documents.[78] Against all forecasts Commissioner Malmström got the Declaration signed in March 2014 without significant concessions to Tunisia. Some cosmetic adjustments of the wording sufficed to include in the Declaration the so-called readmission clause of third countries nationals, a provision that Tunisia tried to resist, before giving up on bargaining with 'a strong and united counterpart'.[79]

In the case observed, perceptions played a pivotal role in shaping the outcomes of the negotiation. Not only did the Tunisian government give up on the issue of readmission; it manifestly refused to put forward its priorities regarding migration and mobility – such as visa facilitation for Tunisian citizens or stronger integration of Tunisians living abroad – because 'there was no room to bargain with a representative of 28 member states, all committed to externalizing their borders'.[80]

If it is true that, in times of transition, the government of Tunisia needed and craved international legitimacy and that the step back of the weakened Ministry of the Interior from its traditional role of last resort negotiator strongly limited the Tunisian leverage, the many references to the 'EU as a strong and strategic partner', as an 'irreplaceable partner for Tunisia' not only throughout the migration dossier but also in overarching documents[81] suggest that the European counterpart was pervasively perceived as a powerful actor and a fortress that 'a small state like Tunisia could in no way oppose during the transition'.[82]

Conclusions: bringing perceptions back into the analysis of Euro–Mediterranean relations

In this chapter we have pointed to the role that perceptions of Europe may have in shaping the relationship between the EU and third countries. By relating the European discourses – the 'speaking Europe' to put it in Smith's terms[83] – to the way in which others 'speak Europe', perceptions enable or constrain dialogue and policy choices.

The analysis of EU–Tunisia bilateral interactions in the realm of migration and mobility demonstrated that Tunisian elites perceived the EU as a powerful and steady actor, able to find internal coherence to pursue its interest. This was possible because the European Commission succeeded in conveying a discourse on effectiveness and unity in relation to a highly fragmented policy area. The more the EU strengthened its discursive practice, the more the Tunisian government perceived strong and sometimes hegemonic agency. This held true especially after the fall of the authoritarian regime, whose persistence relied for a long time on a pervasive self-representation of Tunisia as a successful and trustable partner for International Institutions.[84] From 2011 on, although the EU was experiencing a deep political crisis and could have been challenged by Tunisia during the negotiations of the Mobility Partnership, perceptions affected Tunisian decision-making and narrowed its leverage over the EU.

External perceptions proved to be relevant in deepening the asymmetry between the two counterparts, adding to a long-lasting asymmetry that has historical and cultural roots. In doing so, they helped constructing a counter-narrative to the EU discourse on partnership and co-ownership that framed, and is still framing, Euro-Mediterranean policies. From the Tunisian perspective, the EU did not substantially change its attitude towards the MENA countries over the last fifty years, despite its promises of privileged relationships and strengthened cooperation. Indeed, the study demonstrated that 'perceptions of the other' not only frame decision-making processes in international relations, they also affect discursive struggles underlying specific issue-areas. In opposition to mainstream representations and analysis, the EU can be perceived by external actors as powerful and unified when negotiating strategic issues for its security and stability.

Overall, by considering the role of perceptions and discursive practices in bilateral interactions, this case suggests new ways of looking at Euro–Mediterranean relations before and after the Arab uprisings, at the same time filling a gap in the debate on the EU external image (and agency), mainly focused on the internal impact of outward perceptions.

Notes

1 On this point see Smith 2001.
2 See Diez 2013.
3 See Elgström 2007.
4 See Chaban and Holland 2014.
5 See Chaban and Holland 2013; Chaban and Magdalina 2014.
6 See Lucarelli 2007.
7 See Mišík 2013, 445.
8 On this point see Mohavedi 1985.
9 On this issue see Seeberg 2013.
10 The others countries are Moldova, Cape Verde, Armenia, Azerbaijan, Georgia and in the Mediterranean region Jordan and Morocco.
11 On the external perception see Fioramonti and Poletti 2008.

12 Fieldwork was carried out by the authors after the 'Jasmine Revolution'. Rosita Di Peri between 2013 and 2014 and Federica Zardo between 2014 and 2015.
13 On this point see Lucarelli and Fioramonti 2009.
14 On the conceptualization and analysis of EU actorness see Bretherton and Vogler 2006.
15 On this point see Mišík 2013.
16 On this point see Alexander *et al.* 2005.
17 On this point see Herrmann and Keller 2004.
18 For a focus on role theory see Aggestam 2006.
19 On this point see Chaban and Holland 2008; Chaban and Holland 2013.
20 On this point see Elgström 2007; Sicurelli 2010.
21 On this point see Lucarelli and Fioramonti 2009.
22 European Commission 2004.
23 European Commission 2002.
24 On this point see Mišík 2013.
25 On this point see Bruter 2004; Ilonszki 2009.
26 On this point Jones 2009.
27 On this issue see Kantner *et al.* 2008.
28 On EU discourses and diplomacy see Carta 2008; Carta 2013.
29 On this issue see Schmidt and Radaelli 2004.
30 See especially Barbé and Herranz Surrallés 2010.
31 See Jervis 1976.
32 On this point see Keohane 1969.
33 On this point see Tiilikainen 2006, 73.
34 An extremely interesting view is Hoh 2014.
35 See especially Said 1979. More recently, this view was used to analyse the practice of 'exporting democracy' to the region.
36 On this issue see, especially, Tanner 2014; Tuastad 2003.
37 On the 'privileged relations' see Powel Brieg 2009.
38 On this point see Tovias 1997.
39 On the asymmetry see Panebianco 2012.
40 On security issue see Pace and Cavatorta 2012; Teti, Thompson and Noble 2013.
41 See especially Bauer 2013; Dandashly 2015.
42 The EU's commitment in the Mediterranean basin is not recent. In fact, it finds its legal basis in the EC Treaty, signed in Rome in 1957, which is mainly aimed at improving the economic and political relationships between Europe and the MENA region countries. In order to promote the development of MENA region countries and to consolidate its prominence in such a strategic region, the European Community established a common commercial policy according to the general rule contained in Article 113 of the Rome Treaty.
43 See European Commission 1982.
44 See EU Council 1996.
45 See MEDEA 2013.
46 On this point see King 2007.
47 See EU Council 2005.
48 See Van Hüllen 2012.
49 On this see, in particular, Hibou 2006a.
50 See Brumberg 2002.
51 On this aspect see Powel 2009.
52 See European Commission 2012.
53 On the tourism sector in Tunisia see Di Peri and Giordana 2013.
54 Here the reference is to Camau 1987, 1997.
55 On the point see, especially, Di Peri 2015; Tsourapas 2013.
56 On this vision see Langan 2015.

57 EU Council 1999.
58 See especially Kunz *et al.* 2011; Cassarino 2005.
59 On this point see Joffé and Vasconcelos 2014.
60 Database developed by the EU-funded Borderlands project. With Bulgaria and the United Kingdom, negotiations are still on going. This database is retrievable at: http://data.borderlands-project.eu/data/?p=mapB&topic=migration&year=&country=Tunisia#moretr7. Accessed 31 December 2015.
61 European Commission 2011a.
62 See especially Zardo and Cavatorta 2016; Cassarino 2014.
63 On this point see Baldwin-Edwards 2006.
64 Migration Policy Centre 2013.
65 On this point see Cassarino 2014.
66 For a complete overview of EU migration policies see Boswell and Geddes 2010.
67 See especially Barbé and Surrallés 2010.
68 Interview by Federica Zardo with a Tunisian official, Ministry of Foreign Affairs, held in Tunis in March 2014.
69 See especially Hibou 2006b.
70 On this issue see Cavatorta and Merone 2013.
71 Interviews with EMHRN and FIDH representatives held in Tunis, October 2013. Further information on the position of major human rights organisations active in Tunisia on the political declaration can be found on the official websites of the *Forum International des Droits de l'Homme* (FIDH), *Migreurop Observatoire des Frontières*, Euromediterranean Human Rights Network.
72 Kapitalis 2014; La voix de la Libye 2015.
73 See especially Del Sarto 2015.
74 On this point see Teti *et al.* 2013.
75 European Commission 2011a.
76 See especially Del Sarto and Limam 2015.
77 European Commission 2009.
78 This topic was also discussed in many interviews conducted during the fieldwork.
79 Interview by Federica Zardo with a Tunisian official, Ministry of Foreign Affairs, held in Tunis in March 2014.
80 Interview by Federica Zardo with a Tunisian official, Ministry of Foreign Affairs, held in Tunis in October 2014.
81 EU-Tunisia 2013; EU Council 2015.
82 Public speech of the Secretary of State in charge of migration Houcine Jaziri during the Conference 'Après la fermeture du camp de Choucha: La Tunisie face au défi de l'asile' organized by CeTuMA-SODMUF, October, 22nd, 2013 – Hôtel Majestic, Tunis.
83 See Smith 2001.
84 See on this point Hibou 1999.

Bibliography

Aggestam, Lisbeth. 2006. 'Role Theory and European Foreign Policy: A Framework of Analysis'. In O. Elgström and M. Smith (eds) *The European Union's Roles in International Politics. Concepts and Analysis*, 11–29. London: Routledge.

Alexander, Michele G, Shana Levin and Paul J. Henry. 2005. 'Image Theory, Social Identity and Social Dominance: Structural Characteristics and Individual Motives Underlying International Images'. *Political Psychology* 26: 27–45.

Baldwin-Edwards, Martin. 2006. 'Between a Rock and a Hard Place: North Africa as a Region of Emigration, Immigration and Transit Migration'. *Review of African Political Economy* 33 (108): 311–24.

Barbé, Esther and Anna Herranz Surrallés. 2010. 'Dynamics of Convergence and Differentiation in Euro–Mediterranean Relations: Towards Flexible Region-Building or Fragmentation?' *Mediterranean Politics* 15 (2): 129–47.

Bauer, Patricia 2013. 'European–Mediterranean Security and the Arab Spring: Changes and Challenges'. *Democracy and Security* 9 (1–2): 1–18.

Boswell, Christina and Andrew Geddes. 2010. *Migration and Mobility in the European Union*. London: Palgrave Macmillan.

Bretherton, Charlotte and John Vogler. 2006. *The European Union as a Global Actor*. London: Routledge.

Brumberg, Daniel. 2002. 'The Trap of Liberalized Autocracy'. *Journal of Democracy* 13 (4): 56–68.

Bruter, Michael. 2004. 'On What Citizens Mean by Feeling "European": Perceptions of News, Symbols and Borderless-ness'. *Journal of Ethnic and Migration Studies* 30 (1): 21–39.

Camau, Michel, ed. 1987. *La Tunisie au présent. Une modernité au-dessous de tout soupçon?* Paris: Editions du CNRS.

Camau, Michel. 1997. 'D'une République à l'autre. Refondation politique et aléas de la transition libérale'. *Monde Arabe Maghreb-Mashrek* 157: 3–16.

Carta, Caterina. 2008. 'The EU's International Image As Seen by the Commission's Diplomats'. *European Foreign Affairs Review* 13 (4): 473–91.

Carta, Caterina. 2013. *The European Union Diplomatic Service: Ideas, Preferences and Identities*. London: Routledge.

Cassarino, Jean-Pierre. 2005. 'Migration and Border Management in the Euro-Mediterranean Area: Heading towards New Forms of Interconnectedness'. *Mediterranean Yearbook* 227–31.

Cassarino, Jean-Pierre. 2014. 'Channelled Policy Transfers: EU–Tunisia Interactions on Migration Matters'. *European Journal of Migration and Law* 16 (1): 97–123.

Chaban, Natalia and Ana-Maria Magdalina. 2014. 'External Perceptions of the EU during the Eurozone Sovereign Debt Crisis'. *European Foreign Affairs Review* 19 (2): 195–220.

Chaban, Natalia and Martin Holland. 2008. *European Union and the Asia-Pacific*. London: Routledge.

Chaban, Natalia and Martin Holland. 2013. 'Special Issue. Lisbon and the Changing External Perceptions of the EU: Visions from the Asia-Pacific'. *Baltic Journal of European Studies* 3 (3).

Chaban, Natalia and Martin Holland. 2014. *Communicating Europe in Times of Crisis*. London: Palgrave Macmillan.

Dandashly, Assem. 2015. 'The EU Response to Regime Change in the Wake of the Arab Revolt: Differential Implementation'. *Journal of European Integration* 37 (1): 37–56.

Del Sarto, Raffaella, and Mohamed Limam. 2015. 'Periphery Under Pressure: Morocco, Tunisia and the European Union's Mobility Partnership on Migration'. *Robert Schuman Centre for Advanced Studies Research Paper* No. RSCAS 2015/75.

Di Peri, Rosita. 2015. 'An Enduring "Touristic Miracle" in Tunisia? Coping with Old Challenges after the Revolution'. *British Journal of Middle Eastern Studies* 42 (1): 104–18.

Di Peri, Rosita and Raffaella Giordana, eds. 2013. *Revolution with Revolutions. The Challenges of the Tourism Sector in Tunisia*. Bologna: I Libri di Emil, University Press.

Diez, Thomas. 2013. 'Setting the Limits: Discourse and EU Foreign Policy'. *Cooperation and Conflict* 49 (3): 319–33.

Elgström, Ole. 2007. 'Outsiders' Perceptions of the European Union in International Trade Negotiations'. *JCMS: Journal of Common Market Studies* 45 (4): 949–67.

EU Council. 1996. Council Regulation (EC) No. 1488/96 of 13 July 1996 on Financial and Technical Measures to Accompany (MEDA) the Reform of Economic and Social Structures in the Framework of the Euro-Mediterranean partnership. OJ L 189/1.

EU Council. 1999. Tampere European Council 15–16 October 1999. Presidency Conclusions.

EU Council. 2005. The European Union Strategy for Combating Radicalisation and Recruitment to Terrorism, Justice and Home Affairs Council Meeting. 1 December.

EU Council. 2015. Adoption de la position de l'Union européenne en vue de la onzième session du Conseil d'association. 6926/15.

European Commission. 1982. EEC–Tunisia Cooperation Agreement, X/86/1982, Brussels.

European Commission. 2002. A Wider Europe – A Proximity Policy as the Key to Stability 'Peace, Security And Stability. International Dialogue and the Role of the EU' Sixth ECSA-World Conference. Jean Monnet Project. SPEECH/02/619.

European Commission. 2004. European Neighbourhood Policy Strategy Paper. COM (2004) 373 final.

European Commission. 2009. Mobility Partnerships as a Tool of the Global Approach to Migration SEC (2009) 1240.

European Commission. 2011a. Communication from the Commission to the European Parliament, the Council, the European Economic and Social Committee and the Committee of the Regions. The Global Approach to Migration and Mobility. COM(2011) 743 final.

European Commission. 2011b. Cecilia Malmström Member of the European Commission Responsible for Home Affairs. Immigration Flows – Tunisia Situation. SPEECH/11/106.

European Commission. 2012. Memo – Mission for Growth: Creating Economic Ties to Benefit Tunisia and the EU. Memo/12/920, Brussels.

EU-Tunisia. 2013. Relations Tunisie–Union Européenne: Un partenariat privilégié. Plan d'action 2013–2017.

EU-Tunisia. 2014. Déclaration Conjointe Pour Le Partenariat de Mobilité Entre La Tunisie, l'Union Européenne et Ses Etats Membres Participants.

Fioramonti, Lorenzo. 2009. 'African Perceptions of the European Union: Assessing the Work of the EU in the Field of Democracy Promotion and Peacekeeping'. *SSRN Scholarly Paper* ID 2100508. Rochester, NY: Social Science Research Network.

Fioramonti, Lorenzo and Arlo Poletti. 2008. 'Facing the Giant: Southern Perspectives on the European Union'. *Third World Quarterly* 29 (1): 167–80.

Herrmann, Richard K. and Jonathan W. Keller. 2004. 'Beliefs, Values, and Strategic Choice: US Leaders' Decisions to Engage, Contain, and Use Force in an Era of Globalization'. *Journal of Politics* 66: 557–80.

Hibou, Béatrice, ed. 1999. *La privatisation des Etats*. Paris: KARTHALA Editions.

Hibou, Béatrice. 2006a. 'Domination & Control in Tunisia: Economic Levers for the Exercise of Authoritarian Power'. *Review of African Political Economy* 33 (108): 185–206.

Hibou, Béatrice. 2006b. *La Force de l'Obéissance*. Paris: La Découverte.

Hoh, Anna-Lena. 2014. '"Voir l'Autre"? Seeing the Other, the Developments of the Arab Spring and the European Neighborhood Policy toward Algeria and Tunisia'. *Journal of Borderlands Studies* 29 (2): 203–16.

Ilonszki, Gabriella. 2009. *Perceptions of the European Union in New Member States. A Comparative Perspective*. London: Routledge.

Jervis, Robert. 1976. *Perceptions and Misperception in International Politics*. Princeton, NJ: Princeton University Press.

Joffé, George and Alvaro Vasconcelos. 2014. *The Barcelona Process: Building a Euro-Mediterranean Regional Community*. London: Routledge.

Jones, Erik. 2009. 'Output Legitimacy and the Global Financial Crisis: Perceptions Matters'. *Journal of Common Market Studies* 47: 1085–1105.

Kantner, Cathleen, Amelie Kutter and Swantje Rendfordt. 2008. 'The Perception of the EU as an Emerging Security Actor in Media Debates on Humanitarian and Military Interventions (1090–2006)' *RECON Online Working Paper* 2008/19.

Kapitalis. 2014. 'Tribune: Contre Le "partenariat de Mobilité" Entre La Tunisie et l'Union Européenne'. Kapitalis, Le Portail D'informations Sur La Tunisie et Le Maghreb Arabe. www.kapitalis.com/tribune/21228-tribune-contre-le-partenariat-de-mobilite-entre-la-tunisie-et-l-union-europeenne.html. Accessed 30 November.

Keohane, Robert. 1969. 'Lilliputians' Dilemmas: Small States in International Politics'. *International Organisation* 23: 291–310.

King, Stephen. 2007. *Tunisia: Freedom House country report*. Available from: https://freedomhouse.org/report/countries-crossroads/2007/tunisia. Accessed 1 December 2015.

Kunz, Rahel, Sandra Lavenex and Marion Panizzon. 2011. *Multilayered Migration Governance: The Promise of Partnership*. Abingdon: Taylor & Francis.

Langan, Mark. 2015. 'The Moral Economy of EU Relations with North African States: DCFTAs under the European Neighbourhood Policy'. *Third World Quarterly* 36 (10): 1827–44.

Lavenex, Sandra and Emek M. Uçarer. 2003. *Migration and the Externalities of European Integration*. Lanham, MD: Lexington Books.

La voix de la Libye. 2015. 'Partenariat de Mobilité Entre La Tunisie et l'Union Européenne: Mobilité Réduite et sans Droits'. http://lavoixdelalibye.com/?p=26858. Accessed 15 December 2015.

Lucarelli, Sonia. 2007. 'The European Union in the Eyes of Others: Towards Filling a Gap in the Literature'. *European Foreign Affairs Review* 3 (12): 249–70.

Lucarelli, Sonia and Lorenzo Fioramonti. 2009. *External Perceptions of the European Union as a Global Actor*. London: Routledge.

MEDEA. 2013. *EU–Tunisia Relations*, European Institute for Research on Mediterranean and Euro-Arab Cooperation, Brussels. www.medea.be/en/countries/tunisia/eu-tunisia-relations. Accessed 13 December 2015.

Migration Policy Centre. 2013. 'MPC-Migration Profile. Tunisia'. Robert Schuman Centre for Advanced Studies, Florence. Available at www.migrationpolicycentre.eu/docs/migration/Tunisia.pdf. Accessed 4 October 2016.

Mišík, Matúš. 2013. 'How can Perception Help us to Understand the Dynamic between EU Member States? The state of the art'. *Asia Europe Journal* 11 (4): 445–63.

Movahedi, Siamak. 1985. 'The Social Psychology of Foreign Policy and the Politics of International Images'. *Human Affairs* 8 (19): 18–37.

Pace, Michelle. 2010. 'The European Union, Security and the Southern Dimension'. *European Security* 19 (3): 431–44.

Pace, Michelle and Francesco, Cavatorta. 2012. 'The Arab Uprisings in Theoretical Perspective – an Introduction'. *Mediterranean Politics* 17 (2): 125–38.

Panebianco, Stefania. 2012. *L'Unione Europea 'potenza divisa' nel Mediterraneo*. Milano: Egea.

Powel Brieg, Tomos. 2009. 'A Clash of Norms: Normative Power and EU Democracy Promotion in Tunisia'. *Democratization* 16 (1): 193–214.

Said, Edward. 1979. *Orientalism*. New York: Vintage.

Schmidt, Vivien A. and Claudio M. Radaelli. 2004. 'Policy Change and Discourse in Europe: Conceptual and Methodological Issues'. *West European Politics* 27 (2): 183–210.

Seeberg, Peter. 2010. 'European Neighbourhood Policy, Post-normativity and Prag-matism'. *European Foreign Affairs Review* 15 (5): 663–79.

Seeberg, Peter. 2013. 'The Arab Uprisings and the EU's Migration Policies: The Cases of Egypt, Libya, and Syria'. *Democracy and Security* 9 (1–2): 157–76.

Sicurelli, Daniela. 2010. *The European Union's Africa Policies: Norms, Interests and Impact.* Aldershot: Ashgate.

Smith, Michael. 2001. 'The Quest for Coherence: Institutional Dilemmas of External Action from Maastricht to Amsterdam'. In *The Institutionalization of Europe*, edited by Alec Stone Sweet, Wayen Sandholtz and Neil Fligstein, 171–93. Oxford: Oxford University Press.

Tanner, Rolf. 2014. 'Narrative and Conflict in the Middle East'. *Survival* 56 (2): 89–108.

Teti, Andrea, Darcy Thompson and Christopher Noble. 2013. 'EU Democracy Assistance Discourse in its New Response to a Changing Neighbourhood'. *Democracy and Security* 9 (1–2): 61–79.

Tiilikainen, Teija. 2006. 'Finland – An EU Member with a Small State Identity'. *Journal of European Integration* 28: 73–87.

Torney, Diarmuid. 2014. 'External Perceptions and EU Foreign Policy Effectiveness: The Case of Climate Change'. *Journal of Common Market Studies* 52 (6): 1358–73.

Tovias, Alfred. 1997. 'The Economic Impact of the Euro-Mediterranean Free Trade Area on Mediterranean Non-member Countries'. *Mediterranean Politics* 2 (1): 113–28.

Tsourapas, Gerasimos. 2013. 'The Other Side of a Neoliberal Miracle: Economic Reform and Political De-Liberalization in Ben Ali's Tunisia'. *Mediterranean Politics* 18 (1): 23–41.

Tuastad, Dag. 2003. 'Neo-Orientalism and the New Barbarism Thesis: Aspects of Sym-bolic Violence in the Middle East Conflict(s)'. *Third World Quarterly* 24 (4): 591–99.

Van Hüllen, Vera. 2012. 'Europeanisation through Cooperation? EU Democracy Promo-tion in Morocco and Tunisia'. *West European Politics* 35 (1): 117–34.

Zardo, Federica and Cavatorta, Francesco. 2016. 'What is New in the "Borderlands"? The Influence of EU External Policy-making on Security in Tunisia and Morocco after the Uprisings'. *EUI Working paper. Borderlands project.* RSCAS 2016/02.

Index

Page numbers in *italics* denote tables, those in **bold** denote figures.